MW00526630

# *1864:*
# *A Spoonful of History Every Day*

ISBN-13: 978-1-7334044-7-1
ISBN-10: 1-7334044-7-3

First printing: November, 2020

Front cover description:
Top photos, General U.S. Grant and General Robert E. Lee
Second level, Hostetter's Almanac, Atlanta in 1864, Mexican Emperor Maximilian
Lower left corner, top row, Stanton Edwin, U.S. Secretary of War; wartime Gov. Joseph E. Brown; bottom row, wartime Mayor James M. Calhoun, Rebecca Lee Crumpler.
Lower right corner, Sherman's troops tearing up railroad tracks in Atlanta

Published by:

tm

ThomasMax Publishing
P.O. Box 250054
Atlanta, GA 30325

# *1864: A Spoonful of History Every Day*

**Larry Upthegrove**

ThomasMax

TM

Your Publisher
For The 21st Century

**ACKNOWLEDGMENTS**

I would like to thank all those on Facebook and my daily email lists that have read my work every day for the past nine years and given encouragement for me to publish a book. I would like to especially thank those who have doubted my accuracy of content from time to time, almost never correctly, but still helped me keep focused on the importance of accuracy in such writing. I also thank those who lived in that time for the things they did for me to write about, also the chroniclers who let me know about those things.

Thanks to my wife, Kat, for her patience in my absence from the family while roaming the 1800's daily.

*I would like to dedicate this work to the men and women*
*who volunteer their time to Historic Oakland Cemetery*
*to contribute to the discovery and sharing of the memories*
*of the people who have preceded us in life.*
*This dedication applies to all volunteers for all organizations*
*that help to describe our histories as they really were so that*
*we might find the values in their actions*
*and avoid their failures in the same.*

# Foreword

1863 has drawn to a close and there is a bad feeling in the South and North for the coming year. As winter is now upon the torn Nation, the armies will mostly spend the next few months in winter camps, always cold from lack of proper clothing and shoes, and always hungry from interruptions in the supply lines because of inclement weather or actions by their enemy.

The population of the South is largely in the same shape. Almost three years of war has depleted resources on both sides, especially in the South where the ever-tightening noose of blockading vessels has closed most ports to any outside help with imported goods. While this is not a "Civil War Book" as such, the War is the "elephant in the room." There is no ignoring it if writing about this time-period.

The Confederate Army of Virginia, under General Lee is finally winter-quartered about sixty miles northwest of Richmond, near the Rapidan River. The Union Army under General Meade is on the other side of the Rapidan between Lee and Washington. General Longstreet is in a very forage able area of Tennessee near Morristown, with Union General Corse nearby to keep an eye on him.

In Dalton, Georgia, the Confederate Army of Tennessee has a brand-new leader. Two days after Christmas, General Joseph Johnston was appointed its new commander. He has inherited a badly demoralized army with many men missing from wounds and desertion. He immediately set up a system to give each man a long furlough, knowing that the Georgia roads would not dry out enough to sustain an army until May. Through recruits, furlough return and equipping the men, he will be able to accomplish a fine fighting force by spring, just not enough of the men.

The Union Army is being reorganized also in their winter camps at Chattanooga. General William T. Sherman will be Army commander over three Armies: The Army of the Ohio, under General Schofield; The Army of the Tennessee, under General James B. McPherson; and the Army of the Cumberland, under General George Thomas. They too will be in good fighting shape by Spring and twice in personnel numbers as their opponents.

Together, you, the reader, and I will observe the happenings of this year, one day at a time. You will probably follow the armies through your own community, learning what your own kinfolk experienced in this time. Even if you had no army movement near your home, you probably had relatives that were part of the army or civilian efforts to learn about.

Now that we know enough to be able to keep up with any major actions in the war, we can go ahead and step into 1864, not a giant leap, but a tip-toe will do at first.

## January 1, 1864

The new year is started off on a bitter cold note. Low temperatures ranged from -35 degrees in the Midwest to a balmy 8 degrees in Georgia.

Union cavalry commander Major Henry Cole, with about 350 men has moved into the northern tip of Virginia, into the area known as Mosby's "Confederacy." An element of his force, about 80 men, under Captain AN Hunter, is near Middleburg when they are discovered by Confederate Captain William "Billy" Smith. Mosby is off on a scout in Fairfax and has most of his men with him. Smith only has 32 of Mosby's Rangers but charges the Yankee force anyway. Captain Hunter quickly deploys his men into battle line as the charge strikes, and the line crumbles when Hunter's horse is killed, tumbling him to the icy ground. The Union cavalry begins to run toward Middleburg, leaving 57 of their number killed, wounded, or captured, plus 60 horses captured by the Rangers. Major Cole and the rest of his force is camped in a hidden area on Loudoun Heights where Mosby will find him next week. No one in the South is optimistic about the year ahead.

***

***Harpers Weekly*** **depicts the difference in outlooks for the North and South for 1864.**

## January 2, 1864

The Confederate government has a new Attorney General. George Davis, the Senator from North Carolina succeeds Wade Key today and will be the last one to fill the position in the Confederacy. He is no relation to Jefferson Davis.

***

In Missouri, a slave child is born today, a boy-child that will become a giant of agricultural intellect. Raiders will come to Moses Carver's farm and steal the boy, his sister, and his mother. Carver will hire an agent to recover them, but the only one that he can find is the infant named George Washington. When the war is over and slaves are freed, the boy will be raised by Mr. and Mrs. Carver.

At first, he will be taught at home by Susan Carver, then his education will progress well beyond most other children of his race and his age. Graduating from college with a degree in botany, he will be able to secure a research and teaching position at the Tuskegee Institute under Booker T Washington.

His greatest accomplishment will be in developing crop rotation procedures for Southern farmers. Also, his discoveries of uses for new crops that the farmers can substitute for cotton, approaches genius in magnitude: 300 uses for peanuts and hundreds more for soybeans, pecans, and sweet potatoes. The peanuts and soybeans restore nitrogen into "tired soil" that has been over-farmed.

**George Washington Carver**

## January 3, 1864

In the area of eastern Tennessee near Jonesville, Union Major Charles Beeres has been terrorizing the population of the area. Jonesville is the County seat of Lee County and Beeres has burned down the courthouse for no apparent reason, but the area is attractive to him because of the abundance of forage and food to be taken from the Tennessee citizens in the area. Jonesville is centrally located and connected by roads to Harlan County, Kentucky, Hancock County, Tennessee, Cumberland Gap, Tazewell, Tennessee, and the Confederate camps at Rogersville, TN.

Confederate General "Grumble" Jones has led a force across the Powell River in the bitter cold because it is reported that Beeres has left Tazewell heading to Jonesville. At least four of Jones' men have frozen to death on the way. A smaller portion of Jones' men are the first to engage the Yankees that outnumber them by double, and the battle ebbs and flows until the superior numbers begin to push the Rebels back. Just in time to avoid disaster, Jones' main force comes up and traps Beeres. He surrenders himself and about 350 others, including 48 wounded and 12 dead. Jones loses four killed and 12 wounded.

For the remainder of the war, this action will be known as "the frozen fight". All day it is below zero with a stiff wind blowing. General Jones is much loved in this area of the country and will be sorely mourned when he falls on the field in June.

**Confederate General William E. "Grumble" Jones**

## January 4, 1864

In Atlanta, Ga, Carrie Berry writes in her diary, " Wed. Jan. 4. Miss Mattie reviewed us in the multiplication table and she said that we knowed the multiplication table very well. I had all of my lessons purfect This is mostly the diary of a little girl, not a war correspondent, most similar to today's post.

In Savannah, Sherman's right wing is slowly making its way to Beaufort by transport. Since most of the US transport fleet is tied up with Grant's troops and Fort Fisher, it is taking multiple trips and most of a week to move Sherman's Division......In Savannah, Union Lt. Platter writes about his day, " Had Battalion drill this A.M so that the officers could attend the review of Genl Kilpatricks cavalry which had been assumed to come off today. Major Henry Capt Vanpelt "Hank Comstock & myself rode down to see the reviews but were disappointed as the review was post - poned The wharf presented quite a business like appearance. Quite a number of boats were up. Rode all over town. hunting for " Sutler Stones", but couldn't find any. bought some apples 8 for a dollar. Saw Duke Welfry of the 69th After waiting a while for an "extra" Savannah republican, we rode back to camp Wrote a letter to Father. A very small mail arrived this evening - one letter for me - from Tom. Retired late".........

In New York City, near Wall Street, the New York Stock Exchange opens its doors in its first permanent headquarters, 10-12 Broad St, New York City......

In Virginia, at Bermuda Hundred, Union General Grant meets with General Terry as his 8,000 soldiers are loading on transports for Fort Fisher on the North Carolina Coast. Grant goes over all the details of his plan, and in the strongest of words insists that Terry cooperate with and follow the suggestions of Naval Admiral David Porter, whom Grant has found to be invaluable in his operations on the Mississippi River. Grant has also requested the removal of General Butler as Department Head in a correspondence with General Halleck.

**Admiral David Porter**

**January 5, 1864**

In Washington, tempers between Congress and the Presidency are flaring today about the enlistment bounties the Nation is paying for recruits. Early in the War, with enthusiasm high, recruits were easy to come by. In some areas that it was more difficult to meet quotas, a county, a city, or even a state might use some bounty to live up to the assigned obligation. Over the years, the responsibility for paying these bounties has moved to the Federal Government, and today, Congress says, "No more" by issuing a resolution to not pay the $300 ever again.

Lincoln counters with a request for Congress to reconsider. He needs the recruits immediately so they can be trained to be effective in the field in the spring when armies can again maneuver. He asks that the bounties be extended for another month, and he emphasizes his request, by also asking the bounties to be increased.

In New York, inventor, Mary Jane Montgomery, the only technical woman inventor is issued a patent today for war vessel design improvements. Her design uses corrugated steel and heavy wood boards in various layers for ships' hull construction. The remarkable thing in this day and time is that the designs are done by a woman. Things will change in the future.

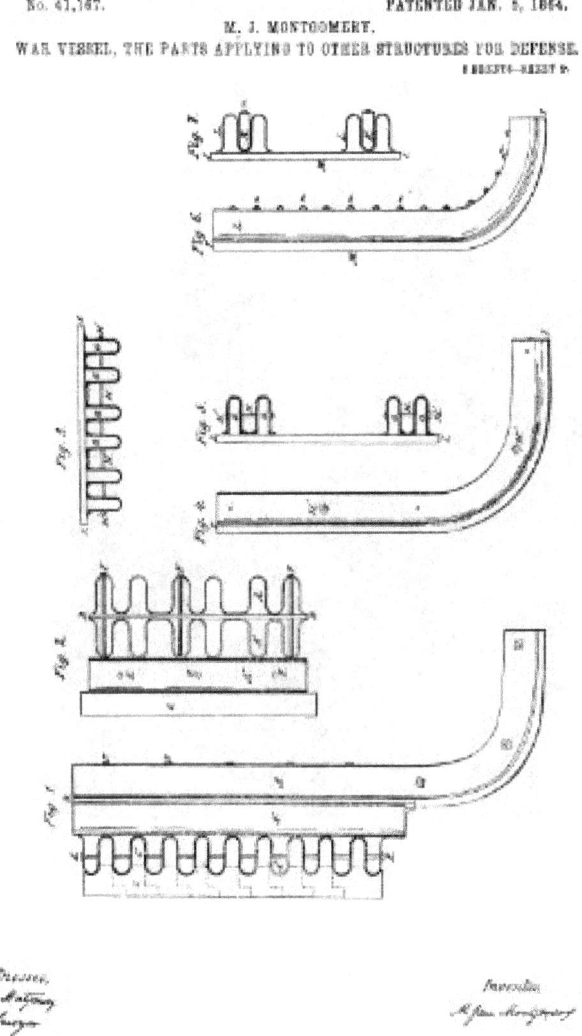


**In the drawing, you can see the new structural steel ribs and other members that the ship's hull will attach to.**

**January 6, 1864**

The Mississippi River is controlled by the Federal army; all the forts are taken so that Northern traffic can go by them. However, there is a Confederate presence along the river that can attack river traffic at any time, severely limiting the amount of shipping that actually goes on in spite of the retributions that General Sherman and other Union officers have assailed on the Southern towns and population along the river. Today there is an action that I will let the participating officer explain his own story, in his report to his commander, Major Holt, Assistant Adjutant-General:

*"Major: the transport "Delta" was disabled by my battery at 12 PM today, run to the opposite shore, and abandoned. Large gun-boat, name not visible, came up; received three raking shots and sought safety in flight, having fire but once. Have but one inferior flatboat and cannot cross for high wind and waves. Looking for Colonel Harrison's forces on the other bank every minute. He has not come to time. Carried 2,000 stands of arms 50 miles on horses. Succeeded in crossing some and hid them in the cane with small guard. Tried to haul is boats from the "Sunflower", but wagons could not pass over the road. Broke the axle-tree of one of my rifled pieces in the action today. Will save the piece. Great many boats running the river. I will be forced to leave the river in two or three days on account of the mud and scarcity of supplies.*

*Very respectfully, your obedient servant, L.S. Ross, Colonel, 6th Texas Cavalry."*

**Lawrence Sullivan Ross (later in life when he is the 19th Governor of Texas)**

## January 7, 1864

In Washington, President Lincoln commutes the death sentence of a soldier accused of desertion, following Jeff Davis' lead who did the same thing, yesterday, with a letter to Lee from Richmond (Neither of them knows about the other).....A curious event happens today, told tomorrow, on the coast of South Carolina: *"Hdqrs Fourth Mil. Dist. of South Carolina Georgetown,*

*January 8, 1864*

*General: I have the honor to report the capture of 4 officers and 20 men belonging to one to the enemy's blockading vessels on this coast, under the following circumstances: the steamer Dan, from Bermuda, in attempting to run the blockade into Wilmington was discovered and chased off. finding escape impossible she was beached at about 12 Pm. yesterday, on the Waccamaw Beach, at a point some 12 or 15 miles north of the Georgetown entrance. Her officers and crew and her passengers were all landed in safety, the steamer having been first fired. The enemy, in attempting to reach her in barges, encountered a very rough sea and their barges were capsized. Three of their men were drowned; the remainder succeeded in reaching the shore and soon after surrendered to Maj. William P. White, 1 officer and 1 man, without firing a shot, though with arms in their hands...."*

***

The Confederate Government names Harvard Law School graduate, General William Preston as envoy to Mexico. He served the United States as envoy to Spain before the war.

Preston was born and raised in Kentucky. General Albert Sydney Johnston was his brother-in-law and preceded him from United States into Confederate service. Preston will survive the war and return to Kentucky where he will practice law and participate in Kentucky State politics.

**Confederate General William Preston**

## January 8, 1864

Confederate General John Hunt Morgan, who has recently escaped from a prison in Ohio, arrives in Richmond with his wife today. He receives a hero's welcome and is introduced to General JEB Stuart whom he has never met before. Tomorrow will be the big event thrown by the City for him.

***

President Davis writes to Governor Zebulon Vance, regarding his plea for the Government to negotiate with the Lincoln Government, that he has tried that and it didn't work, and that *"....this struggle must continue until the enemy is beaten out of his vain confidence in our subjugation..."*

***

In Little Rock, seventeen-year-old David Dodd a former citizen of Little Rock is hanged there today by the Federal Army. Being under age, Dodd was able to gain papers that allowed him to pass into Union controlled Little Rock to conduct some business for his father. As he was returning home, his pass was revoked as he re-entered Confederate territory, but he became confused in the woods and re-entered the Yankee occupied territory illegally. When he was stopped and questioned, it was found that he had troop information in a notebook, written in Morse Code. He was tried and convicted by a military court-martial and today he is placed on the tailgate of a wagon with a rope around his neck. When the prop of the tailgate is kicked away, he swings to his death, except the rope stretches, and he dangles and strangles for a full five minutes as the soldiers and 5,000 onlookers dismay at the horrible sight. He will be treated as a Confederate martyr, because of his refusal to give up the name of the person, who furnished him with his information, in order to save his own life.

**David Owen Dodd**

## January 9, 1864

**Confederate Cavalry Colonel John Mosby**

In Richmond, John Hunt Morgan and his wife arrived in the City yesterday with much fanfare. Today, there are receptions, and Morgan gets to meet with President Davis and Secretary of War, Seddon to plan to get as many of his men back together as possible and increase his command to Regimental size.

Also, from Richmond, President Davis sends warnings to all his commanders in Alabama, Georgia, and Mississippi of reports that Union Adm. Farragut is preparing to attack the fortifications at Mobile bay by running past the forts as he did in New Orleans.

***

Last week a contingency of Union Cavalry under Major Henry Cole, invaded "Mosby's Confederacy" and have been terrorizing the local citizenry in the uppermost tip of Virginia, near Harper's Ferry. On January first, 32 of Mosby's men encountered a portion of Cole's men, numbering about a hundred and defeated the superior force handily. Today Cole's camp with 300 men is discovered and Mosby makes a night time raid to try to capture Cole and as many of his men as he can, but the initial effort is botched, and when Mosby attacks the camp the Federals are in dismounted battle line, enabling them to pour a murderous fire into the Graycoats on horseback. The battle lasts for about 45 minutes, and the Yanks are driven from the camp, but their fellows from Harper's Ferry hear the action and come to force Mosby's men to withdraw. Mosby loses 14 men of a force of 100. The Federals lose 26 from a force of 300 and are considered the winners of the battle because they did not run from Mosby and his men.

## January 10, 1864

In Dalton, Georgia, General Johnston is rapidly converting the Army of Tennessee from a disorganized group of down-hearted losers into a fine, small army.

***

Union General Sherman arrives in Memphis today to start organizing his planned assault on the Mississippi Citizenry and the City of Meridian, in February.

From Memphis, Tennessee, Federal Cavalry General William Sooy Smith begins an operation between Memphis and Meridian, Mississippi to disrupt the activities of Confederate Cavalry under Nathan B Forrest and so occupy him while the rest of the Federals under Sherman can begin their path of destruction and decimation so that the Southern will to fight can be reduced in the area.

***

Off the coast of South Carolina, in Lockwood's Folly Inlet, the Union blockader, "U.S.S. Iron Age" is grounded while trying to salvage a Confederate wreck. When the Federals determine that it is useless to continue trying to float the ship, they destroy it with fire. The fire reaches the magazine and the ship explodes.

**"U.S.S. Iron Age" in its watery grave 150 years from now**

## January 11, 1864

In Washington, President Lincoln is meeting today with former Ohio Governor William Dennison and Postmaster General Montgomery Blair considering campaign strategy if there is a third-party candidate this fall, possibly Secretary of the Treasury Salmon P. Chase or General John C. Fremont.

*John B. Henderson*

.Congress is convened, but many of the members have not been able to arrive as yet, because of the bitter weather blanketing most of the East and Midwest. However, the Democratic Senator, John Henderson, from Missouri is present and today introduces a Joint Resolution into the Senate proposing "*that slavery shall not exist in the United States.*" Of course, Charles Sumner of Massachusetts will hold up the Resolution until the wording is "just right" (his words)

***

The State of Texas loses one of its finest citizens today. Augustus Allen, a native New Yorker, who came to Texas with his brother John, as land opportunists, helped the cause of the rebelling Texans in their efforts against Mexico by outfitting a ship that became half of the Texas navy. With the "Brutus" they could protect the coast and keep shipping avenues open. The brothers also transported troops and supplies to and for Sam Houston's army. After the war was over, the brothers, using money that Augustus's wife Charlotte inherited, bought 6,600 acres of land for the purpose of establishing a new city that was named for the great hero of Texas, Sam Houston. Allen is in Washington today for the purpose of resigning the two US Consulships he has been serving as, in Mexico. Failing health is his reason for the resignation. He will be buried in his home state of New York, in Brooklyn.

**Augustus Chapman Allen, co-founder of Houston, Texas**

## January 12, 1864

Francis Poteet has recently returned to his unit from a trip home to North Carolina. He was promptly placed in the guard house for desertion of which he is guilty. He took off home when he learned of his child's serious illness; when the child died, he returned. Here is a letter written from him to his wife today: *"My Dear Wife and Children I take the pleasure to drop you a few lines to let you now that I am well at this time hoping these lines may Reach your kind hands and find you injoying the same blessing I want you to Rite to me as soon as this comes to hand you Rite tha have to Read the letters that I git from you and Read my letters I want you to Rite to me whether tha have taken ashville are not I could not git to come Back I want you to Rite to me whether you have got your hogs killed are not I am in the gard house and I dont now when I will git out I hope that god will Bless you and my littel Children and give you plenty to eat as long as you live Dyrect to NC Weldon gard House in care of the prov Marchel ofis I could [Provost Marshal's Office] not Rite till now and I doo hope that you may git this letter and hear from me and hear that I am well if it can Reach you and find you all well I would be glad I must come to A close by saying that I remain your loving Husband until death F. M. Poteet to M. A. E. Poteet god bless you"*

***

Today, a contingency of American troops from General Banks army arrives in Matamoros, Mexico to guarantee the safety of the American Consul, Leonard Pierce. There is wide unrest in the Country and sympathizers loyal to Juarez and those who support the French government of Maximillian are fighting in the street with anarchy prevailing. The troops will escort Pierce to safety in Texas.

**American Consul, Leonard Pierce Jr., final resting place Old City Cemetery, Brownsville, Texas, Masonic burial ground, in 1872.**

## January 13, 1864

On Morris Island, South Carolina, Federal Brigadier General Gillmore has a visitor deliver a letter from President Lincoln. Major John Hay explains that Lincoln wants him to not worry about pounding on Fort Sumter, but to take a force and invade the coast of Florida, hoping to recruit 10% of the population to take a loyalty oath, for Florida to be admitted back in the Union.

***

Confederate President Davis communicates to Joe Johnston in Dalton, Ga to not adopt any measures that would have his army to "fall back." --Davis now has General Braxton Bragg as his principal military advisor.

***

America's most beloved songwriter is dead today, in Belleview Hospital where he is taken after a fall in a flophouse hotel at 30 Bowery on the lower East Side of Manhattan, New York. Stephen Foster has in his wallet a scrap of paper that says "Dear friends and gentle hearts" along with 38 cents in Civil War scrip and three pennies. Although the South has identified with him more than any other area, he was only in the South one time, during his honeymoon trip to New Orleans. He never once saw the Suwannee River.

**Perhaps his best effort, the wonderful, "Beautiful Dreamer," will be published after his death at 37 years old.**

January 14, 1864: In Dalton, Georgia, General Johnston receives a communication from President Davis that, if necessary, he should send troops to Mobile or north Mississippi (I wonder if he has any idea of how many troops Johnston has or how many he is up against.)

***

In Montana Territory, gold is booming, miners are plentiful, and there is no law. The towns of Bannack and Virginia City have been plagued with thieves, armed robbers, and murderers. Now, a newly-formed Vigilance Committee has gone to war against the lawlessness. Last week the Sheriff of Bannack, Henry Plummer, was found guilty of being the boss of a local crime gang and was executed by hanging. Today, in Virginia City, five more members of that gang are hanged from a beam in a half-constructed building. The most disgusting of the quintet is Boone Helm who has admitted to killing eleven men over the past thirteen years, some for survival (he ate them), some for money, (two for sure), some in duels, and some just for meanness. As 6,000 men watch the hangings, the hangman approaches the box that Helm is on, but Helm does not wait. He springs off the box, yelling: *"Hurrah for Jeff Davis! Let her rip!"* In the first two months of this year, the Vigilance Committee will similarly, rid the Territory of Montana of 24 human dregs of society.

**Boone Helm before his moments of glory**

## January 15, 1864

With the Federals in Knoxville huddled down for the winter, and the Confederates about twenty miles away, both armies are hurting for food and equipment. The main supply to Knoxville is from a couple of unreliable river boats and forage parties working the civilian population, paying in Confederate money and script. Under Longstreet almost all of the Confederates' food supplies are from foraging, and so far, it has gone pretty well. The Yanks know the area around Dandridge is fat for forage, and they want to graze it themselves. The Rebels think of it as their own rice bowl and are determined to keep it their own. Yesterday, a substantial Union force came up to Dandridge, forcing the Johnnies to withdraw their foraging parties. Today, Longstreet sends a sufficient number of troops to halt the Union progress, but the weather turns surly enough to prevent fighting today. There will be engagement tomorrow.

***

Today, even in this time of desperation, the "Richmond Dispatch" finds a small bit of humor to print. The following cartoon, I added from another source:

**"--A correspondent of the *Southern Recorder* says that the Legislature of Georgia, at its last session, whilst hastily tampering with the Code, unintentionally repealed the law making the marriage license. If this be so, the people of that State are at liberty to go back to the primitive ceremony of jumping the broom."**

## January 16, 1864

The day before yesterday, the Union cavalry and Rebel cavalry bumped together at Dandridge, Tennessee, forcing the Confederates away. Yesterday the Confederates brought up reinforcements, and today, Yankee General Sam Sturgis' cavalry corps encounters a fortified Confederate infantry brigade under General Micah Jenkins. They fight all afternoon, but the Rebels hold tight, and the Yankees retreat at sundown back to Dandridge. (stay tuned for tomorrow)

***

One of the most treacherous stretches of river in the Confederate States is in Tennessee at Chattanooga. The Tennessee River at the base of Lookout Mountain is infamous in the 1700's and 1800's for its "whirl and suck". In fact, one riverman used to tell a story about how, once on a trip through the Suck, he passed a shack with a man playing a banjo out front, then another, then another, then another. It was only then that he realized that the current was spinning him around, and that he was passing the same shack over and over again. Today in New York, "Harpers Weekly" prints a short article and picture illustrating how such a vicious occurrence can look so docile.

"THE river at the "Suck" is about 300 yards wide and very deep, but the current is so rapid that steamers can not head against it, and are obliged to be pulled up by a windlass. The water runs comparatively smoothly until within a short distance from the "Suck," when it breaks into waves and dashes against a rock on the left, flinging the foam high in the air. Waldron's Ridge, on the left bank, resembles the Palisades on the Hudson; the trees, however, run nearly to the top. On the right is Raccoon Ridge."

## January 17, 1864

In eastern Tennessee, about twenty miles northeast of Knoxville, three days ago, Union cavalry forces encroached into the grazing grounds of confederate General Longstreet's winter area in a hope to force him out of winter quarters and out of the area. They occupied Dandridge and prepared to advance further. Day before yesterday, Longstreet sent reinforcements from Morristown to meet them and threaten their base at New Market. Yesterday, Union Brig Gen Sturgis pushed from Dandridge toward Kimbrough's Crossroads where he ran into Longstreet's infantry under Micah Jenkins, who was dug in, with artillery. After the Bluecoats tried the afternoon to break the line, they withdrew last night to Dandridge. Today, Jenkins Confederates advance toward the expecting Federals, who are formed in line of battle, late in the afternoon, about 4 o'clock. The Rebel attack comes, and the Yankees stiffen their defense, but it soon becomes apparent that the men in gray will prevail. Complete darkness halts the fighting, and the Northerners leave in the direction of New Market and Strawberry Plains. Lacking cannons, ammunition and shoes, Jenkins cannot pursue, but for the time being all Union forces are leaving the area, and Dandridge belongs to Longstreet.

**Confederate Brig. Gen. Micah Jenkins**

**Union Brig. Gen. Samuel Sturgis**

## January 18, 1864

In North Carolina, there is much opposition to the Confederate Conscription law, and protest meetings will be held all winter.

***

In New York City, "The New York Times" lead story is not about the war at all, but the tragedy, of the church fire in Santiago, Chile, last month, the news just now reaching the United States. The day was a celebration of the Feast of the Immaculate Conception, being celebrated in the "*Church of the Company of Jesus*" with about 3,000 in attendance. The temple was festively adorned with candles, wall coverings, and oil lamps suspended with string. The huge building was packed with people, and the huge, inward-opening doors had been secured to allow the ceremony to begin without distraction. Somehow, flame from an oil lamp ignited some of the veils adorning the walls, and the fire began. Flames burned the suspension strings of the oil lamps, causing them to become fire bombs on the attendees below. Within seconds, fire was consuming the entire church interior, and the crowds were pushing against the doors and those nearest them, but the doors could not open outward; they were inward-opening. More than 2,500, mostly women, died in the fire.

## January 19, 1864

In Tennessee, near Tazewell at Big Springs, on the Morristown Road, about 125 members of Confederate, Longstreet's cavalry, surrounds and captures about 40 men of the 6th Indiana Cavalry. The only Federal to escape is the Indiana Captain, Captain Stepp.

***

In Arkansas, the Unionized State Government opens a Constitutional Convention for the purpose of revising the State constitution to emancipate the slaves. Only a few counties are represented.

***

Last September, the voters of Nevada Territory approved of the concept of statehood by 6,660 votes to 1,502. Thirty-nine delegates have met and drafted a state constitution, based on California's because most of the population came from California. Today, the voters reject the new constitution by 8,851 to 2,257. Evidently the part about heavy taxation of mine owners is distasteful to most of the people

**Happy 57th Birthday to General Lee!!!**

***Confederate General Robert E. Lee***

## January 20, 1864

In Washington, President Lincoln again angers some of his general officers by suspending army executions for desertion. This time there were five soldiers spared the rope.

Lincoln also, orders General Frederick Steele, commander of Arkansas, that he should order an election at once on the new anti-slavery constitution that has been proposed.

***

Union naval vessels scout out the Forts Morgan and Gaines, protecting Mobile Bay, anticipating the coming invasion by Farragut and others.

***

From Richmond, General Lee sends orders to General George Pickett, head of Confederate forces in North Carolina, to assemble a force and cooperate with the navy in taking the Federal supply depots at New Berne. Along with the orders are specific operational details to implement the complicated plan. Lee urges the utmost "secrecy, expedition and boldness" in preparation and execution of the plans. In fact, to be sure that the written instructions are perfectly understood, he sends the package by Brig. Gen. Robert Hoke, who will explain the movements to Pickett. This will be Pickett's first battle command since his disaster at Gettysburg one year ago this month.

**Confederate Major General George Edward Pickett**

## January 21, 1864

In Boston, "The Boston Medical and Surgical Journal" today publishes an article By Dr. John Bacon on the poisonous action of the green arsenical pigments used to color wallpaper. He says that in the duller green color there is 55 percent arsenious acid and emerald green over 58 percent. The problems of health arise with the fine dust particles of the paper deteriorating being inhaled, leading to major sickness and death.

***

In the Union Department of Ohio, distillation of whisky is forbidden because of the low supply of grain.

***

From Chattanooga, a Union patrol occurs today to Ooltewah, Tennessee for the purpose of requisitioning the records of the County Registrar and arresting Miss S. Locke and Miss Barnet, who are accused of passing contraband information.

***

In Nashville, Former Governor and present military Governor, Andrew Johnson is trying to organize a constitutional convention to draft a new State Constitution that denies slavery. There is substantial interest in this effort among the population.

**Tennessee Military Governor Andrew Johnson**

## January 22, 1864

In Missouri, Federal General Rosecrans is replacing General J.M. Schofield as commander because of the political uproar between moderate and radical Union men. Schofield will soon be made commander of the Department of the Ohio, making him the head of that army, and will march with Sherman into Georgia in late spring.

***

Fifty years ago, on this date, because of short enlistments, American General Andrew Jackson was down to about 100 troops until one week ago, when he was reinforced with 900 raw recruits with 60-day enlistments. Leaving a small garrison, he departed Fort Strother toward the country of the Tallapoosa River, joining two hundred friendly Cherokees and lower Creeks who are skeptical that his force is strong enough for such a venture. Last night the group camped near a Red-Stick Indian camp, Emuckfaw, where much ceremony and whooping and dancing was observed, after the warriors sent away their women and children.

This morning, just before dawn, the Red Sticks attack, but Jackson and his men are prepared and waiting. After half an hour the Indians can make no headway, and Jackson attacks them, pushing them back through their village, which the Americans destroy, and before the day is over, despite counter-attack after counter-attack, the Red Sticks fall back about three miles. Jackson is critically short of supplies, has numerous wounded, and the Indians are sure to be reinforced, so he now has to make it back to the safety of Fort Strother, quickly. Emuckfaw is located where the black balloon shows in southeastern Alabama.

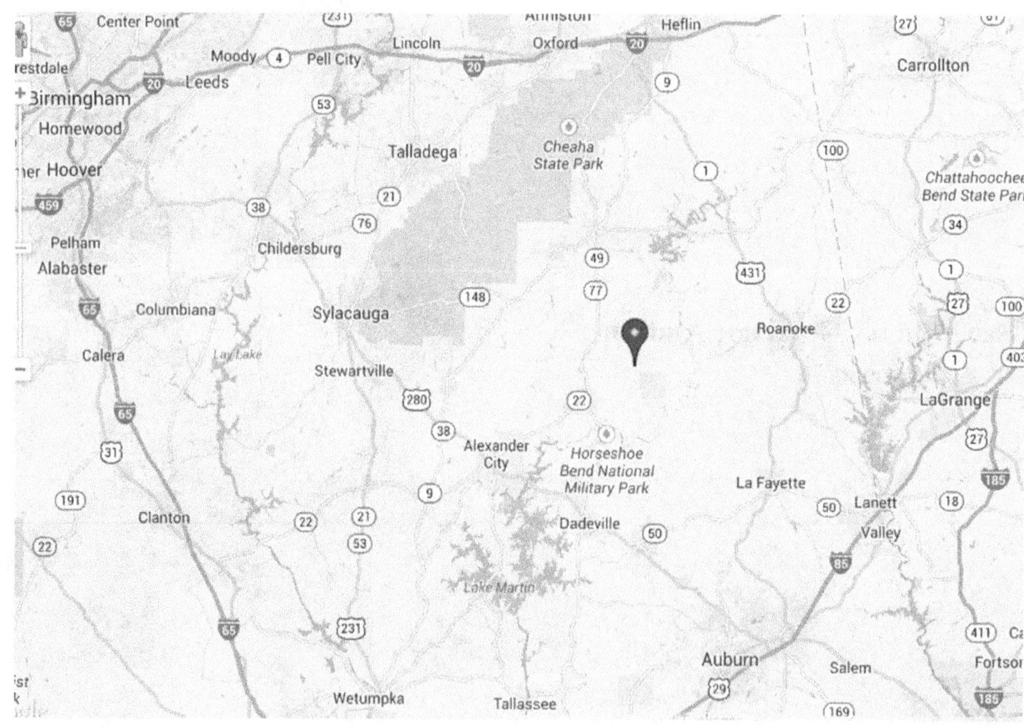

## January 23, 1864

In Washington, President Lincoln approves a policy that will allow plantation owners to officially recognize the freedom of their former slaves and hire them, under contract, in order to "re-commence the cultivation of their plantations." Also, the Treasury Department removes most restrictions of trade in Kentucky and Missouri.

***

There is a sudden mildness in the weather over much of the East and there are many small cavalry movements and conflicts today, especially in Tennessee, Arkansas, and Virginia.

***

From Memphis, Federal General Sherman writes a letter to Major General Steele congratulating him on his promotion to head of the Department of Arkansas and telling him of his plans to cut the railroad service from Meridian to Selma to set the stage for a major campaign in early spring: "*I believe in the move on Red River and would engage in it at once, but Red River is too low at this time. I will start in a few days for Meridian, and think I will be back on the river by the end of February, by which time I think I can spare you a force of about 10,000 men to ascend Red River in boats....*".

***

**With the armies not able to make major troop movements because of winter weather, it is time to rotate the troops, reducing strength to save groceries with furloughs. Today's "Harpers Weekly" depicts a Union volunteer company returning for furlough. It could just as easily have been a Confederate unit. The scene would be the same.**

## January 24, 1864

In Tennessee and Virginia, the main armies are dug in for the winter except for Union General Foster, in charge of the Federal troops around Knoxville and the forces between Knoxville and Rebel General Longstreet at Dandridge and Morristown. He still believes that Longstreet is coming after him in the bad weather. In truth, Longstreet would, if his men all had shoes and supplies enough for such a campaign. There is skirmish fighting north of Longstreet in Tazewell, and other minor actions near Natchez, Mississippi.

***

Fifty years ago, in 1814, American General Andrew Jackson has led an untried force of 900 recruits from relative safety at Fort Strother to the land of the Tallapoosa where the "Red Stick" Creeks are on the warpath (about mid-way between Talladega and Auburn, Alabama). After a bitter fight at the Indian village, Emuckfaw, which Jackson won, he was able to disengage and head for home, with wounded and a reinforced enemy on his tail. This morning, as the Americans with their Indian allies are crossing Enotichopco Creek, the Red Sticks attack in force. Jackson knows they are close and has left a rear guard with orders to attack at the first sign of the enemy closing, and they do. The unexpected action throws the Indians into confusion, then they retreat, and they cannot get organized to come after him again. He will make it to Fort Strother, returning for more war in mid-March.

BATTLE OF ENOTICHOPCO.

## January 25, 1864

It is a beautiful winter day over many of the states in the East and Midwest; cavalry units are active, with foraging and raiding parties numerous. Late this afternoon, in Tennessee, on the Fair Garden Road, Union Col. Edward McCook's division attacks Maj Gen William Martin's Confederates with sabers, routing the men in gray. The Federals continue to chase the disorganized Rebels during the night. Tomorrow, they will find and kill more of them. This continues until they reach the French Broad River near Dandridge, where they run into Longstreet's infantry. No match for this force, they pull away to look for another, smaller force to attack.

***

In Memphis and Nashville, Union doctors are battling rampant syphilis and gonorrhea outbreaks, affecting 82 of every thousand men.

***

In Memphis, Federal General Sherman is preparing heavily for his Mississippi expedition. He has all the blacksmith shops working on nothing but Union army horses, re-shoeing all of them.

***

In Richmond, during the night someone breaks into the Davis' residence storeroom, steals what they can carry and sets fire to the building. The family is awakened by the strong smell of smoke and evacuated into the cold night. Prompt action by the Richmond Fire Dept. saves the structure.

**The Confederate White House, President Davis' home in Richmond**

## January 26, 1864

In Memphis, General Sherman is ready for his invasion of Mississippi and today writes in his journal: " *I have organized the army for the march. We will have 3 divisions commanded by Tuttle, A J Smith and Veatch. General Buckland will be detached from Tuttle and administer Memphis in the absence of Hurlbut.*" He also writes to Captain Porter of the US Navy that he will only take his force to Meridian, then return to Memphis to organize the Red River Campaign.

***

In Washington, President Lincoln approves new trade regulations for the Southern areas that are now under secure Federal control.

***

In Washington the U. S. Patent applications, most of the time are for farm equipment, boilers, or industrial equipment, but today, the following:

No. 41,382.—**Rufus Leavitt**, Melrose, Mass.—*Ladies' Skirt Lifter*.—January 26, 1864.—This invention consists in the employment of two series or rows of eyelets placed one above the other and attached to the inner side of a skirt near the waist. Through these eyelets is passed a cord, by drawing the ends of which the skirt may be shortened as desired.

*Claim*.—Making the skirt with a series of eyes attached at or near the belt, and another series at a suitable distance below the same, and interlacing them by a cord, substantially in the manner and for the purpose described.

***

**In Athens, Alabama, in Federal controlled, Northern Alabama, near the Tennessee line, a contingency of 100 Union infantry soldiers successfully defends the town against 600 Confederate Cavalry. Sources state that the defenders are not fortified, and they do not mention if the defenders have repeating rifles. Both of these forces are veterans, not greenhorns.**

## January 27, 1864

In Sevier County, Tennessee, after a several-day bump and battle with Confederate forces, Union Cavalry General Sturgis wants to try the Rebels, under Maj. Gen. William Martin, just one more time. In an attack on the 25th Sturgis did very well, driving the Confederates, then hunting down the stragglers the next day until he encountered a strong Confederate infantry force that he was able to avoid. Today, he tries a Cavalry division under General Frank Armstrong that he thinks is small enough for him to run over, like Martin the day before yesterday, but this one is reinforced with 3 infantry regiments and Sturgis' troops suffer heavy casualties and have to withdraw. In fact, they will leave the area, leaving prime foraging grounds for Longstreet's, ever-hungry, boys in gray.

***

In the six-year-old State of Minnesota, in the town of Rochester, there appears today, a small advertisement that marks the dawn of an important era in medicine. An Englishman, Dr. William Worrall Mayo opens a private practice for the first time. At age 27, he came to America for the first time, not yet completed in his medical studies, nor qualified to practice. He received his degrees at Indiana Medical College where they had a microscope, not a common fixture in the medicine of the times. In 1862, Dr. Mayo helped to set up and staff field hospitals in southwest Minnesota for victims and refugees of the Dakota War. Last year he was engaged as a military surgeon for the Rochester draft board, and now he is set up to go into a promising private practice. He will be later joined by his sons and a system of hospitals will grow from them. 150 years from now there will be 55,000 doctors and nurses working in Mayo Hospitals, serving over one million Americans each year.

**Dr William Worrall Mayo**

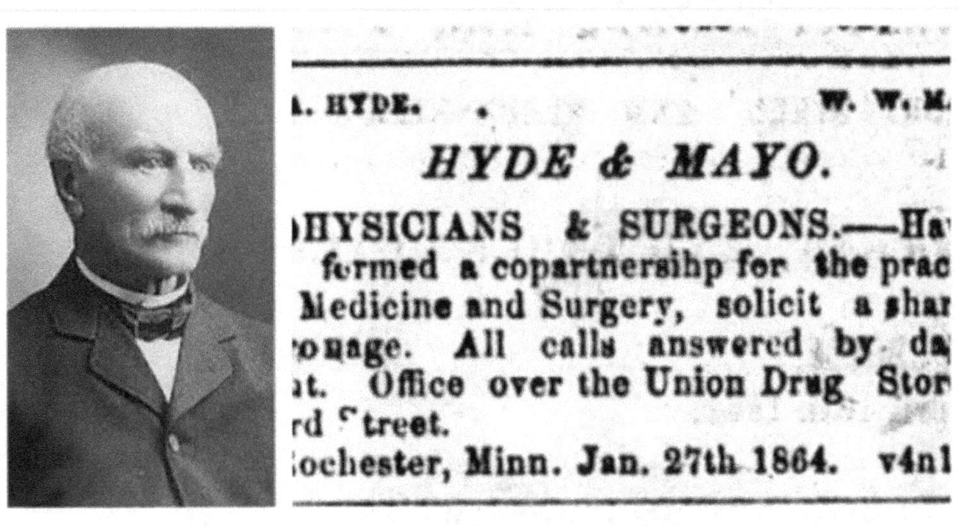

L. HYDE. W. W. M.

*HYDE & MAYO.*

PHYSICIANS & SURGEONS.—Ha formed a copartnersihp for the prac Medicine and Surgery, solicit a shar onage. All calls answered by da at. Office over the Union Drug Stor rd Street.
Rochester, Minn. Jan. 27th 1864. v4n1

## January 28, 1864

Union General Sherman has left Memphis, on his way to Vicksburg, by the gun boat "Juliet", and now has time to catch up on his personal correspondence. He writes a long and rambling letter to his wife, Ellen, that talks about the pomp and laurels that are piled on him by the Union loyal: "*...I cannot speak consecutively, but it seems that what I do say is vehemently applauded.*" He goes on to tell her that he is about to go into 200 miles of danger and when he leaves Vicksburg, she will not hear from him until he returns, except through the Southern press. His mission is mostly punitive, and he states: "*...We will take all provisions and God help the starving families. I warned them last year against this last visitation, and now it is at hand.*"

***

In Washington, William Henry Johnson is dead. William has served as personal valet to Abraham Lincoln since his days in Illinois. He has had a bad time of it in the White House because of his very dark color. Most of the White House servants are light-skinned Negroes and look down on the darker ones. Early this year, William was with the President when he contracted the Smallpox that he is just recovering from and nursed him through the sickness while becoming ill himself. He does not survive, and Lincoln personally, takes care of his burial arrangements, probably in this place, in Arlington National Cemetery.

## January 29, 1864

In Charleston Harbor, the Confederate Ironclad, "Charleston" joins the small Confederate defensive fleet today. The other two ships are "Palmetto State" and "Chicora"

***

On the Mississippi River, the US Steamer "Sir William Wallace" is fired upon from Islands Nos. 70 and 71. From 50 to 75 Confederates, behind a breastworks made of logs, are able to get 27 cannon shots into the boat, killing 3, and wounding 4 more severely. This is the sort of thing that sends General Sherman into a family-killing rage.

***

In Washington, members of Congress have been required to take an oath of loyalty since the first Congress of 1789. Back in 1862, congress enacted the "Test Oath", requiring all Civil Service and military officers to swear not only to future loyalty, but also to affirm that they have never previously engaged in disloyal conduct. This Test Oath was not required for members of Congress, but many of them have taken it anyway. In another act of political bullying, Massachusetts Republican Charles Sumner engineers a rule change making the Test Oath mandatory for all Senators.

Delaware Democrat, James Bayard is outraged, and declares that the Senate has made it impossible for any Southerner to hold the office even if he has a Presidential pardon, if and when the country becomes reunited. Today, Senator Bayard takes the Test Oath and immediately resigns from the Senate in protest. When his successor dies in office later, he will again be elected to the Senate. His father was Senator from Delaware, and his brother was. His son will be Senator from Delaware and so will his Grandson.

**James Asheton Bayard Jr.**

## January 30, 1864

Union General John Schofield turns over the Federal Department of the Missouri to General William S Rosecrans.

***

Also, today, Union General Frederick Steele assumes full command of the Department of Arkansas.

***

There is fighting in Georgia, on Chickamauga Creek, by opposing army patrols.

***

Union General Sherman arrives today in Vicksburg where he will stage his invasion into Mississippi to Meridian, punishing the population along the way for the attacks on Northern shipping on the Mississippi River.

General William Sooy Smith is moving his 7,000 cavalry from Memphis toward Meridian.

Joining Sherman will be General Hurlbut with the Sixteenth Corps, and General McPherson with the Seventeenth Corps.

All this will give Sherman approximately 20,000 Yankees to go against a perceived 10,000 Rebels under Confederate General Leonidas Polk.

**Union General James Birdseye McPherson**

## January 31, 1864

Union General Grant, who has rushed to St Louis to be by his son's deathbed two days ago, finds his son much better so he is able to return to Nashville today. In order to receive permission from General Halleck to make the trip, Grant had to bring his entire staff with him, so that he could remain in charge of the Department.

In a letter to Union General Banks, Abraham Lincoln answers to Banks' complaint about the wording of the loyalty oath he has to administer to those that want to return to the Union: ".....*So you see it is not even a modification of anything I have heretofore said when I tell you that you are at liberty to adopt any rule which shall admit to vote any unquestionably loyal free-state men and none others. And yet I do wish they would all take the oath. Yours truly.....*"

***

In a letter, a Northern soldier asks his brother to propose for a friend of theirs: "...*he forgot to tell you to do the erand for him so he wanted i should put it in for him he wants you to tell Miss Jennie Cateret that if he had only been maried instead of enlisting he would have been a good deal better of than he is now he says he would a good deal rather be sleeping with her in his house in a good warm bed than to be here where he is so he says if she will Consent to the termes he will try and Accomodate her wal i shall have to stop this is fun*".

***

In Missouri, Governor Gamble is dead. On a train, with his arm out the window for some reason, he was struck, and his arm took blood poisoning and passed him away, today. Gamble was the Provisional Governor, voted in place by the Unionists when that part of the State was conquered by General Lyons early in the war.

**Missouri Governor Hamilton Rown Gamble**

## February 1, 1864

In Washington, President Lincoln, using the Conscription Act, orders that 500,000 men be drafted on March 10 for a term of 3 years, or the duration of the war.

***

As a prelude to the Red River Campaign this spring, Union Col William Phillips leads a raid into Indian Territory, bound for Texas with fifteen hundred men determined to leave nothing but scorched earth behind them. He gives his men orders to take no prisoners. His purpose is to defeat Confederate resolve in the area; there being no force of any size to oppose him.

***

In North Carolina, at New Berne, Confederate General George Pickett's Division is organized into 3 attack prongs. The first to attack is Brig. General Hoke who has initial success and captures over 300 Federals, then stops to allow the others to do their job and catch up. The second to attack is Brig Gen Barton, but when the Union artillery opens up on him, he believes the defenses are too formidable and withdraws from range. The third attack is by Col. James Dearing against Fort Anderson, and he also found the defense well-fortified and not assailable. During the night Pickett will have to begin withdrawal, leaving the bulging storehouses of desperately needed goods with the Federals.

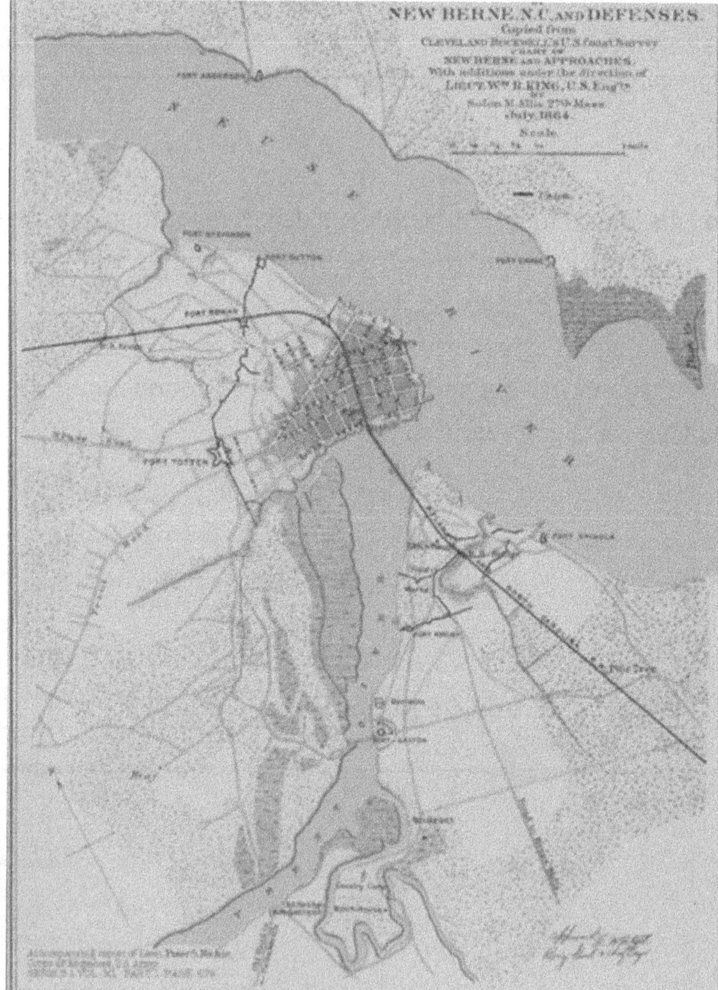


**New Berne, NC in 1864**

## February 2, 1864

At Chattanooga, Tennessee, 129 Confederate deserters take the oath of allegiance to the United States, thus earning the label that will stick with them the rest of their lives as "galvanized Yankees."

***

Yesterday, the detachment of Confederate Marines and sailors led by Commander John T. Wood were working with George Pickett in the actions about New Bern, North Carolina, but not directly involved in the fighting. Early this morning, about 2:30AM, the 250 mariners, in 14 small boats and launches, led by Cdr. Wood, quietly descend the adjacent Neuse River from Kinston and attack the Federal gunboat, USS "Underwriter" as she lies near the west bank just above New Bern.

After an initial murderous volley from the ship, the Confederates are able to board and engage the Yankees in hand-to-hand combat, defeating them and capturing the ship. They want to take the ship down the river and attack the Navy shipyard there, but the boiler fires are banked, and the ship is tightly moored. The Union shore batteries open fire on the ship when they realize it is captured, even firing on their own men, the captured and wounded. Since they cannot use it, the Rebels set fire to the "Underwriter" and evacuate their own men and the Federals, just reaching safe distance before the fires reach the magazine and blow the whole ship skyward, then bottomward.

**"USS Underwriter" in it last moments**

## February 3, 1864

Finally, after weeks of planning and organizing, Union General Sherman is off on his expedition across Mississippi toward Meridian, and probably on down to Mobile, Alabama. His purpose is twofold. He will punish the Southern people for the transgressions of guerrilla fighters firing on Northern shipping on the Mississippi River, and he will damage Southern shipping and manufacturing in critical places.

He has scouted his enemy well and has more than an adequate force for the job. He has about 26,000 troops, including two corps under Generals Stephen Hurlbut and James McPherson, along with a small contingency of cavalry. He has Cavalry General William Sooy Smith with 7,600 horsemen heading from Memphis to meet him near Meridian, but Smith is detained, waiting on the remainder of his force to reach him before he can leave. Smith will really be detained; he will run into Nathan Bedford Forrest at West Point, Mississippi.

Sherman will not need Smith because of the spacing of the Confederate positions in the area. To oppose the Yankee force is about 20,000 widely scattered Rebel troops under Bishop Polk, with cavalry under Stephen Lee doing much of the initial opposition.

**Union Maj. Gen. William T Sherman**

**Confederate. Lt. Gen. Bishop Leonidas Polk**

## February 4, 1864

In Mississippi, the two columns of Sherman's army advance into the State, with Confederate skirmishers contesting the ground hotly, but the two corps easily push the opposition away, only staggering their lines somewhat with the effort. They will arrive at the old battleground of Champion's Hill today and move beyond

***

In Hartford Connecticut, the Colt Armory was built in 1855, then a huge addition was built in 1861, known as the West Armory. Together, the Armory complex covers 260 acres. At about 8:15 this morning, workers discover smoke coming from the attic and fail at their attempts to extinguish the flames which quickly spread to the roof.

Once the roof is involved, by 9:00 the East Armory is completely engulfed and soon destroyed, along with several outbuildings. The West Armory is saved with little damage.

At this time, the factory employs about 900 men and will keep producing the pistols and revolving rifles to honor the contract commitments for the Union Army.

There is much suspicion that the fire was started by Southern sympathizers, but the real cause will never be discovered.

**February 5, 1864**

In Mississippi, the expedition of Union General Sherman moves eastward into Jackson, despite vicious, snarling, attacks from Confederate forces under Stephen D Lee, Wirt Adams, Samuel French, and William Loring, who have insufficient numbers to do more than create delays along the way of the 25,000 Yankee soldiers, giving Confederate Lt. General Polk all the time they can, to organize as much defense as he can.

***

The Federal expedition into Florida under Brig. General Truman Seymour moves out from Hilton Head, South Carolina to Jacksonville, Florida this morning.

***

In Kinston, NC, Confederate General Pickett, who has squandered an attempt to take New Berne and is in an ill mood, discovers that among the captured Federal soldiers there are two "galvanized" Yankees, Southern deserters that have taken oaths to the Union Army. He convenes a court-martial that finds the two guilty, and has a scaffold erected. A hangman is recruited from a card game at the railroad depot, and a rope is borrowed from the Navy. The prisoners are marched up on the scaffold, their heads covered with corn sacks, and the lever is pulled that drops them. Their brass buttons are stripped from the uniforms, and they are buried nearby.

***Confederate General George Pickett***

## February 6, 1864

In Mississippi, Federal troops with General Sherman occupy Jackson today and begin to prepare the City for their departure by destroying all the public buildings and many of the private residences also. From Memphis, Union General William Sooy Smith and his 6,700 horsemen are finally ready and leave toward Meridian to meet Sherman and his force for venture further, to Mobile.

***

In Atlanta, it is one of the biggest days in the City's short history. Confederate General John Hunt Morgan and his staff are here to be honored at a huge reception at the Trout House, the largest, finest hotel in town. A parade from Col Calhoun's (Mayor of Atlanta) through throngs of people, with admirers pulling the General's carriage, slowly flows to the Trout House, where there are speeches by General William Campbell Breckinridge, General Morgan, and Col Robert Alston, Morgan's Chief of Staff and Atlanta Resident.

Colonel Alston owns the land that will someday be Eastlake Country Club. Such a festive day bears no hint that neither the Trout House nor General Morgan will survive this year. Colonel Alston will also die violently, in a gunfight within the State Capitol Building in 1879.

**Confederate General John Hunt Morgan**

**Confederate Colonel Robert Alston**

## February 7, 1864

In Mississippi, the Federal troops under Sherman complete the destruction of Jackson and move on to Brandon, the Confederates only harassing them with no major attempt of solid defense.

***

Union troops, under General Truman A. Seymour, land at Jacksonville, Florida to establish the Federal supply base for the push into the center of the Sunshine State, a push that will culminate with the Battle of Olustee on February 20. Many of the African-American troops in the Union force are former free blacks and runaway slaves from the north Florida area.

***

In Virginia, the Federals under Sedgwick organize a major demonstration of aggression against Lee's troops at Morton Ford, to threaten Richmond, in order to force Lee to pull back his North Carolina force under George Pickett. The Yanks cross over the Rapidan about 9:30 this morning and have initial successes with the Rebel pickets falling back, but when they encounter heavy organized fire, the attack stalls and then is pushed back, leaving 262 fallen in blue and 60 of the men in gray, 30 of whom are members of the Stonewall Brigade captured, pickets that were overwhelmed by the initial attack.

**Fighting at Morton's Ford (Picture from "Harpers Weekly")**

## February 8, 1864

In Mississippi, Union General Sherman's forces leave Jackson in ruins and move to Brandon where they find an abundance of food and feed.

***

In Washington, Senator Charles Sumner introduces a bill into the Senate that will eventually be the 13th amendment, the freeing of all slaves.

***

In Florida, as the Federal expedition begins, there is a significant skirmish at Ten-Mile Run, near the evacuated Confederate Camp Finnegan. The push is due west and Rebel resistance is mostly slight.

***

At Libby Prison in Richmond, Federal prisoners, led by Colonel Thomas Rose have spent the last 17 days and nights, working in shifts, digging a tunnel from their cell under the prison wall. The tunnel is almost complete and tomorrow night the escape attempt will be made. Among those who will attempt the escape is the notorious General A. D. Streight, who was captured, with his whole command, last spring by Reb General Forrest as his raiding party was pushing to destroy railroads and Rome, Georgia.

**Libby Prison**

**Union Col. Thomas E. Rose**

## February 9, 1864:

In Mississippi, Reb General Polk now seems to think that Sherman's intent is directly toward Mobile, not Meridian, so he weakens his harassing force to strengthen the defenses of Mobile, leaving Gens Loring and French to go it with Stephen D Lee's cavalry.

***

In Richmond, tonight, 109 Union officers will crawl through the tunnel it has taken 17 days to dig, from a rat-infested cellar of Libby Prison to the yard of a nearby tobacco warehouse. From there, in groups of 2 or 3 men, they wander into the population of the City. Their absence will not be noticed until tomorrow morning's roll call. Of the group, 59 will succeed in reaching Union lines safely, but 48 will be recaptured, including the leader of the group, Col. Rose. Two others will drown in the James River.

The Confederates will hate that Rose is back in the place and will arrange a prisoner exchange for him in April. He will return to the 77th Pennsylvania and eventually survive the war.

***

In Washington, President Lincoln, and his son Tad, go to the studios of Mathew Brady where Anthony Berger takes the most famous shots of Lincoln. One of them is the source of the famous picture that will be on the American five-dollar bill for many years.

## February 10, 1864

North of Atlanta, Georgia, just north of Peachtree Creek on the Peachtree Road near the hamlet of Buckhead, the Wesley Gray Collier family is preparing to retire for the evening. Suddenly, there is a group of 12 men in the yard and on the porch demanding that they be allowed to enter the home. Collier inquires through the door the nature of their business, but they do not explain, just arrogantly demand entry.

The thugs are Confederate soldiers that have been sent to the area to rid it of thieves and deserters, but they are young and drunk, and not to be reasoned with. The group then starts breaking the glass out of the windows, and one of them pushes his way through a window, just in time to catch a shotgun blast to his trunk area from Collier.

The family has crouched in a back shed room, all surviving the hail of bullets that now crisscrosses through the structure. When the attackers say they are going to burn the house down, Collier and the family run from the house to the woods amid a swarm of passing gunshots, none of which do any damage. One of the children is sent to a neighboring brother's house to get him to go into Atlanta and locate authorities to help with the situation.

Future Oakland Cemetery resident, Oliver Jones, the City Marshall, and two men locate the group, camped at future 16th St and Peachtree. Mr. Collier's buggy is there, stolen to transport the wounded man, and so is the dying Lt. Knight. The group are charged with aggravated riot and will be convicted in Fulton County Superior Court. No charges are pending on Collier.

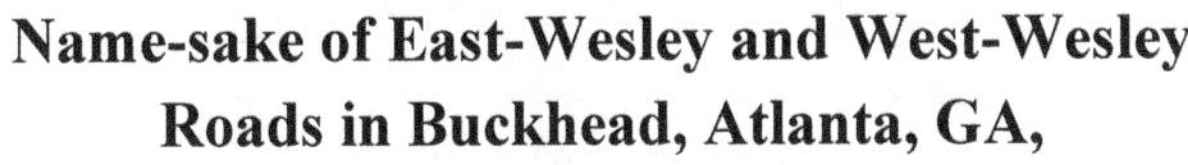

**Name-sake of East-Wesley and West-Wesley Roads in Buckhead, Atlanta, GA,**

**Wesley Gray Collier**

## February 11, 1864

In Mississippi, Union General Sherman's 26,000 troops continue their creep toward Meridian, hoping to meet Cavalry General W. Sooy Smith and his 6,700 horsemen coming from Memphis. Union General Smith is just past Collierville in his journey. His only danger is the piecemeal force of about 2,500 that Confederate General Forrest commands. This should not be a real threat, and Smith has stated how much he desires a chance to go at Forrest.

***

Today, Union Major, Thomas Jackson Rodman, famous arms designer, and developer, oversees the casting of the largest gun ever made. The gun will fire a 20" half-ton projectile a distance of about five miles at 25-degree elevation. The casting will have a plate mounted on it reading thus "20-inch, No. 1, Fort Pitt, 116,497 lbs.", the 116,497 being the weight of the barrel.

***

In Washington, last night a fire broke out in the stables at the White House. Inside were six horses, two ponies and several goats that perished. Saved were the carriages and coupe. When the President discovered what was burning, he ran to the barn, outrunning his Secret Service protection, and tore the barn door open with his fingers, but the entire interior was a ball of fire, and he could save nothing. An especially dear loss are the two ponies, one belonging to Lincoln's son Tad, and the other to his dead son Willie. Today Lincoln consoles Tad by saying, the horses are: *"gone where the good horses go."*

**White House Stables before the fire**

## February 12, 1864

Today is Abraham Lincoln's fifty-fifth birthday.

***

In Mississippi, the two Federal columns continue to fight their way toward convergence at Meridian. Cavalry General W Sooy Smith is moving from Memphis southward, and the main force of Sherman's infantry sees action at Wall Hill and Holly Springs.

***

As a part of the overall strategy, today, Grant orders Federal General Thomas to take his army in Chattanooga toward Dalton, GA. in a move to keep Confederates under Johnston from reinforcing Polk in Mississippi.

***

In Nashville, the theatre audiences are loving the talented 25-year-old John Wilkes Booth. He came to Nashville, known by reputation only, and the crowds have increased with each passing performance. Tonight, is his final performance of his engagement and he will commence with Shakespeare's tragedy, "The Merchant of Venice," and close with "Catherine and Petruchio," a Shakespearean comedy. The Nashville "*Daily Union*" reports about tonight's performance: "We expect to see the house literally overflowing tonight. Gentlemen with ladies should make it a point to go early to be sure of getting seats.

**John Wilkes Booth, actor**

## February 13, 1864

In Oklahoma, a portion of the Federal force Under Col. William A Phillips that has invaded the Indian Territory, attacks the Confederate outpost at Middle Boggy with 350 men plus artillery. The 90 defenders fight bravely but futilely, and withdraw, leaving about half their force dead or wounded. The Yankees execute the wounded and ride on.

***

In Richmond, the Confederate Congress passes legislation doing away with the "substitute" provision of draft deferment

***

In Florida, the Federal expedition across the State fights a skirmish at Peas Creek

***

.In Port-au-Prince, Haiti, the reformist President, Fabre Geffrard, calls the Nation together to witness the execution of 8 vodou-practicing murderers. They seized the 12-year-old girl on December 27 and hid her for four days, bound and gagged beneath the alter of a vodou temple. In a ceremony on New Year's Eve they strangled, decapitated, and dismembered her body. They then bled her body into a jar and cooked her. They all participated in the meal wherein they ate the body and drank the blood. President Geffrard is trying to outlaw the pagan religion that makes his country appear so backward.

## February 14, 1864

Union General Sherman has accomplished his goal. He has taken 20,000 men across the State of Mississippi from Vicksburg on the Mississippi River to Meridian, near the Alabama line.

As his troops near Meridian, the weaker forces of Confederate General Polk evacuate the City, leaving it to Sherman. Now if Cavalry General W. Sooy Smith will just get here with his 7,000 horsemen, Sherman will lead all to Selma, Alabama where the coal mining and industrial center can be destroyed from the South's usage. Then maybe they will continue on down to Mobile and help Admiral Farragut take over the port City.

Sherman will wait almost a week on Smith, utilizing the time in destruction. Later his own words will describe it: "For five days 10,000 men worked hard and with a will in that work of destruction.

Meridian, with its depots, store-houses, arsenals, hospitals, offices, hotels, and cantonments, no longer exists."

Map of the area of the campaign so far

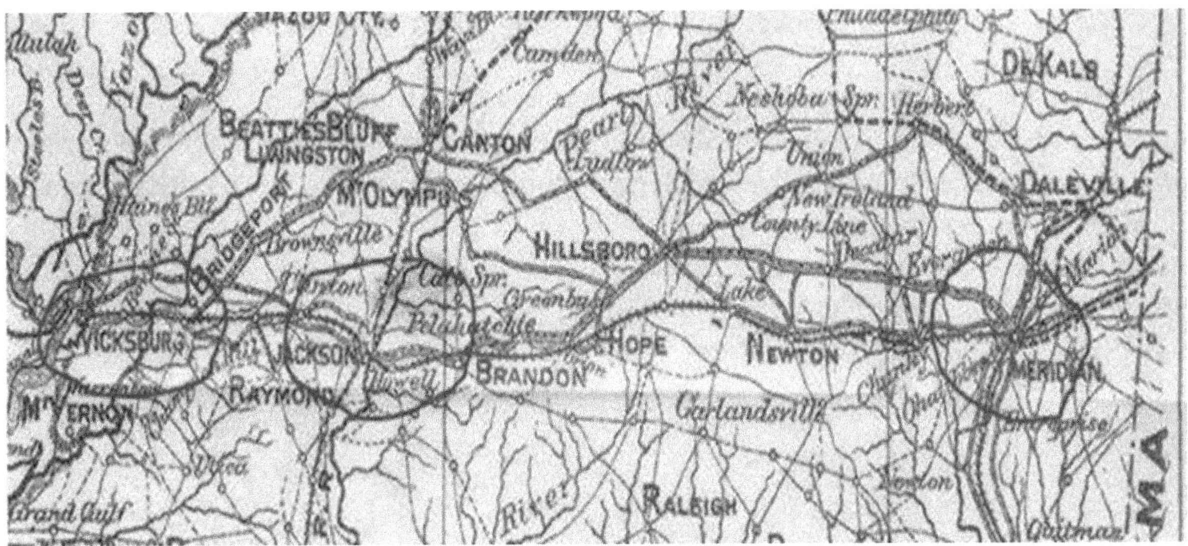

## February 15, 1864

In Washington, the House of Representatives votes today on the 13th Amendment bill submitted by Charles Sumner of Massachusetts, and the bill gains a plurality, 78 to 62, but does not have the required 2/3 of the votes for a majority. Many of the legislatures, including Republicans are having trouble with the phrase "giving equal protection under the law".

***

In Florida, another Federal expedition leaves Fernandina Beach toward Woodstock and King's Ferry Mills.

***

After the Confederate debacle at New Berne NC under George Pickett, Pickett discovered that 22 of the captured enemy soldiers were "galvanized Yankees" Southern deserters in the Union Army. After a trial, two of these men were executed on February 5, five more three days ago, and 13 more die in one hanging today.

***

The attempt on New Berne was not entirely unsuccessful, Commander John Wood of the Confederate Navy successfully captured, then sank, the Federal gunboat, "USS Underwriter". Today the Confederate Congress gives thanks to Commander Wood, his officers, and his men for his most recent capture, US transport steamer "Elmore". Other captures are "USS Allegheny", USS Golden Rod", "USS Coquette", and "USS Two Brothers".

**Confederate Naval Commander John Taylor Wood**

## February 16, 1864

In Meridian, Mississippi, as Union General Sherman's 20,000 men are taking the City apart, Union Cavalry Commander W. Sooy Smith with his 7,000 horsemen and twenty pieces of cannon are moving their way from Memphis to join Sherman, stopping along the way to have some fun in destruction themselves.

His opposition, who has failed to show up, is Confederate Major General Nathan B. Forrest who in the last several months has recruited enough deserters and absentees to raise a command of about 2,500 men of whom he has made into soldiers. He has drilled them, practiced them, and executed some of them, while instilling a fierce attitude and pride in them that they, as individuals, have not experienced before. They have not been tried in battle, only 300 veterans in the group, but they will do what Forrest expects of them, when the time comes.......

***

In Charleston Harbor, the underwater vessel "Hunley" has been operating under muscle power for three months, both in the daylight and in the dark, hoping for conditions to be right for an attack on the blockading fleet of Federal gunboats that have stopped shipping into Charleston. The crew is preparing for an attack tomorrow night if weather conditions are right. This is the third crew, the other two crews died in their seats in the cramped little steel cigar tube, including the inventor, Horace Hunley.

**"CSS Hunley"**

## February 17, 1864

From Charleston Harbor, conditions are prime for the underwater craft "CSS Hunley" to strike against the blockading Yankee fleet just offshore. The first submarine is commanded by George E Dixon and crewed by 7 others. It is powered by muscle power as each person pushes and pulls on a crankshaft to turn the propeller.

The night is moonlit to silhouette the enemy ships, and there is a low-lying fog to help hide the attackers. The "USS Housatonic" lies at anchor 7 miles out and casually spies "a plank in the water" approaching the ship. The nose spar of the submarine, with its 90 lbs of explosives sinks into the hull of the ship, and the underwater craft backs away, leaving the deadly charge attached to the ship with a line connecting the "Hunley" and the triggering device. When the line becomes taut, the device explodes the charge, and a gaping hole is made in the hull of the "Housatonic" just forward of the mizzen mast. Trembling from the shock, the big warship heels to port and goes down stern first.

Five of the crew are killed, but the water is shallow enough that the remainder climb into the rigging which is still above water and await rescue. The "Hunley" signals its success to the shore and is never seen again. Over a hundred years later, she will be discovered lying side by side with the "Housatonic" on the sandy bottom.

**"USS Housatonic"**

## February 18, 1864

In Meridian, Mississippi, the troops of Union General WT Sherman are laboring hard to completely dismantle the small city. Work parties are going out every day to destroy the railroads toward Selma. Sherman is also waiting on W. Sooy Smith with his cavalry contingency to show up. Sherman is getting nervous about the absence of cavalry now. He has patrols out to keep an eye on things, but they tend to get occupied with pillaging the farms and not covering the terrain like cavalry does.

***

In northern Florida, Union Brigadier General Truman Seymour landed 5,500 troops in Federally held Jacksonville a couple of weeks ago and has been raiding on day-trips the surrounding area. He is trying to disrupt the beef and salt supply from Florida to points in the Confederacy and to recruit black troops. Seymour's orders are to not venture into the interior of the state, but he has decided to cross North Florida and take Tallahassee. By the time he was underway, the Confederates in the area, bolstered by reinforcements from General Alfred Colquitt, have become organized under Brig. Gen. Joseph Finnegan, who with 5,000 men, will make a stand the day after tomorrow near Ocean Pond, at Olustee Station.

**Yank General, Truman Seymour**

**Reb General Joseph Finnegan**

## February 19, 1864

In northern Florida, the Union Brigade, under Brig Gen Truman Seymour, draws closer and closer to the 5,000 Confederates under Brig. Gen. Joe Finnegan, constructing fine entrenchments near Olustee Station. They will meet tomorrow......

***

In Mississippi, finally, it becomes clear to Confederate Major General Nathan B Forrest where the 7,000 horsemen of Union General Sooy Smith are heading. He observes the blue force following and destroying the M&O Railroad that will lead them to Meridian, and he knows what to do. He divides his force into three divisions and sends one division, under his little brother, Colonel Jeffrey Forrest, to take place in front of the Bluecoats allowing themselves to be pushed back through West Point and into a pocket that will be formed by the two other divisions, creating a trap for the much superior force. Over the next several days, I will refer to the brothers Forrest as Col. Forrest and Gen. Forrest for clarity's sake......

***

In Washington, a new secret fraternity is born today by Justus H. Rathbone. The Order of Knights of Pythias will become an international, non-sectarian fraternal order, initially designed to bring men of the North and the South together with common benevolent projects. The order will grow to over 2,000 lodges and total membership over 50,000 in the next 150 years and be the first fraternal organization to receive a charter under an act of the United States Congress. Too bad the members of Congress will not practice the tenets of the order.

## February 20, 1864

In Mississippi, not knowing the whereabouts of the cavalry force under Sooy Smith, Union General Sherman orders his expeditionary force turned back toward Vicksburg. He cannot know that Smith is being lured into a trap by Rebel General Forrest's baby brother........

***

In northern Florida, the Union expedition of 5,500 men are moving in the direction of Lake City, and the Confederate defending 5,000 are in fortifications near Olustee Station, waiting on them in a pine forest. The Rebels have pickets forward of the fortified area, and they become engaged with the forward units of Yankees about 2:30 in the afternoon. As the Confederate pickets fall back to their lines, the Federals under Truman Seymour fail to take the bait, and they reinforce themselves well in front of the earthworks. The Confederates under Joseph Finnegan and Alfred Colquitt move out of the fortifications and give battle face to face. The Union forces continue to attack all afternoon but are savagely repulsed with every effort. Late in the day, Finnegan commits the last of his reserves into the fray, and it is enough to tip the battle to his advantage. The Union line moves back slowly, then breaks into a flood of running blue. No major attempt is made by the Confederates to pursue, but a small force of Rebels offers one attempt at the retreating rear, just before dark, which is handily repulsed by the rearguard, composed mainly of negro troops. After the battle, it is likely some of the wounded negroes were executed in individual acts of brutality. This is the largest action that Florida will see in the war. Federal losses are 1,861 and Confederate losses are 946.

**The lithograph below is largely inaccurate, showing the Confederates fortified and on an open plain.**

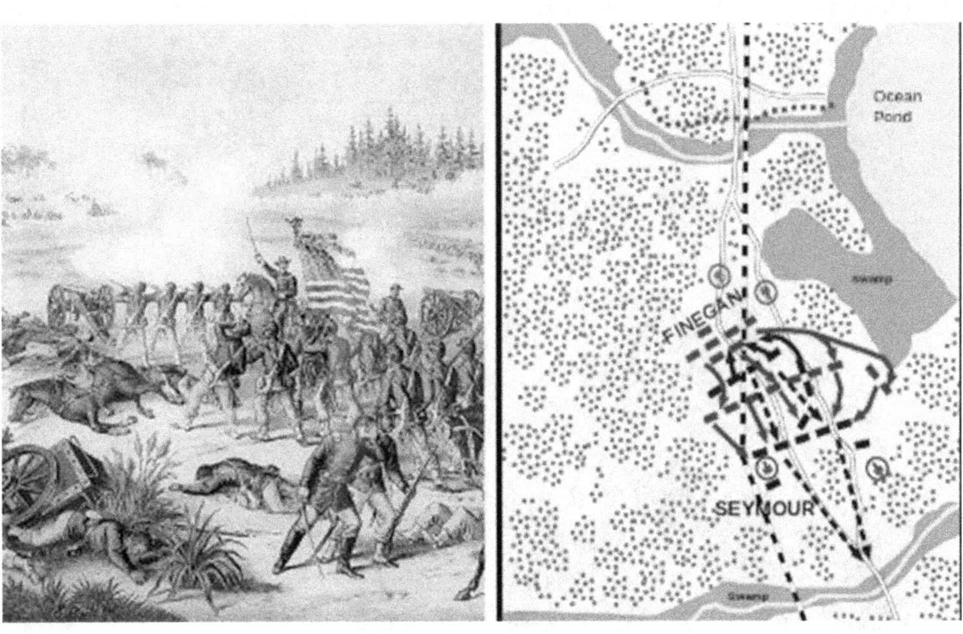

## February 21, 1864

In Atlanta, Ga., the City's only theatre, the "Athenaeum", serving the city for 9 years, is about to be closed and converted into a store. Seating over 800 people, it has been a cultural diamond in the South. According to the "Intelligencer": "*....some local Puritans combined with authorities to ban entertainments as being either indecent or too frivolous for the times.*"

***

In Mississippi, Federal Cavalry commander W. Sooy Smith has had his spoken wish come true; he has found Confederate General Nathan B Forrest's newly formed rag-tag force and has attacked. One division of Johnny Rebs under Col. Jeffrey Forrest has made violent contact, then relented, allowing themselves to be driven through the town of West Point and into the swamps, where two other gray divisions lurk to apply pincers to the pursuing Yankees. However, Smith smells a rat, and learns of General Sherman's return toward Vicksburg.

He does not want to be left deep in enemy territory all by himself with only 7,000 men and horses. Also, Smith has accumulated (number depends on which book you read) about 3, 000 freed slaves, for whom he feels responsibility for their safety. Therefore, he decides to break away from action and go back to Memphis.

When General Forrest perceives Smith's intent, he is not about to let him get back to safety without a fight. Forrest has about 2,500 ill-trained men, and Smith has about 7,000 seasoned fighters, so Forrest feels he has enough advantage, and he will attack Smith with all force tomorrow morning.

**Union Cavalry General W Sooy Smith**

**Conf. Maj. Gen Nathan B Forrest**

## February 22, 1864

In Chattanooga, the troops under Union General Thomas move out toward Tunnel Hill, GA, Rocky Face Ridge and toward Dalton, GA in demonstrations designed to force the Confederates out of their winter camps and make them too cautious to send any troops to Mississippi to help against Sherman.

***

In Mississippi near Okolona, Union Cavalry General Smith yesterday began a withdrawal of his 7,000 troops, but Confederate General Forrest will not let him leave without a fight. This morning at dawn, General Forrest himself leads the frontal assault and probing flank attacks that cut gaps in the Blue battle lines, prompting a hasty retreat that leaves five cannons on the field. The Yankees reform on a ridge and in a series of attacks and counterattacks, Colonel Jeffrey Forrest, Nathan's youngest brother who he has raised like a son, is struck in the neck by a bullet that takes his life. He dies in the arms of his older brother who returns to the fight with a fury.

All Union forces withdraw and a running battle of 11 miles begins. Every defensive position the Federals employ is overrun until late in the day, the bluecoats draw into three lines on a field and charge the gray ones, who use volley fire to break up the charges with 40 yards separating the forces. Smith has really had enough and begins another withdrawal. Forrest, being almost out of ammunition, lets him go, except for small, harassing attacks on the perimeter of the main force, all the way back to Tennessee.

**Battle of Okolona by Historical Artist Don Troiani**

## February 23, 1864

In Washington, Treasury Secretary Salmon P Chase is a secret candidate for the Republican nomination for President. US Senator from Kansas, Sam Pomeroy has authored a circular that has been passed around to top Republicans, demeaning the Lincoln Presidency and touted the virtues of Chase. Lincoln has found out about the circular and today answers a letter written by Chase that he will comment more fully later on the matter. In the letter Chase swears his loyalty and offer to resign. Lincoln really does not want him to resign. That would allow Chase to campaign openly against him.

***

In Georgia, under the orders of Union General Thomas, John Palmer's corps move into position to move on Rocky Face Ridge and Mill Gap. Confederate General Johnston is establishing strong defensive lines that will hold the Yankees on the western side of Rocky Face and not let them come through Mill Gap.

**Union General John Palmer**

*Rocky Face defenses plaque installed on U.S. 41 in 1930*

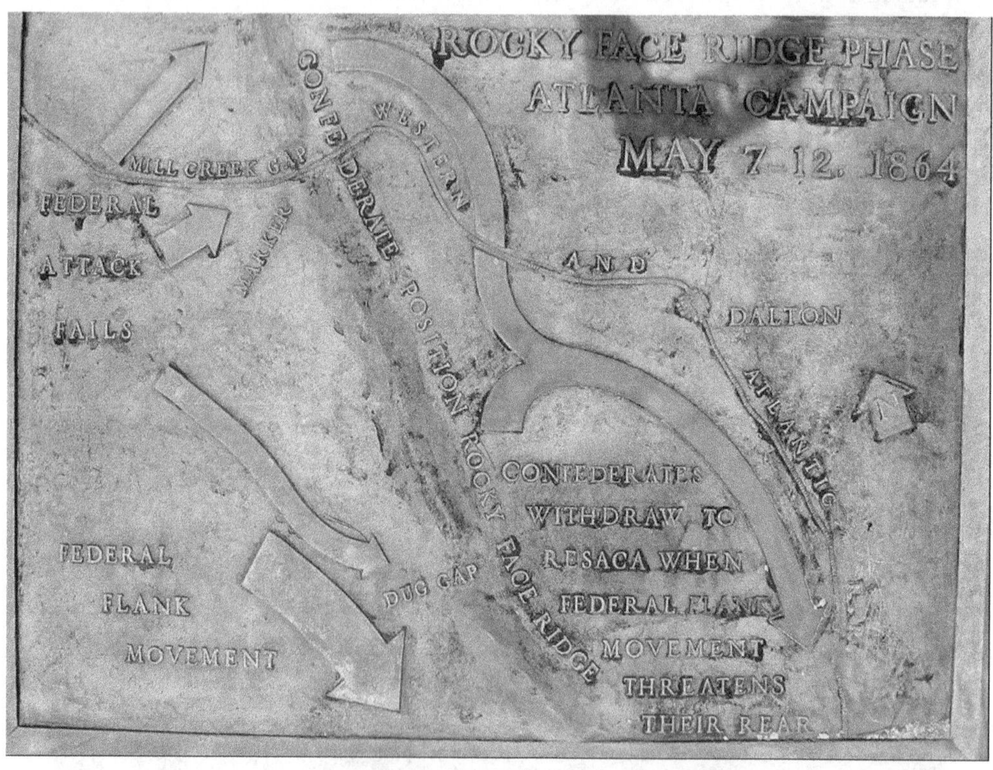

## February 24, 1864

In North Georgia, the half-hearted attempts at invading Dalton, GA by the Federal army begins in earnest today. Elements of General John Palmer's corps move by Tunnel Hill and try to take the natural gateway through Rock Face Ridge, called Buzzard's Roost, into Crow Valley, but stiff Confederate resistance, reinforced by artillery, smothers the advance.

***

In Southwest Georgia, the new prison, Camp Sumter, at Andersonville, receives its first Union prisoners today, even though the facility is not yet ready for operation. In fact, it will never get entirely ready for operation. The initial structure will be finished soon but will have to be expanded immediately.

Originally planned for 10,000 inmates, its number will swell to 30,000 because of US General Grant's refusal to allow prisoner exchanges. His logic is that when most of them are exchanged, they are in such bad shape that by the time they recover, their enlistment is almost up, and if he leaves them in the camps they use resources of the Confederacy to feed and guard them, also bury them.

***

Rebecca Davis Lee, a native of Delaware and Pennsylvania, found her calling early in life helping the aunt that raised her to care for infirm neighbors. She became a nurse in Charlestown, Massachusetts, where the doctors she worked with issued letters that allowed her to enter the New England Female Medical College, and today, four years later, she becomes the first Black female medical doctor in the United States. She will soon marry Arthur Crumpler, thus becoming Rebecca Lee Crumpler.

**Rebecca Lee Crumpler, M.D.**

## February 25, 1864

In Washington yesterday, the Senate passed a measure to revive the rank of Lieutenant General so that Ulysses S. Grant can become the third officer in the Nation's history to hold such a rank.

***

In North Georgia, several pushes by Union forces around Rocky Face Ridge to force the Confederates out of Dalton will be abandoned after today's futile efforts.

***

Confederate General Robert E Lee gets some great news. His son, William Henry Fitzhugh Lee, known as "Rooney Lee" is exchanged from prison in New York State. Brigadier General Lee was seriously wounded at Brandy Station last June and captured while convalescing at his Father-in-law's plantation several weeks later. While Lee was in the prison, his wife Charlotte died, the day after Christmas last year

***

Former First Lady Anna Harrison dies today at 88 years old. She is the widow of our ninth President, William Henry Harrison who died 32 days into his office, and she will be the Grandmother of our 23rd President, Benjamin Harrison. Anna and William raised ten children in spite of the grueling family life of a military General, especially during those days of the War of 1812. She was against her husband running for the Presidency, and when he was inaugurated, she was sick and could not attend. When he died a month later, she was not physically able to attend his funeral. She never entered the White House.

**Anna Tuthill Symmes Harrison**

## February 26, 1864

Three significant Union Army misfortunes end today: 1. Yesterday afternoon Union General Thomas was feeling better and visited the camp of General Palmer, who is heading up the effort to pry the Confederates loose from their winter camps at Dalton, GA. After personally assessing the information about his adversaries' strength and placements, he orders his men back to Chattanooga, leaving the Rebels alone. They leave today.

2. Union cavalry commander W. Sooy Smith has had enough of Confederate Generals Nathan Bedford Forrest and Stephen D Lee. Forrest, with a force one-third the size of his own, whipped him badly five days ago at Okolona, and Lee's men have been unrelenting in their harassment of his perimeter on his journey back to Memphis, which he gladly concludes today.

3. As of this afternoon, the US Army is no longer in the camel business. Some 75 camels were imported in the mid-1850's for desert transportation usage, and the results of the experiment are mixed. The camels could carry four times as much as a mule, and live on a third of the forage and water that it takes for a mule, but they did not pull well in harness, they stink, they spit on you, and they bite, nobody wanted to work with them. Also, the soft pads of their feet, well-adapted to the hot sands of the Sahara, become very sore in the rocky Mojave Desert of California where they were mostly used. Today, only 34 remain, and they are auctioned off at Benicia, California for $1945.00.

**The only known remaining photograph of an Army camel**

## February 27, 1864

In North Georgia, the citizens of Rome, Georgia and other related communities are breathing a sigh of relief that the Union force pushing at Dalton has been stopped and is beginning to retreat back to Chattanooga. Rome has been preparing for evacuation for several days.

***

In Florida, operating along the Gulf coastal waters the Federal ship "USS Tahoma" reports the successful results of its latest expedition of destruction of Confederate salt works, at Goose Creek, near St. Marks.

Commander Harmony sends three boats under his executive officer with orders to destroy the works unless he is seen by Confederates, known to be patrolling in the area. The group is not discovered, and upon landing, they immediately surround the houses, capturing all the people inside them. The boats then return to the ship bringing twelve prisoners, a captain of an infantry company, an ex-Rebel soldier amputee, missing his leg, and ten workmen and women, employees of the salt plant. The amputee and two aged others will be paroled tomorrow at St. Marks.

The expedition has successfully destroyed two plants capable of producing 2,400 bushels of salt daily. Since the Confederate government buys part of the salt at market value, all who are captured are legitimate prisoners of war, as they are aiding and abetting the enemy.

**"USS Tahoma"**

Photo # NH 57826 USS Tahoma, artwork by R.G. Skerrett

## February 28 & 29, 1864

Today, Confederate General Robt. E. Lee reminds his troops of the value of the local "stewards of the earth" in the following order: "*In order to afford every facility and encouragement to the farmers to prepare for planting the coming season, the general commanding directs that particular attention be given to the preservation of the fencing and the closing of roads through fields which the owners may desire to cultivate.*".

***

Also, today, Kilpatrick's raid into Richmond begins, with its stated mission, to free the Union prisoners in the city and increase awareness among the population about Lincoln's amnesty offer. Kilpatrick has about 3,500 men in his assembled group and is supported by Col. Ulric Dahlgren, son of US Naval Captain John Dahlgren, the Father of the Union's heavy ordinance.

Dahlgren, with his 460 men leaves late tonight from Ely's Ford on the Rapidan, following Kilpatrick who left just after dark. Earlier, a cavalry diversion began demonstrating on the Confederate left, so the raiders have opportunity to slip around the right of Lee's army and head straight to poorly-defended Richmond, Kilpatrick from the North, and Dahlgren from the West.

By tomorrow afternoon, after a fine day of travel, Kilpatrick's men are tearing up track at Beaver Dam station when a train from Richmond approaches, sees their activity, and backs in a return to Richmond, spreading the word. Confederate home guard units mobilize, and late tomorrow night, Confederate General Wade Hampton with 300 regular Confederate cavalrymen will ride all night to try to intercept the raiders. Whereas yesterday and today have been beautiful weather, all changes for tomorrow. By the time Hampton gets in the saddle, clouds and rain will have turned into snow and sleet, making men dressed in both colors perfectly miserable.

**Union General Judson Kilpatrick**

**Union Col. Ulric Dahlgren**

## March 1, 1864

Unbeknownst to Union General Judson Kilpatrick (known to his men as "killcavalry") and to Colonel Dahlgren, the population around Richmond is in an uproar, but in the morning, the two leaders of the raid to free prisoners still believe that no one knows they are coming.

The lightly-defended city is active with preparations to receive them. Confederate General Wade Hampton is desperately trying to get there with a force of about 300, to stop 3,500, and militia leaders are organizing a defensive position. Through the snow and sleet Kilpatrick encounters the defense of the wounded, veterans, office and factory workers, and home guards, all seem determined to stop him, and he believes them. The defense looks too formidable, and he now believes that Dahlgren did not enter the City from the other side as planned, he would be right about that.

To attack Richmond on the south side, Col Dahlgren has to cross the James River and has hired a freed-slave guide to show him where. When the crossing is reached, the water is so high they cannot get across. Dahlgren demands to be shown another way, but when the guide cannot respond positively, Dahlgren orders him executed; the man is hung without delay.

Now, Dahlgren has learned that Confederate General Custis Lee is coming after him, and Kilpatrick knows that Wade Hampton, with god-only-knows how many men, is coming after him, so they make their decisions independently, to do anything possible to get back to the comfort and safety of their lines.

## March 2, 1864

For only the third time in American history, the army has a Lieutenant General, Ulysses S. Grant, who follows George Washington and Winfield Scott. His nomination is confirmed by the Senate today, making Grant the supreme commander of the United States Army. Just three years ago he was a clerk in his father's leather store.

***

In Virginia, General Kilpatrick continues to withdraw back across the Rapidan, and Colonel Dahlgren continues to try to dodge elements of Confederates under Custis Lee until tonight. A small group of Rebels under Lt. Pollard have been successful in short-cutting around the fleeing Yankees and have set up an ambush, hoping the Federals will pass their way. As they approach, Dahlgren draws his revolver, rides to the front of the column and shouts: "Surrender you damned rebels, or we will charge you".

A similar demand issues from the shadows of the roadside, and Dahlgren tries to fire his weapon which misfires, but the Rebel guns do not misfire. A murderous volley pours forth, and the entire Yankee line, in mass confusion, bolts to the rear, leaving dead, wounded, horses, and their leader, lying in the mud. Col. Dahlgren has been hit five times and is probably dead before he hits the ground. Tomorrow morning his pocket contents will make for remarkably interesting discovery.

AMBUSCADE AND DEATH OF COLONEL DAHLGREN.—[See P... 78.]

**March 3, 1864**

In Virginia, last night a 13-year-old boy, one of the improvised defenders of Richmond, crawls from his wooded position to see about the fallen Yankee Colonel, Ulric Dahlgren, finding him to be dead with papers in his pockets. He takes the papers to his school teacher, also one of the defenders, who, in the morning light, discovers a rambling speech to Dahlgren's troops that the Colonel never had occasion to deliver.

Also present, is a copy of his orders, which reads: "*The men must keep together and well in hand, and once in the city, it must be destroyed, and Jeff Davis and Cabinet killed.*". Both the Northern and Southern press will have a field day with that statement, and some scholars will give credit for it planting the seed of thought that will lead to Lincoln's assassination

***

In New York, this morning the Archbishop of New York, John Hughes, known to friend and enemy alike as "Dagger John", speaks his last words: "Bury me in the sunshine". John is the most famous Catholic in the United States. His passion and eloquence are felt in the Irish community all over the North. He is probably the key to tens of thousands of Irish Catholic boys dedicating their service to the American Army and not going to join with the South, as many have. Abe Lincoln loses a fine ally today.

**Archbishop John Hughes**

## March 4, 1864

Union Major General Sherman writes to Union Major General Banks that his venture force is returning to Vicksburg today, and that, on the day after tomorrow, he will send Banks 10,000 hand-picked men for his campaign up the Red River, but he wants the men back in 30 days so he can prepare to take the Union army south of the Tennessee River in late April.

***

In Tennessee, Andrew Johnson is confirmed by the US Senate as the Military Governor of Tennessee.

***

In Louisiana the new Governor, Michael Hahn, takes office.

***

The new US Lieutenant General, U.S. Grant, is ordered to Washington by the President so they can start planning the coming spring's warfare.

***

Also, in Washington, word is out about the devastating loss suffered by the Kilpatrick raid against Richmond, but word is not out about the fate of Col. Dahlgren. Today, Dahlgren's Father, Adm. John A. Dahlgren, the inventor of the Dahlgren Gun and many other heavy ordinance pieces for the Union, visits the White House to see if Lincoln can give him any information about his son.

**Rear Admiral John A. Dahlgren**

## March 5, 1864

As anticipated, the Press of the North and of the South have picked up on the outrageous orders that the late Col. Dahlgren carried in his pocket. The Richmond Papers call for reprisals and execution of Federal officers captured in the raid, and the New York Times gloats over the reports of damage to public and private property inflicted on the Southerners during the raid and states that the slave, Martin Robinson, who was lynched by Dahlgren because the James River was too high to cross, has met a fate that he "*so richly deserved, because he dared to trifle with the welfare of his country*", whatever that means

***

The Confederate Government today orders that all ships will give one-half of their cargo capacity to government shipments. This, to help the army get the things it needs to continue.

***

Former Vice-President of the United States and former Senator from Kentucky, John Breckinridge assumes command of the Confederate Department of Western Virginia today, his first command since being relieved of command, for alleged drunkenness-in-battle, by Braxton Bragg. His charge will be to protect Confederate interests in the mountains and Shenandoah Valley of Virginia.

**Confederate Major General**

**John C.**

**Breckinridge**

## March 6, 1864

In Richmond, the papers have built a feverous indignation about the discovered statement of intent of Union Colonel Dahlgren, listing the destruction of Richmond and execution of Jefferson Davis and his cabinet, as his ultimate goals for the raid of three days ago. Members of the Confederate Cabinet and top legislatures want to try the officers of the captured as war criminals and execute them. Davis asks General Lee his opinion of this business, and he nixes the idea of execution: "*I think it better to do right, even if we suffer in so doing, than to incur the reproach of our consciences and posterity*." He, also says that the South has men just as cruel as Dahlgren, and we should worry about retaliation and what history may say of us

***

"CSS David" is a surface-operated torpedo boat that looks like a submarine. In fact, it operates mostly underwater, with only the conning and the smokestack above the waves. It holds 134 lbs of explosives on a pole, well out front of it, with a percussion detonator.

Tonight, in the North Edisto River, "David" attacks the blockader, "USS Memphis". The attack goes perfectly, but the charge fails to explode. The "Memphis" starts firing at her with small arms, but "David" turns around and strikes again with the torpedo misfiring again. Now, "Memphis" opens up with her big guns, and "David" loses her stack and retreats up the river out of range. Although there were about 20 of the torpedo boats built by the Confederacy, the successes were extremely limited.

**"CSS David"**

THE BEGINNINGS OF SUBMARINE WARFARE

A CONFEDERATE PHOTOGRAPH OF '64—THE FIRST "DAVID," FIGURING IN AN HEROIC EXPLOIT

## March 7, 1864

In Richmond, Confederate General Bragg has resolved to keep a permanent garrison of 1500 cavalry to discourage Federal raids like the one last week by Kilpatrick.

***

From Richmond, President Davis writes to Confederate General Longstreet, at Greenville, Tennessee, "*It is needless to point you to you the value of a successful movement into Tennessee and Kentucky, and the importance _ I may say necessity _ of our taking the initiative.*" You will notice that there is not one word of reinforcements coming to Longstreet, who has repeatedly insisted that he is not moving without being reinforced, except, maybe, to return to Lee in Virginia.

***

In Richmond, the newspapers report the arrival of the first Negro prisoners of war in the city.

***

There is little fighting going on today, just skirmishes at Decatur, Alabama, and Brownsville, Mississippi.

***

MR. LINCOLN FINDS A BROOM TO HIS LIKING.

***(Leslie's Illustrated, March 7, 1864)***

**Major General U.S. Grant is on his way to Washington to receive his new commission as Lt. General. "Leslie's Illustrated" has the following comment about that:**

## March 8, 1864

Union General Sherman has initiated his contribution to General Bank's Red River Campaign, his mission being to ascend the river, do damage, and wreak havoc all the way to Shreveport in an all-out effort to deny supplies reaching the South from Mexico via Texas..

Today, Sherman writes to General Steel, head of the Department of Arkansas, explaining the plan underway, *"By tomorrow General A.J. Smith with 10,000 of my men will be at the mouth of Red River, and will go up Red as far as Alexandria to meet General Banks by or before March 17. Water in the Red is very low, and I doubt if the fleet can get over the falls or rapids there, in which event they must await a rise or go up by land alone. I think the expedition should not attempt Shreveport until the gunboats can participate...I am going to Memphis and thence around to Huntsville, to prepare for the big fight in Georgia that is sure to come off in all April or May."*

***

This afternoon Union General Grant arrives in Washington to receive his promotion and new command. After an evening meal, he is about to retire for the evening when a messenger summons him to the White House to attend a reception already underway. There, General Grant meets his boss, President Lincoln, for the first time ever.

After an hour or so of introductions, Grant and Lincoln have a few minutes to talk, with Lincoln informing him that the official promotion ceremony will be tomorrow at 1 Pm and he will have to make a short speech. Lincoln gives him his talking points, and Grant leaves, pretty much overwhelmed by the whole scene.

**Grant and Lincoln meet for the first time**

## March 9, 1864

In Washington, the coronation of Union General U. S. Grant as Lieutenant General is completed today. In the Cabinet chambers, in the presence of every Cabinet member, Lincoln speaks: "*....With this high honor, devolves upon you also, a corresponding responsibility. As the country herein trusts you, so, under God, it will sustain you. I scarcely need to add that with what I hear speak for the nation goes my own hearty personal concurrence.*"

Grant, as you will remember, was given "talking points" last night. He was to say things to not make other officers jealous, and boast about the Army of the Potomac, but he disregards all that and has this to say: *"Mr. President, I accept this commission with gratitude for the high honor conferred. With the aid of the noble armies that have fought on so many fields for our common country, it will be my earnest endeavor not to disappoint your expectation. I feel the full weight of the responsibilities now devolving on me, and I know that, if they are met, it will be due to those armies and, above all, to the favor of that Providence which leads both nations of men."*

.

## March 10, 1864

In Washington, President Lincoln signs a directive that his newly-installed Lt. General, US Grant be made Commander of all the armies of the United States. Grant does not wait around town for this, but is in Virginia today, meeting with General Meade, trying to figure out how the two of them can work together. Meade is different from most of the Union Generals, in that, he is not an egotistical man. It will work out fine for Grant to command the army in the field, and Mead remain in command of the Army of the Potomac, relieving Grant of many details and administrative duties.

***

The Red River campaign of Louisiana is under way. Union General Banks with 17,000 troops is moving up from New Orleans via Bayou Teche to link up at Alexandria, with 10,000 of General Sherman's troops under General Whiskey Smith. At the same time, General Steele is advancing south from Little Rock with 15,000 men to join the others at either Alexandria, Natchitoches, or Shreveport, as their progress develops.

Union Brigadier General Andrew J Smith (Whiskey)

## March 11, 1864

Union Lt. General Grant concludes his meetings with General Meade in Virginia and returns to Washington. Staying there no longer than he absolutely has to, he boards a train bound for Nashville, arranging for a meeting with General Sherman, who he intends to place with the responsibility of heading up all the Western military efforts. (West, meaning anything west of Virginia).

***

In Sheffield, South Yorkshire, England, tonight, the 185,000 occupants awake to rushing, flooding waters. The, brand new, Dale Dyke Dam has failed, breaking apart. The structure, being under the process of filling for the first time, showed cracks this afternoon, and orders were given to start draining the retained water, but the discovery comes too late, and 238 people and 700 animals are in the process of drowning. 130 buildings are destroyed completely, and about 500 buildings are, partially to heavily, damaged. 15 bridges are swept away, and six others are badly damaged. This is considered to be the worst flood in English history, both now, and one hundred fifty years to come.

**Sheffield, South Yorkshire, England, aftermath**

## March 12, 1864

The Federal force of 10,000 men under Union General Whisky Smith today starts up the Red River, being transported By Adm. David Porter's naval vessels numbering over 100, including transports and gunships. The water in the Red is quite low, and the ships are only clearing bottom by inches in places despite heavy rains in the area all last week.

General Banks has not left Bayou Teche yet, with his 17,000 men, nor has General Steel left Arkansas with his 7,000.

To oppose these named forces is Confederate General Kirby Smith, with about 30,000 men, equally distributed, under three different leaders, widely apart from each other. General T.H. Holmes is near Camden, Arkansas, General J.B. Magruder is on the Texas coast, and General Richard Taylor is in Louisiana. It looks like General Taylor will be the prime Confederate opposition, since he has about 10,000 men in the area.

Taylor's men have already cut many trees, to fall across the river and aggravate the upstream movement of the Blue-coated invaders. Taylor is also ridding the countryside around Alexandria of sustenance; anything the approaching armies can use is being moved and hidden.

**Confederate General Richard Taylor**

(Son of President Zachary Taylor)

## March 13, 1864

From Washington, President Lincoln, in a letter to newly seated Governor Hahn of Louisiana, hints that he should seat some of the "very intelligent" Negros in a convention which would "define the elective franchise"

***

50 years ago, from this date, March 13, 1814: In Georgia, under orders from General Pinkney, First Lieutenant George Gilmer arrives at the confluence of Peachtree Creek and the Chattahoochee River for the purpose of building a fort. The fort will be a part of a chain of forts the United States is building for military presence in the Creek Nation.

Gilmer is in command of 22 newly recruited soldiers (poorly armed), a contractor named James Montgomery, and a boatwright named Bowman. Of these men, none have seen a fort before, but Gilmer has a copy of the military manual, "Duane's Tactics," and will be able to conceive from that.

Across the river from the selected construction site is an old Cherokee Indian village called Standing Peachtree, with a mixed population of Creeks and Cherokees, because of refugeeing Lower Creeks, trying to escape the areas of the more war-like Red Stick Creeks. The Lower Creeks and Cherokees are allied at this time against the Red Sticks and their British sponsors, this being during the War of 1812.

The newly established military presence here will be called Fort Standing Peachtree, and the creek entering the Chattahoochee at the same place is called Peachtree Creek. Bowman will construct a small fleet of boats to connect this fort with Fort Mitchell miles down the river. Soon a road will be built that will connect Standing Peachtree with Fort Daniel at Hog Mountain, the Peachtree Road.

**Lt. George Gilmer later as Governor of Georgia**

## March 14, 1864

The Red River Campaign began two days ago as Union General "Whiskey" Smith with 10,000 men, transported and supplied by Union Admiral David Porter's 100 vessels, entered the Red from the Mississippi. Other than downed trees blocking the way, the first real challenge for the bluecoats will be Fort De Russy, recently rebuilt and guns fortified with steel plating. Not wishing to sustain vessel damage from the fort's guns, the 10,000 land soldiers disembark about 30 miles from the fort and approach from there.

The 3,000 Confederate defenders, under General John Walker, leave about 350 men, to man the river guns, and pull out of the fort, hoping to catch the Yankees in an unprepared, flanking position, but the Federal commander is too wary, properly positioned, and there is nothing Walker can do but withdraw after minor contact.

Late this afternoon, the 10,000 Union soldiers storm the fort and force the surrender of the Confederates that are not killed in the action.

***

In Missouri, John Luther Jones is born. While he is still a boy, his family will move to Cacey, Kentucky, from whence he will take his nickname, "Casey". He will become the most famous railroad engineer in history with his heroism during his fatal train crash in the year 1900 in Vaughn, Mississippi. He, like Ben Dewberry, will be immortalized in song, in future years....

**Casey Jones**

## March 15, 1864

In Louisiana, Union General Banks receives a letter from General Grant informing him of Grant's promotion to Supreme commander. Also, Grant tells Banks that he approves of what he wants to do on the Red River, and that it is important work, but it must be concluded or given up by mid-April to allow his borrowed troops to participate in the spring campaign with General Sherman. He also tells Banks to have his men live off the land, as much as possible, taking what he needs from the population, unless the victims can document that they have taken the loyalty oath, in which case, Banks can pay for the plunder. The first Federal gunboats begin to arrive at Alexandria, as the expedition slowly makes its way up the Red River

***

The United States has a new fifty-dollar bill, issued for the first time today. The front features a picture of Alexander Hamilton and a female figure that represents loyalty. Each bill will have a red seal and serial number and is interest bearing. One year from the issue date the note can be exchanged for the 50-dollar value plus five dollars interest, at which time it will be destroyed. Because of the destruction, the bills will become rare in the future and very valuable to collectors.

## March 16, 1864

Just last month, Confederate General Nathan Bedford Forrest could barely field 2,500 troops when he met Union General Sooy Smith at Okolona and defeated his 7,000 bluecoats. Now Forrest has recruited up to total strength of 7,000 and begins today, an expedition into western Tennessee and Kentucky.

***

In Louisiana, on the Red River, Union Admiral Porter, and General "Whiskey" Smith, after overwhelming the fortifications at DeRussy yesterday, leave a destruction force there to render the fort useless, and they have moved on up the river to the town of Alexandria. Confederate General Richard Taylor, has just moved his much inferior force out of the town as the Northerners move in, taking all military supplies, but 3 cannons, with him. Although a token chase was directed at Taylor, most of the Navy personnel fell to wanton looting of private homes and warehouses. Although Porter has given orders to "respect private citizens", he turns a blind eye as great stores of cotton are taken from private warehouses and stacked on the gunboats. Sailors enter every private house and steal what they can, gleefully congratulating themselves for getting to the booty before the army can reach the town to beat them to it.

**Union Admiral Porter's boats at Alexandria taken on today's date**

PORTERS FLEET AT ALEXANDRIA LOUISIANA IN 1864 , DURING THE CIVIL WAR BETWEEN THE STATES, THIS PICTURE WAS TAKEN AT ALEXANDRIA LOUISIANA ON MARCH 16 1864.

The fleet boats names from the front are-- SOUTHWESTERN, W.L.EWING, CLARA BELLE, EMERALD, DES MOINES, CHOUTMARS, SIOUX CITY, THOMAS E. TUTT STARLIGHT, LIONESS, RED CHIEF, BELLE CREOLE, ROB ROY, BELLADONNA, DIADEM, MATTIE STEPHENS, ARIZONA, SILVER WAVE, ADRIATIC, LIBERITY, AND ALSO TIN CLAD GROSSBEAK.

## March 17, 1864

Union Lt Gen. Grant and Major General Sherman are in Nashville to meet and plan strategy. Grant issues today the following order to all Union Generals: "*—I assume command of the armies of the United States. Headquarters will be in the field, and, until further orders, will be with the army of the Potomac. There will be an office headquarters in Washington, D. C, to which all official communications will be sent, except those from the army where the headquarters are at the date of their address.*"

With the attention of the press and many dignitaries trying for Grant's attention, he is not able to have a productive meeting with Sherman, and it is important that it happens, so they plan for Sherman to accompany Grant as far east as Cincinnati to talk on the train. As it happens, the train will make so much noise they will have to shout and still not be heard. In Cincinnati, they will rent a room and have a sentry stand at the door so they can converse uninterrupted.

***

In Arkansas, Union General Frederick Steele issues his initial orders to get his army moving toward Louisiana to meet General Banks and go against Shreveport. He is having to pull troops from three different areas of the state and have them converge on Arkadelphia. Steele's forces are not in good shape for travel. They do not have enough supplies for travel, not enough forage, not enough draft animals; the animals they do have are poor and not able to do much work. Initially, travel will be exceedingly difficult with heavy rains quagmiring the roads.

**Union Major General Frederick Steele**

## March 18, 1864

In Nashville, Union General Sherman assumes command of all Union forces in the West.

***

To illustrate the importance of Texas to the Confederacy: Today, there are 5,000 bales of cotton stacked in San Austin Plaza, in downtown Laredo, Texas, defended by 42 Confederate soldiers, commanded by Colonel Santos Benavides, ex-mayor of Laredo and descendent of the city's founder. Union Major Alfred Holt has 200 men and is just outside the city. He has come to destroy the cotton, but he is met by entrenched Confederates at Zacate Creek, just outside Laredo.

Holt's first attack is deterred with stiff resistance. He attacks again, and yet again, but cannot dislodge the stubborn Rebels from their defenses. Finally, he goes away, with his remaining force, and Colonel Benavides moves the cotton across the Rio Grande where it is sold for the benefit of the Confederacy.

***

In Washington, the Fair for fund-raising for the Sanitary Commission closes today with a speech from Lincoln. The Sanitary Commission works in the Yankee camps to help provide a more sanitary environment and to aid with wounded on the battlefield and in long-term recovery. It is run by men, but mostly administered by women, and Lincoln says this about them: *"If all that has been said by orators and poets since the creation of the world in praise of women applied to the women of America, it would not do them justice for their conduct during this war."*

## March 19, 1864

In Milledgeville, Georgia, the Georgia Legislature expresses its confidence in President Davis and resolves that the Confederate government should, after each victory, make an offer of peace to the North based on independence of the South and self-determination by the border states (Is Joe Brown going to sign this?).

***

Confederate President Davis is pushing Joe Johnston to agree to a plan that would have him take his available force to a point between Nashville and Chattanooga to destroy the railroad between Chattanooga and Nashville. He would then move northward to Kingston where General Longstreet would bring his force to meet him. Together they would march across the mountains to Sparta where the army can be self-sustaining, living off the land. Davis says that if Johnston will agree to advance in this manner, he will build his total force to 75,000 men. Both Johnston and Longstreet are arguing that they would each be too vulnerable until the meeting of the forces could be affected.

***

The picture today, is from "Harper's Weekly" and shows a map of the rebellion, comparing the areas controlled by each faction in 1861, and currently. With the Federals now controlling the coast lines, and great areas of the South are isolated from the others you can see how Major General Winfield Scott's constriction of the "Anaconda Plan" is working in this map.

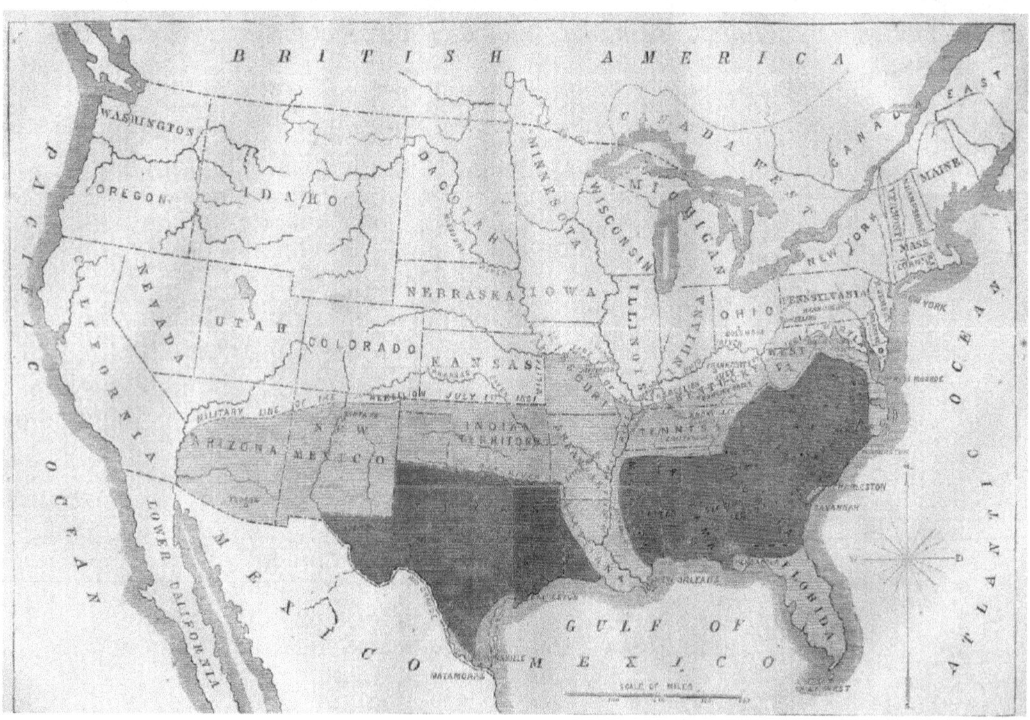

## March 20, 1864

In California, the light shaking of an earthquake is felt, but in the areas around Stockton, Sacramento, and Santa Rosa, the shock is quite severe.

***

In Louisiana, forward units of Union cavalry under General Banks reach the area around Alexandria and have light contact with Confederate cavalry in the area. Confederate General Taylor (President Zachary Taylor's son) is assembling all his forces in the area to be able to block the soon-to-be combined force of Yankees that will outnumber him, at least two to one, much more than that if Union General Steele can make it here from Arkansas.

***

In Cincinnati, Union Generals, Grant, and Sherman are meeting in a hotel, discussing this year's strategy to end the war.

***

Off the coast of Cape Town, South Africa, the world famous, "*C.S.S. Alabama*" arrives, as a part of its world-wide campaign of attacking United States shipping wherever it can find it. Commenting on the absence of Union cruisers in the area, Captain Semmes states in later writings: "That huge old coal-box, the Vanderbilt, having thought it was useless to pursue us further, had turned back, and was now probably doing a more profitable business, by picking up blockade-runners on the American coast. That operation will pay-- the Captain might grow rich upon it. Chasing the Alabama did not pay nor will not."

***"C.S.S. Alabama"***

## March 21, 1864

In Washington, desirous of putting 3 more electoral votes into play for the coming fall election, the Republican Congress decides to admit Nevada Territory into the union as a State, even though the population requirement of 60,000 free inhabitants is lacking by one-third. Some argue that the country needs the minerals of the territory and the salt, but those things will be available as a Territory as well as a State.

***

President Lincoln's genuine, Republican meanness is displayed today in remarks he makes to the New York Workingmen's Democratic Republican Association: :

*"Property is the fruit of labor...property is desirable...is a positive good in the world. That some should be rich shows that others may become rich, and hence is just encouragement to industry and enterprise. Let not him who is houseless pull down the house of another; but let him labor diligently and build one for himself, thus by example assuring that his own shall be safe from violence when built."*

***

In Louisiana, Union Colonel Thomas Lucas, commanding a full brigade of cavalry, is able to find and surround Confederate General Richard Taylor's entire cavalry force, barely a regiment in size. This is a real blow to Taylor who now has no way of keeping an eye on his enemies as the two forces unite against him.

**Union Colonel Thomas J. Lucas**

## March 22, 1864

In Baltimore, Union General Lewis Wallace (later in life will author "*Ben Hur*"), today assumes command of the Middle Department, superseding Brig. Gen. Henry Lockwood.

***

In Dalton, Georgia, five inches of snow fell last night, and the bored Confederates make the most of it, in this novel environment. In Cleburne's Div., Lucius Polk's (nephew to Maj Gen Leonidas Polk) Brigade attacks Brig. Gen. Govan's Brigade with snowballs. It is quite a fray, with pounding, thumping, and rolling around in the snow. Soldiers are wrestling and smearing the iciness all over their opponents with hand-to-hand combat, in great heaps of wriggling, gauging, humanity. General Pat Cleburne himself, takes over his old brigade and gets into the fray, organizing an overwhelming barrage of snowballs, driving Govan's men back, but Govan rallies his troops and they charge forward, yelling for all they are worth, and manage to surround and capture General Cleburne. ....With a break in the action, a mock trial is held, and after some solemn deliberation it is decided to parole the Division Commander. Suddenly, the snowball fight begins again, and Cleburne is back in the thick of it. After some ebb and flow of superiority, Cleburne is again captured and placed on trial for violation of parole. After much bluster and pontification, the General is again placed on parole, and he parries by issuing a ration of whiskey to the troops. Great bonfires are built, and the former combatants stand around the warmth and sing the popular songs of the day at the top of their voices.

## March 23, 1864

In Virginia, a Confederate soldier reports in a letter to home: " *Snow fell all night, and was eight or ten inches deep this morning; but it was a bright morning, and glorious sunshine all day".*

***

In Dalton, only two more inches of the frozen white fell last night, but it is enough to produce similar rough play as the day before. In Virginia, the snowball war really blossoms. In snow so deep walking is difficult, thousands of troops organize into their normal lines-of-battle and go against their comrades in a rare frolic.

***

Union General Grant returns to Washington from his meetings with Sherman and others in the West. To please certain "radical" Republicans, he replaces several of his generals that lean toward the "democratic" party.

***

In terrible weather, Union General Steele finally is ready and leaves Little Rock to push into Louisiana to join General Banks in the Red River Campaign. Almost immediately he encounters light Confederate resistance, but nothing that delays him. He follows a route that roughly parallels a future Interstate 30. He will cross the Ouachita River at Rockport and continue southwest toward Texas with 8,500 men.

**Union General Frederick Steele**

## March 24, 1864

Union Army Commander, Grant, has returned to Washington and spends the evening conferring with the President. He will be making Culpepper Courthouse his headquarters for the time being.

***

In western Tennessee, as Confederate General Forrest moves toward Paducah, Kentucky, he has dispatched a small force of 500 men under Colonel William Duckworth to take Union City, Tennessee. Union City is defended by 500 Yankee soldiers within strong fortifications, and Duckworth has no artillery with him, so he tries to convince the defenders to surrender.

The US Commander is Colonel Isaac Hawkins who has been captured by Forrest before and paroled, so when surrender is demanded of him, he asks to meet with Forrest. The Confederate voice yells back and says that Forrest will not meet with an officer of inferior rank but will send in a Colonel (that being Duckworth) to arrange terms. The trick works, the fort contingency surrenders at about 11 AM, just several hours before a 2,000-man US force reaches the area and turns back after hearing of the surrender, not knowing exactly how big Forrest's force is. Since the Lincoln army has stopped paroles, the surrendered men will be taken to the new Confederate prison facility at Andersonville, Georgia, only about a third of them will ever make it home from there.

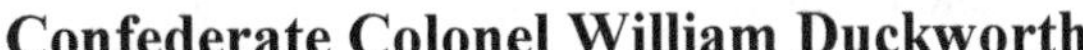

**Confederate Colonel William Duckworth**

## March 25, 1864:

In Louisiana, much of General Banks' army from New Orleans arrives in Alexandria today, and General Banks himself will arrive tomorrow.

***

In Paducah, Kentucky, shortly after noon today, Confederate General Nathan Bedford Forrest and 2,800 of his cavalrymen descend on the town that lies next to the Ohio River. Forrest has ridden 100 miles in 50 hours on this raid designed to recruit new soldiers to the South and to capture and destroy Union supplies. The defenders of the town, 665 in number, under the command of Union Col. Stephen Hicks, withdraw into Fort Anderson, a strong earthen fort just west of town, heavily supported by two gunboats in the river. Forrest demands the fort's surrender, but orders some of his men to keep the Yanks penned down inside the fort while the rest gather up the Union stores, destroying what they cannot use or carry.

Conf. Col. A.P. Thompson, a native of Paducah, disobeys Forrest instruction and orders an ill-advised assault on the fort, in which he is blown apart by the resulting artillery fire from the gunboats. The boats continue to fire on the town, not hitting the Confederates, but destroying much of the town. Forrest will complete his mission and leave the area about midnight, with about 50 prisoners and much needed stores.

In a few days Forrest will read a northern newspaper that boasts that he missed 140 excellent army horses that were hidden in a foundry, so he will send a detachment back, to again run Hicks into the fort, find the horses, and take them back to Mississippi with him.

**Paducah commemorative of Forrest's raid**

## March 26, 1864

In Paducah Kentucky, as Forrest's troops pull out, word has spread of his presence on the Ohio River, and panic is developing throughout Ohio, but Forrest is not going to stick around until all the Union forces in the area can be organized against him.

Union Lieutenant General Grant is now ensconced in his new quarters at Culpeper Court House, in Virginia, and Union Major General James McPherson, now working for Sherman, takes his position at the head of the Army of the Tennessee.

"Harper's Weekly", this week, on today's date, describes the difficult military condition of Mobile Bay and tells of the obstacles that Admiral Farragut faces in his campaign of conquest of that city. Here is some of it and a set of three pictures published today: "*.....At last accounts Admiral Farragut was bombarding Fort Powell, which commands Grant's Pass, on the left of the picture. This fort is bombproof, but under the vigorous fire directed against it, could not, it was believed at the date of the latest advices, long hold out......Fort Morgan is a very strong work, protected on the sea front by a strong water-battery of masonry and turf. The fort and battery, with their full battery, mount forty-five guns, mostly Columbiads of heavy calibre. Fort Gaines is situated on Dauphin's Island Point, three miles and one fourth from and nearly opposite Fort Morgan and is heavily mounted. Vessels drawing more than seven and a half feet are compelled to pass between these forts; and obstructions placed in the channel will make the passage for Farragut still more difficult......*

## March 27, 1864

In Georgia, Henry Wirz takes command of the prison inmates at Camp Sumter, near Andersonville, Georgia.

***

In Atlanta, Rev. Dr. Charles Quintard holds Easter services for Episcopals, calling the gathering, St Luke's. Property will be acquired, and construction will begin on a new Episcopal Church in Atlanta to accommodate the new refugee population. This is being done with the blessings and aid of St Phillip's Cathedral with gifted land and materials, built with volunteer labor.

***

50 years ago from this date, March 27 1814: It is the day of reckoning for the warlike, Upper Creek Indians in Alabama and Georgia. Following the philosophies of Tecumseh and his idiot brother, known as "the prophet", the Upper Creeks have revolted against the Creek Nation and declared war on the white population. After initiating massacres at the Battle of Burnt Corn and Fort Mims the "Red Sticks" (so-called because they all carry red war clubs) are headquartered on about 100 acres, tucked into the sharp bend of the Tallapoosa River, with river water on three sides of the camp, and the land entrance heavily fortified. Chief Menawa has about 1,000 warriors, and today a combined force of 2,700 Tennessee, Georgia, and Alabama militia, with Lower Creek and Cherokee warriors, under Andrew Jackson comes calling. Very much impressed with the land fortification, Jackson sends 1,300 of his men, under John Coffee, to cross the river and surround the encampment. At first, Jackson tries to reduce the breastwork with his light-weight cannon, but no major results are achieved. He then orders a straight-on charge with bayonets which does not succeed at first, but after a few hours of constant hand-to-hand battle, a young lieutenant, Sam Houston, manages to scamper over the wall and others follow with devastating fury on the Indians. Chief Menawa and about 200 of his warriors manage to escape into safety among the Seminole tribe in Spanish Florida. The others are all killed.

**Sam Houston receiving a wound at Horseshoe Bend**

## March 28, 1868

In Bonham, Texas, Ohio native and guerrilla leader William Quantrill is arrested by Confederate forces. Quantrill is famous for his lead in the sacking and destruction of Lawrence, Kansas two years after the target of the raid, Jim Lane, and his band of Jayhawkers, destroyed Osceola, Missouri. Once a legitimate Confederate soldier, Quantrill participated in the Battle of Wilson's Creek, early in the war, but soon thereafter, collected a group of thugs and renegades to run amuck in Kansas and Missouri. After murdering Union prisoners at Baxter Springs, he took his merry men to Texas where he has lived off the population by preying on the citizens of Fannin and Grayson Counties. He is arrested today but escapes his capture this afternoon and takes his men across the Red River into Indian Territory.

***

In Charleston Illinois, friction between the Copperheads (Southern Sympathizers) and the furloughed Union soldiers erupts into violence between the two factions. A Democratic rally, attracting hundreds of Copperheads, is disrupted by 40 or fifty soldiers who have been drinking and forcing citizens down on their knees to take a loyalty oath to the US Government. Much yelling and shoving has already passed between the groups, and when the soldiers approach Copperhead Nelson Wells and begin to hassle him, he draws a gun and kills a soldier, who is able to return fire and kill Wells before he dies. At this the Democrats uncover the weapons they have hidden in the wagons and in a matter of only minutes the death toll stands at 6 soldiers, 3 Copperheads and 1 innocent by-standing shopkeeper. 12 others are wounded. Tomorrow the town will be flooded with soldiers to restore order and arrest guilty parties.

## March 29, 1864

In Virginia, Confederate General Lee has been convinced the Federal effort will be concentrated on the west this year, but evidence is piling up that it is coming straight at him, so he is beginning to recall troops from furlough and create as many stockpiles as he can..

***

In Louisiana, Union General Banks has assembled his forces at Alexandria, and began pulling out yesterday, pushing up the Red River toward Shreveport. Meanwhile, in Shreveport, Confederate General Kirby Smith is assembling as many graycoats as he can to support his General Taylor's defense.

***

Today in North Carolina, a Rebel soldier excitedly writes home about a speech he heard his Governor deliver today in Charlotte, and a speculation about the origins of the term "tar-heel":

"Lee, Walter, ?-1865(?). "Letter from Walter Lee, March 29, 1864" "*...in an uproar in less than two minutes after he arose. He said it did not sound right to him to address us as "Fellow Soldiers," because he was not one of us-- he used to be until he shirked out of the service for a little office down in North Carolina, so now he would address us as "Fellow Tar Heels," as we always stick. I was in a good place to hear every word that he said, and I don't think I ever listened to a more able speech of the kind in my life. It was very able and deep, interspersed with anecdotes, illustration of his subject, which kept the men from feeling fatigued.* "

**North Carolina Governor Zebulon Vance**

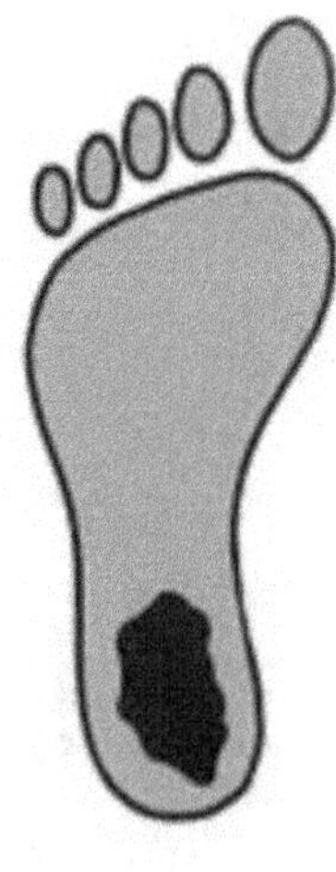

## March 30, 1864

In Virginia, on the Rappahannock, General Lee issues General Order 23 which states that the Army will comply with the Presidential and Congressional wishes that April 8, be set aside as a Day of Thanksgiving and Prayer. Only the most essential of labor is to be performed on that date.

***

.In Arkansas at the Saline River crossing, Union Lieutenants Grover Young and Frank Greathouse, each with 50 hand-picked men find the Rebel wagon train they have heard about, and they arrive at the camp in the wee hours of the morning. Under darkness they charge into the enemy camp and demand a surrender. The Confederates, completely surprised, immediately acquiesce, losing 35 wagons of supplies, 260 prisoners, and a payroll chest with $60,000 in it.

***

The Great Lakes Steamer the "*Maple Leaf*" has transported the entire baggage of the Brigade of Union Troops that has left Folly Island, S.C. for Jacksonville, Fla. Upon arrival today, the troops are unloaded, but before their gear and baggage can be unloaded, "*Maple Leaf*" is ordered to transport cavalry to Palatka, 70 miles up the St Johns River. On the return trip, "*Maple Leaf*" strikes a Rebel torpedo and sinks immediately, losing almost everything the Brigade owned, the Companies' books, uniforms, swords, gear; most end up with what they have on, and their rifles.

***"USS Maple Leaf"***

## March 31, 1864

In Albany New York, it is snowing to a depth of 13 inches, but in the South it is budding Spring; the fields are busy as you can tell from this letter written in Texas: "*Today the boys are at work planting corn in the new ground. Hicks assisted me at the mill. we ground 5 bushels of wheat & 6 bushels of corn. I let Mr. Leatherman have calf skin & sole leather enough to make five pairs of shoes. He took the measure of the little woman [Margaret Hall Stewart nee Sharp], Nellie [Mary Alexandrien Sharp nee Lemaire], Mother [Mahala Sharp Hall nee Roberts], Fawn [Florence Mahala Hall] & myself and promised to have the shoes back in six weeks. I paid him 25$ for making them or 5$ per pair. He then left for home. Weather clear & cool. So closes my notes for the month of March.*".

***

Union General Sherman reports to the Adjutant-General the following: "*Chattanooga, Tennessee, March 31, 1864 9 p. m. Am just down from Knoxville. Longstreet is doubtless moving out of East Tennessee for Virginia. General Schofield will occupy Bull's Gap with infantry and fill up the valley with cavalry. Forrest was badly worsted at Paducah and is still between the Mississippi and Tennessee. I hope to catch him and break him up. Veatch is near Purdy with infantry, and Grierson's cavalry is operating from Memphis. I will go to Nashville tomorrow, where I can better direct the movement. All well here. W. T. SHERMAN, Major-General* "

***

In Louisiana, Union Admiral Porter is having the devil of a time leaving Alexandria, because of the rapids and low water. He is not going to be able to go further with most of his fleet, but Union General Banks' army is still making good progress as it crosses the Cane River, as you can see in the picture from

***Leslie's Illustrated***

## April 1, 1864

In Arkansas, while Federal General Banks moves up the Red River, with Admiral Porter slowly groaning his way through the maze of boulders, plagued with low water in the River, Federal General Steele, moving south through Arkansas to join them, is plagued with high water and sloppy, muddy roads. Every time he comes to an existing ford the water is too high and he has to stop and bridge it

***

It is "All Fools Day" today, especially in the North. One Union soldier receives a letter from his little brother back home, "*April 1- Went to May Eldridges and Anne Fuller's birthday party. We had some fun. We put karosine oil on the birthday cake. It was a April fool joke. A boy don't have no fun having fun unless somebody jumps.*"

Below is an original Thomas Nast illustration from tomorrow's edition of "*Harper's Weekly*". It pertains to today, so we are previewing it. The cartoon features about a dozen images of April Fool's day pranks, and is captioned, "All Fool's Day". Some of the pranks in the picture include women paying a visit to an older man, with the women wearing beards and moustaches. Another image shows Civil War Soldiers playing April Fool's tricks on one another. In one case, a soldier is seen holding his hand on in front of the binoculars of a friend, and in another case, a sailor is seen holding his hat over the telescope of a friend. In one of the lower images, a young boy can be seen tying a string on the dress of a little girl, and in another image a school teacher is seen with a sign on his back that says, "Old Fool".

## April 2, 1864

In Louisiana, Union Major General Banks has concluded his supervision of elections in Alexandria and boards a gunboat that will take him, in few hours, to join his men at Natchitoches, where they are arriving today.

Admiral Porter's naval force is nearby at Grand Ecore, on the Red River. Just before leaving, Banks sends this message to his boss, General Halleck, "Our troops now occupy Natchitoches, and we hope to be in Shreveport by the 10th of April. I do not fear concentration of the enemy at that point. My fear is that they may not be willing to meet us." When President Lincoln occasions to read the dispatch, he has this comment: "I am sorry to see this tone of confidence," he says. "The next news we shall hear from there will be of a defeat."

But how can that be? Reb General, Taylor, only has just over 7,000 men while Banks musters a force of around 35,000. Even if Taylor is reinforced as his boss, Kirby Smith, promises, he will still be greatly outnumbered, especially when General Steele can get here from Arkansas. Taylor is sick and tired of retreating, and he is about to pick a spot and converge what support he can get at that point.

***

In Today's issue of "Harper's Weekly", there is a great drawing of a scene of the rearguard of Sherman's army as it moved across Mississippi back in February.

## April 3, 1864

In Louisiana on the Red River, Union Admiral David Porter's gunboats are moving the last of the troops and officers from Alexandria to Grand Encore. They will then march overland to Natchitoches to join the rest of General Bank's forces already there.

Meanwhile, in Arkansas, Union General Steele is fighting terrible roads, dense undergrowth, and the Rebel cavalry of John Marmaduke in his efforts to join Banks from the north. The two combatant forces are about equal in strength, but both of them are scattered so much that neither can get a good fight going. The Confederates are attacking on the flank, in the front, and in the rear, trying to prevent the Federals from crossing the Little Missouri River at Elkin's Ferry. Steele, however, manages to get enough of a force together to seize control of the crossing and manage to hold off the Graycoats until his men can be reassembled and over the river, in a two-day fight involving 8,500 Federals and 7,500 Confederates. There are only about 90 total casualties.

***

On the Outer Banks of North Carolina, the lighthouse at Cape Lookout is attacked by a small band of Confederates, trying to cripple Federal shipping in the area. The structure was built in 1859, replacing a smaller lighthouse built in 1812. The light is 163 ft from the ground and is visible 19 miles until it hides beneath the curvature of the Earth. There are very mixed reports about the Rebels' success, ranging from complete destruction, to minor damage, but the populace of the area will celebrate the event for at least 150 years.

**Cape Lookout Lighthouse**

## April 4, 1864

In Louisiana, the fighting for the crossing of the little Missouri River, while hotly contested yesterday, never came to a general engagement. 8,500 Infantry and cavalry under Union General Frederick Steele was successful in fending off the 7,500 cavalry under Confederate John Marmaduke. Early this morning, one division of Marmaduke's horsemen tries to take the ford back and are handily defeated. Fighting is quite scattered, and the two days' casualties are 38 for the Yankees and 54 for the Rebs. Marmaduke will retreat his men about 16 miles further south to have another go at Steele's men before they reach Shreveport and can join up with Banks and Smith against Confederate leader Kirby Smith.

***

Last night, after midnight, fire is discovered under the second flight of stairs of the Masonic Fraternity Building in Boston. The mammoth-sized building serves a dual purpose. The top three floors accommodate the Masonic order with the Grand Lodge of Massachusetts occupying one of them. The three lower floors compose the Winthrop House hotel and has 200 residents who barely escape with their lives. 16 different Lodge Rooms are total losses, as well as the Grand Lodgeroom. There is some insurance money, but not nearly enough. The Masonic order will have to come together nationally to solve this problem. The residents will all be relocated today, because of the great availability of rooms in Boston.

The original Winthrop House and Freemasonic Hall, Boston -- after the great fire.

## April 5, 1864

The Federal Army has a new cavalry commander, Maj. Gen. Philip Sheridan, brought from the Western theatre to Virginia and converted from a foot-soldier to head of Grant's cavalry.

***

The U.S. House of Representatives passes a joint resolution that states the nation will not permit the establishment of a monarchy in Mexico. It is feared that the French will establish trading with the Confederacy if they get a foothold on this continent.

***

In Louisiana, Federal General Banks has moved up the Red River some 60 miles toward Shreveport and has about 60 more to go. Union Admiral Porter with his fleet of transports and gunboats also has come that distance. Both factions of the expedition are resting and preparing at Grand Encore before moving on up the state. Porter has found the going getting rougher and rougher in the waters of the Red, but Banks is in high spirits. He has determined that Confederate General Taylor will not dare to make a stand against him and obviously lose, to a finer, more numerous, and better equipped fighting force.

Progress of the Red River Campaign…Keep in mind that the further they go up the rivers, the shallower the waterways become.

## April 6, 1864

On the second anniversary of Shiloh, in New Orleans, the puppet State Government set up by the Lincolnites today adopts a new state constitution, very much the same as the old one, except this one abolishes slavery.

***

In Louisiana, on the Red River at Grand Ecore, Union General Banks and Admiral Porter have everything ready for departure on up the Red toward Shreveport. This time they will separate, with Porter's fleet holding to the River and Banks taking an inland road that curves west, then northwest through Pleasant Hill and Mansfield, then back to the Red, where they will again meet up at Springfield Landing before continuing on to Shreveport. Banks has explained to his wife in a letter. "The enemy retreats before us and will not fight a battle this side of Shreveport, if then."

In Bank's army, in the 95th Illinois, is Jennie Irene Hodgers, an Irish-born immigrant woman, serving as a male soldier, Albert Cashier. From childhood, Cashier found she could find enough work to survive if she were male, and she enlisted in November of 1862. She will serve the Union army in approximately forty battles, including the siege of Vicksburg, The Red River Campaign, and the combat at Guntown, Mississippi. Her sex will be discovered several times in life, once in the military, and she will be thrown out, but will enlist again. Several times doctors and nurses will discover her secret but keep their findings private. She will work at various manly jobs and late in life will draw a military pension. Late in life her mind will deteriorate, and she will be admitted to the Watertown State Hospital for the Insane, where they will discover her sex and require her to wear a dress. By this time, she will be completely crazy and deserve the attire.

**Albert D.J. Cashier (Jennie Irene Hodgers)**

## April 7, 1864

In Tennessee, Confederate General Longstreet is ordered to leave Tennessee to the Union and take his troops back to Virginia to rejoin Lee's Army of Northern Virginia. Longstreet was detached last September and sent to aid General Bragg at the battle of Chickamauga, then to take Knoxville. He was unable to take Knoxville and has spent the winter in quarters just northeast of there.

***

In Louisiana, Confederate General Richard Taylor has managed to assemble a force of about 8,800 men to oppose the Union force, under Banks, of about 12,000. Banks has left the Red River and is approaching the town of Mansfield with much confidence. If he were on the Red, he would have the guns of Admiral Porter's gunboat fleet to cover him, but he feels secure with his own field artillery and his superior army. There is contact between the two forces this afternoon at Wilson's plantation, when a small group of Union horsemen are driven back by a larger group of Rebel cavalry. Banks is not concerned with this; many times, on this expedition, the Confederates have hit, and pulled back, retreating northward from the approaching Federals. They do not intend to retreat tomorrow.

**Confederate General Richard Taylor**

## April 8, 1864

The day of Thanksgiving and fasting that President Jefferson Davis called for two weeks ago, is being observed all across the South today. The churches are filled with those praying for help in this anticipated brutal year.

***

In Louisiana, Reb General Dick Taylor is not fasting, but mustering, and placing his "inferior" force of cavalry and infantry in a huge field at Sabine Crossroads, about 3 miles from Mansfield, where he will stop retreating. Taylor now has less than 9,000 men with, 4,000 more on the way to reinforce him. When the Yanks discover him in line of battle, they quickly start bringing their 20,000 up to the front, much hampered by the narrow roads and line of supply wagons mixed in the troop formation. When the Federals have pulled about 12, 000 to the front, Taylor decides to not wait any longer on his reinforcements and begins hostilities. The Feds are about to organize an attack, when Taylor attacks them with ferocity, "like a cyclone", one Union defender will say after the war. The blue line of the Yankees wavers and breaks, with the gray horde pouring in, and the best of Banks, turning and running. One reporter with the army will say afterwards, they were "a disorganized mob of screaming, sobbing, hysterical, pale, terror-stricken men.". After retreating several miles, Banks is able to utilize some of his reserves and assemble a line that stops the rout. The Confederates try it, but can only push it, not break it. After the third effort, darkness stops the fighting. Tonight, the Yanks will withdraw back to Pleasant Hill to await more action. Of the 12,000 Federals involved today , there are 2235 casualties, and the Confederates lose about 1,000 of their 9,000.

## April 9, 1864

In Virginia, US Grant is issuing campaign orders which I will discuss tomorrow.

***

In Arkansas, Federal General Steele is still trying to get his army to the party Union General Banks is throwing in Louisiana, but the horsemen of Reb General Marmaduke are making his journey a nightmare.

In the village of Pleasant Hill, Louisiana, General Banks waits most of the day for the onslaught from the reinforced Confederates that he knows will come. About 11:00 AM, he sends his supply wagons and cavalry back to Grand Ecore on the Red River, preparing for a general retreat. About 4 PM, the Confederates charge hard and are able to push his line of battle back, but this time his men do not break and run like yesterday. Banks is able to organize a counter-charge that is successful, and the Rebels are pushed from the field as darkness falls.

This morning at 4 AM, Confederate General Taylor notified his boss, General Kirby Smith of yesterday's fighting, and Smith left Shreveport immediately for the battlefields. When Smith arrives, the fighting has been over for hours and the Yankees have begun to pull out, toward the safety of the gunboats on the Red River. Forces are about equal in number today and losses similar. The Yanks lose just over 1300 and the Rebs lose over 1600.

**The Battle of Pleasant Hill from *"Harper's Weekly"*, published in New York City**

## April 10, 1864

In Louisiana, Federal General Banks is retreating back toward Grand Ecore where he can summon the fleet of David Porter to protect him with their big guns. Since he had sent his supply train back hours before the battle yesterday, he has no food or water for his men, and he has no medical supplies. He has to leave his wounded for the Confederates to nurse and capture.

***

In southern Arkansas, Union General Steele has been reinforced by General John Thayer and together they are able to defeat and push the Rebel defenders under Sterling Price back at the Prairie D'Ane, where skirmishing will continue for several days.

***

In Virginia yesterday, Union Lt. General Grant issued campaign orders as follows: "*Meade will go after Lee, Banks will move against Mobile, Sherman will go after Joe Johnston, Sigel will march south into the Shenandoah, and Benjamin Butler will move against Richmond from the south side of the James River.*"

***

In North Georgia Dr. Mary Edwards Walker, an assistant surgeon for the 52nd Ohio Volunteers, is captured by the Confederates and accused of spying. She will be held until August, then exchanged. Next year, she will become the only woman to receive the Medal of Honor.

**Dr Mary Edwards Walker with her Medal of Honor**

## April 11, 1864

In Louisiana, Federal General Banks reaches Grand Ecore and gets word to Admiral Porter to turn his gunboats around and come back down the river, where they will help each other retreat back out of the hell they created. They would have a lot worse time of it if Confederate General Kirby Smith had allowed Richard Taylor to have his way and actively pursue their destruction, but Union General Steele is making too much progress in his southward push through Arkansas and needs more attention from the boys in gray. He will get that soon.

***

In lower Kentucky, Reb General Forrest continues his raid , arriving in Columbus today. He will move on Fort Pillow, in Tennessee, tomorrow.

***

In upper Tennessee, Confederate General Longstreet has received his order to return his command to Virginia and to the Army of Northern Virginia. His men learn of this today, and there is much good feeling in the ranks. Brig. General Tige Anderson's Brigade of Georgia troops are very happy. They know that being close to Lee means big-time warfare, but just knowing he is watching the field makes the fighting less fearsome. A soldier of the 11th Georgia speaks for all of Longstreet's Corps when he writes, "We have seen the worst part of this war since we came to Tennessee."

**Confederate Brigadier General Tige Anderson**

## April 12, 1864

On this, the third anniversary of the start of the War at Fort Sumter and the second anniversary of the Great Locomotive Chase in northern Georgia, Reb General, Nathan Bedford Forrest, approaches Fort Pillow in the western part of Tennessee. With 1500 men, Forrest surrounds the fort and under white flag demands the surrender in twenty minutes or immediate assault. There is much bluster and taunting from the fort with the occupants feeling safe behind their strong walls. Union Major William Bradford, with 557 (half of them Negroes) heavily fortified defenders, sends a note saying, "I will not surrender".

Forrest turns and orders the bugler to sound the charge immediately. With Rebel sharpshooters pouring a murderous fire on the top of the parapets, the first charging wave runs to the base of the wall and into the six-foot deep ditch, using their backs as a stepping-stone for the second wave, who gain footing across the ditch and pull their comrades up with them. In another orchestrated movement, the sniper fire suddenly stops, and both waves go up the embankments, over the parapets, and fire their guns with deadly accuracy into the massed defenders who are beaten immediately. Although Forrest yells to cease fire, shooting goes on longer than necessary, with many of the defenders running toward, and swimming in the adjacent river. About half of the defending Federals are killed in the action and another 100 wounded.

The casualty rate is so high, especially among the colored soldiers, that the Northern papers will scream that it is a massacre. No doubt it is a brutal affair. Forrest loses about 100 men total.

**Fort Pillow**

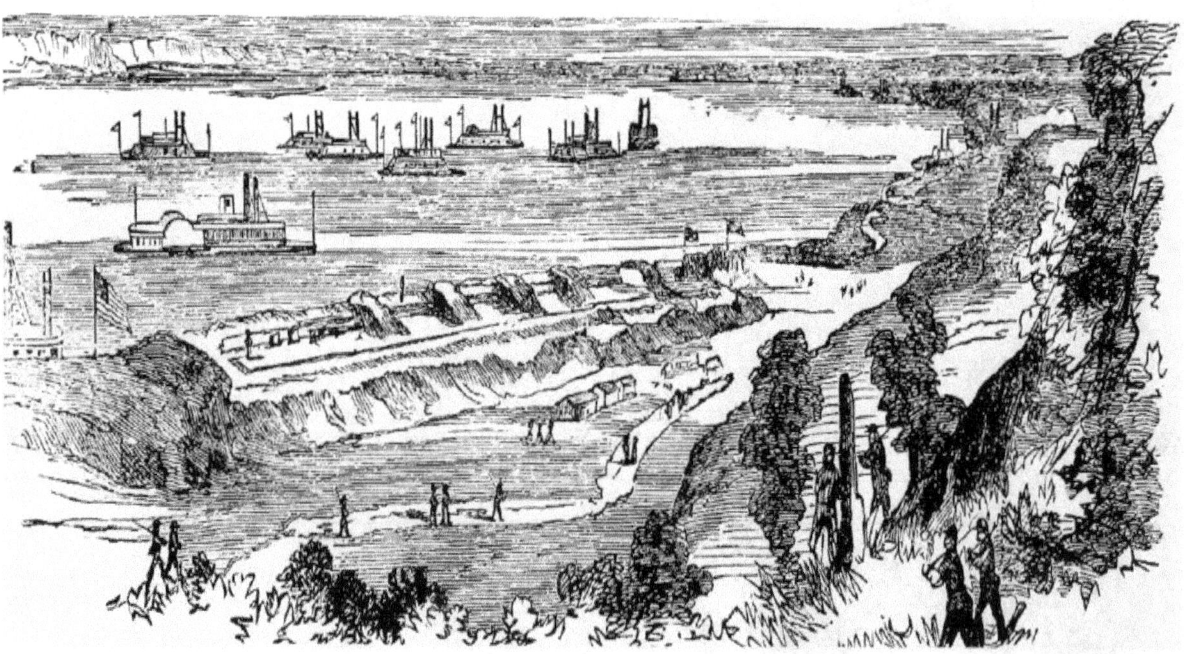

## April 13, 1864

In Louisiana, on the Red River, Admiral Porter's gunboat fleet safely arrives downstream to Grand Ecore, despite falling water levels and Rebel harassment. They will hang there, near Bank's army for a few days until Banks can figure out how to proceed with the expedition.

***

In Dalton, Georgia, Confederate General Johnston is carrying on a letter-argument with Bragg in Richmond concerning troop movements. Bragg wants him to move against Sherman and drive the Yanks from Tennessee, and it is Johnston's position that, since his 39,000 men would have slim chance against the 103,000 opponents, he wants to fight defensively, to try to keep his army in the field.

Evidently Bragg has chosen General Hood to be his in-camp spy because on this date Hood pens the following: "*I received your letter, and I am sorry to inform you that I have done all in my power to induce General Johnston to accept the proposition you made to move forward. I regret this exceedingly, as my heart was fixed upon going to the front and regaining Kentucky and Tennessee...To regain Tennessee would be of more value to us than half a dozen victories in Virginia.*" Hood goes on to recommend that Polk's army in Louisiana be moved to Dalton in order to strengthen Johnston's forces.

**Confederate General John Bell Hood**

## April 14, 1864

In Kentucky, there is fighting near Paducah with elements of Forrest's cavalry involved.

***

In Arkansas, in the Confederate efforts to slow the advance of Union General Steele's army going to reinforce Bank's withdrawing army, there is fighting at Bayou Saline, Dutch Mills, and White Oak Creek near Camden.

***

.In Washington, President Lincoln spends the day reviewing court-martial appeals. He reviews 67 cases today and issues several pardons. He has exactly one year to live.

***

In northwestern Georgia, there is a major skirmish between scouting parties of Reb General Johnston and Union General Sherman at Taylor's Ridge.

***

In New York City, the Sanitary Commission Fair begins today and will outshine the stellar production of its older sister in Chicago last year. The Sanitary Commission is administered by ladies and is to promote health and healing among the soldiers and wounded. The first two days of this event will result in collecting over $150,000......

**Sanitary Commission Fair at Metropolitan Fair Building NYC.**

**April 15, 1864**

In Knoxville, Federal Governor Andrew Johnson "*vociferously*" supports emancipation at a huge pro-Union rally. (This may seal his deal as the Republican nominee for Vice-President).

***

In lower Arkansas, today Federal General Steele's forces move into Camden, given up yesterday by Confederate General Price. The Rebs in the area keep falling back but delaying the larger Union army as they do.

***

In Shreveport, Confederate General Kirby Smith has left only a demonstration force to fool, not oppose, Union General Banks and brought most of his men north to move against Steele, who is having a hard time feeding his men and animals. All food was taken from the town of Camden by the retreating Rebs and the wells were spoiled by the citizens placing dead animals in them.

***

On the Red River, trying to get back down to Grand Ecore, the Federal iron-clad "*Eastport*" strikes a torpedo (mine) that tears a gaping hole in her bottom that is not repairable, but efforts will be made for several days before she is destroyed completely by her crew.

***"U.S.S. Eastport"***

## April 16, 1864

In Washington, the Army reports that since the beginning of the War they have captured 146,634 Confederate soldiers.

***

In Richmond, quoting from the diary of John Beouchamp Jones, a Rebel war clerk: *"APRIL 16TH. —Rained all night, and in fitful showers all day... Troops are passing northward every night. The carnage and carnival of death will soon begin!"*

***

.In Louisiana, Union General Banks receives the following correspondence notifying him that he is about to lose half his Red River force, and his expedition is over. He now has to retreat completely, losing as little as possible to the Rebs along the way.

*" General: The last of my transports having arrived from above, I take this the earliest opportunity of notifying the commanding general of the Department of the Gulf that I have received orders from Maj. Gen. W.T. Sherman, commanding Military Division of the Mississippi, to return with my command immediately to Vicksburg, Miss.*

*I have the honor to be, very respectfully, your obedient servant, A.J. Smith, Brigadier-General."*

**Brig. Gen. A.J. (whisky) Smith**

## April 17, 1864

The Confederate Government is very much interested in recovering the North Carolina coastal region and has detached Conf. Gen. Robert Hoke from the Army of Northern Virginia with 800 men to try to take Plymouth. He will have the aid of a new Confederate ironclad ram, "*CSS Albemarle*", that has been under construction for a year, in a makeshift shipyard, in a cornfield, up the Roanoke River at Edward's ferry.

A twenty-year-old Confederate Lieutenant, Gilbert Elliott, of North Carolina, is the contractor that has built this fine example of a armored gunship in a remote location, chosen by him, that does not permit heavy-drafting Union gunships to come close enough to destroy it. The Union Navy has known about the ship for some time and begged Washington to send a land force to destroy it, but the weather and bureaucracy has not allowed that until now, when it is too late.

The ship launches today, the same day that Hoke begins his attack on Plymouth. Only drawing nine feet of water, "*Albemarle*" has displacement of 376 tons, and she is 158 ft long and 35.4 ft wide. She has two steam engines of 200 horsepower each, and a top speed of 4 knots. She has a complement of 150 officers and men, armed with two 6.4 Brooke double-banded, rifled cannon. Her mission is to clear the river of all Union traffic, and all gunships and other, around Plymouth.

***"C.S.S. Albemarle"***

## April 18, 1864

In Arkansas, Union Major General Steele, after much fighting and swamp crawling, reached Camden three days ago, expecting large stores of supplies to be waiting for him. However, the supplies still have not arrived today, and his army is hungry. He sends a 1,200-man foraging party to take 200 wagonloads of corn from a Rebel storehouse, but on the way back the group is attacked, defeated, chased, and scattered into the woods at the Battle of Poison Spring. Steele will have to wait on the cornbread.

***

At Plymouth North Carolina, Reb General Hoke with 7,000 men is capturing some of the outer defenses and doing well with his attack, but will not be able to take the city without the aid of "CSS Albemarle" to bomb the city from the river and defeat the Yankee gunboats that are bombarding the Confederate forces. "Albemarle" is on her way but has been delayed with mechanical difficulties, and now she has reached a Union barricade of the river composed of old ship hulks that have been sunk to block her passage.

Tonight, after dark, the young Lieutenant, Gilbert Elliott, who has built the big ram, takes a couple of men and a small boat, and with a long probing pole, he is able to find a passage that the new iron-clad can cross, exploiting her shallow draft of nine feet. She will be ready for war and knee-deep in it, tomorrow morning.

***

***

Today, Confederate General Beauregard is officially notified that he will head up the newly-created Department of North Carolina and Cape Fear (which he will rename the Department of North Carolina and Southern Virginia). His job is to prepare to protect Richmond from the threat from Union General, Benjamin (the beast) Butler.

**Confederate General Pierre Gustave Toutant Beauregard**

## April 19, 1864

In the Roanoke River of North Carolina, the newly-constructed iron-clad ram of the Confederacy, "*CSS Albemarle*", eases over the sunken obstructions placed to keep it out of Albemarle Sound. The crossing occurs at four o'clock, and by first light her commander, James M Cook, sees the four Union ships that are waiting on him.

The two largest, "*Miami*" and "*Southfield*" are lashed loosely together to try to trap Albemarle between them so it can't ram them, and they can toss explosives down the smokestack, but Commander Cook is too wary for that and steers near the south bank, then turns abruptly and steams toward the two shackled ships. They are pouring solid shot on "*Albemarle*" as fast as they can load, but the Rebel armor is deflecting the balls, suffering only minor dimples with each shot.

"*Albemarle*" strikes "*Southfield*" in the flank and buries its snout all the way to the engine room, so deep that "*Albemarle*" has trouble pulling out and away. The captain of "*Miami*" fires three explosive shells point-blank at the Rebel monster, and all three shatter against the iron casement only 20 feet away. The third shot rebounds from the iron surface and knocks down the gun crew and kills the captain with shot fragments lodged deep in his face and chest. As "*Albemarle*" is able to free from "*Southfield*", "*Miami*" runs with all her speed toward open water with the other two Union gunboats running with her, leaving "*Southfield*" headed for the bottom.

Cook cannot chase them because shot holes in his smokestack prevent proper fire-drafting, but he can turn his guns on the fort. Now General Hoke's guns open on the fort also, and for the first time it is the Federal's turn to find out what it's like to try to hold the fort while under attack from land and water at the same time.

**"*CSS Albemarle*" in action with "*USS Southfield*" and "*USS Miami*"**

## April 20, 1864

In Albemarle Sound, Plymouth, North Carolina, the fortified City received quite a bashing yesterday from the guns of Confederate Brig. General Hoke and Commander James Cook, skipper of the brand-new iron-clad ram, "CSS Albemarle".

During the night, last night, the smokestacks of the ship were repaired, and it has plenty of maneuvering power this morning. At daylight all the Rebel guns open up again, pounding and pounding, without any return fire. "Albemarle" is in position to destroy any gunners who could fire on Hoke, and Hoke is in position to protect "Albemarle" in a like manner. Later the fort's commander will report: "The breast-height was struck by solid shot on every side, fragments of shell sought almost every interior angle of the work, the whole extent of the parapet was swept by musketry, and men were killed and wounded even on the banquette slope..."

At 10 AM, the white flag goes up and 2,834 prisoners, thirty guns and many supplies are taken for the Confederacy, at a cost of 300 casualties. Richmond is ecstatic, and President Davis wires Hoke directly: "Accept my thanks and congratulations for the brilliant success which has attended your attack and capture of Plymouth. You are promoted to be a major general from this date."

**Confederate Major General**
**Robert Frederick Hoke**

## April 21, 1864

On the Red River at Grand Ecore, Union General Banks has bemoaned his misfortunes long enough and accepted his failure to succeed in his grand expedition to Shreveport, and on then to Texas. He has spent several days writing excuses to Grant and asking for permission to continue his folly for several more weeks, but Grant has had enough of Banks. This spring, Banks has tied up 20,000 of his own men, 10,000 loaned to him by Sherman, another 10,000 with General Steele, still trying to make it to Shreveport, and the entire river fleet of Admiral David Porter.

At Porter's insistence, today Banks' army pulls out in retreat toward Alexandria. The Red River Campaign is not over. Now it remains to be seen if Banks can make it back to the Mississippi with his expeditionary force.

***

General Beauregard has taken over the responsibilities of defending northern North Carolina and southern Virginia.

***

In South Carolina, yesterday Confederate General Samuel Jones succeeded General Beauregard as commander of the Department of South Carolina.

**Confederate General Sam Jones, commander of South Carolina**

## April 22, 1864

In southern Arkansas at Camden, Union General Steele has been able to have corn bread and other sustenance since the day before yesterday when his supply train finally arrived. Steele now has word that the force under General Banks has been defeated and is not moving forward so he is biding his time in Camden, because he feels safe here.

Confederate General Kirby Smith has been pulling most of his forces to north of Shreveport in order to block Steele from further progress. Steele better think about going back north to Little Rock before Smith gets strong enough to come at him. Smith has left Confederate General Taylor only one division to harass Banks' withdrawal, but Taylor has Banks believing that he is as strong as he was at Pleasant Hill

***

Today the US Congress passes an act that calls for US coinage to be changed in chemical composition and include the word "God" in the stamping of the coinage. Treasury Secretary Chase has asked the Director of the Mint to submit designs, and Chase has written the following to him: "*I approve your mottoes, only suggesting that on that with the Washington obverse the motto should begin with the word OUR, so as to read OUR GOD AND OUR COUNTRY. And on that with the shield, it should be changed so as to read: IN GOD WE TRUST.*". It is this slogan that Congress approves today. The first time it will appear is on the two-cent coin. The chemical change is from a combination of nickel and copper to a combination of copper with small amounts of tin and zinc.

## April 23, 1864

Union General Banks' force retreats toward Alexandria where they will meet the Union Fleet of David Porter and be under the protection of his guns from the Red River once more. They are pushing hard to get there. Before the last of the men leave Grand Ecore, the lead units are twenty miles ahead of them. But they are not moving so fast that they cannot linger and pillage the countryside. Wanton destruction is following them down the river. The small Confederate Army in the area is kept busy helping the citizens fight the fires the spiteful blue army is setting, even burning the cabins of the Negroes who turn out to welcome them.

Confederate General Dick Taylor has sent Brig. Gen. Bee to hold a river crossing at Monett's Ferry. With 2,000 men to encounter 25,000, it is the Rebs best shot at a major victory, but it is not to be.

Fighting with his men dismounted, Bee fails to fortify his position properly and allows himself to be flanked by two divisions of cavalry. When his position becomes untenable, Bee retreats 30 miles instead of attacking disorganized elements of the main Union army. Taylor is livid with Bee and frustrated with his own lack of human resources to punish these torch-wielding monsters.

***

Around the world, including the United States and the Confederate States, today poetic and literary organizations are celebrating the 300th birthday of William Shakespeare.

**Happy birthday Bill!!**

## April 24, 1864

In Andersonville, Georgia, Confederate inspector Major Thomas Turner is quoted in the "*Columbus Daily Enquirer*" that an additional stockade is already needed at the new prison facility because of overcrowding, and that the inmate hospital that is now inside the stockade should be located somewhere else, on or near the post.

***

In Chattanooga, Union General Sherman issues orders today that when time comes to march, tents will be left behind. Each man is to carry bacon for five days, bread for twenty days, and a months' worth of salt, sugar, and coffee. Each regiment will have only one supply wagon including the headquarters staff, only one wagon for the entire staff, including Sherman.

***

In Virginia, General Lee writes to his son, Rooney, in an attempt to comfort him about the recent death of his wife from tuberculosis. Rooney was a prisoner of war when she died and has been deep in depression since his recent release.

Lee writes: "*I recd last night My dear Son your letter of the 22nd. It has given me great Comfort. God knows how I loved your dear dear Wife, how Sweet her memory is to me, & how I mourn her loss. My grief Could not be greater if you had been taken from me. You were both equally dear to me. My heart is too full to Speak on this Subject, nor Can I write. But my grief is not for her, but for ourselves. She is brighter & happier than ever, Safe from all evil & awaiting us in her Heavenly abode. May God in his Mercy enable us to join her in eternal praise to our Lord & Saviour. Let us humbly bow ourselves before Him & offer perpetual prayer for pardon & forgiveness!*"

**Confederate Brig. Gen. William Henry Fitzhugh Lee (Rooney)**

## April 25, 1864:

In Arkansas, Confederate cavalry commander, Brig. Gen James Fagan, operating under Kirby Smith near Camden, gets word of a large supply train that has been sent by Union General Steele back to Pine Bluff for supplies. The train is large and well-guarded by some 1800 soldiers, about half the force that Fagan commands.

At dawn, this morning Fagan has placed some of his men in front of the train to block the way, while others attack from the flanks, with still others cutting off the retreat. As the supply train approaches Mark's Mill in a large clearing, the Rebels strike. In fighting that lasts about four hours total, the Confederates are able to reach around the Yankees and smother out their battle efforts, capturing all but about 150 of the Union forces.

Confederate losses are estimated at about 300 killed and wounded. The victorious Southerners hold about 1,300 prisoners, 300 wagons with their teams, and six cannons. This action leaves Union General Steele in a very precarious position at Camden with his enemy becoming stronger each day and his pantry dwindling rapidly. He has a big decision to make tonight.

**Confederate Brigadier General James Fleming Fagan**

## April 26, 1864

In North Carolina, Federal troops are beginning to evacuate Washington, North Carolina, following the fall of Plymouth and anticipating the further success of Confederate General Hoke and the ram, "*Albemarle*".

***

At one o'clock this morning in Camden, Arkansas, the troops of Union General Steele silently steal from their fortifications and begin their journey to Little Rock and safety. The Camden expedition of the Red River Campaign is over, except for the Confederate defenders who are becoming the aggressors. To help delay the Rebs pursuit, the Yanks take the pontoon bridge that crosses the river with them. The men in gray will have to swim their cavalry across and build a bridge for the supply trains and big guns before they can follow.

***

In Louisiana, remember the portions of US Admiral David Porter's gunboat fleet that could not get over the rapids at Alexandria Falls? Well they are in much better shape than the ones that did. The river continues to fall to a level where there is not much more than 3 feet of water, and the upper river boats are having to drag each other over rocks and sandbars to make any progress at all. I do not know what they will do when they again encounter the rapids at the falls. There simply is not enough water to take them over, and the Rebels keep raking their ships with cannon and small arms fire, relentlessly.

**U.S. Naval Admiral David Porter**

## April 27, 1864

In north Georgia, there is skirmishing every day around Chickamauga, Taylor's Ridge, and Ringgold, with scouting groups on both sides trying to see what the other side is up to.

***

.In Arkansas, the Confederates spend the entire day and most of tonight in swimming the cavalry and ferrying the infantry and artillery across the Ouachita River, so they can begin pursuit of the fleeing Union Army under General Steele. They build a floating bridge (huge raft), and the crossings are many, also they are slow, but they finally will get the job done early tomorrow morning.

***

In Richmond, President Davis meets with and instructs Jacob Thompson on a secret mission to Canada. Thompson was the 5th United States Secretary of the Interior and is familiar with many Canadian Government officials. He resigned his post at the beginning of the War to become Inspector General of the Confederate States Army. His secret mission is to obtain Canadian help to contact certain United States officials as to possible peace or truce agreements.

**Confederate Inspector General Jacob Thompson**

## April 28, 1864

In southern Arkansas, a desperate race is underway. The Federal troops under General Steele are putting forth an all-out effort to make it across the Saline River before the Confederates of Kirby Smith can catch them in force. Just before he began his retreat, Steele issued to his men, all the remaining food rations. Each man received two hardtack crackers and a half-pint of cornmeal, with a warning that this is all there would be until they get across the Saline River and meet a friendly wagon train.

It has started to rain, really blow, and storm, and the roads are quickly becoming quagmires. The poorly fed draft animals are having an extremely hard time pulling the ammo wagons, the cannon, and the wagons that are transporting the pontoon bridge that will take them to safety, across the Saline.

The men in blue are trembly in the legs and short in endurance because of the lack of nourishment, but they manage to make it to the little town of Princeton where they will bed for the night, in the dismal rain.

**April 29, 1864**

In Arkansas, the race between the Confederates and the Union army of General Steele is almost over. Today Steele will make it to the banks of the Saline River but will not get across it before the Confederates hit him. The cavalry units of Rebel General Marmaduke are dicing and chopping at the outer edges of the soggy force, with the rain continuing in an absolute downpour.

The Yankee engineers make it to the river and start launching their pontoons, linking, and flooring them. The other troops rapidly construct breastworks and corduroy the road in the low areas on both sides of the bridge. The work goes on most of the night, by firelight, when they can keep the fires lit in spite of the rain.

The Confederates are exhausted, but they keep pushing on, and arrive, only to collapse into the mud for a few hours rest before the battle starts at first light.

***

In Virginia, the Seventh and Eighth Georgia Regiments, with the rest of Anderson's Brigade and the whole of Longstreet's army are proudly marching in review for General Lee. Although they know the fighting will soon begin, they are somehow comforted to know that Lee will be on the field with them this time. When Lee reviews the troops, all know the fighting is imminent. The Battle of the Wilderness will begin in four days.

General Lee on Traveler

**April 30, 1864**

In Arkansas, on the Saline River at Jenkin's Ferry, the Union force under General Steele has started crossing the pontoon bridge assembled during the night. The Confederates under General Kirby Smith have a hard time getting to the fortified protection of the bridge.

The Yanks have built sturdy fortifications of logs and mud between impenetrable swamps of Toxie Creek that protect the left and the right. The only avenue of attack is straight up, head on to the breastworks and that does not do well. A heavy fog is over the field, thickened with gun smoke, impenetrable by light but stops no Yankee bullets, and the Southern boys are driven back time after time, while the Federals keep on crossing.

Finally, the rear guard is pulled over the bridge, and it is cut loose, breaking out with fire as it swings down the river. The Federal army is saved, what's left of it.

***

In Richmond, late this afternoon, tragedy strikes the household of President Jefferson Davis. His five-year-old son, Joseph Evan is killed in an accident at the Confederate White House. He attempted to climb to the top of a portico and fell 15 feet onto a brick walkway. He is discovered by a servant who tries to revive him, but to no avail. His parents are gone when it happens but arrive home in time to have the boy die in their arms.

**Devastated, President Davis will have the portico removed, and the children of Richmond will consort to furnish the marker for his child. No pictures were ever taken of Joseph Evan.**

## May 1, 1864

In Arkansas, Union General Steele is not being pursued in force, but he thinks he is, just as soon as the Rebels can get across the Saline River. Instead of pursuit of Steele, Confederate General Kirby Smith has decided to rest his men for a couple of days and head them down the Red River to help General Taylor damage the retreating Federals under Banks as much as they can.

Meanwhile, from dawn today until 4 AM tomorrow the starving, staggering, troops of Steele's are moving toward Little Rock and safety. In the afternoon tomorrow, they will encounter a supply train and have the first real food in several days. Today, as wagons are stuck in the muck, the teams are cut loose, and the wagons are burned. Tonight, the cavalry will light fires along the road for the exhausted troops to see the route by.

***

On the Red River at Alexandria, the weary troops of General Banks have completed their retreat to Alexandria, but the upper fleet of Admiral Porter is stuck in the low water of the Red. There is only three feet four inches of water and the fleet needs seven feet to get over the natural dam and rapids' boulders at Alexandria. Porter is in complete despair. He knows he will have to destroy millions of dollars of equipment and his naval career will be blemished beyond repair, but his chief of engineers, Lt Col Joseph Bailey, has a plan.

He will use his logging experience in building dams to float logs to design a dam and raise the river level. After some initial scoffing Porter has warmed to the idea, and Banks gives Bailey 3,000 men to do the job. They begin work today.

**Lt Col Joseph Bailey, Union Chief of Engineers**

## May 2, 1864

In northwestern Georgia, near Ringgold and Tunnel Hill, skirmishing occurs between the Yanks of Union General Sherman and the Rebs of Joe Johnson as the armies maneuver and gather themselves for the imminent action ahead.

***

In Virginia, along the Rapidan, General Lee meets with his Generals and discusses their flexible defense, the ability to shift to meet the thrust of the Federals when it comes. Lee seems to know that Grant is giving orders now to begin movement tomorrow, on Lee's right......

***

In Richmond, speaking to congress, Confederate President, Jefferson Davis has the following: " *...The unjust war commenced against us in violation of the rights of the States, and in usurpation of power not delegated to the government of the United States, is still characterized by the barbarism with which it has heretofore been conducted by the enemy. Aged men, helpless women and children, appeal in vain to the humanity which should be inspired by their condition, for immunity from arrest, incarceration or banishment from their homes. Plunder and devastation of the property of non-combatants, destruction of private dwellings and even of edifices devoted to the worship of God, expeditions organized for the sole purpose of sacking cities, consigning them to the flames, killing the unarmed inhabitants and inflicting horrible outrages on women and children are some of the constantly recurring atrocities of the invader."*

**Jefferson Davis**

**May 3, 1864**

In northwest Georgia, Union General Sherman with 98,500 men (he has a large number on furlough that will return by June 1, raising his force to 112,000) makes final preparations and gives final orders that will begin the Atlanta campaign tomorrow, against the Confederate army of General Joseph Johnston who initially has about 50,000 men that will be reinforced with another 15,000, bringing his force to 65,000.

***

In Virginia, along the Rapidan River, there is great movement and excitement by the forces of Union Generals Grant and Meade, pushing the army up to the Rapidan for imminent crossing. In a movement that will begin shortly after midnight tonight, Grant will bring 102,000 men across the river, and Lee will oppose with 61,000. When Grant clears the river, his destination is around to the right of Lee and into the open country where he can maneuver his huge force to advantage. Lee will not allow that to happen. He will not oppose the river crossing but will make Grant fight in the wilderness near the river to limit his maneuverability and artillery power.

**Union General Grant**

**Confederate General Lee**

## May 4, 1864

Federal General Sherman has his whole army moving from Chattanooga and Ringgold toward the western edge of Rocky Face Ridge and will be in position to fight Joe Johnston's Confederates in three days.

***

On the Rapidan in Virginia, General Lee has correctly guessed the direction of the Federal movement across the river that began shortly after midnight, but in case he was wrong, he had placed General Longstreet's corps forty miles away at Gordonsville. Now Longstreet has to hustle up to get to Lee before the fighting starts. Lee's other Generals, Ewell, AP Hill, and cavalry commander Stuart are ordered to oppose the Federals but not bring on a general engagement until Longstreet can reach a point where he can, at least, strike a flanking blow.

By late this afternoon, Federal General Grant will have his 122,000 men across the river and in positions to rest for his intended attack at dawn tomorrow, not knowing that the Rebels are only about a mile away. Longstreet will march his men for most of the night to try to get in place, and Lee will prepare to meet the onslaught, outnumbered two to one, slightly better odds than a year ago when he defeated Joe Hooker at nearby Chancellorsville...maybe he can attack the Yankees before they attack him

***

.Meanwhile, Union General Benjamin (the beast) Butler has 30,000 troops on about 200 transport ships heading up the James River to strike a lethal blow on Richmond, only defended with 5,000 men. Confederate General Beauregard is on his way to reinforce the Richmond garrison.

The Overland Campaign May 4, 1864

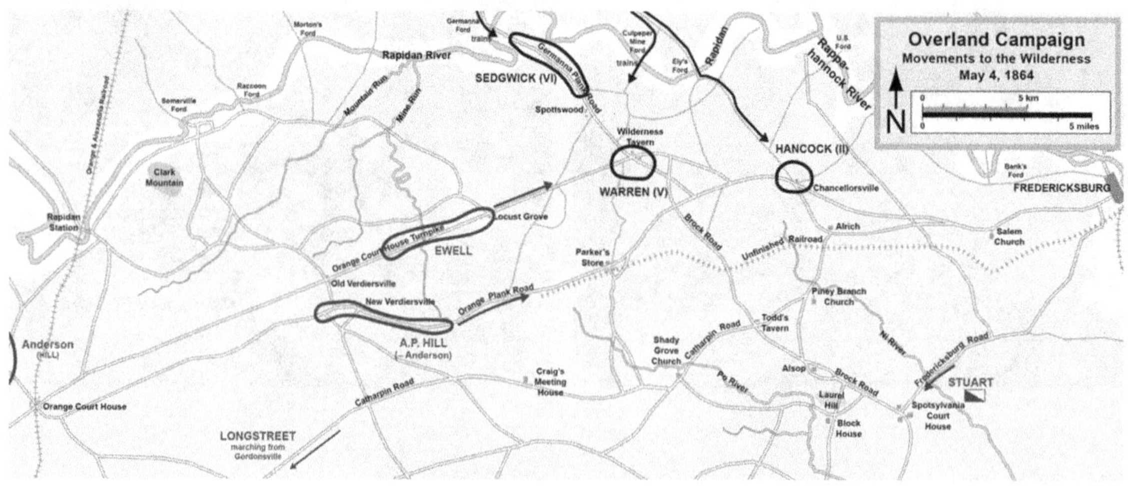

**May 5, 1864**

There is much cavalry skirmishing in North Georgia as Sherman's Army moves toward Buzzard's Roost, a gap in Rocky Face Ridge.

***

In the wilderness, south of the Rapidan of Virginia, dawn brings a beautiful spring day. Union General Gouverneur K. Warren's Fifth Corps meets, in a mutual attack, Confederate General Ewell's Second Corps on the Orange Turnpike with initial success, driving the Rebels back, but Ewell recovers and is able to drive back Warren and his Fifth Corps.

Meanwhile, the Confederates of A.P. Hill, who early advance on the Orange Plank Road, slam into Union General Hancock, and sharp fighting ensues with basically the same results as the other field of the battle. Many of the Northern units are struggling through the briars and bushes trying to get their army together and artillery into position to be effective.

Reb General Longstreet is still trying to get to the action and will march his men through much of the night tonight so they can participate tomorrow. Darkness halts the action today, and both armies will fight as whole tomorrow. Where the fighting has occurred today, neither side was fortified and casualties are very high on each side, with the Federals losing many more than the Confederates.

**Battle of the Wilderness by Kurz and Allison**

**May 6, 1863**

In northwest Georgia, the Union troops of General Sherman move ever closer to the gap in Rocky Face Ridge, known as "Buzzard Roost", and will attack the Confederates there tomorrow.

In Virginia, fighting continues in the Wilderness south of the Rapidan. On the Federal right, along the Orange Turnpike, Union Generals Warren and Sedgewick are finding Reb General Ewell tough to conquer, and on the left the Yankee troops of Hancock have discovered that not only are they fighting Reb Gen. A.P. Hill, but Longstreet's Corps has joined the party. Shortly after noon, Longstreet finds a weak spot where the Yanks can be flanked and sends in two divisions to overwhelm the Feds and start them running. As Longstreet is pushing to supplement their efforts with a charge of his own, he is wounded in the base of his neck with the bullet passing into his right shoulder. He blows the bloody froth from his mouth to shout, "Tell General Field to take command, and move forward with the whole force and gain the Brock Road".

The Yankees are in bad shape all over the battlefield, but holding on tightly in many places, then the battlefield catches fire. Soldiers are running, pulling wounded to safety, and fighting as best they can in the smoke and flames.

Toward the end of the day, Reb General John B Gordon is finally given permission for a charge against the Union right flank, which is quite successful but not supported, forcing him to withdraw from his gains.

Grant has discovered, on this day, what a parade of Union Army commanders before him already have known about Lee. He comes to the battle to fight. It is a resounding Confederate victory; the Federals remove from the field, leaving 17,666 casualties of an engaged force of over 100,000. Of the 60,000 Confederates, there are about 7500 casualties.

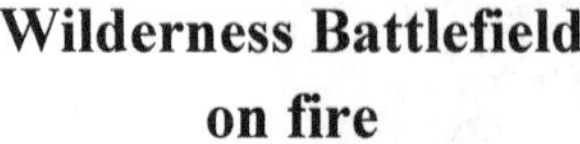

**Wilderness Battlefield on fire**

**May 7, 1864**

In Virginia, at the Wilderness Battlefield, both armies are licking their wounds from the last two days of fighting. Essentially, neither army has destroyed the other, and Grant is not going to try again today. He wants to be in open country where he can bring all his artillery to bear and take advantage of his two-to-one personnel advantage.

Grant orders his army to Spotsylvania Courthouse, in direct line to Richmond. Lee will have to follow to try to get between Grant and the Confederate Capital.

Lee orders Maj. Gen. Richard Heron Anderson, commanding in place of wounded Longstreet, to take his corps and beat Grant to the vital crossroads at Spotsylvania, while Stuart's cavalry delays the Federal movement as much as possible.

***

In southeastern Virginia at the James River, Union General Butler has landed his 33,000 troops and is fortifying himself before making his move on Richmond.

***

In northwest Georgia, as part of Sherman's Union Army under Thomas moves toward Rocky Face Ridge, Another Portion under Schofield moves north to go around Rocky Face between Dalton, GA and Cleveland, Tennessee. Still another portion, under McPherson, is moving southward to steal through Snake Creek Gap and move against the railroad at Resaca. There is fighting at Tunnel Hill as Thomas' advance troops take control of this, another way to get across the mountain barrier that the Confederates of Johnston have wintered behind.

**Tunnel at Tunnel Hill**

## May 8, 1864

In Georgia, near Dalton, the army of General Thomas, under Sherman demonstrates heavily against the impenetrable fortifications of the Confederates on Rocky Face Ridge while Union General McPherson sneaks his Army of the Tennessee through Snake Creek Gap and moves toward Resaca in a plan to entrap the Rebs between armies.

***

In Northern Virginia, after an all-night race, the Confederates of Calvary Commander Fitzhugh Lee manage to fortify high ground near Spotsylvania Courthouse, at a place they call Laurel Hill, just in time to be attacked by lead units of Grant's Federals. The initial attacks are repulsed, and more are attempted as the Union army comes up. However Confederate, General Richard Anderson, commanding Longstreet's corps, begins to arrive and fortify, so all attempts to drive Johnny Reb away and out of the wilderness areas are foiled.

Late in the day, Confederate General Ewell's Corps arrive, just in time to help stave off a late-day assault on the now-growing trench works. Ewell is very sick and not fit for command, so he is temporarily relieved by Jubal Early, who appoints General John B Gordon to command his Division.

The Confederate cavalry, both mounted and dismounted, have given Lee great service over the last two days, but Grant is disappointed in his Cavalry commander, Phil Sheridan, and he orders him to take 10,000 horsemen and raid toward Richmond, in order to draw Confederate Stuart away from the army activities.

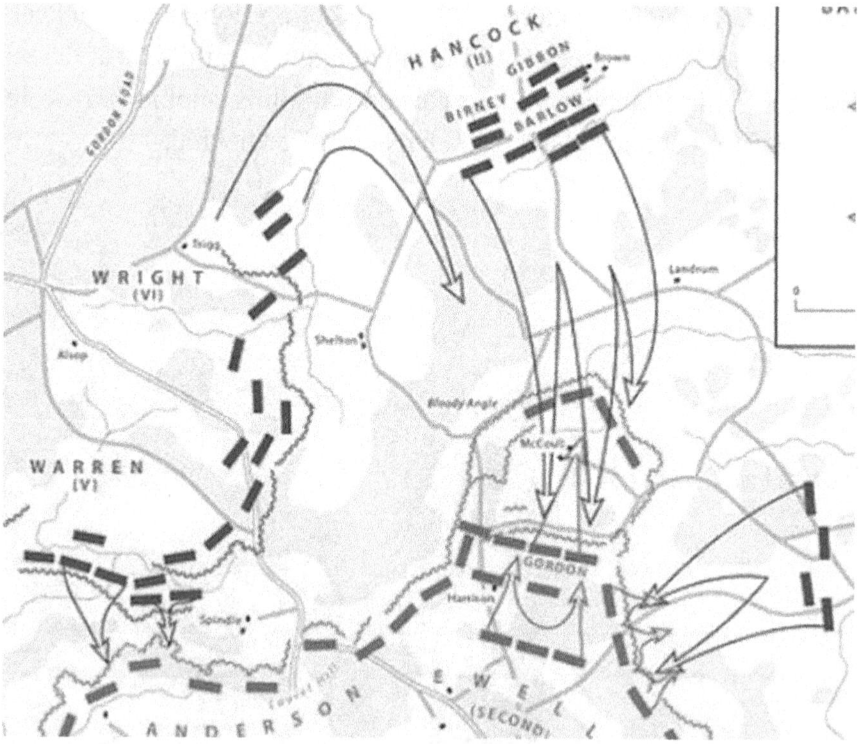

**In the map, remember Richard Anderson is commanding Longstreet's Corps, and Tige Anderson's Brigade is part of that corps. Gordon is commanding Early's Division**

**May 9, 1864**

Near Dalton, GA, the Army of the Cumberland, under Union Gen. Thomas is attacking and demonstrating the main Confederate force at Rocky Face Ridge, west of Dalton. The Army of the Ohio, under Schofield, is demonstrating and attacking the Confederates north of Dalton. The Army of the Tennessee, under McPherson, is moving out of Snake Creek Gap, captured yesterday, and engaging minor Rebel units as they push toward the railroad at Resaca; they are well behind enemy lines and without cavalry.

McPherson's job is to cut the railroad and fortify between Resaca and Dalton to prevent the Rebs at Rocky Face from being able to withdraw southward, but Southern resistance is stiffer than is was supposed to be, and McPherson is traveling blind with only a few horsemen out scouting for him. All the Yankee Generals know that Confederate General Polk is on his way from Louisiana to reinforce the Confederates, but they do not know when the arrival will be or how many are coming. McPherson decides to pull back and dig in near Snake Creek Gap, but the fact that he has been near to Resaca is enough to draw the Confederates out of their strong defensive positions to thwart their enemy behind them.

***

In Virginia, fighting is sporadic at Spotsylvania Courthouse today, limited to artillery exchanges and sniper fire. One Rebel sniper is especially effective. Firing from about 800 yds, his Whitworth rifle is whistling bullets near the staff of General Sedgwick.

When Sedgwick sees his men dodging from the close rounds, he says, "What? Men dodging this way for single bullets"..."They couldn't hit an elephant at this distance". Those are his final words, as the bullet slams into his face, creating a fountain of blood, pumping his life into the Virginia soil. He will be shipped to Cornwall Hollow, Connecticut for interment in the Berkshires.

**Union Major General John (Uncle John) Sedgwick**

## May 10, 1864

In Northwest Georgia, Union General Sherman, disappointed in McPherson's performance at Resaca yesterday, begins to move his entire army down through Sugar Valley and Snake Creek Gap, with Resaca as a destination.

***

In Virginia, Union cavalry General Sheridan's 10,000 raiders are skirmishing with Jeb Stuart's cavalry all along the North Anna River and near Beaver Dam Station. Stuart is placing his force between Richmond and Sheridan, barely 20 miles from Richmond.

***

At Spotsylvania, the Confederate defenses are about four miles long and sparsely manned in places. General Lee has Brig. Gen. Gordon, temporarily Division commander, hold his division behind the center angle so that he can move to assist any threatened area. There have been two major assaults today, and the Federals have been thrown back handily.

Late this afternoon, around 6:00, Union Major General Upton masses his division and strikes the "mule-shoe" shape of the center of the line. His charge carries over the trenches and into the Rebels, driving and scattering the defenders. Gordon's Division races to the rescue, surrounds and kills many of the Federals, capturing many of them before Upton can free himself and get back to his friendly lines.

On the Federal left, Burnsides Corps, not engaged today, moves close to the town, entrenching in front of Early's Corps.

**Upton's Charge at Spotsylvania Courthouse**

## May 11, 1864

In Virginia, downpours of rain most of the day keep the armies apart. Grant wants to try the bulge in the center of the Rebel line again, but that will have to wait until tomorrow.

In Virginia, the 10,000 horsemen of Union General Sheridan defeat the 4,500 cavalrymen of JEB Stuart in a three-hour action at Yellow Tavern. Each of the Union riders is armed with Spencer repeating rifles, but it is a 44-caliber pistol shot that mortally wounds Stuart. He is carried to the rear, and Maj. Gen. Fitzhugh Lee assumes temporary command.

Sheridan will not try the defenses of Richmond but will go around and join Butler's forces opposing Beauregard. Grant will be without cavalry eyes for a couple of weeks.

***

In Louisiana, on the Red River Union Admiral Porter has watched his Chief Engineer, Lt. Col. Bailey, design and oversee construction of a dam that is hoped to float his flotilla over the rocks of the rapids at Alexandria. The dam is constructed and almost filled with water when the center begins to fail from the pressure. Porter orders three nearby vessels to line up near the potential breach, and when the dam breaks, the three of them are able to pass over and float on down the river. The dam will be repaired, and a supplemental dam will be built to float the remainder of the fleet up and over, out of harm's way.

BAILEY'S DAM ON THE RED RIVER.

## May 12, 1864

In North Georgia, Union General Sherman is assembling his armies as they make their ways through the mountain passes and narrow valleys to the open country, moving close to Resaca.

Confederate General Johnston will pull his army off Rocky Face Ridge and Dalton, heading them to Resaca tonight.

***

On the Spotsylvania battlefield, this morning at 4:30 Union General Hancock creeps his corps up to Ewell's lines and begins to pour through in a concentrated effort that is largely undiscovered until daylight. Tens of thousands of Yankees are behind the lines and more are coming. Brig. Gen. John B Gordon, acting Division Commander, assembles his division for a counter-charge and, when ready, notices General Lee, hatless, in front of his men, intending to lead the charge in person, out front.

"Go back, General Lee," yells Gordon. "We will drive them back!" "These men are Georgians, Virginians, and Carolinians. They have never failed you on any field. They will not fail you here. Will you boys?" The reply is resounding, and when General Lee is led to the rear, Gordon leads the charge and is able to stop the Federal advance and hold until Generals Rodes and Jim Lane reinforce him to push the federals back enough that lines can be re-established. This is a very bloody day; with prisoners included, the Federals lose about 7,000 and the South loses about 9,000 men. General Lee is so grateful for Gordon's efforts, he applies for, and is granted, a new commission for Gordon. Day after tomorrow, he will be Major General John B Gordon.

**Future Historic Oakland Cemetery
Resident Major General John B Gordon**

## May 13, 1864

In Louisiana, on the Red River, the last of the federal ships that have been hung above the falls at Alexandria are saved by use of a system of dams to increase the water level on that part of the river so they can clear the rocks of the rapids. Bank's Federal army will leave Alexandria today, under the protection of the guns of that river fleet of Admiral Porter.

Starting about 9 AM, Banks will repay the citizens of Alexandria for their forced hospitality by burning the town completely, including all courthouse records, all churches except one Catholic Church, schools, houses, barns...everything. He has also taken all food and forage.

***

In Virginia, after the fierce fighting yesterday, wounded are tended and armies reposition themselves, with Grant preparing to move away from Lee toward the south, then east.

***

In north Georgia, skirmishing has begun around Resaca between Confederate General Polk's Louisianans and forward elements of Sherman's three armies. The main Confederate force is mostly moving by train out of Dalton and into the prepared lines of fortifications at Resaca. There is sporadic fighting in the area the entire day, but the main event will begin tomorrow.

**Confederate positions at Resaca**

## May 14, 1864

Just northwest of Resaca, Georgia, General Johnston has his 60,000 Rebels heavily fortified in a line that is four miles long, with his left at the Oostanaula River and the right touching the Conasauga, with steep-banked Camp Creek, in front of his lines. Late this morning, Maj. Gen John Schofield and Maj. Gen Oliver Howard charge their Yankee divisions across the Camp Creek and into the breastworks, suffering heavy casualties in their repulsion. The only Union success on the field this day will be to push General Polk's line back, closer to Resaca. After several such attacks, by 3 PM the Union Army settles in for a heavy artillery bombardment of the impregnable Rebel lines.

Meanwhile, Union General Sherman is having a brand-new pontoon bridge, along with an older one, moved into position to be installed across the Oostanaula River, downriver about five miles at Lay's Ferry. Union Brig. General Sweeny, who works for James McPherson, today secures the Ferry, and moves the bridges into position for installation tomorrow morning. This will give the Federals the threat they need to the Confederate life-line (the railroad south), in order to pull them from their strong defensive position into the open where the disparity in numbers of troops matters more. That is....if they can hold onto their river crossing......

**Resaca, by Kurtz and Allison, first day of real fighting, from a Union perspective**

**May 15, 1864**

Yesterday at Resaca, Georgia, the Federals attacked multiple times trying the defenses of Joseph Johnston's Confederates. One attempt was moderately, but temporarily successful and the day ended with everyone still in place. Today is not much different. The battle line is loaded with Union General Hooker's corps concentrating attacks down the Dalton-Resaca wagon road and overrunning Reb. Captain Max Van Dem Corput's four-Napoleon gun battery. Counter attacks and counter- counter attacks are the order of the day over the ground occupied by four unmanned cannon, with the Federals finally sneaking up to the battery, digging down a corner of the earthworks, and dragging the guns out with ropes.

Meanwhile, at Lay's Ferry, downstream about 5 miles, just east of Calhoun, Union General Sweeny has built two pontoon bridges across the Oostanaula River to move soldiers across and flank the Rebels out of position. Despite opposition by Reb General Walker, Sweeny is able to establish foothold and flood the area with Yankees. Tonight, General Johnston will remove his force down to the south, to keep his supply lines from being severed.

***

This morning there is drama at Farmer's Bridge on Armuchee Creek, just north of Rome. A force of horsemen of Union General Garrard, under Colonel Minty, three regiments and artillery, arrive on the road just north of the bridge. They are opposed by a company of Johnnies under Captain William Lokey, the defenders being successful in repelling the initial charge, but Minty pins the Confederates in place and sends flanking units across the creek at fords upstream and downstream, forcing the Rebels out of works and into retreat. Their Captain, Lokey is wounded mortally and ten of his command killed. Their bodies will be temporarily interred where they are killed but will soon be moved to a family graveyard. Later the family graveyard will be surrounded by the New Armuchee Baptist Church graveyard where my Great-Grandparents, my Grandparents, Great Aunts and Uncles, and Aunts and Uncles will join them on the peaceful knoll above the gentle waters of Armuchee Creek.

## May 16, 1864

In North Georgia, Confederate General Joe Johnston, not liking his battle position at Calhoun, begins movement toward Adairsville. Sherman will follow.

Union General Jefferson C Davis, following the cavalry of General Garrard, is plaguing the countryside north of Rome and approaching the City.

***

In eastern Virginia, Union General Butler who landed 30,000 men at Bermuda Hundred on May 5, has taken his substantial force to cut the railroad between Richmond and Petersburg. In opposition, Confederate General PGT Beauregard has hastily assembled a force of about 18,000 to defend this part of the State. Beauregard is in stout defenses at Drewry's Bluff, and when Butler approaches, he decides not to attack the Confederates, but to fortify himself.

This morning at 4:30, in a heavy fog, Beauregard slams the Federal right with Ransom's Division, collapsing Heckman's Brigade before the line can be reinforced, then hold. Then Reb General Hoke attacks the center with two brigades and has initial success, but the line manages to hold by shifting units from the left to center. More brigades from Hoke hits the Union left, and they have had enough.

In an orderly withdrawal they pull back and begin to make their way back to safety at Bermuda Hundred. They will stay there too because Beauregard will fortify to block them in. Richmond and Petersburg, lightly defended, have just dodged a huge bullet.

**Union General Benjamin (Beast) Butler**

## May 17, 1864

In North Georgia, there is skirmishing in various places, especially around Rome and Adairsville as the two mighty antagonists feel for each other in their southward movement. In Adairsville, Confederate General Johnston calls a meeting of his corps commanders Hood, Hardee, and Polk, for two purposes:

1. To describe a plan whereby they will lure the enemy into thinking the main army movement is toward Kingston; the enemy will then move its major portions in that direction and allow the smaller portion under Schofield to move on the road to Cassville, then back to converge on their attack at Kingston. One Rebel corps, under Hardee, will demonstrate as if they are the rear guard of the main Rebel force, and move on toward Kingston. The other two corps will really move ahead to Cassville where they will lie in wait for Schofield's troops to appear without the main body of Federals to protect them. Once Schofield is defeated, attention can turn to one of the other elements of Sherman's forces.

2. General Johnston's wife has written to General Polk with a request of him as a Bishop in the Episcopal Church: "*...lead my soldier nearer to God. General Johnston has never been baptized. It is the dearest wish of my heart that he should be, and that you should perform the ceremony.*" --Tonight, in the candlelight of the tent, in full robes, and in the presence of God and other Generals, the rite of baptism is performed on the Army Commander.

**General Joseph Johnston**

**General Bishop Leonidas Polk**

## May 18, 1864

In Louisiana, Union General Banks' ordeal is almost over. Yesterday, he reached the Atchafalaya River, and today he is building bridges to cross it, then he will be able to continue his journey without the continuous Confederate harassment of Rebels under Richard Taylor. Today he sends a brigade to attack elements of Taylor's force that are at nearby Yellow Bayou. At first the Rebs retreat until they reach the main body, then attack with success. The two forces ebb and flow until the woods develop a horrific forest fire. The fire ends the fight, and hostile action in the Red River Campaign ends here as well.

***

In North Georgia, both armies continue their moves toward Kingston and Cassville.

***

In Virginia, over the past days, Union General Grant has been extending his left lines so far that his right now opposes the original center of Lee's Confederates where brutal action occurred on May 10 and 12. Grant believes that Lee has moved so many men to his (Lee's) right to counter the shifting fortifications of Grant that he has weakened his forces at Lee's left, the old center of the line.

This morning Grant has moved a major portion of his force from his left all the way to the right and attacks on the same ground as the 10th. and 12th. Lee has, however, fortified and strengthened the position. Artillery is in place and amply supplied. As the attacking legions cross the field, they are cut to ribbons by enfilading cannon fire. The storm of rifle fire is just thrown in for good measure, because the Rebel artillery has handed Grant, yet another, defeat on this battlefield.

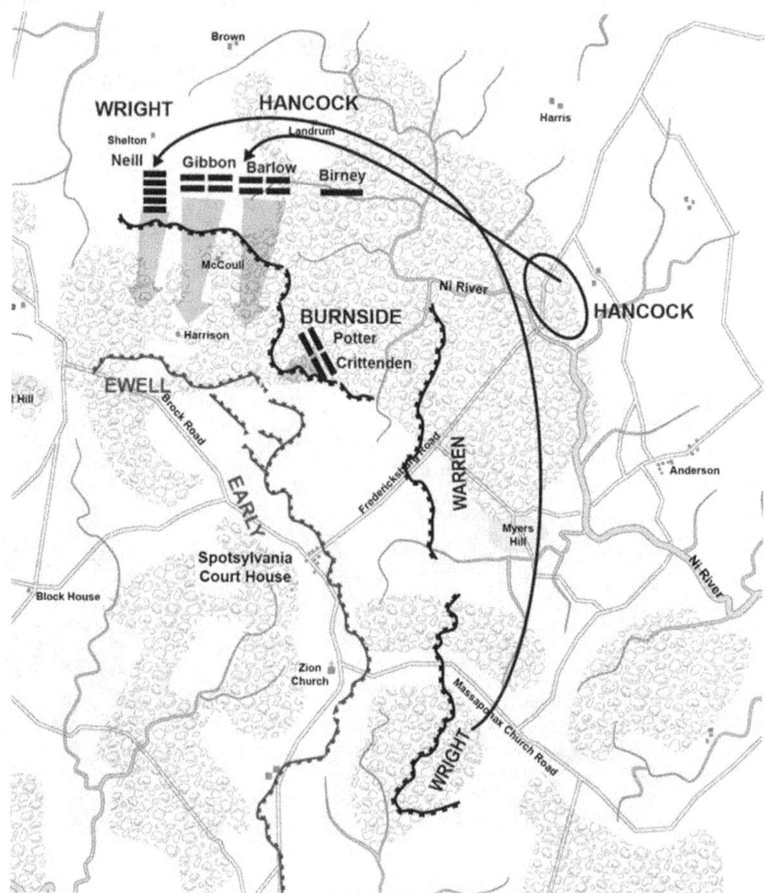

## May 19, 1864

In Virginia, at Spotsylvania, Reb. General Lee orders General Ewell to demonstrate against the Federal right to see if Grant is once more moving to the right. It is discovered that Grant is indeed moving to the right, and east, now heading for the Po River.

***

In north Georgia, everything is going right for Johnston's plan to ambush Schofield's Army of the Ohio. Hardee's fake movement toward Kingston has Sherman fooled, and he is following that. Schofield is moving on the Cassville Rd, as planned, with Hood's corps lying in wait for him near Cassville. Suddenly a column of Yankee cavalry appears on Hood's rear, and he, not knowing the strength of the force, turns to face that and withdraws back to the main Confederate Army, spoiling the trap.

Johnston then assembles his Army on a high, good defensive position to wait to be attacked, but both Generals Polk and Hood declare their positions are not defendable, so Johnston withdraws his army to, and through, Cartersville to the Etowah River. They will cross the river tomorrow.

***

The American continent is saddened today by the death of Nathanial Hawthorne who has died in his sleep in Plymouth New Hampshire while on a sight-seeing trip with his best friend, President Franklin Pierce. Hawthorn, not quite 60, has been complaining of stomach pains for the past few days.

**Nathanial Hawthorne**

## May 20, 1864

In North Georgia this morning, Confederate General Johnston, and his Confederate Army of Tennessee (remember the "Army of The Tennessee" is in blue uniforms. The Union armies are named for rivers, The Southern armies are named for States.) are crossing the Etowah River moving toward the Allatoona Mountains where they will establish strong fortifications in excellent geographically defensive terrain. The Yankees under Sherman are sitting still, resting, in Kingston, except for Schofield's Army of the Ohio which moves into Cartersville as the Rebels pull out.

***

In Virginia, the Army of the Potomac, led by Union General Hancock, moves by its left and then across the Mattaponi River, heading to Guiney's Station. Confederate General Lee is made aware of the large movement and prepares to move to the south to block Grant again.

***

In southern Virginia, Reb General Beauregard has Union General Butler trapped on the peninsula at Bermuda Hundred, but he is not bottled up as tight as he can be, so this morning Beauregard launches a "vigorous attack" on the Federal outposts, driving them back toward the river, and occupying their defensive works. When the works are improved, Beauregard will be able to send reinforcements to Lee and still keep Butler out of the war. This action is known as the Battle of Ware Bottom Church.

**Confederate General Pierre Gustave Toutant-Beauregard**

## May 21, 1864

In North Georgia, Rebs under Johnston are heavily fortified in elevated positions at Allatoona Pass, praying that Union General Sherman will attack them there. Sherman, however, is familiar with this area from work he did here before the war, and he is not about to attack under these unfavorable conditions. He wants Johnston away from mountains, out in the open so he can utilize his two-to-one ratio of troops and abundance of cannon. This day is spent with his army near and within Kingston. His men are repairing railroad and bridges so that he can be well supplied by trains from Chattanooga before starting again.

***

In Virginia, US Grant has sent 20,000 men under Hancock toward Guiney's station hoping that Lee will go after them, bringing his army on to open fields where Grant can take his other corps and numerical superiority to render a major defeat. But Lee is not moving, at least not until late in the day, but at that time he orders movement, not toward Hancock and Guiney's Station but toward the North Anna River to get into blocking position, between Grant and Richmond. The Race is on!

**Grant war Council Massaponax Church, near Guinea Station, on May 21, 1864**
**(Grant is sitting, smoking with his back to the smaller tree)**

## May 22, 1864

In Kingston, GA, while his army rests, Union General Sherman spends the day catching up on his dispatches and other correspondence. He knows that Confederate General Johnston can find places to attack him if he follows the railroad through the hills around Altoona and can find places to defend attack in those same hills, so he will remove his army to the southwest.

He orders all his forces to prepare to leave tomorrow destined toward Dallas, GA. From there he will go to Marietta, then Atlanta.

***

In Virginia, the race is on again. Union General Grant is moving as fast as his huge force can move from Guiney's Station toward the North Anna River. Reb General Lee has pushed all night to arrive first and defend the River crossings, keeping themselves in between the Northern enemy and Richmond. This morning two corps of the men in gray arrive at Hanover Junction, beating Grant's men. Lee will have a strong defensive position, between two rivers, but he will have to be careful of exposure to Union artillery.

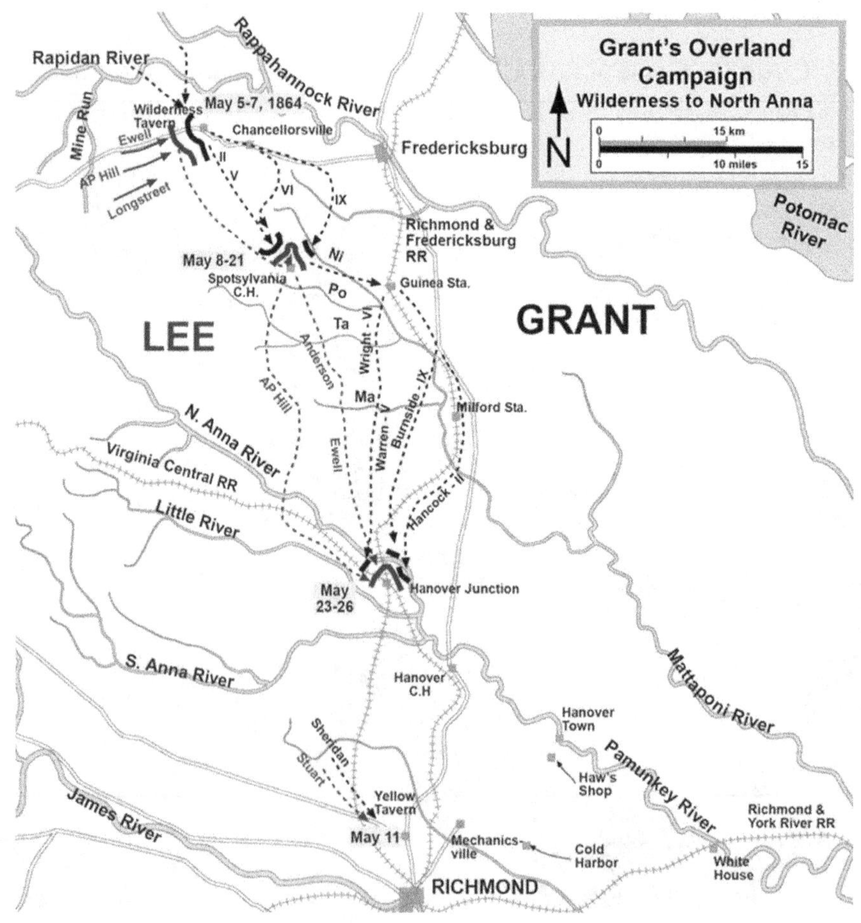

## May 23, 1864

In North Georgia, the Federal Army moves out in entirety from Kingston toward Dallas, GA. So many men require the use of several roads to keep from being strung out too thinly for their self-protection. McPherson is moving his Army of the Tennessee to Van Wert to approach Dallas from the west. Schofield and Stoneman's cavalry move to approach Dallas from the east by way of Burnt Hickory, and Thomas' Army of the Cumberland moves due south through Euharlee and Stilesboro, to maintain the center and approach Dallas from the north. From the reports of Johnston's cavalry, he is strongly suspecting that Sherman is moving everything to the west away from the railroad and begins to prepare to move to intercept him.

***

In Virginia, on the North Anna River, near Hanover Junction, General Lee has not anticipated Grant's objectives correctly and has left several river crossings unprotected. A couple of corps are able to take advantage of this before artillery can be trained to stop it. The II Corps under Maj Gen Winfield S Hancock storms a small fortified Confederate force and seizes the Chesterfield Bridge but does not advance further. Also, the Union V Corps, under Maj Gen Warren fords the river and establishes a beachhead at Jericho Mills, then constructs a pontoon bridge and fortifies. Confederate Maj Gen AP Hill, thinking it is a small force participating in a feint only sends a division to push them back, and it is almost successful anyway, driving the Federals back to the bridge. However, at the river the Union artillery opens up with twelve guns and moves the Confederates back and away.

General Lee is really peeved at General Hill for not removing the Yanks. He says: ""General Hill, why did you let those people cross here? Why didn't you throw your whole force on them and drive them back
as Jackson would have done?"

**Pontoon Bridge at Jericho Mills**

## May 24, 1864

In North Georgia, Reb General Johnston has figured out the intent of Union General Sherman's march toward Dallas. To get started, Sherman had to cross the Etowah River, then travel about the same distance that Johnston does, but he does not have to cross any rivers and will arrive near Dallas and fortify before Sherman can get there. They will meet tomorrow at New Hope Church.

***

In Virginia, on the North Anna River, the Johnnies have worked all night to establish strong forts in an inverted V-shaped line that effectively cuts the Union Army in two after they cross over the North Anna. It is a trap that the old Master has set, and Grant has taken the bait, crossing his men as fast as he can, not realizing what Lee is doing. Lee wants to be fortified so that he can defend each Union force on his side of the River, then attack each force separately. For whichever half that is attacked, the other half will have to come around, crossing the river two times to be of any assistance. By that time defeat will be the order of the day.

Unfortunately for the Rebels, General Lee's guts are boiling. He is having severe stomach pain, much more severe than his normal suffering from angina. He is plagued with diarrhea so bad that he cannot function and is bed-ridden. He has his plans in his head, not in notes, and he has no leader capable of carrying them out, so he just lets Grant attack him, sacrificing his Boys in Blue, until he has enough of it and will begin another withdrawal.

**Lee's brilliant defense is evident on the map below.**

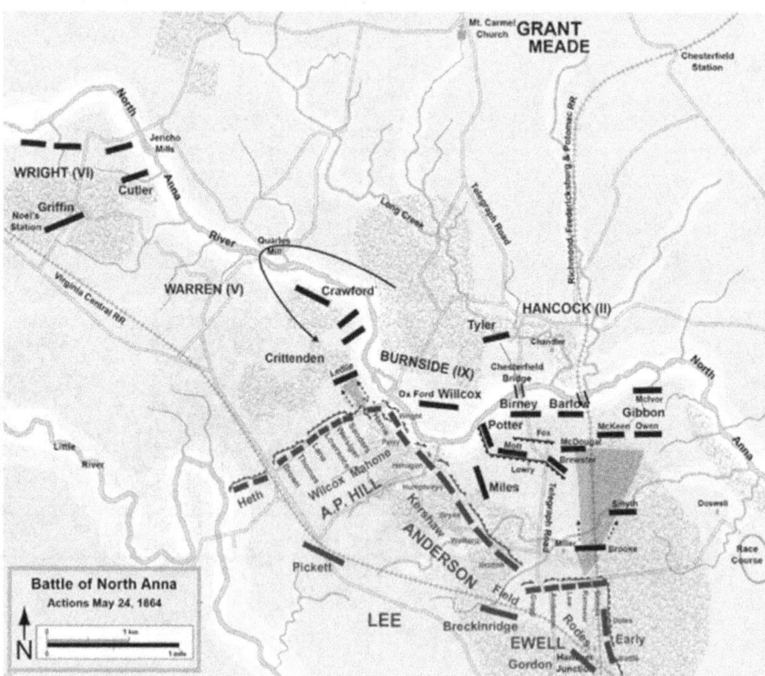

## May 25, 1864

In Virginia, on North Anna River, General Lee is still suffering from stomach ailments with no let up. He is able to dictate some correspondences from his sick bed but is planning no offense today. Grant certainly is not either, except for a few demonstrations at Lee's lines to test their strength. In fact, Grant does not know what to do. For three weeks he has been thwarted at every initiative.

***

In North Georgia, near Dallas, Reb General Hood and his Texans have taken position at New Hope Church, where he believes Union General Hooker and his corps are headed. He is right. The two forces come together initially at Pumpkinvine Creek where Hooker finds the pickets easy to drive, pushing them hard for about three miles, then all hell breaks loose. Hood's lines are widely spread, and Major General Stewart's Division bears the brunt of the 20,000-man attack. Concerned, Johnston sends word to ask if Stewart needs help. He replies: "My own troops will hold the position", and he will.

In addition to the horrific noise of the cannon and rifles, the sky opens up with thunder, lightning, and rain. Hooker loses 1,665 men in the action and Stewart loses about 350. The battle is close enough to Atlanta that the rumble of the big guns is heard there and starts many citizens to evacuate.

New Hope Church Battlefield "The Hell Hole"

## May 26, 1864

In Virginia, General Lee is still sick and is frantic that his opportunity to deal Union General Grant a crushing blow on the North Anna is slipping away. Lee has become aware that Grant is not going to fight him in this place but will move away...where?...toward Richmond?...Grant is moving tonight!

***

In the Shenandoah Valley, the new Union Commander, David Hunter, with 16, 000 men, is moving toward Staunton, Virginia, being opposed by Rebel "Grumble" Jones with about 8,500 men.

***

.In North Georgia, after the hard fighting yesterday at New Hope Church, more Federal elements arrive in front of the increasing Confederate lines, and skirmishing is common around the area. We will call these few days the Dallas Campaign, consisting of yesterday's Battle of New Hope Church, tomorrow's Battle of Pickett's Mill, and day after tomorrow's Battle of Dallas.

Union General McPherson has moved his men up on the Federal right, General Thomas in the Center, and General Schofield on the left. Fortifications in trenches are the order of the day as both armies are digging as hard as they can.

**Period map of the Dallas area and how it relates to Marietta and Kennesaw Mountain**

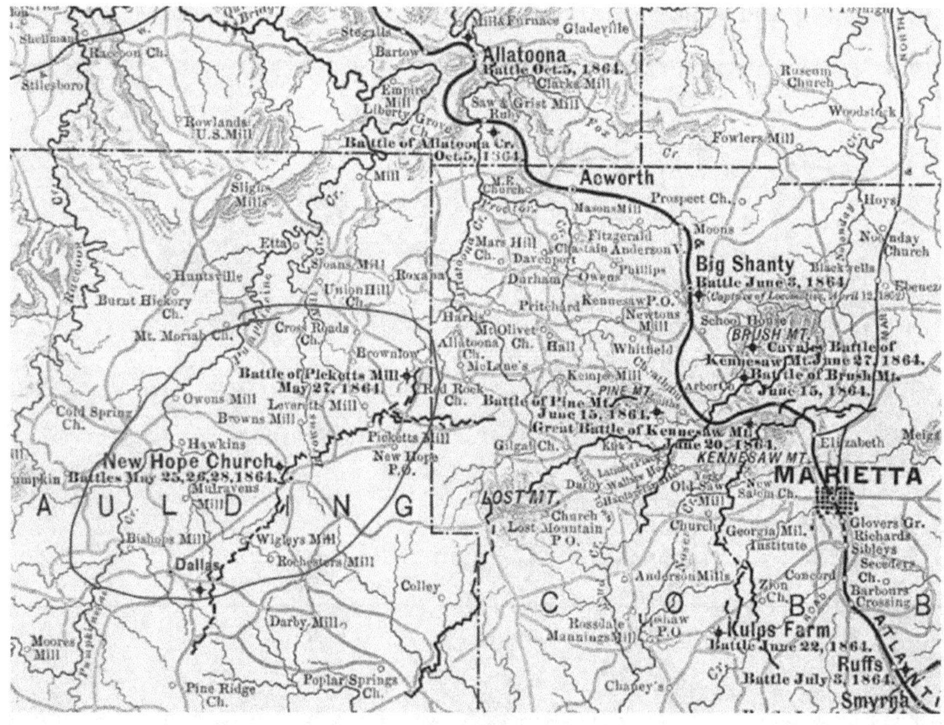

## May 27, 1864

In Virginia by first light, General Lee is moving his army closer to Richmond. When he is nine miles away, he beds the army down for the night, hoping, by morning, to have discovered Grant's intent. Lee is a little better in the stomach, but General Ewell is now sick and turns his Corps command over to General Early, temporarily

***

In Georgia near Dallas, the lines of opponents still face each other on the New Hope Church Battlefield, and Union cannon start bombarding the Rebels at daylight. Union General Sherman sends General Oliver Howard to try the Confederate right at Pickett's Mill, defended by Brigadier General Hiram Granbury of Cheatham's Corps.

Howard's lead brigade, under William Hazen, is met with a storm of shot and artillery fire but makes some progress before Granbury is reinforced and drives the Federals back. After several bloody tries, the Yanks establish defensive lines before dark and prepare to wait out the night. About 10:00 PM, Sherman orders the attacks called off, but Granbury's Texans are charging in the dark with the Rebel yell resounding through the woods. Panicked, the Federals fire a token volley and run for their lives, many surrendering.

Losses are about the same as the day before yesterday in the fighting for New Hope Church, about three Yanks lost for each of the 448 Johnnie Rebs.

**Confederate Brig. Gen. Hiram Granbury**

**Union Brig. Gen. William Hazen**

## May 28, 1864

In Virginia, Confederate General Lee is hurrying his Army of Northern Virginia from the North Anna River north of the Chickahominy, then southward toward Cold Harbor to get between Richmond and Union General Grant who is crossing the Pamunkey near Hanovertown. The Union Army has been reinforced to where the strengths of the two forces are about even. Grant has 108,000 and Lee has 59,000

***

In Georgia, Reb General Johnston orders General Hardee to take a part of his corps and challenge the Federal right to see if the opposition is moving out and to the east. The probe is to check strength and then pull back, but Hardee's men move so quickly behind the lines and find the Federals so strong they have to be reinforced in order to disengage. Losses are high for such a small engagement.

***

In Mexico, Austrian Maximilian Ferdinand, arrives today in Veracruz to take the throne as Emperor of Mexico. He is supported by the French Army that has successfully invaded the country, the Catholic Church, and the conservative elements in the upper class of the Country. He will rule with his wife Charlotte of Belgium, who has taken the name of Carlota. In reality he is a puppet monarch of the Second French Empire.

**Emperor Maximilian Ferdinand**

## May 29, 1864

In Georgia, after yesterday's repulse of elements of Confederate General Cheatham's corps, a council of war was held by Johnston and his corps commanders. General Hood proposed that his corps be shifted eastward, beyond Cleburne, for an attack on the Union left, then Polk would strike the right and Hardee the center. The supporting attacks will begin when Hood's artillery sounds. Johnston likes the plan, so this morning finds the lines waiting, listening for the rumble of the guns that signal the attack. Dawn, then sunup comes and passes before midmorning, when a note from Hood informing Johnston that a newly arrived Yankee division is blocking his way, and he does not think it prudent to continue the attack. He has halted and awaits instructions from command. Johnston cancels the attack and instructs all commanders to further strengthen their defenses.

***

In Virginia Reb General Lee is still trying to figure out where Grant's Army of the Potomac is heading, and he is cautiously wedging his Army of Northern Virginia between the blue horde and Richmond. Lt. General Ewell's physical condition has declined, and Lee decides he needs rest far from the army, so he places Ewell on leave of absence, giving his corps command to Early who has been filling in for several days.

**Confederate Major General Jubal Anderson Early**

## May 30, 1864

In Virginia, Confederate General Lee has fortified his Army of Northern Virginia just south of the Totopotomoy River, with an impenetrable swamp area just in front of his center. Already outnumbering the Rebs by a margin of over 2 to 1, Grant is again reinforced with two corps brought by General Baldy Smith. While Grant is fortifying to face Lee's lines it is discovered that plenty of Yankees are already across the Totopotomoy, and Early makes plans to attack them near Bethesda Church. With Lee's permission, he sends a division forward that makes gains at first, but delays, waiting for supporting attacks, stutters the rhythm of the operation and allows gaps in action that helps the Yanks reinforce and bring guns to bear, finally ripping the attacking Johnnies apart. A bloody repulse of the Rebel forces marks the end of the Battle at Bethesda Church.

***

In Georgia around Dallas, there is a buzzing beehive of activity with almost constant skirmishing and sharpshooting surrounding fortified positions for both sides. There are no big troop movements or any strategy ploys for today.

***

In newly established Arizona Territory, there is a meeting tonight at the store of Don Manuel on Granite Creek for making certain decisions about the new town that is mandated by the Government for the administration of the Territory. The new town will be in the center of the current mining activity, and will be selling lots, surveyed by the Government. It is to be named Prescott in honor of the great American Historian who has recorded all that is written about the history of the area and the war with Mexico.

**William Hickling Prescott**

## May 31, 1864

In North Georgia near Dallas, the armies are at stalemate. Both sides are so well dug in that neither can accomplish much against the other, and Sherman wants to go. He wants to get back to his grocery supply, the railroad. He instructs McPherson to piecemeal, stealthily, withdraw from the lines while other units fill his position. When he can get free of the Rebs, he is to go take the railroad at Allatoona Pass, and Sherman will follow with the rest of the army.

Johnston receives news that Confederate Cavalry General John Hunt Morgan is beginning a campaign against Sherman's supply lines in Kentucky and Tennessee to diminish some of the supply flow from that area.

***

In Virginia, near Richmond, Grant is moving from his new positions at the Totopotomoy River by shifting again to Lee's right. Cavalry elements of both armies are racing to get positions set up at Old Cold Harbor crossroads (so called for a tavern called the Cold Harbor Tavern, that furnishes shelter 'harbor', but only serves food that is not hot therefore "cold").

Grant is reinforced today with 10,000 men sent from Butler who is under siege and cannot use them, and Lee is reinforced with 7,000 from Beauregard in the same area of Bermuda Hundred.

**Troop movements in Virginia**

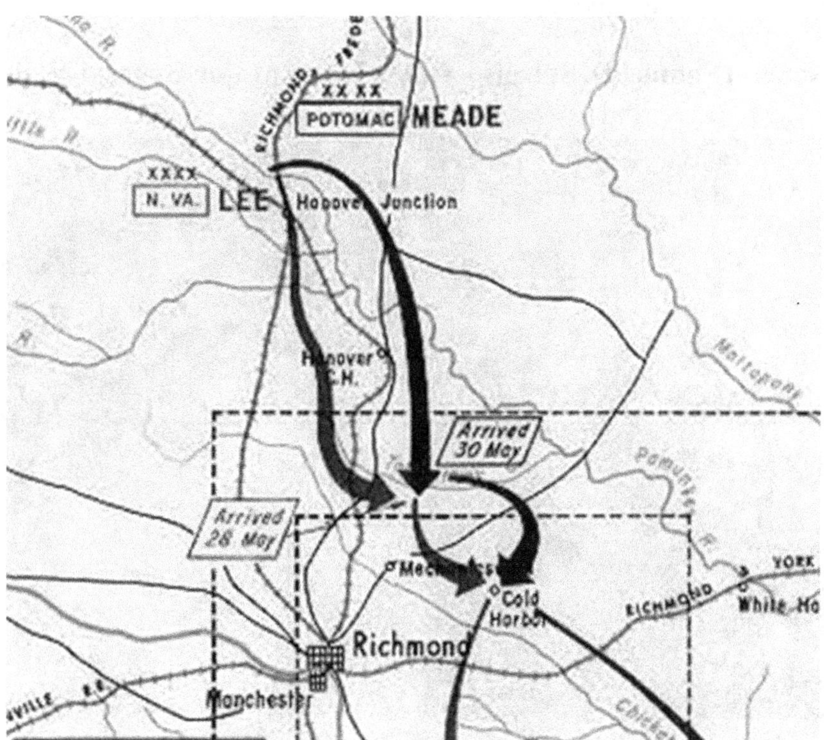

## June 1, 1864

In Virginia, near Cold Harbor, Confederate General Lee ordered, yesterday, an attack on arriving Union troops to begin at dawn, hoping to catch the Yanks off guard and in unimproved positions, but the attack is with a mix of newly arrived troops from Beauregard and Lee's veterans, and the communications between the groups are ill-executed, plus the Union soldiers have dug in quite well after their arrival. No victory for the South on this field this morning.

This afternoon, the newly arrived, Federal Wright's Corps, assails the Confederate lines, and at first make some gains, but the Rebel resistance stiffens and stops the advancement. At dark everybody starts entrenching where they are, with the Federals having big attack plans for tomorrow morning. The battles for Cold Harbor are on.

***

In Georgia, Federal General Stoneman secures the railroad at Allatoona Pass for General Sherman, and he is having his army do the crawfish movements that will allow them to protect themselves as they withdraw from their lines near Dallas and move back toward the railroad in the east. Much skirmishing and sharpshooting in actions associated with this movement.

To keep General Sherman from having to worry too much about Reb General Forrest interrupting his supply lines in Tennessee, he has ordered Union General Sturgis with 8,500 men to go after, and engage Forrest, who has 3,200 men, to destroy him...Is he crazy?...Do you think Sturgis can beat Forrest with only this many men?

**Union General Samuel D. Sturgis** **Confederate Major General N. B. Forrest**

## June 2, 1864

In Georgia there are sharp skirmishes at Acworth and Raccoon Bottom (I believe this to be about half way between Cartersville and Rockmart, south of Euharlee), as the huge Federal army sidewinds left to attach itself to the Western & Atlantic railroad near Allatoona Pass, moving away from the Dallas area and closer to Kennesaw Mountain.

***

In Virginia, the two armies face each other along five miles of entrenchments with the Federals wanting to attack this morning, but they are tired from the hurry-up marching of yesterday and digging-in last night. Also, not everybody is up to the lines and in position. The attack is postponed until 5:30 this afternoon, and at that time things will still not be ready so tomorrow morning is when the big battle will be.

On the map below, I have highlighted in yellow where the main thrust will come and drawn a shaky red arrow to General Gordon's position. Anderson's Brigade is with Anderson's Corps (no relation to Tige Anderson and is now substituting for the wounded Longstreet) about half way from Gordon to Cold Harbor. They will see plenty of action tomorrow morning. This afternoon, men in gray and in blue are sewing bits of paper inside their uniforms, paper with their names, and who should be notified when they are killed on the bloody field tomorrow.

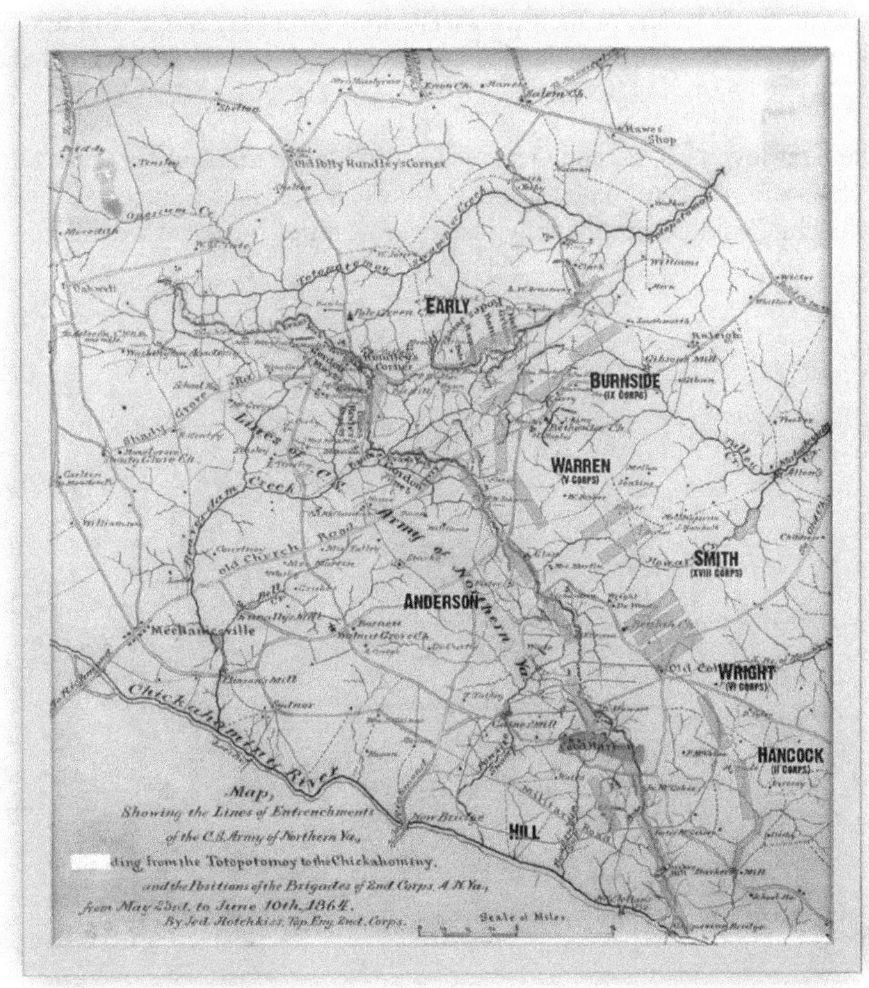


Only the officers of the Union Army know what time the attack will be, but all those on the field know it will be tomorrow.

## June 3, 1864

In Virginia, near Cold Harbor crossroads, moving through a heavy fog, tens of thousands of blue uniforms charge through the woods and open fields to storm the defenses of Confederate General Lee's Army of Northern Virginia. In hand-to-hand combat, Union Commander Hancock's Corps is able to overrun the breastworks of Reb General Breckinridge, but nearby Rebel artillery opens up and slaughters the only victorious Federals of the day.

As daylight exposes the charging horde, the guns, big and small, open up a sheet of lead, iron, and fire that sweeps the field, blasting the assaults, and decimating the retreats. When forward progress is stopped, many of the Union soldiers fall into ground depressions and use their weapons, canteens, or whatever they have, as digging tools to establish protection from the deadly missiles.

By 7 a.m. Union General Grant is ordering his corps commanders to keep striking at the Confederates, but they have had enough. They will keep firing from position for several hours, but they are not going to throw good men into that killing machine again today. Finally, about noon, Grant concedes that his army is done, but he has thousands of wounded caught between the lines without food, water, or medical assistance. Grant is reluctant to ask for a formal truce that will allow him to recover his wounded because that would be an acknowledgment, he has lost the battle.

Over the next few days, he and General Lee will trade notes about truce terms but will not come to agreement until it is too late for most of those suffering. Canteens of water flung into the area by Confederate soldiers are the only instances of relief for those wounded.

**June 4, 1864:**

In Georgia, Union General Sherman is increasing his efforts to move his armies to the east before Joe Johnston catches on and begins to set traps for him. Sherman writes to General Halleck in Washington, "*It has been raining for three days, making roads bad and swelling all the small mountain creeks, which, however, are easily bridged, and run out very soon. It is still raining. As soon as I hear of General Blair (who has been sent to occupy and destroy Rome, Ga), I will swing east by north over to the railroad, leaving Johnston to my right. He is in force, occupying blind and difficult ground, and we continue skirmishing along the whole front, each party inviting the other to attack.*"

***

In Virginia, from today's "Richmond Dispatch" :" *According to the accounts of prisoners, Grant on the night of Thursday caused a quart of whisky to be distributed to each of the soldiers, and about four o'clock yesterday morning, having primed them well for the work, commenced an assault upon our works. repulsed again and again, with unprecedented slaughter, he constantly renewed the attack with fresh troops, sending his men up in columns ten deep, and, in great part, so drunk that they knew not what they were about, and pressed on with the most reckless audacity. Nothing could exceed the coolness with which they were received by our troops, who, standing behind their breastworks and suffering but little, shot them down by thousands, with as much deliberation as though they were firing at so many marks. At one o'clock the action ceased along the whole line, our troops having repulsed the enemy, who left several thousand behind him, dead or wounded, on the field.*" In fact, Grant lost about 7,000 men in a foolish attack yesterday and caused about 1,500 Confederate casualties. He wires Washington today that he "gained no decisive advantage" and that his "losses were not severe,".

**Cold Harbor Tavern**

**June 5, 1864**

In rainy North Georgia late last night, the Army of Tennessee of Joseph Johnston pulled out from its strongly fortified positions around New Hope Church and has travelled all night to occupy new positions that reflect the eastward movement of their enemy. General Hardee is now occupying the Confederate left, on Lost Mountain and Gilgal Church, General Polk, the center, from Pine Mountain to the Western & Atlantic Railroad, six miles below Acworth, and General Hood the right, across the railroad at the base of Brush Mountain. Kennesaw Mountain is two miles to the Confederate rear in case of more necessary retreats. Much to Union General Sherman's chagrin, these new positions are every bit as good as those abandoned.

***

In the Shenandoah Valley of Virginia with 5,600 men Reb General W.E. (Grumble) Jones is moving to stop the raiding of Union General Hunter with his 8,500 men, and they meet near Piedmont. At first the lesser Confederate force is able to hold off the charges of the larger force, but in order to do it, units have to be consolidated, leaving gaps in the battle line. During heavy hand-to-hand fighting, the surplus Federals are able to charge into the gap and isolate units, capturing over 1,000 unwounded Confederates in one instance.

Trying to keep his men from fleeing the field, General Jones is charging his enemy when one of them is able to shoot him in the head, killing him. The Rebs are defeated with casualties about the same for both forces except for the 1,000 Southern prisoners.

**Confederate General W.E. (Grumble) Jones and his death in battle**

## June 6, 1864

In Virginia near Cold Harbor Crossroads, Confederate General Early shams an attack across the lines of General Grant, just to let them know that there is still danger on the other side. Grant and Lee exchange notes about a truce to collect the wounded Federals still lying in the zone between the two armies. Late in the day, Grant finally agrees to asks for a formal truce of two hours which Lee agrees to, but nothing will happen until tomorrow morning.

***

In Georgia, in the rain, the Federal headquarters is at Allatoona where Sherman has set up his supply depot. Track is being repaired from this point northward to be able to receive trains in a couple of days. Sherman is anxious to get on to Marietta and has issued orders today to leave on June 9, for Marietta and then to the Chattahoochee (Does he not know where Joe Johnston's army is right now?).

Sherman is expecting Major General Francis Blair with 10,000 men to reinforce him day after tomorrow, and Blair will participate in the movement planned for that day. The following are the last two articles in Field Order number 20 issued for today, which is Monday:

*III. On Thursday morning at daylight, Major-General Stoneman will be on the right, reporting with all his effective cavalry to Major-General Schofield, and General Garrard will be on the left, reporting with all his effective force to Major-General McPherson. The utmost care must be taken to graze all horses and mules at every chance. The growing wheat, oats, and rye, if used in moderation and frequently, will not injure a mule or horse.*

*IV. The whole army must be ready to move at daylight Thursday, supplied for ten days, all empty and surplus wagons to be sent back to the neighborhood of Cartersville and Etowah bridge.*

**U.S. Major General Francis Blair**

**June 7, 1864**

In Baltimore, the Republicans, and some war Democrats, open the National Union Convention for the purpose of nominating a candidate for the President of the United States. For sure the candidate will be Lincoln, but Hannibal Hamlin wants no more to do with the Vice-Presidency, so that candidate has to be decided.

***

In Virginia, between the battle lines, Union burial and rescue details are utilizing the two-hour truce to find live wounded men that have spent 4 days lying, waiting for rescue. There are only 2 men found still alive, but hundreds of swollen, rotting corpses are gathered for burial. At the end of the two hours a single gunshot signals for hostilities to start again, with many unburied still remaining on the field.

In Virginia, Grant has a new plan. He will send Cavalry General Phil Sheridan to destroy about thirty miles of the Virginia Central Railroad, then join Maj Gen Hunter in the Shenandoah Valley to help destroy Lee's supply source. Meanwhile, after the Railroad is destroyed, Grant will move his army across the James River and take the City of Petersburg. By then Hunter and Sheridan will have destroyed the Shenandoah and can come and attack Richmond from the north while Grant does the same from the south. General Lee must cooperate for this plan to work. Sheridan leaves today on this expedition.

**Union Cavalry General Phillip (Little Phil) Sheridan** ....Lincoln has described him thusly: "A brown, chunky little chap, with a long body, short legs, not enough neck to hang him, and such long arms that if his ankles itch he can scratch them without stooping."

## June 8, 1864

In Mississippi, Confederate cavalry commanders Forrest and S.D. Lee establish their headquarters at Baldwyn. Union General Sturgis' main force is still near Ruckersville, trying to cross the flooded Hatchie River.

***

In Baltimore, the republicans and war democrats conclude the nomination of Abraham Lincoln as candidate for the Presidency, and they nominate war democrat Andrew Johnson of Tennessee for Vice-President.

***

In the Shenandoah Valley the Cavalry commands of Union Brig. Gens. George Crook and William W. Averell, USA, join up with Maj. Gen. David Hunter's, making Hunter's force now 18,000 strong, a real worry for Robert E Lee.

***

In Georgia, the Confederate army under Johnston continues to occupy and fortify the line from Lost Mountain to Brush Mtn, and Sherman gets his reinforcements from General Blair, arriving today with his 10,000 seasoned veterans, but I don't think he is going to be able to push off south tomorrow as he has planned.

***

In Virginia, learning of Union General Phil Sheridan, with 9,286 men, heading to destroy the Virginia Central Railroad, General Lee sends his nephew Fitzhugh Lee, under Wade Hampton, with a combined force of 6,762 men to intercept him and prevent the harm of the railroad.

**Confederate Cavalry Commanders Wade Hampton (left) and Fitzhugh Lee**

**June 9, 1864**

In Mississippi near Tupelo, Reb General NB Forrest knows the destination and the route of the Federal force of General Samuel Sturgis, and he knows that Sturgis' infantry is marching about 3 hours behind the cavalry, so Forrest plans to fight two battles at the same spot tomorrow, 1st the cavalry, then the infantry, at Bryce's Crossroads.

***

In Virginia, Union General Butler sends 3,400 infantrymen and 1,300 cavalrymen, to attack and hold lightly-defended Petersburg. Two brigades of infantry attack on the east side and the cavalry swings to enter from the south. The infantry attacks are poorly coordinated, and the Rebel resistance makes the Federals believe the defenses are formidable.

The south side is defended by a battalion of Virginia reserves, numbering 125 old men, boys, recuperating wounded, and city jail prisoners. The dismounted cavalrymen attack and are repelled. They attack again and again for nearly two hours before Confederate reinforcements arrive to chase away the frustrated Federals. Battalion Commander Fletcher Archer says this of his men :

"heads silvered o'er with the frosts of advancing years," while noting that others of his men scarcely deserved to be called men at all, unable to "boast of the down upon the cheek."

**June 10, 1864:**

In Atlanta, Georgia, Samuel Pierce Richards writes in his diary today: "*Friday, June 10. Today was appointed by our Mayor as a day of fasting and prayer, especially for the safety of our city from invasion by the enemy...*"

***

In Mississippi, near Tupelo, a brigade of General Sturgis' Union cavalry reaches Brice's Crossroads at 9:45 a.m. By 10:30 enough of Reb General Forrest's cavalry has arrived to be able to hold the Federals in position until both sides can be reinforced, and by 11:30 Forrest is hitting them in force.

General Sturgis has ordered his infantry up at double-time, and they left camp this morning 3 hours after the cavalry, so they have a long way to run on the rainy, mud-soaked roads. Forrest is fighting with 3,200 men, and at last Sturgis is able to get most of his 8,500 men to the fight, but most of the infantry is exhausted upon arrival.

When Forrest starts shelling the line with grapeshot, the Federals try to withdraw across the bridge across the Tishomingo River, but the Confederates attack that bridge and at two more places on the lines. The bridge attack fails but creates confusion in the blue ranks and panic ensues. The retreat becomes a terrified rout, and the wild flight and pursuit back toward Memphis flows over six counties before everyone is too exhausted to play anymore. The Confederates suffer 492 casualties and the Union 2,240. Forrest captures huge supplies of arms and ammunition including 16 cannons.

**General Nathan B. Forrest at Brice's Crossroads**

## June 11, 1864

For the ninth day in a row, it is raining in northern Georgia. The Federal army under Sherman pulled out from its Allatoona line yesterday, and as it discovers the Rebel lines today, heavy skirmishing is the order of the day from the slopes of Lost Mountain to Brush Mountain.

***

In Virginia, last week General Grant sent Cavalry General Phil Sheridan and 9,300 riders to destroy the Virginia Central Railroad and move on into the Shenandoah Valley to join General Hunter, who is destroying the Virginia Military Institute today. To counter this move, Reb General Lee sent his nephew, Fitzhugh Lee, and General Wade Hampton to block the Yankee attempt. Hampton and Lee moved to different places on the railroad line with a force totaling 6,762 men.

Hampton encounters his enemy early this morning and in stubborn dismounted fighting pushes Alfred Torbet's division back up the Trevilian Station Road. At the same time Fitz Lee encounters General George A Custer's brigade on the Louisa Court House Rd. Lee has to fall back, and that creates a gap between he and Hampton, which Custer quickly exploits with an attack on Hampton's rear. Custer manages to capture Hampton's wagon train, 800 horses and three caissons, then realizes that Hampton is attacking his flank and Lee is attacking his rear so that Custer's men are almost in a defensive circle and have lost their spoils.

About the time Custer is in extreme danger, Sheridan attacks Hampton forcing the Confederates to retreat to a point several miles west of the train station, and Fitz Lee falls back to the east, to Louisa court House. If the fight ends now, and Sheridan goes on to Meet Hunter, the victory is his, but what will happen tomorrow?

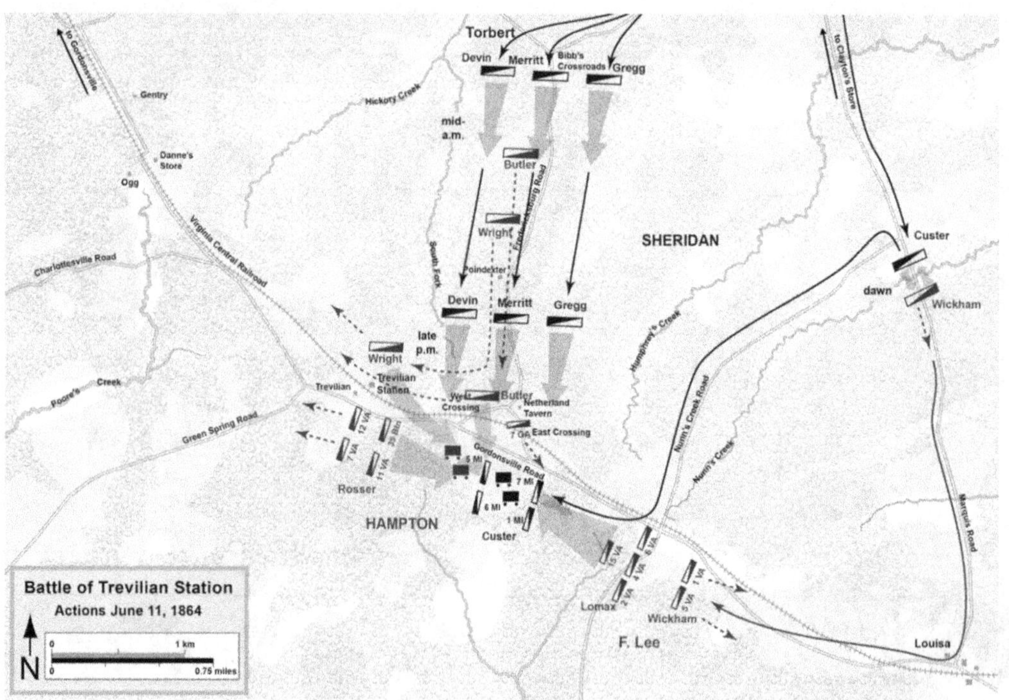

## June 12, 1864

In Georgia, the rain continues to fall as the Southerners continue to strengthen their lines, and the Northerners continue to move up and fortify themselves within rifle shot of their enemy. Sherman's supply trains are now rolling across the Etowah, loading him up with all necessaries.

***

In Virginia, two miles northwest of Trevillian Station, the Confederate cavalry under Fitzhugh Lee and Wade Hampton has fortified behind hastily constructed log breastworks before the onslaught of Union General Sheridan's superior force. The attacks begin about 3 pm and are repulsed with heavy losses. Fitzhugh Lee detaches from the fortifications and swings around to the right to slam into the flank with a strong counterattack. The battle ends about 10 o'clock with both forces on the field, but late in the night Sheridan begins a withdrawal back to Cold Harbor. He will withdraw and move slowly, hoping that Hampton will follow and be kept occupied for days, unavailable to Robert E. Lee.

***

At Cold Harbor, the battle is finally over, the Union Army is pulling out tonight, moving around Lee's right and toward the James River. So far, since the first of May, Grant has lost about 52,000 men, 20,000 more than Lee, causing the anti-war voices to resound across the northern States. However, Grant has been reinforced back up to his starting strength, and there are no reinforcements for Lee.

**Bodies, on the Field of Cold Harbor, being collected in April of 1865**

## June 13, 1864

In Georgia, the rain ends today after a solid week of mud, and things are active around the entrenched lines of the Blue and the Gray. There is heavy skirmishing around the Burnt Hickory area.

***

In Virginia, Grant's Union Army crosses the Chickahominy and lead elements, including Grant, will bed the night at Wilcox Landing on the James, planning a crossing tomorrow.

In Virginia, General Lee has discovered that Grant is gone, but does not know where he is going, so Lee embarks his Army of Northern Virginia toward the south to keep between Grant and Richmond.

Not knowing the enemy would be moving today, Lee, yesterday, ordered General Early and his corps to go to the Shenandoah Valley to defeat Hunter and get the Yankees out of that breadbasket. Since the Valley is the back door into Washington, the expedition might threaten the Lincolnites enough that Grant has to send some of his men away from Lee's army.

Early leaves this morning with a much smaller force than he will be facing, but Lee has confidence in Early's abilities, and he has a fine staff of Division Commanders, Rodes, Gordon, and Ramseur. Early and Gordon do not get along well, but Gordon will fight for him.

**General Rodes** **General Gordon** **General Ramseur**

## June 14, 1864

In Virginia, the Union Army is constructing a huge pontoon bridge across the James River for them to move over on. Lead elements of the army are being transported over by the U.S. Navy transports, as the army continues to assemble from the various roads of travel.

***

In Georgia, Confederate General Johnston knows his defensive lines are too long and is trying to decide the best way to shorten and strengthen them; he wants to have the front lines manned by Hardee's and Polk's Corps with Hood's Corps in second line, able to aid either of the front line corps if attacked. To aid in the planning, a meeting is called with Generals Hardee and Polk at a lookout point on Pine Mountain, a high hill sparsely wooded with pine trees. From this elevation, a view of the positions of both armies can be had. Also, from this elevation, one can be viewed and shot at from below.

When General Sherman sees the small party observing him with field glasses, he orders a battery to fire three rounds at the group to make them take cover. Upon seeing the puff of smoke and hearing the first round, Generals Johnston and Hardee move away from each other and toward safety, but General Polk stays a moment longer and is nailed by the second round. The three-inch ball strikes his left arm, passing through his heart and lungs, then exiting, blowing his right arm almost off.

Despite pleas from the staff members, Johnston and Hardee both rush to the downed General and hold him as his life slips away. Johnston with tears in his eyes, holding Polk's head says, *"We have lost much! I would rather anything but this."*

## June 15, 1864

In Virginia, preceding the arrival of Grant and his main army, is the cavalry of Union General Baldy Smith under instruction to attack the northeastern end of the Southern lines at Petersburg. Smith has 16,000 men and is attacking a defensive force of less than 2500, many of whom are old men and boys.

At first Smith's progress is good, but then he meets with enough stiff opposition to make him believe he is dealing with a lot larger force. He allows the attack to falter instead of pushing harder, and he decides to wait until he is reinforced. Overnight the Confederates will be reinforced from the Bermuda Hundred Line, and Grant has lost an opportunity to end the war early.

***

In North Georgia, between Gilgal Church and Pine Knob, along the Sandtown Road, Union Major General Joe Hooker sends three divisions (15,000) men against the sparsely defended, but well fortified, Confederate line. When the Rebel pickets came running in, announcing the attack, the Confederates disassembled Gilgal Church to use the wood in strengthening breastworks. In every place along the one-mile-long attack the Federals are repulsed with moderate losses. Two of the leaders of the Federal attack are Major General Dan Butterfield, composer of "Taps", and Benjamin Harrison, future President of the United States.

## June 16, 1864

In North Georgia, Reb General Johnston has made the adjustments to his lines that were discussed on Pine Mountain two days ago. He has pulled off Pine Mountain and pulled the Gilgal Church line back south to Mud Creek. Sherman is late to realize this movement and, upon discovery, issues this order to General Thomas: "*Get down to your command as soon as you can this morning, and if you can, put your whole army between the two wings of the enemy, do it; or if he show a force on Kenesaw, push his center and try to get on the Marietta to Vining's Bridge road that is to the rear of Marietta.*"

***

In Virginia at Petersburg, defending Reb General Beauregard has given up the Bermuda Hundred and pulled all his men (14,000) into the fortifications of Petersburg. Lee still thinks Grant's intent is Richmond and is defending the approaches to that city.

Early this morning, Yank General Baldy Smith continues his assaults from yesterday and has some success in breaching a redan of the fortifications, but the defenders establish new lines quickly.

*Yankees under Baldy Smith attacking Confederate forts*

Federal troops continue to arrive from across the James River all day, and late in the day, under the command of General Hancock, 40,000 troops assault the works in various places. The attack goes on until 2 am by moonlight (3/4 moon, full on 19th), and the Feds are able to take three more redans and some trenches, but the Confederate lines do not break, just retreat and dig back in, inflicting heavy losses on the blue-coated enemy.

Then the Confederates counterattack and drive the offenders back, taking numerous Union prisoners and re-occupying their own captured forts. The survivors of the counterattack dig in close to the Southern works.

## June 17, 1864

In Virginia, just before sunrise, the 9th Corps of Union General Burnside has quietly assembled in a ravine just outside the Confederate lines of Petersburg and is able to surprise the sleeping Rebels with a bayonet charge over the lines. The lone division in blue captures a mile of the line and 600 prisoners. Miles away Reb General Lee is still in denial that the whole Federal Army is crossing the James and building up outside Petersburg. He has sent General A. P. Hill's Corps toward Richmond, and Beauregard is begging for help because he is trying to stand off the entire Army of the Potomac with only 14,000 men.

Union General Meade, sharing command with Grant, knows they have to do as much as they can to Beauregard before Lee gets his army here in force so he schedules another attack this afternoon by Generals Hancock, Warren, and Wright, three corps, about 60,000 men. At 6 O'clock PM they charge and make much gain, then Beauregard concentrates his forces and countercharges, pushing the bluecoats back and out of his fortifications by midnight.

***

In Georgia, because Confederate General Johnston adjusted his lines by pulling back from Gilgal Church, Union General Sherman is sure that the Rebs are in retreat, and he wants them attacked while vulnerable. However, everywhere that the lines are being tried, the Union troops are finding stiff resistance behind good earthen protection, and they quickly fortify themselves, much to Sherman's chagrin. Sherman does not understand the timidity of his men in forested conditions, encountering fresh red clay breastworks. He was not in those conditions on May 27, in the horrors of Pickett's Mill, like they were.

**The lines position today, Rebs on the green line, Yanks are blue, Railroad is red, dirt roads are black, notice the new blue line is south of Gilgal Church.**

## June 18, 1864

In North Georgia, the morning begins with heavy rain, and the day will pass with debilitating rainfall on both armies.

***

In the Shenandoah Valley, Union General Hunter and Union Cavalry General Averell have blazed enough of a trail of devastation across that part of Virginia to entitle them to a hatred, in that part of the Country, equal to that of Sherman in the deep South. Today they try for Lynchburg, the rail hub and supply depot for the Confederacy. However, during the night and continuing today, the incoming trains are delivering Confederate Maj Gen Early and 14,000 Rebel troops to stop the 16,000 of Hunter.

Timid attacks come from Hunter early, but they increase as the day goes on, and every hour Early grows stronger. All Federal efforts are repulsed. By tonight Early will be at full strength, and he plans to counterattack first thing in the morning.

***

In Virginia at Petersburg, Reb General Lee has finally realized that Beauregard is correct, and Mead's Army of the Potomac is knocking on his door. Lee has ordered both remaining corps into Petersburg, and most of them are inside, giving Beauregard much needed support for today. Grant has ordered Meade to issue orders for general assault on all lines, but division commanders are unwilling to go against the reinforced lines and refuse. Those that do comply see their forces shot to ribbons with no gain to show for it. Grant finally admits the works are too formidable in his report to Union Gen Halleck: "*"I am perfectly satisfied that all has been done that could be done,"* came Grant's reply, *"and that the assaults to-day were called for by all the appearances and information that could be obtained. Now we will rest the men and use the spade for their protection until a new vein can be struck."* Grant has sacrificed over 8,000 men the last four days. The siege of Petersburg is on. **Below is a sketch, drawn today, of Petersburg from the Union lines**.

## June 19, 1864

In Virginia, the two armies are resting and digging in today. Grant has lost enough men trying to get into Petersburg, defended by a skeleton force, he is not going to attack now that the defenders approximate one third his own. There are still three of five railroads operating into Petersburg

***

In North Georgia, during last night as the Federals slept, the Johnny Rebs of General Johnston fell back once more into very strong positions that will become known as the Kennesaw line. Hood's Corps covers the area west of the railroad where it bends around Kennesaw Mountain, Loring's Corps fortifies on the mountain, and Hardee's Corps is on a chain of hills above Nose's Creek. The front extends seven miles and Wheeler's cavalry protects the right flank and Jackson's on the left.

The Yankees spend the day discovering the new lines and bombarding them. It is still raining.

***

Today the "*CSS Alabama*" under the command of Confederate Captain Raphael Semmes finally meets its match when the "*USS Kearsage*", under the command of Captain John Winslow, challenges and lures "*Alabama*" outside the harbor at Cherbourg France where "*Alabama*' is waiting for much needed repairs to be started on the ship. When "*Alabama*" comes out into international waters the two ships begin traveling parallel in a series of loops, firing broadsides at each other. Semmes can never get quite close enough and although his gunners are firing twice as fast as Winslow's, they are accustomed to close-in fighting and are not focused on accuracy. Winslow's guns are slow, powerful and accurate, and soon the great "*Alabama*" begins to sink. Most of the crew and Semmes are rescued by private yacht and by the "*Kearsage*". Semmes will make it back to CSS Naval command. In its two-year career, "*Alabama*" has taken 65 American merchantmen and battleships.

## June 20, 1864

In North Georgia, rain is falling for the 18th day in a row; action is quiet except for lively skirmishes over a couple of small hills. Field fortifications are being improved by both armies, and tonight, the Confederates will try to haul cannon to the top of Big Kennesaw and Little Kennesaw.

***

Just outside Petersburg, at nine this morning there is a strange execution taking place. William Henry Johnson, a Baltimore native and a private in Company E, 23 Regiment, United States Colored Troops has been accused and convicted of desertion and "*of attempting to commit an outrage on a white woman at Cold Harbor.*" This execution is being performed in full view of the Confederates in order to allow the population of Petersburg to see that when the Union Army finally enters, no outrages from the colored troops will be permitted. At first when the gallows were being constructed, the Rebels shelled the work detail, until, under a flag of truce, it is explained to them that it is a negro to be executed and the reason for it. The hanging then proceeds with the Union Provost Marshall offering this description: *"The Execution came off this morning. I went out early, & examined the gallows, with other arrangements & then went back for the troops & prisoner—they arrived, just after a shelling commenced, upon the very place where the gallows were erected so that I had to form the troops below the crest & leave as few exposed as possible—The Chaplin prayed with him he acknowledged that he was a deserter, that he had changed his name and committed the crime charged upon him—The rope was adjusted the bandages placed over his eyes & the drop fell—He ever knew anything after. A shell killed the Sergt. Major of a Mass. Regt. Just at the time."*

The Confederates then parade all the negro laborers (Whose number has been dwindling because of desertions to the Northerners) by the gallows so they can see what happens to blacks who go to the other side. This will greatly reduce the number of desertions among the colored labor force for the immediate future.

## June 21, 1864

In Virginia, President Lincoln visits the camp of General Grant and congratulates him on all his accomplishments this spring. Grant has ordered his siege lines extended from the Appomattox River on the right to the Appomattox River on the left, completely encircling Petersburg.

***

In North Georgia, Federal General Sherman awakes to more rain. He telegraphs Washington, "*The roads are impassable, and fields and woods become quagmires after a few wagons have crossed.*" So he orders both Thomas and McPherson to hold where they are until the world dries out to where they can properly move their armies. Schofield however, he orders to continue moving to his right until he is about to be detached from Hooker, then go no further unsupported.

Anticipating the westward move by elements of Sherman's armies, Reb General Johnston has ordered General Hood's Corps from their strong positions on his right to beyond the fortified positions on the left in order to thwart Schofield's flanking movements. The evacuated line will be manned by spreading out Loring's Corps (Remember Loring has taken dead General Polk's Corps). This movement is carried out early this morning, in the rain, and it is a good thing for Schofield that he stops where he does because by now Reb. Gen. Hood's Texans are occupying Powder Springs Road in force.

**"Map by Hal Jespersen, www.cwmaps.com" shows the Armies positions at the end of the day today except that, during the action tomorrow at Kolb's farm, Hood will be pushed back to the shown position where he will dig in.**

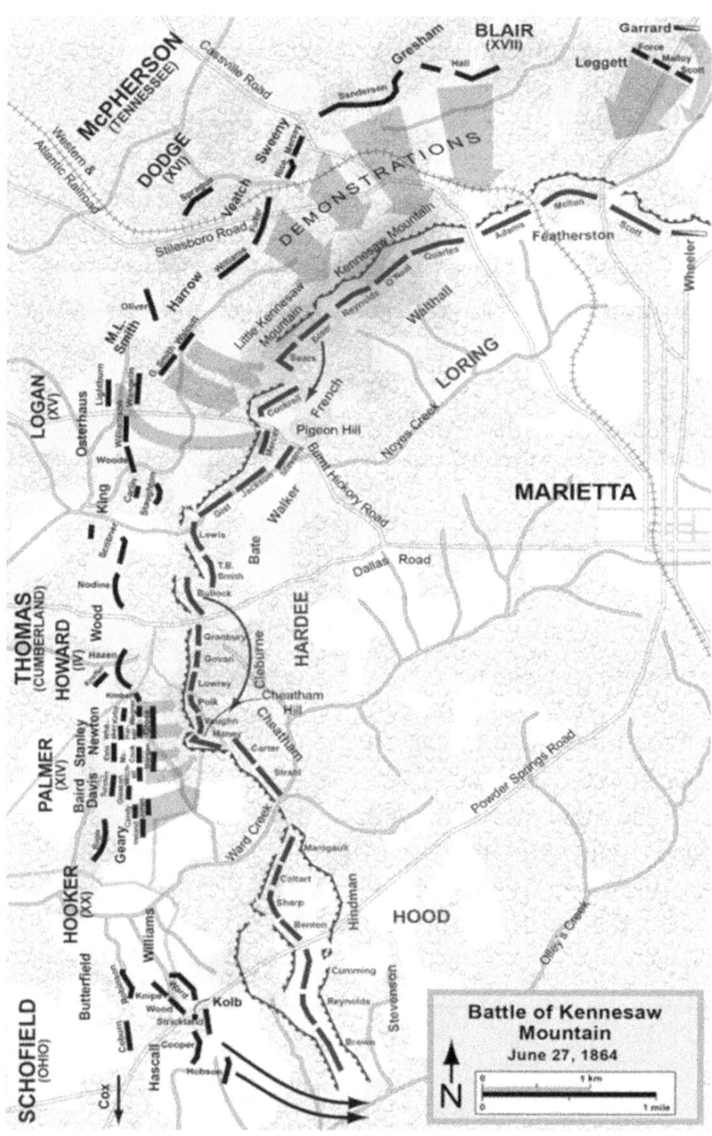

## June 22, 1864:

In Virginia, Union General Grant has ordered that his lines be extended, and the Weldon Railroad into Petersburg be destroyed. As the Union 2nd Corps moves to its new position in a coordinated effort with the 6th Corps which is going after the railroad, Confederate General A. P. Hill attacks the 2nd Corps wedging between the two Federal Corps and causing panic in the ranks. Hill manages to force the Federals back into their lines, handing Grant another defeat. Approximately 27,000 disorganized Federals against 8,000 well-commanded Rebels generates 2,962 Federal casualties and 572 Rebels lost. The railroad is damaged but will be running in a few days.

***

In Georgia on the Kennesaw line, as Confederate General Hood is concluding his move of his Corps from the east side of the line, through Marietta, to the west side of the opposing lines, his men encounter elements of Union General Schofield's Army of the Ohio under the command of Major General Joe Hooker. Hood assumes that his opposition is the extreme right of Sherman's line, thus unsupported, so without reconnaissance, he attacks at once, at Valentine Kolb's farm.

Schofield had no intentions of staying in this place but to continue to move to the right to flank Johnston out of his strong positions, but he prudently had his men fortify themselves until he could find out what is coming at him. Charging blind, Hood's Texans find themselves on a killing ground when the encountered trenches open up with fire. At first repulsed, Hood regroups and charges the works again, losing even more men. When he finally withdraws and entrenches his command, he is 1500 men fewer, and has created 250 casualties for Sherman's Army. When General Johnston finds out he has squandered over 1,000 men, he is livid at Hood.

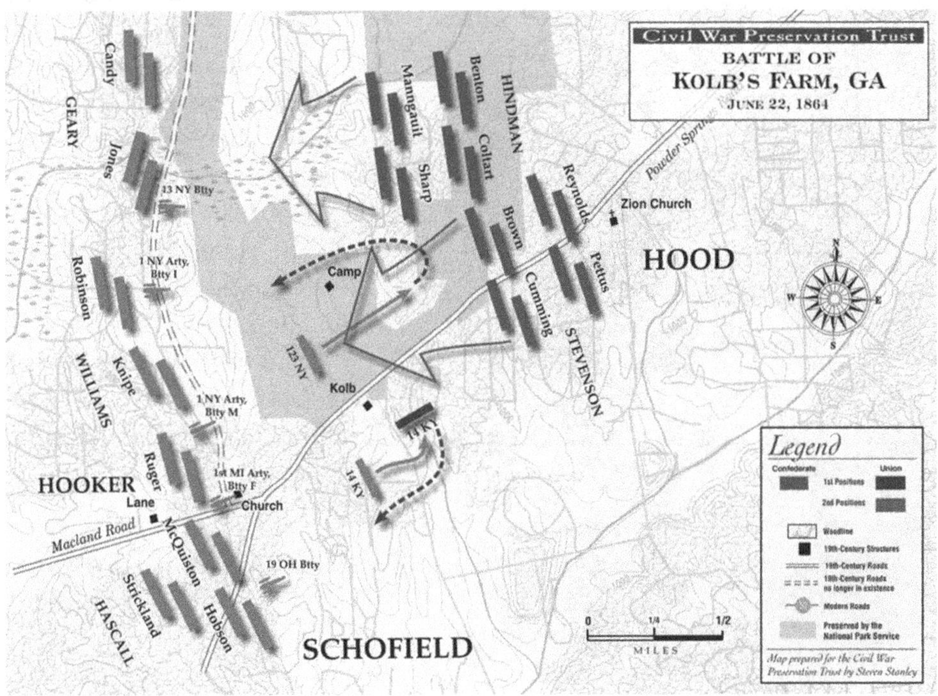

## June 23, 1864

In Georgia, both army commanders are mad at their Generals this morning. Reb General Johnston is very mad at General Hood for his squandering of 1,500 experienced men yesterday, and Union General Sherman, last night, received a dispatch from victorious General Joe Hooker that he had repulsed two heavy attacks and wants reinforcements immediately or he will be overrun . He also said, "*Three entire corps are in front of us*". Sherman knows that Johnston only has three corps, and he knows that both Hardee and Loring's Corps are still entrenched in front of him. This morning Sherman takes advantage of the clearing weather and rides to Kolb's farm to chew Hooker out and see for himself.

After Sherman chastises Hooker for misrepresenting and boasting, he inspects the situation and finds Confederates heavily entrenched in front of Schofield. This means his army has stretched as far west as it can without turning loose of the supply lines on the eastern end at the railroad. Sherman will have to find a weak spot in the mountain defenses and attack it. After all, he did it at Missionary Ridge, and it worked out just fine.

***

In Virginia, in the Shenandoah Valley, Confederate General Early's corps has been chasing an equal-sized Union corps under General David Hunter for days now. In addition to running from Rebels, Hunter has declared war on the civilian population. In a manner that would make Sherman proud, he steals or destroys their food and crops and burns their houses with all their clothing inside. Hatred for him will last at least 150 years in this valley. When Hunter reaches the mountains, Early stops his chase, rests for one day, and heads his 14,000 gray-backs in the direction of Washington DC. He and General Lee have a plan not talked about before with anyone else.

**Union General David Hunter**

## June 24, 1864

In Virginia, as Union Maj. Gen. Phil Sheridan's cavalry returns from their unsuccessful raid against the Virginia Central Railroad and their loss at the Battle of Trevillian Station, they pick up about 200 abandoned wagons at White House and are heading to meet up with Grant near the James River when Reb General Wade Hampton with about 4,000 of his men attacks Union Brig. Gen. Gregg's division at St Mary's Church. The attack is more an encounter with both armies dribbling onto the field of battle allowing each other to entrench. When Hampton pushes the issue, the Federals have to yield the field in a hurry, but since they have been traveling parallel to the path of the wagons, the teamsters are able to continue with the supplies while the fighting occupies the Rebs, on out of harm's way.

***

In North Georgia, General Sherman has made his plan and submits it to his top Generals today. They are under orders to tell no one yet, other than the Army Commanders, and all troop movements are to be done at night.

"SPECIAL FIELD ORDERS, HDQRS. MIL. DIV. OF THE MISS Numbers 28. In the Field, near Kenesaw Mountain, June 24, 1864

"*The army commanders will make full reconnaissance and preparations to attack the enemy in force on the 27th instant, at 8 a. m. precisely. The commanding general will be on Signal Hill and will have telegraphic communication with all the army commanders. I. Major-General Thomas will assault the enemy at any point near his center, to be selected by himself, and will make any charges in his troops necessary by night, so as not to attract the attention of the enemy. II. Major-General McPherson will feign by a movement of his cavalry and one division of infantry on his extreme left, approaching Marietta from the north, and using artillery freely, but will make his real attack at a point south and west of Kenesaw. III. Major-General Schofield will feel well to his extreme right and threaten that flank of the enemy with artillery and display, but attack some one point of the enemy's line as near the Marietta and Powder Springs road as he can with prospect of success.*"

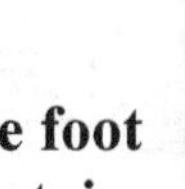

**Federal lines at the foot of Kennesaw Mountain**

## June 25, 1864

In Northwest Georgia, near Kennesaw, the armies of Union General Sherman are quietly repositioning themselves, secretly preparing for the attack on the defenses of Kennesaw Mountain that will begin at 8:00 AM, the day after tomorrow.

***

In Virginia, to help to starve out the forces of Reb General Lee, Yank General Grant has sent 5,000 riders to destroy the Richmond and Danville Line and the bridge at Staunton. The raiders have destroyed about 60 miles of line and as they approach Staunton, the populace is able to develop their own defensive force from Confederate Reservists, old men, boys, and volunteers from adjacent towns. The 938 Rebels can hold off the Union force's five charges for about five hours, then Rooney Lee arrives with about 3,000 regular cavalry to completely defeat the enemy and save the railroad bridge. The rail line will be back in operation in a couple of weeks.

At Petersburg, the siege is in stalemate, and Union Colonel Henry Pleasants has an idea. The men of his unit, 48th Pennsylvania, are mostly miners and are capable of mine construction. Pleasants' idea is to dig a 500 ft long tunnel under the Confederate lines, pack it with explosives, and blow a tremendous hole in the lines to pour an attack force through. The plan was approved yesterday by Burnsides, sneered at by Grant and Meade, but work is beginning today. You will not hear very much about this for about six weeks, until the tunnel is completed, then you will.

**Entrance to the tunnel at the Petersburg line**

## June 26, 1864

In Virginia, Union Cavalry General Phil Sheridan is able to escape back into the folds of US Grant by crossing the James River on the ferry at Couthard's Landing, rejoining the main army.

***

In North Georgia, Union General Sherman's army commanders are in place with their men. Preparations are made for tomorrow's attack. Sherman feels that General Schofield is too sparsely deployed to participate in the actual attacks, so his role is downrated to demonstrative. He will try to make the Rebels think he is coming, to prevent them from reinforcing the actual targets of the blood fest planned. This means that the left and right of the Federals will play-act attack, and the middle of the Confederate line will be attacked in two places. The soldiers still do not know; they will be awakened early in the morning and informed at that time.

Today is Sunday, and both armies have multiple services well attended. It is also Pentecostal Sunday, the celebration of the reunion of the Apostles with their Savior, seven weeks after the resurrection, the time the Mormons believe, Christ spent in the United States. While Pentecostal Sunday is the order of this day, Tomorrow will be hell in Georgia.

**The First Pentecost, the beginning of the Christian Church**

## June 27, 1864

In North Georgia after dawn, 200 Federal guns erupt in thunder and flame, slamming explosive rounds against the entrenched Rebel army on the slopes of Kennesaw mountain. Quickly, with the exploding shells and answering artillery, the mountain becomes almost hidden in smoke. The left and right side of the Federal lines begin to demonstrate as if the attack is in progress, trying to draw forces from the Confederate center, but the Rebs are not falling for it. They can see the massing of the blue coats in two areas near the center.

It is a bright morning, already warm, that will heat up to one hundred degrees, adding heat exhaustion to the miseries of men on the field of battle. The first attacks begin around nine am with Union Division commander Logan sending his men toward the point between Little Kennesaw and Big Kennesaw at Pigeon Hill, and General Palmer sending his Division against General Ben Cheatham at the defensive salient to be known as "Cheatham's Hill". In both attacks, the terrain is rough, brambled and stony, uphill and dangerous with flying lead.

The Yankees begin to fall yet push on. As the defenses are approached the ground becomes littered with the dead and wounded. At Pigeon Hill the defenses will not be touched by Federal hands, but at Cheatham Hill the Confederates only prevail with fierce hand-to-hand combat protecting their works. After three major assaults, at all attack points, the Union army is repulsed with very heavy losses. The field commanders can see how futile further offensive action will be, but Sherman orders another attack.

Major General Thomas refuses the order saying: "We have already lost heavily today without gaining any material advantage; one or two more such assaults would use up this army." Union losses for the day are about 3,000, and Johnston loses about 1,000. In actual combat the number of men are about equal with the Southerners fortified.

During the Battle of Kennesaw Mountain, on June 27, 1864, Brig. Gen. Daniel McCook Jr. was mortally wounded when he personally led his old regiment, the 52nd Ohio. He died at the home of his brother George on July 17.

## June 28, 1864

At Kennesaw Mountain Battlefield, the battle is over, and it is time for reflection about certain events that happened yesterday. One of the obstructions the Confederate Soldiers have placed in front of their works are huge trees, cut down, with the tops facing the enemy, and the limbs sharpened into points, very effective in slowing down an enemy charge. It is call abatis, and the trees have been down for several weeks now with the leaves having dried and fallen down.

Yesterday, as the Federal soldiers are attacking the Confederate works just north of the "dead angle" on Cheatham's Hill, the wounded are numerous, and the leaves catch fire, bursting into quite a blaze. The helpless wounded are screaming and in great danger of being burned to death. Reb Colonel William H. Martin from Arkansas shouted, *"Boys, this is butchery."*

He mounted the parapet waving a white handkerchief to call a truce so the men could be removed from the fire. He shouted: "Come get your wounded, they are burning up". Blue and Gray alike pulled wounded from the flames, and while the Federals were tending their injured, moving them from the field, the Confederates stomped out the fires. When the field was cleared of men and fire, a shot rang out, and the battle resumed, just as fierce and bloody as before the respite.

Today, Union Colonel John I. Smith of the Thirty-First Indiana, under Stanley's Division offers a brace of pearl-handled pistols in a presentation case to Confederate Colonel Martin in appreciation for his Samaritan act of yesterday.

## June 29, 1864

At Kennesaw Mountain in North Georgia, reflecting back on the day before yesterday, many stories need to be told. One is of Colonel Dan McCook Jr., a member of the Ohio family, known as the "Fighting McCooks", who will reach prominence as officers in the Union Army during this war. Two brothers, Daniel and John McCook and thirteen of their sons are actively involved with the army, and six of them will rise to the rank of Brigadier General and higher.

Dan McCook, before the war was law partner in a firm with Hugh Boyle Ewing, Thomas Ewing Jr. , and William T. Sherman in Leavenworth Kansas. All those lawyers will become Union Generals before the war is over, with McCook working for Sherman on this day, in Thomas' Army of the Cumberland. He is designated to command the lead brigade in the assault on Cheatham's Hill at what will become known as the "dead angle". His men are assembled and witness the tremendous cannon barrage on the targets across the fields, through the woods, and up the hills where they have to go. To steady them McCook recites portions of Thomas Macaulay's poem of "Horatius" as he paces the ground in front of them:

Then out spake brave Horatius,

The Captain of the Gate:

"To every man upon this earth

Death cometh soon or late.

And how can man die better

Than facing fearful odds,

For the ashes of his fathers,

And the temples of his gods?"

McCook leads the ones who do not fall through the hot morning, through the flying lead, past the abatis, and up to the very parapet of the works he is trying to take, and that is where he receives a bullet through his lung, a mortal wound. He has faced his "fearful odds" and failed, as did all men in the blue this day.

**Colonel Dan McCook**

## June 30, 1864:

In Virginia, the battle lines are stable with the siege of Petersburg. Confederate General Lee is still able to keep the Richmond Danville Railroad open, and the Pennsylvania Yankees are still digging their tunnel under the lines and under the no-man's land between

***

In Washington, political intrigue has caused the Treasury Secretary, Salmon Chase, to submit his resignation for the third time. Each time before, he has been granted concessions and his resignation denied. This time, to his dismay, it is accepted by Abe Lincoln.

***

In North Georgia, near Kennesaw Mtn., Union General Sherman has planned and issued orders for his next move. He will move to the right, away from the railroad, with his entire army just as soon as he can accumulate ten days rations for each man. He thinks he can flank Johnston off Kennesaw Mountain and reach Marietta in five days, so he should be carrying plenty of supplies.

Tonight, Sherman writes to his wife Ellen to tell her of his plans. His psyche is grim, reflective of the dismal month in the mud and the disastrous attacks of three days ago. He says, "*It's enough to make the whole world start at the awful amount of death and destruction that now stalks abroad. Daily for the past two months has the work progressed, and I see no signs of a remission till one or both, and all the armies are destroyed. .I begin to regard the death and mangling of a couple thousand men as a small affair, a kind of morning dash---and it may be well that we become so hardened. The worst of the war is not yet begun.*"

**Ellen Ewing Sherman**

**July 1, 1864**

In Washington, President Lincoln appoints a new Secretary of the Treasury, William Pitt Fessenden, a long-time Senator from Maine.

***

In Virginia, at Petersburg, the armies are mostly quiet today as they face each other in the trenches. The blue-coated Pennsylvanians continue to dig their tunnel.

***

In Georgia, July has entered the State in a dry mood. Contrasting with the last few weeks, the weather and the roads are drying out and the Union army is discretely becoming much more active on its outer right-hand side. Union General Jacob Cox of Schofield's Army has made his way far around the Confederate lines, with the remainder of Schofield's men following him in a perilously thin line that would be devastated if the Confederates should discover it.

At Confederate headquarters, there is distinguished company today. Benjamin Harvey Hill, Confederate Senator from Georgia is here to try to discover what Plan General Johnston has to stop the Federal invasion into the State. Johnston says to him the same thing he has been preaching to President Davis. If Davis will get General Nathan B Forrest or General John H Morgan to destroy the supply lines of Sherman, then his, Johnston's, tactics of defense from good positions will work. Sherman will not be able to defeat him and will have to retreat in order to feed his army. Hill promises to go straight to Richmond and plead with Davis to send Forrest against Sherman's supply line. Meanwhile Sherman is still accumulating his ten days of supplies, preparing to leave the railroad and push his army around to the right, forcing Johnston off Kennesaw Mountain.

**Confederate Senator Benjamin H Hill future Oakland Cemetery Resident**

## July 2, 1864:

In Virginia, Confederate General Jubal Early occupies Winchester and drives the Federals off Bolivar Heights, West Virginia. He has his eye on Harper's Ferry next, pushing his way toward the Potomac.

***

In North Georgia, Kennesaw Mtn., despite a heavy thunderstorm yesterday afternoon, the surrounding roads are hard-packed and usable. Union General Sherman is able to expand General Schofield's hold on the left of Johnston's Rebels and begin a subtle push toward the Chattahoochee. He hopes to get enough resources behind Johnston that he can force him off Kennesaw Mountain and attack him while he is in the open. He thinks Johnston will pull off the mountain, head for the Chattahoochee, cross over, and fortify. His army will be very vulnerable making that trip.

What Sherman does not know is that Johnston has had engineers constructing fortifications at Smyrna Campground close to the Chattahoochee, and his real plan is to withdraw to there, fortify, then protect his withdrawal on across the river. Sherman has his flanking movement planned for tomorrow, but Johnston is withdrawing tonight.

When twilight is gone and it is dark enough, about 10 o'clock PM, Loring's Corps pulls out of the trenches, an hour later, Hardee's, then Hood's follows, leaving behind skirmishers to protect the rear. By the time Sherman discovers they are moving, they will be arriving at their new defensive line.

**The Smyrna Line of entrenchments**

## July 3, 1864

In North Georgia, during the night, Union General McPherson's Army left the fortified line on the Union left, pulled out behind General Thomas' Army, and moved into positions for an attack on the Confederates' left flank.

Very early this morning it is discovered that the Rebels have pulled away from the Kennesaw line and through Marietta. Union General Sherman is desperate to try to attack them while they are traveling out in the open, but by the time the Federals find Confederate General Johnston's Army, they are nestled into strong temporary entrenchments midway between Marietta and the Chattahoochee River. The new line is six miles long, centering on the Smyrna Campground and reaching from Nickajack Creek to Rottenwood Creek.

Shortly after dawn the Union Army enters and begins to occupy Marietta. General Sherman establishes his headquarters at the Kennesaw House, and General Thomas utilizes the buildings of the Georgia Military Institute for his headquarters, but both generals are too occupied with chasing Johnston at the moment to be thinking about administrative duties.

Late in the day Sherman orders General Thomas to attack the new lines at dawn, "*...Press with vehemence at any cost of life and material. Every inch of line should be felt and the moment there is a give, pursuit should be made.*"

**Federally occupied Marietta**

## July 4, 1864

In West Virginia, Confederate General Jubal Early and his 15,000 soldiers are operating near Harpers Ferry, preparing to cross the Potomac River.

***

In North Georgia, Union General Sherman comes to his senses and rescinds the "attack" order he issued at sundown yesterday. This morning he can see the Rebs are well-fortified and would love to give him a blood bath like they did on the slopes of Kennesaw Mountain, so he spends the day probing the lines and moving McPherson's Army further to the right, to good flanking positions for tomorrow.

Elements of Sherman's right reach all the way to the Chattahoochee at Campbellton. In feeling-out operations there is fighting at Burnt Hickory, Rottenwood Creek, Campbellton, Neal Dow Station, Mitchell's Crossroads, and at Ruff's Mill, Union Brig. General John Fuller's Brigade attacks Stephenson's Division early this morning and is repulsed, but late this afternoon, they return, reinforced by Sweeney's 2nd. Div, and with bitter fighting are able to seize the first line of works near the Gann Cemetery, but stubborn resistance limits them from further advance.

With the gains that McPherson has made to the Union right, Johnston knows his position is tenuous and uses the cover of darkness tonight to remove back to the series of very strong forts on the north side of the Chattahoochee that will be known as the "River Line".

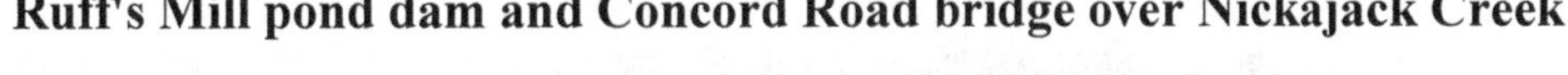

**Ruff's Mill pond dam and Concord Road bridge over Nickajack Creek**

## July 5, 1864

In West Virginia, Confederate General Early has found Harper's Ferry too well defended by the artillery on adjoining heights for him to try to occupy. After raiding Federal storehouses, he crosses portions of his force over the Potomac into Maryland at Shepherdstown. The crossing will be completed tomorrow.

Washington and Maryland are seriously alarmed by Early's nearness and obvious threat with no substantial Yankee army in the area, and the call is out for 24,000 volunteers to come help defend against Early's forces.

***

In Georgia, near Vinings last night, Reb General Johnston removed his army from the temporary defenses of the Smyrna Line and into the strong River Line just on the north side of the Chattahoochee River. Constructed by General Francis Shoup, in less than a month, with over 1,000 slaves, the line consists of 36 small triangular-shaped forts, connected with breastworks. The redoubts are very functional for a small defending force and will become known as "Shoupades" in future years. Upon Sherman's observation, he remarks, "*...the best line of field intrenchments I have ever seen.*"

Today, Sherman gets his first look at Atlanta. From a high elevation beside Vinings, in the Pace's and Randall's graveyard, he, and other Federal officers, can behold the church spires of downtown Atlanta.

**Picture is by this author from the Pace family graveyard in 2006**

## July 6, 1864

In Maryland, Confederate General Early, and the remainder of his corps, cross the Potomac today, and General McCausland occupies the City of Hagerstown.

***

In North Georgia, cavalry operations continue as the Federals of Sherman's Army probe for river crossings that they can use to flank the Rebs out of their river-line fortifications. Searching for a crossing, Union Cavalry General Kenner Garrard rides all the way to Roswell, finding all bridges destroyed, but also, finding the industrial complex of Roswell Mills. The mills are mostly run by women, some 400 of them. Garrard's men dismantle the mill equipment and the buildings, using the building materials to rebuild the bridge that crosses the Chattahoochee River at that point.

Acting on orders from Sherman, Garrard loads the women, with their children and some of their things, on wagons for transport to Marietta where they will be housed temporarily in buildings of the Georgia Military Institute until shipment for them to Indiana can be arranged. The workers of the Manchester Mills at Sweetwater are joined with the Roswell Women, those mills being rendered useless also.

Most of these families will never return to Georgia. The ones that survive will eventually find employment in the cotton mills of the area, but destitution will be their immediate fate because of the lack of employment opportunities for this many people in the new area.

**Employees of Roswell Mills**

## July 7, 1864

In Virginia, trainloads of Union troops are making their way to Washington for protection from Confederate General Jubal Early, who has just crossed the Potomac River with Washington in mind.

***

Another major bombardment of Fort Sumter in Charleston Harbor begins today. 784 rounds are thrown at the heap of rubble. Four times, the Rebel flag is knocked down, and four times it is restored.

***

In North Georgia, near Vinings, Federal armies still are searching the banks of the Chattahoochee River for any place a foothold on the south side of the river might be gained. Already General Kenner Garrard is rebuilding the bridge at Roswell, and this afternoon, near the confluence of Sope Creek and the paper mill that was destroyed yesterday by Garrard's men, elements of General Schofield's Army of the Ohio discover an old underwater Indian fish dam, constructed of stones, that can allow wading soldiers to cross.

The crossing is lightly defended with a handful of Confederate soldiers and two old field pieces. When Schofield reports this to Sherman this evening, he orders Schofield to affect a major crossing at that place tomorrow.

This evening when Confederate General Johnston convenes his meeting with his corps commanders, there is a new Lt General present. It is Alexander P. Stewart, who is taking permanent command of Polk's Corps, relieving General Loring who will return to his Division command. Stewart is a favorite of Braxton Bragg, but unlike Bragg, he has fought well in the past, especially at Chickamauga.

**Confederate Lt. General Alexander P. Stewart**

## July 8, 1864

In Maryland near Frederick, Union General Lew Wallace is gathering miscellaneous units to assemble a defense to stop the advance of Confederate General Jubal Early's advance toward Washington. One division of the Federal Sixth Corps has just arrived in Baltimore from the Petersburg lines and will be able to help. They will meet General Early tomorrow at Monocacy Junction.

***

In North Georgia along the Chattahoochee River, Union General Schofield assembles his Army of the Ohio at the burned-out ruins of the paper mill on Sope Creek, where it is wide and deep, before flowing into the Chattahoochee. He sends Cameron's Brigade of Cox's Division across the rain-swollen river, carefully walking on an ancient fish dam, constructed of heavy stones acting as a submerged causeway. The soldiers arrive on the other side undetected by the small contingency of Confederates who are quite casual about their duties in this isolated post.

When Cameron is in place, 25 hidden pontoon boats, laden with Yankee soldiers, move down Sope Creek and into the river heading for a beachhead on the other side. When Cameron's men appear and the boats come into view, the confused defenders fire a few token shots and hightail it to spread the news that a major Union force is across the river. Actually, it is not a major force across, but it soon will be, as the Yankee engineers assemble the pontoon bridge before dark, allowing Cox's entire Division to cross over and establish field fortifications.

Confederate General Johnston will receive the word that he is outflanked about midnight and will start making plans to pull back across the river.

**Ruins of the paper mill on Sope Creek**

## July 9, 1864

Near Roswell, Georgia, while the work is continuing on the construction of the Roswell Bridge, Union Cavalry General Garrard sends four dismounted companies, wading across the 200 yards wide Chattahoochee River. Using an ancient ford and firing Spencer repeating rifles, and under the protection of supporting fire from their shore, the invaders are able to drive away the defending Johnnies on the southern side.

When Confederate General Johnston learns that Yankees are on the Atlanta side of the river in two places now, he prepares, and pulls out of the River line under cover of darkness tonight. He burns the railroad bridge, destroys the pontoon bridges, and nestles his army into the prepared fortifications encircling Atlanta. The abandoned home of a Boston slave-dealer, Dexter Niles, on the Marietta Road, becomes the new Confederate Headquarters.

***

In Maryland, Union General Lew Wallace (later author of "Ben Hur"), has assembled a hodgepodge of defenders to try to delay or defeat the invading Rebels under Jubal Early. At Monocacy Junction on the Monocacy River. Early has about 10,000 men with him at this point, and Wallace has slightly less than 6,000, but he is well-fortified behind a stone wall on the opposite side of the river. Initial attacks against the defenders stall and fail until future Oakland resident General John B. Gordon takes his division across the river and charges the works.

The Federals begin to run in places and are withdrawing in all places as the other two Reb Divisions cheer from across the river. Federal losses are about 1,300 and Confederates lose about 800, among those are Brigadier General Clement A Evans who is seriously wounded, one of his five wounds in the War. Evans is in command of Gordon's old regiment, will command under him the remainder of the War, and will rest, permanently near him, near the Confederate Memorial of Historic Oakland Cemetery.

**Brig. General Clement A. Evans**

## July 10, 1864

In Maryland, after losing a day's time defeating the Union Army at Frederick, Confederate General Early is moving into the outlying areas of Washington, causing quite a stir among the occupants, including the Lincolns. General Grant has notified General Halleck that in addition to the 6,000 troops he has sent to Baltimore, he is moving an entire corps to the Washington area from Petersburg. These troops will be coming by rail so Early better hurry to do whatever he is going to do. The delay yesterday cost him dearly in time.

***

In Georgia, near Vinings, once again the Federal armies of Sherman find their enemy has disappeared in the night and left open fortifications in front of them. Sherman has not yet heard from cavalry General Stoneman who is exploring the river south of his position, therefore he cannot make a final decision on movements yet, so everybody takes a bath, including Sherman.

Inside Atlanta, everyone is loading wagons, boarding trains, or hiding their valuables. Most will be gone in a couple of days, but there will be many that have no place to go, or no means to get there. The local newspapers are moving out to Macon, but the Memphis "Appeal", that has already moved several times fleeing the Yankees, has decided to stay in Atlanta for the time being.

The map gives you an idea of the recent and future troop movements. The Union movements all stop at the Chattahoochee today. The right of the Chattahoochee will be in days to come. Notice McPherson will move from the extreme right to Roswell, then to Decatur to sever the Georgia Railroad.

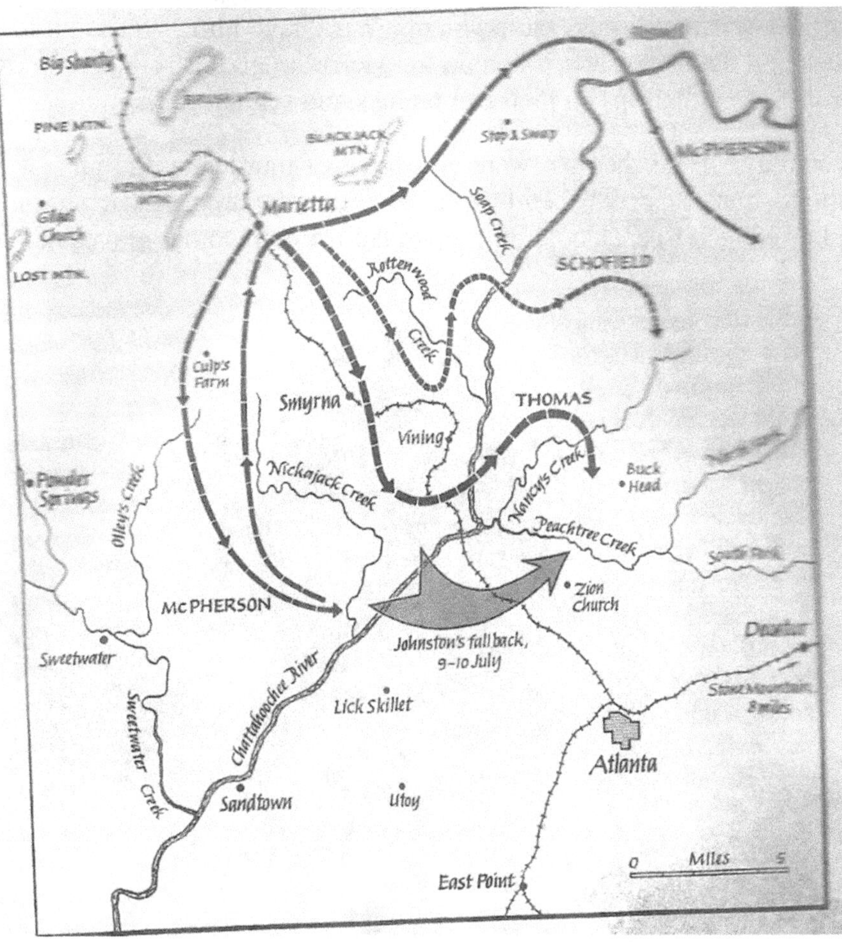


**Map scanned from Shelby Foote's "The Civil War"**

## July 11, 1864

In Maryland, near Washington City, Confederate General Early and 10,000 of his corps are knocking on the door. As they approach Fort Stevens the exhausted Southerners believe the works to be sparsely manned, but as they prepare to take possession, their enemy seems to emerge from nowhere to fully occupy the position. Early is too late. The battle at Frederick on the Monocacy River day before yesterday delayed his travel enough that Grant has gotten his reinforcements to Lincoln in time to thwart him. There is much skirmishing today, and the decision as to attacking the fort will be made in the morning.

***

In Georgia, positions have changed little around Atlanta. Sherman continues with bridge building, and Johnston continues to improve fortifications.

***

In the prisoner of war camp at Andersonville, Georgia, there has been a group of inmates who call themselves "raiders" operating against their fellow prisoners as thieves, and in some cases, murderers. As new prisoners come in, they rob them of everything they have, and if they resist, they kill them. One spokesman, Big Pete McCullough of Illinois has gone to the camp commander, Colonel Wirz to discuss the problem. Wirz gave him permission to organize a resistance to the thugs and act as he saw fit to stop it. McCullough has rounded up over 200 men and tried them for various violations on their campmates and sentenced them to varying degrees of punishment.

Yesterday, six of the men were convicted of murder by the jury of their peers, and today, with gallows materials furnished by the Rebel guards, they are hanged until they are dead. They will be buried next to each other but separated from the other graves of Camp Sumter.

*Frank Leslie's Illustrated Newspaper* artist James E. Taylor captured the gruesome scene of the mass hanging of the Raiders.

## July 12, 1864

In Richmond, the debate is on about keeping Johnston as the commander of the Army of Tennessee. Most of President Davis' cabinet and his military advisor, Bragg, recommend that he be removed because of his purely defensive strategies. It is a bad time to remove an army commander, on the eve of major military events, but Davis is afraid that Johnston will continue to withdraw, surrendering Atlanta and Georgia to the Federals. Just in case Johnston has imminent plans to attack and is afraid to communicate them by telegraph, Davis sends Braxton Bragg to see Johnston personally to determine if there are any such plans.

***

Outside Washington D.C., over night the defensive works of the City have been reinforced with veteran troops, and Confederate General Early's heavy demonstrations against the lines have found no weak spots to exploit. Visiting the defenses at Fort Stevens, President Lincoln, despite pleas from the soldiers, is exposing himself on the parapets when a sniper's bullet falls the man beside him, Assistant Surgeon Cornelius Crawford . Early makes the decision that he would only waste men in an attack and turns his force back toward Virginia, saying to a staff member, *"We didn't take Washington, but we scared Abe Lincoln like Hell."*....he really doesn't know how close he came.

**Lincoln on the parapet of Fort Stevens with an officer pleading for him to come down.**

## July 13, 1864

In Maryland, Confederate General Jubal Early has not taken Washington, but even if he had, he would not be able to hold it. He has, however, accomplished his goal of forcing Grant to weaken his forces around Petersburg where the Pennsylvania miners are still digging that tunnel under the defensive lines. And now, some of those forces are coming after him. Today Grant dispatches Maj. Gen. Horatio Wright and 15,000 men to pursue Early's retreat toward the Potomac

***

In Atlanta, Major General Braxton Bragg meets all day with General Johnston, learning his exact situation and plans for the immediate future. The condition of the army is poor, and its future is bleak. The report Bragg wires to Richmond late tonight will firm the decision to remove Johnston from command. Now the decision must be made as to his replacement.

Outside Atlanta, Union General Sherman's worst fear is that somehow Reb General Forrest will get into his supply lines and force a retreat with starvation. To that end he has sent Union Maj. Gen. A.J. Smith with fourteen thousand men into Mississippi to find Forrest and kill him. His stated mission is to protect the supply lines, but everyone knows the real mission. For a couple of days Forrest has been stalking and skirmishing the larger force with his 2,000 men but has been ordered to lay off the Federals until Stephen D Lee could get there with 6,000 reinforcements.

Lee has arrived and assumed command because he is the senior officer. The Yanks are fortified just outside Tupelo on a low, open ridge. The Rebels will attack them at dawn tomorrow......

**Confederate Major General Stephan Dill Lee (no relation to Robert E Lee)**

## July 14, 1864

In Poolesville, Maryland, Union General Wright has arrived at the Potomac River just after the retreating Confederates under Jubal Early have completed their crossing into Virginia and secured the southern shores. Knowing his own force is approximately equal to Early's, Wright doesn't think it wise to go after him in Virginia, and he wires Halleck in Washington for advice. After checking with Grant, Halleck tells him to follow Early, but not too close, in case there is an opportunity to reinforce him, then attack the Rebel force.

***

From Atlanta, after extensive interviews with General Johnston and his corps commanders, Confederate General Bragg writes a long letter to President Davis then sends it by courier to Richmond. The letter includes the following statement: "*....if any change is made, Lt. General Hood would give unlimited satisfaction, and my estimation of him, already high, has been raised by this campaign.*".

***

Near Tupelo Mississippi, Reb General Forrest is unsure of the wisdom of attacking the 14,000 Yankees under A.J. Smith on his fortified hillside. He had rather wait until the enemy moves then slice at him with his inferior numbers, but his superior officer, Stephen D Lee, decides to charge the works and be done with it. The attacks begin at dawn today, and although they are poorly coordinated, the trenches are too strongly manned, and the Confederates suffer a resounding repulse, losing over 1,300 men to 674 of the Federals. The attacks are called off about noon, and the two forces watch each other for the remainder of the daylight.

**Union General Andrew Jackson Smith**

## July 15, 1864

In Northern Virginia, Confederate General Early continues to move toward Richmond with just a handful of Johnnies holding the Potomac River crossings, preventing any pursuit by the Federals under Wright.

***

In Atlanta, Confederate General Braxton Bragg is meeting with General Hood today to advance his plot to relieve General Joe Johnston with Hood as soon as possible. General Lee has advised President Davis that Hardee would be a better choice, but Bragg hates Hardee because of criticism of his management of the Army after the fiasco at Missionary Ridge.

***

In New York, at Elmira, a newly prepared prisoner of war camp, Camp Rathbun, is ready for prisoners, and a shipment of 833 Confederates, captured at Cold Harbor, is in route by train, on the last leg of their journey. Because of a drunken telegraph operator, the train of prisoners with 128 Union guards, runs head on into a coal train at "King and Fuller's Cut" near Shohola, Pennsylvania. At least 51 Confederate prisoners and 17 Union guards die today and tomorrow from their wounds.

There will be other dead during the days to come in spite of heroic efforts from the population of the little town of Shohola who take the wounded into their homes and into the train station to nurse them back to health, Northern and Southern alike. All the dead are buried near the train track at the accident scene and will remain there until 1911 when they will all be moved to Woodlawn National Cemetery.

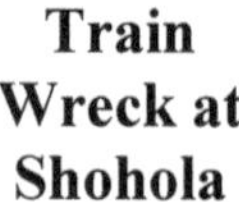

**Train Wreck at Shohola**

## July 16, 1864

In Mississippi, yesterday afternoon, the Federals under Whiskey Smith decided they were too low in supplies to play any more war with Stephen D Lee and Nathan B Forrest so they pulled out of their strong positions and began a retreat back to Memphis. The Confederates immediately started attacking them as they pulled away. During the actions, Forrest is wounded badly in the foot and will be absent from his men for about three weeks, during which time rumors will be about that he is dead.

***

In Richmond, Confederate President Davis decides to give General Johnston one last chance to stay in command. He sends this message to him: "*...I wish to hear from you as to present situation, and your plan of operations so specifically as will enable me to anticipate events.*" Johnston's reply is not going to be Davis' favorite anthem: "*...As the enemy has double our number, we must be on the defensive. My plan of operations must, therefore, depend on that of the enemy. It is mainly to watch for an opportunity to fight to advantage. We are trying to put Atlanta in condition to be held for a day or two by the Georgia militia, that army movements may be freer and wider.*"

Meanwhile Union General Sherman is receiving warnings from Grant that Early's Corps is returning to Lee, and Lee cannot afford to feed them so he can expect Lee to put at least a corps on trains to reinforce Johnston as he did with Longstreet last year at Chickamauga.

***

**In New York, today's Harper's Weekly has some fun with the White House intrigue about the resignation of Treasury Secretary Salmon Chase, and Lincoln's acceptance of it, to give the job to former Ohio Governor, David Tod who declined the offer.**

MR. LINCOLN. "MIKE, remove the SALMON and bring me a TOD." MIKE. "The TOD'S out; but can't I fitch something else, Sir?"

## July 17, 1864

In Georgia, near the Chattahoochee River, the respite is over today. The Armies of William T Sherman are moving once more, not together, but at the same time. The Army of the Cumberland under Thomas is crossing the river at Vinings and will move up the Pace's Ferry Road to Buckhead. The Army of the Ohio has already crossed at Sope Creek and is making its way toward Cross Keys, with Decatur as its destination. The Army of the Tennessee has already been moved all the way to Roswell where it is crossing the river and heading south to destroy railroad east of Decatur.

***

From Richmond, President Davis has ordered Inspector General to send the following telegram to General Joseph Johnston:

*"July 17, 1864 (Sunday) General J. E. Johnston: Lieut. Gen. J. B. Hood has been commissioned to the temporary rank of general under the late law of Congress, I am directed by the Secretary of War to inform you that as you have failed to arrest the advance of the enemy to the vicinity of Atlanta, far in the interior of Georgia, and express no confidence that you can defeat or repel him, you are hereby relieved from the command of the Army and Department of Tennessee, which you will immediately turn over to General Hood. S. COOPER, Adjutant and Inspector General."*

Major Charles Hubner (future poet laureate of the South and future Oakland Cemetery permanent resident) is General Johnston's head of communications and is notified when the message is received about 9:30 pm. He elects, personally to deliver the profound document to the General, who he finds at his headquarters on the Marietta Road, conferring about defenses with Col. Presstman. After reading the communication General Johnston proceeds to write a note of congratulations to General Hood and dispatches it, before retiring for the evening.

**Confederate Major General Joseph E. Johnston**

## July 18, 1864

In extreme northern Virginia, the retreating Rebel Army, under Early, is defending river crossings to delay pursuing Federal troops from crossing to cut off their direction. Near Berryville at Cool Spring about 5,000 Federals are defeated by about 8,000 Confederates in a sharp skirmish that costs each side about 400 casualties.

***

Near Atlanta, Georgia, Confederate General Johnston responds, this morning, to the order relieving him of command, last night. His telegram to General Cooper reads:

*"Your dispatch of yesterday received and obeyed. Command of the Army and Department of Tennessee has been transferred to General Hood. As to the alleged cause of my removal, I assert that Sherman's army is much stronger compared with that of Tennessee than Grant's compared with that of Northern Virginia. Yet the enemy has been compelled to advance much more slowly to vicinity of Atlanta than to that of Richmond and Petersburg and has penetrated much deeper into Virginia than into Georgia. Confident language by a military commander is not usually regarded as evidence of competency."*

The Army of Tennessee goes into mourning during the day, lamenting the removal of their beloved leader. Very few consider General Hood worthy of their leadership. We will see.

**Confederate Major General John Bell Hood**

## July 19, 1864

Near Atlanta, Ga, the Federal armies are busy preparing themselves for the conquest of the City. McPherson's Army is in Decatur, sacking and destroying as much property as they can, and Sherman orders them to turn their attention to the destruction of the railroad today and prepare to move in close to Atlanta tomorrow morning. General Schofield is in Brookhaven and Sherman is headquartered with him. General Thomas is mostly in Buckhead with two divisions south of Peachtree Creek securing the foot hold.

Bridges are being built over Peachtree Creek to cross the guns and supplies, preparing for the main force to cross over tomorrow morning. In Sherman's dispatches for the day, the tone is urgent. He knows his forces are too far apart, neither could assist the other in case of major attack, but his cavalry is keeping him constantly informed as to Confederate forces' locations.

Confederate skirmishers are busy resisting the creek crossings the Federals are attempting. A substantial fight happens at Moore's Mill, where a small, well-fortified rifle force manages to deny crossing to the Yanks who will drain the millpond and flank the Rebs out of position tonight.

Meanwhile, Confederate General Hood is preparing to attack Thomas' Army of the Cumberland tomorrow, after they cross Peachtree Creek, before they can fortify themselves; the attack is to come at one PM.

In order to fill the command vacancy caused by his own promotion, General Hood promotes Ben Cheatham to command his Texans.

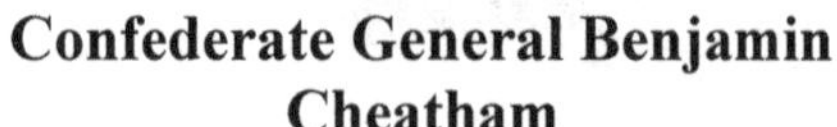

**Confederate General Benjamin Cheatham**

## July 20, 1864

At Decatur, Georgia, Union General James B McPherson's Army of the Tennessee moves out on the Decatur Road toward Atlanta. Moving slowly, tearing up railroad as they advance, about noon, he finds a knoll from which he can see the church spires of the City. He has Captain DeGress unlimber five cannon and commence firing at those churches from what will someday be the Inman Park Marta Station. When shells start falling on downtown the population goes into a panic.

On the north side of the City, Confederate General Hood is planning his assault on the Federals of George Thomas for one o'clock, using Hardee's and Stewart's Corps attacking *en echelon* in a line that stretches from the east side of Peachtree Rd. to just west of Howell Mill Rd. Hood believes that McPherson is still moving toward Decatur, but when the shells start falling on downtown Atlanta, he realizes that the threat from the east is more imminent than he had thought and starts shifting troops to his right to counter it.

This hurts him two ways; It weakens his attacking force, and it delays the main assault until Thomas' army is mostly across Peachtree Creek and fortified with trenches, about four o'clock. Due to the thick, brushy, and briary, woods that the Southerners are attacking through, the attacks are piecemeal and largely uncoordinated. Where the Rebels do break through the woods and into the Collier family fields, well-placed Yankee cannon cut their lines to ribbons.

The fighting continues until almost dark, and Hood gets word that his cavalry commander, Joe Wheeler is heavily engaged with McPherson's troops and needs assistance. He halts the attacks on Thomas and sends General Pat Cleburne's Division to the east where he will fight tomorrow.

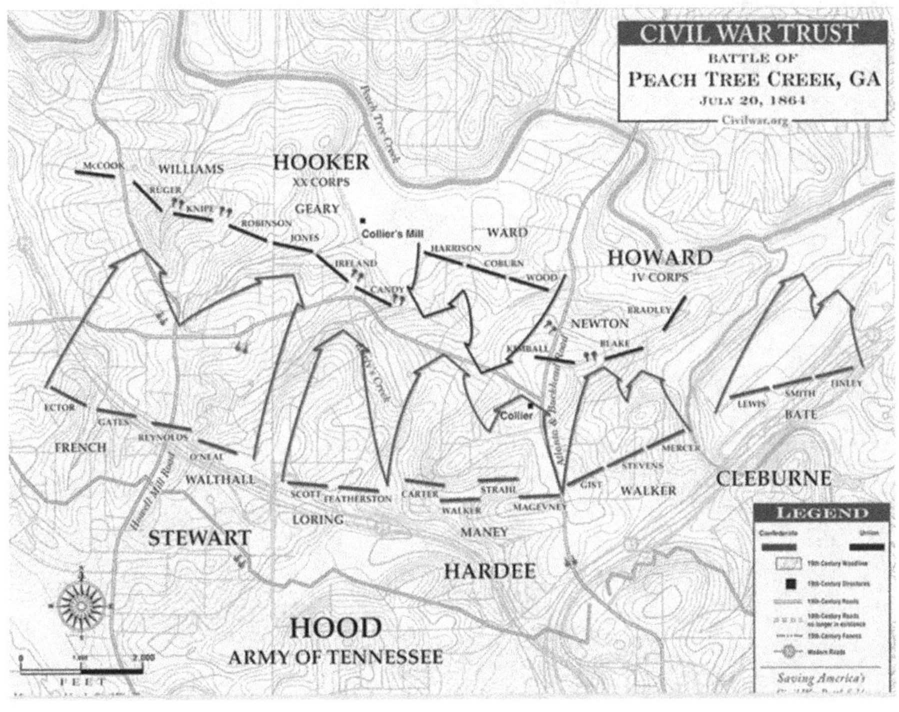


The Battle of Peachtree Creek is over, Hood's first loss as leader of the Army of Tennessee. There were some, initial, successes, but the scattered nature of the attacks and the superior artillery fire of the Federals rule the day. Confederate losses are over 4,500 and Federal losses are about half of that, with approximately 20,000 men on each side being involved in the fight.

## July 21, 1864

Near Atlanta, Ga, as the day closed yesterday, Reb General Hood moved his right-hand corps under General Pat Cleburne further to the right to assist dismounted cavalry under Joe Wheeler to hold a strategic value, a high hill with sloping sides, known as Bald Hill. Cleburne moved into position during the night.

At first light this morning, the Federals open a devastating artillery barrage on the fortified Confederates, rendering many casualties in just a few minutes. The bombardment is followed by several attacks forcing the cavalry under Iverson to evacuate, but Granbury's Texans under Cleburne hold tight and counter-charge. Finally, Union General Leggett charges the works and forces the Confederates off the hill. Reinforced, Cleburne charges Leggett several times, but is unsuccessful in prying Leggett from the hill from which the Federal guns can accurately target positions in downtown Atlanta.

For almost a hundred years, the height will carry the name "Leggett's Hill", until it is graded away with the construction of the I-20 / Moreland Ave. interchange. After dark this evening, Confederate General Hardee will start pulling his men from the lines north of the City and marching them through downtown and around to the southeast where tomorrow at dawn they will be in position to begin the Battle of Atlanta.

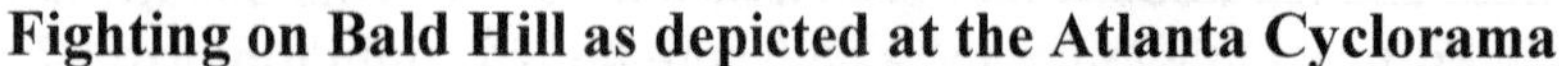
**Fighting on Bald Hill as depicted at the Atlanta Cyclorama**

# July 22, 1864-- page 1 of 2

All night Confederate General Hardee's Corps has been marching through downtown Atlanta, southward, down to the South River where they made an eastward turn, then Maney's and Cleburne's Divisions turn back northward along the future route of Moreland Ave., but Walker and his Division continue on eastward to skirt the large lake and swamp called Terry's millpond. After stumbling around in the darkness and cane for hours, Walker finally breaks through the jungle and takes a bullet that kills him instantly from a Federal picket. General Hugh Mercer immediately takes command of the Division, moving it forward to begin the Battle of Atlanta.

Meanwhile, Federal Major General McPherson has been eating his lunch with staff members in a shelter of trees when he hears the prolonged rattle of musketry indicating action. He leaves with only an orderly to assess the situation. He sees his men pushing back the attacking Rebels about the time another group in gray break out of the woods and order him to stop. Disregarding the command, he wheels his horse and is shot through the lung, a mortal wound. Major General John "Black Jack" Logan will be appointed temporary commander by Sherman for this battle only.

Near Decatur, the occupying Yankees are attacked by Joe Wheeler's cavalry. The Federals flee the town but manage to save the supply trains, getting them back to safety. Wheeler is in possession of Decatur but with the Federals still strong between him and Atlanta, he must pull out and fall back to Atlanta.

The battle now consists of many smaller fights, but the main events are centered around Bald Hill and the DeGress Batteries, the guns that opened up on downtown day before yesterday. On Bald Hill, the Yanks have heavily reinforced the fortifications so further charging is futile, but that is what the Confederates continue to do. They will continue to charge and to die until darkness covers the battlefield.

At the future location of the Inman Park Marta station, the Degress batteries are taken from the Yanks, but not before they spike the touch holes and kill the horses, preventing the use of the guns and their removal from the field. Even so, the Federals are rallied by General Logan who leads a sweeping charge that reclaims the guns for the blue army.

As darkness signals quitting time, the battle ends. The Union has suffered about 3.400 casualties and one Army Commander. The South had lost 5,500 veteran soldiers and one Major General, a devastating loss for the already diminished army, but they still hold the city.

The entire city will be hospitals for a while, private homes, warehouses, churches. At the Confederate high command post adjacent to Oakland Cemetery, there will be field surgeries all night, amputating mangled limbs, removing bullets, setting breaks etc.

**The following page has a map drawn by Wilber Kurtz of the fighting of this day. It was taken it from Franklin Garrett's "Atlanta and Environs" page 616.**

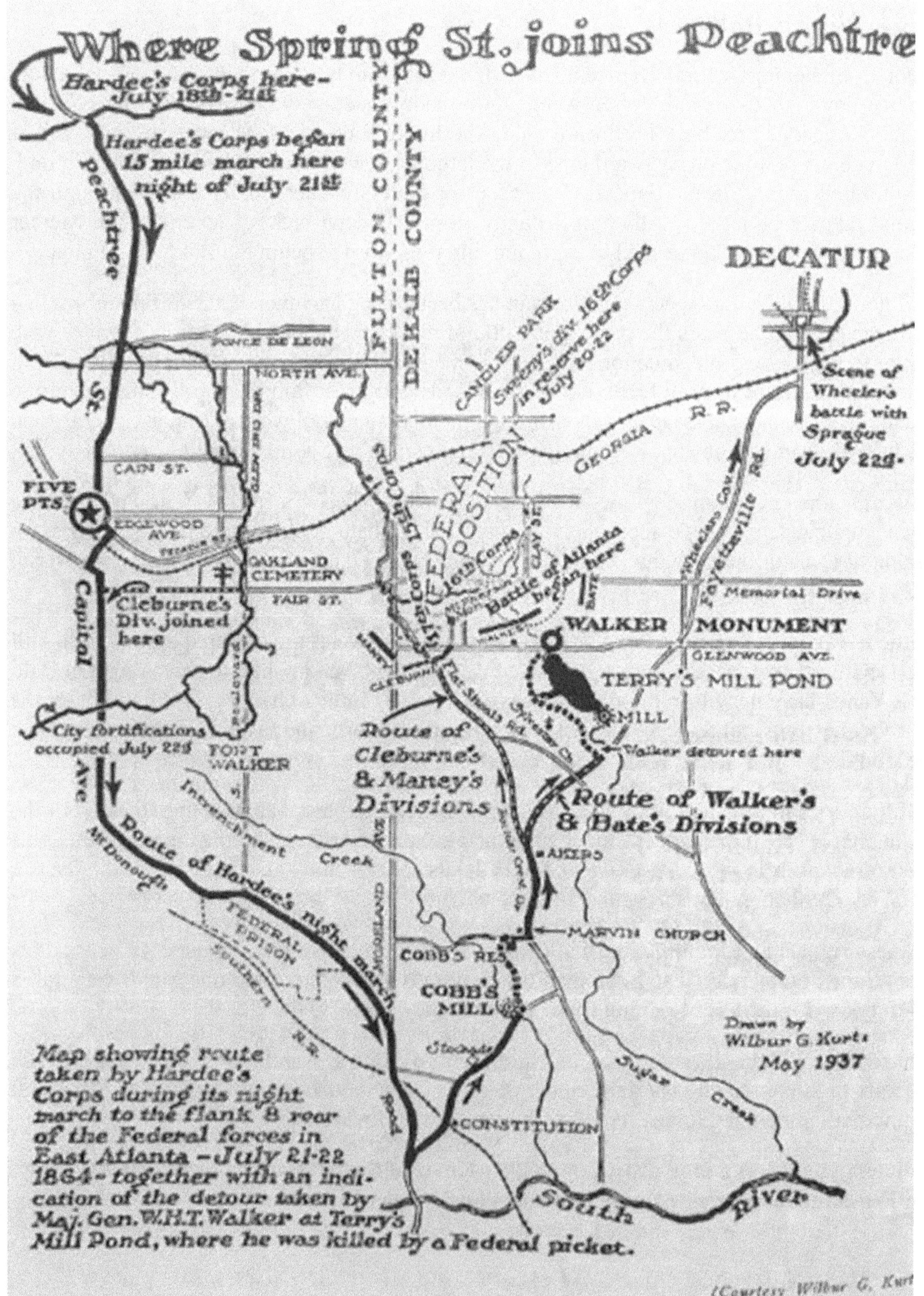


(Courtesy Wilbur G. Kurtz)

**July 23, 1864**

In Atlanta, Georgia, it is cooler today than the blistering heat of yesterday, but the City is awash in misery. Temporary, supplemental hospitals are set up in the City park and at field headquarters near the City graveyard where Drs. Noel D'Alvigny and Joseph Logan performed amputations all night, moving their patients to near the railroad yards this morning, anticipating transport to the south.

With their newly acquired gun positions, the Union gunners are dropping explosive rounds scattered about within the downtown area, filling the population with fear.

On the battlefield the Confederates apply for a truce for removal of wounded and dead. Once the truce is proclaimed by General Logan, soldiers of both sides begin the task of burial and removal.

Lt. Henry O. Wright, a correspondent for "Harper's Weekly" and a soldier in the 20th Ohio writes, "*This, then, is what an assault means, a slaughter pen, a charnel house, and an army of weeping mothers and sisters at home*". At one place Lt. Wright sees 45 slain Confederates in a pile in front of a Union fortification, with a Union soldier looking about with his legs dangling down. Wright takes the time and sketches the scene before him.

Confederate dead after the Battle of Atlanta, July 23, 1864. Sketch by Henry Dwight. Courtesy of Ohio Historical Society.

## July 24, 1864

In the Shenandoah Valley of Virginia, yesterday, Reb General Early's cavalry fought a sharp skirmish with Federal pickets at Kernstown. Learning from prisoners taken there that Union General Wright has taken his two corps back to Grant at Petersburg, Early, with about 13,000, decides to go against the remaining Yankees in the Valley under General Crook who has about 10,000 men.

This morning, the cavalry of both forces engage first, and the attack centers on John B. Gordon's Division. Gordon is able to stop the Federal advance, and Confederate Breckinridge's Division joins the fight, sending the bluecoats into full retreat. Retreat quickly becomes a rout, and Crook's Army is pushed and chased all the way into West Virginia.

***

Near Atlanta Georgia, as the armies patch themselves up and get some needed rest, Union General Kenner Garrard returns today from his raid of the eastern areas begun on July 21. In three days, his men have been in Tucker, Lawrenceville, Loganville, Oxford, Covington, Monroe, Athens, Watkinsville, and Madison. In his report to Sherman Garrard states that he has burned the depot in Covington and over 2,000 bales of cotton. He burned the new hospital in Covington that accommodates 10,000 patients, both Union and Confederate.

In Oxford, in a hospital of 1,000 patients, many of those who could walk ran into the woods. Garrard's men examined those remaining, and the ones that are physically able are taken as prisoners. In general, Garrard and his men have had a great time stealing, destroying, and terrorizing undefended areas of the state, moving rapidly so no force could be raised against them.

**Union Major General Kenner Garrard**

## July 25, 1864:

Near Petersburg, Virginia, Union General Grant, in order to relieve siege boredom and hopeful of weakening the defenders some, sends out his 2nd Corps and two divisions of cavalry to tear up railroads and threaten Richmond any way they can think of, so that Reb General Lee will have to detach some forces to stop them.

Meanwhile, the coal miners from Pennsylvania are still working on the tunnel that will go under the breastworks of the Confederate defenders and will soon be blown to high heaven. Attack forces are practicing daily as to how to circumnavigate the inevitable crater that will be formed and flow themselves into the City, through the breached defenses.

***

Near Atlanta, GA, US General Sherman is preparing two columns of cavalry to strike around Atlanta and destroy portions of the railroad. They will leave day after tomorrow. Also, on that date, acting Commander, Logan will move his Army of the Tennessee around General Thomas to the right, and move against East Point to sever the West Point Railroad. Sherman and Grant have to decide about the permanent replacement of McPherson. Logan performed brilliantly under dire circumstances when he assumed command on the 22nd, but he is not a West Point Graduate, and possibly not capable of handling the administrative part of the job. Joe Hooker is the ranking officer and qualified for the job, but who wants him?

**Union Major General John "Black Jack" Logan**

## July 26, 1864:

Around Atlanta, Georgia, both armies are having to reorganize high command due to loss of General Officers in the recent Battle of Atlanta. The Confederates lost Major General WHT Walker and will disband his division thusly: Mercer's, brigade will go to Pat Cleburne; Gist's Brigade to Maney; and Stevens' brigade to Bate. Stephen D Lee is given Corps Command of Hood's old corps, thereby returning Major General Ben Cheatham to his division. Confederate General Bragg is pushing for Hardee to be exchanged in command for Richard Taylor in Louisiana, but nothing is done yet about that.

There is weeping and wailing and gnashing of teeth in the Federal camps today. Major General Oliver Howard is announced as permanent Army Commander of the Army of the Tennessee, replacing the dead James McPherson who arrives in Nashville today to begin the last leg of his journey home to Ohio. Major General John Logan, who has done a fine job of temporary command is bitterly disappointed that he was not chosen.

The Junior Major General, Schofield, thought he would be moved to command the larger army and is disappointed, but not vocal about his feelings. But, Major General Joe Hooker, Former Commander of the Army of the Potomac, is very vocal and immediately sends a note to Sherman asking to be relieved of command. After consulting with Thomas, Sherman wires Halleck and asks him to get the President to get Hooker out of here and replace him with Henry Slocum. So now Sherman has two new commanding officers, one Corps Commander and one Army Commander.

**Major General Henry Slocum**

**Major General Oliver Howard**

## July 27, 1864

At Petersburg, Virginia, the tunnel under the Confederate defenses is complete, and being stocked with explosives. In order to weaken the force manning the walls in that area, Union General Grant has sent cavalry generals Hancock and Sheridan to attack the defenses of Richmond. This will force Lee to pull men from Petersburg to help defend the Confederate Capital. All goes well until this afternoon when the Federals find the Rebel defenses too hard to crack in the Deep Bottom area of the James River, where they are stopped cold, in a sharp action. Reinforcements are, however, being pulled from critical areas of Petersburg to assist Richmond as Grant has hoped.

The attack at Petersburg is set for July 30, when the tunnel will be blown, and an invasion force will enter the City around the crater.

***

Union General Howard pulls his new command from the eastern side of the City to the north, and around General Thomas' Army of the Cumberland, moving far around the Confederate left, the Middle Georgia expeditions of cavalry generals Edward McCook and George Stoneman begin today with Stoneman moving out, quietly, with about 2,000 of his own men and Kenner Garrard, with about 3,000. This force is to feint toward Augusta, but move south toward McDonough, then up to Lovejoy where they will join forces with McCook and his 4,000 horsemen who will have traveled through, and done damage to, Palmetto and Fayetteville.

McCook and Stoneman will destroy the railroad in the area while Garrard protects the enterprise from Confederate General Joe Wheeler. When destruction is complete, McCook and Garrard are to return to Sherman, and Stoneman will continue on southward to free the union captives at Camp Oglethorpe, near Macon, and Camp Sumter at Andersonville. I just described how Sherman has ordered this expedition be conducted. Stoneman has other ideas.

**Union Generals George Stoneman (left) and Edward McCook**

## July 28, 1864

Just outside Atlanta, Georgia, yesterday, Union General Oliver Howard began, cautiously, moving his new command, the Army of The Tennessee around the far right of Union forces and southward toward East Point in an attempt to get to the Macon and Western Railroad in order to sever that vital supply line of the Confederates that are fortified in Atlanta. This morning, when Confederate General Hood realizes the movement, he sends new corps commander, Stephen D. Lee to block the approach with two division of his corps. Stewart's Corps is to follow and circle around to attack Howard from the rear tomorrow morning.

When Lee discovers Howard's Federals, they are already fortified with logs at the Lickskillet Rd / Sandtown Rd crossroads near Ezra Church. He sends word for Stewart to move up and he sends a blistering attack against the center of Logan's Corps which is easily repulsed. Lee attacks again, and yet again, with no more success than before. He should have waited for Stewart to come up, and a coordinated attack had a chance for success, but by the time Stewart gets into position, Lee's force is so shot up and the men demoralized that the combined effort is just as futile as the prior ones have been. Lee loses about 3,000 casualties, and Howard, about 600, but the Federals are blocked from southward progress, and the Macon and Western Railroad is safe for now.

Tonight, as the two battered forces face each other behind breastworks, just constructed, one of Union General Logan's soldiers cries out into the darkness "Say, Johnny," he calls, "How many of you are there left?"....."*Oh, about enough for another killing,*" came the Rebel reply.

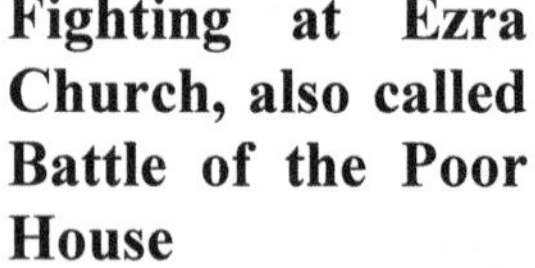
**Fighting at Ezra Church, also called Battle of the Poor House**

## July 29, 1864

In South Georgia, to alleviate some of the overcrowding at the prisoner-of-war Camp Sumter at Andersonville, a, larger, new camp is starting construction today. Camp Lawton, five miles from Millen Crossroads, will be ready for prisoners in late September or early October.

***

In Virginia, near Richmond, the combined Union force under Maj. Gens. Winfield Hancock and Phillip Sheridan have been defeated in their attempts to break the defensive lines of Richmond, and they return to Grant late today in case they are needed at the break-through effort at the mine that is to be exploded early tomorrow morning. They were successful, however, in forcing Confederate General Lee to pull personnel from the mine area to help defend Richmond, so their mission in the "Battles of the Deep Bottom" was accomplished.

At Petersburg, Virginia, the mine is ready, the galleries are stocked with explosives and fuses are being set for a detonation tomorrow morning. Union General Burnsides has been drilling a division of colored troops for weeks so that they know exactly what to do when the explosion occurs, but Union General Grant changes the game plan, fearing the colored troops might be massacred if the attempt fails.

If that should occur, then Grant fears the spin that the media and other critics might put upon it, making him seem heartless regarding the negroes. It will be much better to use an all-white force, ill-prepared, to be devastated if this "untested" plan goes badly. A new force is assembled and made ready. All involved forces move up into position late tonight. The bomb will go off at 3:30 tomorrow morning.

**Mine and galleries 500 feet from the entrance**

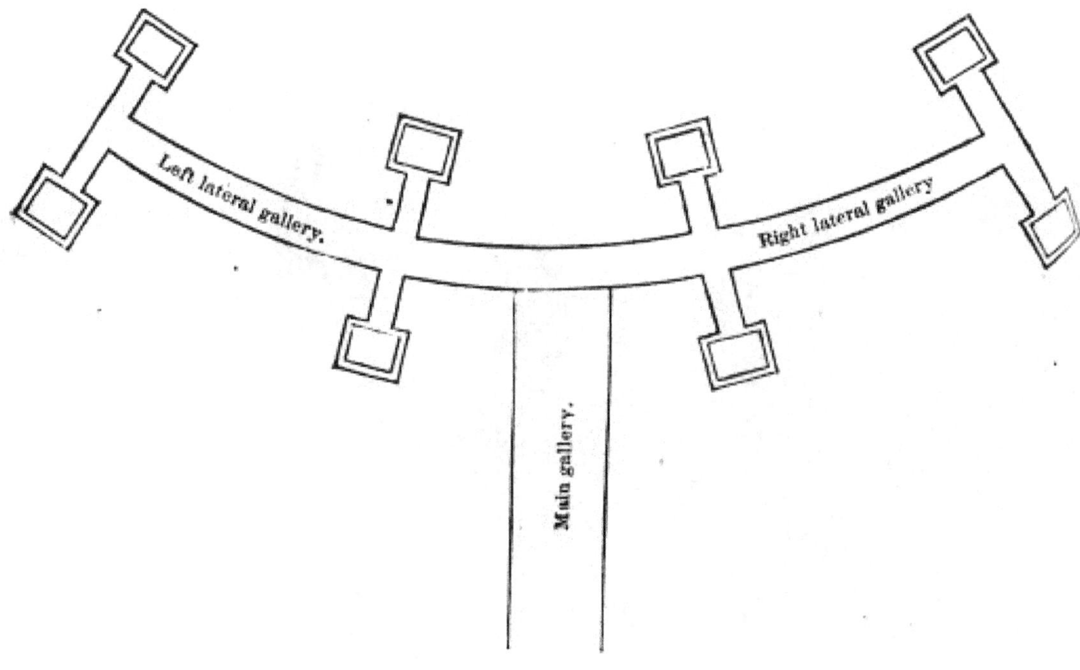

## July 30, 1864

In Georgia, southwest of Atlanta the raid by Union General Edward McCook runs into difficulty today. Leaving the Federal lines on July 27, he, and his 4,000 horsemen, have been through Palmetto and Fayetteville where he did major damage to businesses and homes. He made it to Lovejoy as scheduled and destroyed a Confederate wagon train, but Stoneman never showed up to meet him. After doing much damage to the railroad, McCook starts making his way back to Sherman's lines and is caught up with at Brown's Mill near Newnan by Reb Cavalry General, Joe Wheeler, this morning.

With a force of just over half his enemy's, Wheeler, attacks and devastates McCook's ranks who fold up and begin to run. The Rebels will spend the rest of the day chasing and fighting, and on into tomorrow, rendering almost 1,000 casualties to the Union force. McCook himself, will make it back to Sherman.

***

In the defensive positions of Petersburg, the huge bomb in the tunnels beneath, goes off as scheduled, immediately killing and wounding about 300 Confederate soldiers. Then the attacking Yankees pour through the wall breech and into the craters left by the bomb, many of them are Negroes and are screaming "*No Quarter! Remember Fort Pillow!*" They could climb on through except for the quick-responding Johnny Rebs who pour a deadly fire into their ranks. Other attackers continue to arrive, pushing inward, but there is an unorganized traffic jam at the breech and the Confederates continue to be reinforced. Then the counter attacks, under Reb General William Malone, completely halt all advance and the Federals are ordered back. The entire event is a disastrous debacle for the Union troops, and Grant is furious at General Burnside. Many Union Negroes are killed trying to run away and some while trying to surrender. There would have been an absolute slaughter if it were not for the efforts of General Malone to control his men. Union losses approach 4,000 and Confederate losses are about 1,500.

## July 31, 1864

In Chambersburg, Pennsylvania, Confederate Cavalry General McCausland, under orders from Major General Early, entered the town yesterday and demanded a ransom be paid of $500,000 in greenbacks, or he would burn the town. This is in retaliation for the damage and destruction that Union General Hunter has caused in the Shenandoah Valley. When the citizens could not pay, the torch was applied to most of the buildings of the town.

During the night and this morning many Confederate soldiers feeling the shame of the situation pour their feelings out on paper in letters to home, while others loot and brutalize the population, acting exactly like the worst animals in Sherman's army. This is the Confederates' darkest day, a day with no honor at all.

***

In Georgia, Union General Stoneman's Cavalry expedition has been acting like the Rebels in Pennsylvania all through middle Georgia and having a fine time until yesterday when they are stopped by a hard battle with a contingency of Georgia Militia at Dunlap Hill, near Macon. Reb General Howell Cobb has his men well fortified, armed, and determined. Not able to proceed southward, Stoneman finds that Confederate Cavalry General Iverson (who was sent south by General Lee after a dismal performance at Gettysburg) has him cut off from northward movement at Sunshine Church. Fighting ensues, and Stoneman cannot determine Iverson's troops' strength because of the wooded nature of the terrain, but he knows he can't break through them, and Cobb is moving his Georgia militia up to close the trap.

Stoneman knows that surrender is his only option, so he orders two brigades to escape with tonight's darkness, and he will fight delaying action with the remaining brigade and submit to capture tomorrow morning. Confederate General Iverson has found that he is a much better cavalry General than an infantry General, and it helps that he is fighting in the area that he grew up in; he was born and raised near Clinton, GA. Eventually he will become a permanent "silent citizen" of Historic Oakland Cemetery in Atlanta.

**Confederate General Alfred Iverson Jr.**

## August 1, 1864

In Georgia, near Macon at Sunshine Church, Federal General George Stoneman surrenders the remainder of his command to Confederate Generals Alfred Iverson and Howell Cobb. It is all the two commanders can do to keep the members of the Georgia Militia from hanging him to the nearest tree because of the destruction of personal property in the area, that he and his men have wrought. He will be imprisoned in the very Camp Oglethorpe that he wanted to liberate, and his men will go to Camp Sumter at Andersonville, another "liberation" target of Stoneman's.

***

In Virginia, the Confederates under Jubal Early have had their way for several weeks in the Shenandoah Valley, and have invaded Pennsylvania and threatened Washington. All efforts to stop them have been futilely orchestrated from Washington. From Petersburg, Lt General Grant has sent for General Phillip Sheridan, explained the situation to him, and today orders him to go to Washington where a force of 37,000 men (20,000 more than Early has) will be assembled for him. He is to stay southward of Early, trap him and defeat him.

***

In Atlanta, the population is under siege. The Federal guns are relentless in their pounding of the City, the Rebel guns always answering in kind. Even though there is not much action to report this month, there is much drama within the strong fortifications, with people living in constant fear of the explosive rounds falling from the sky. Ten-year-old Carrie Berry acting on her Father's suggestion has begun to record what each of her days are like. We will share her thoughts throughout the month of August.

"Aug. 1. Monday. It was raining this morning and we thought we would not have any shelling today so I nurst Sister while Mama would do a little work, but before night we had to run to the cellar."

## August 2, 1864

In Atlanta, Carrie Berry writes in her diary: "Aug. 2. Tuesday. We have not been shelled much today, but the muskets have been going all day. I have done but little today but nurse Sister. She has not been well today."

***

Near Athens, Ga. one of the two Federal cavalry brigades that eluded capture at Sunshine Church nears the City, sending the population into a frenzy. A hastily assembled assortment of defenders put forth a united front, bristling with rifles held by factory workers, farmers, home guards, and college professors.

The defense is staged from prepared breastworks at Barber's Creek and supported by two cannons. As Union Col. Silas Adams and his 1st Kentucky Cavalry Regiment approach, the locals open up with squirrel guns and the cannon. Exhausted and almost out of ammunition the Yankees retreat out of range and go on around Athens, desperate to get back to Sherman and safety. Neither side has any casualties in the action.

***

In the Gulf of Mexico, just outside Mobile Bay, the Federal fleet under the command of Admiral David Farragut is preparing for attack on the morning of the 5th of August. In order to get his force into the bay, Farragut will have to pass between Fort Gaines on Dauphine Island and Fort Morgan, on a narrow strip of mainland, the other side of the opening into the bay. The path will have to be close to Fort Morgan because of obstructions and torpedoes (mines) in the bay, and once past the forts, they will have to contend with "CSS Tennessee", a strong iron-clad, and two Confederate gunships. The first step of the campaign is to take Fort Gaines by land and that will begin tomorrow morning.

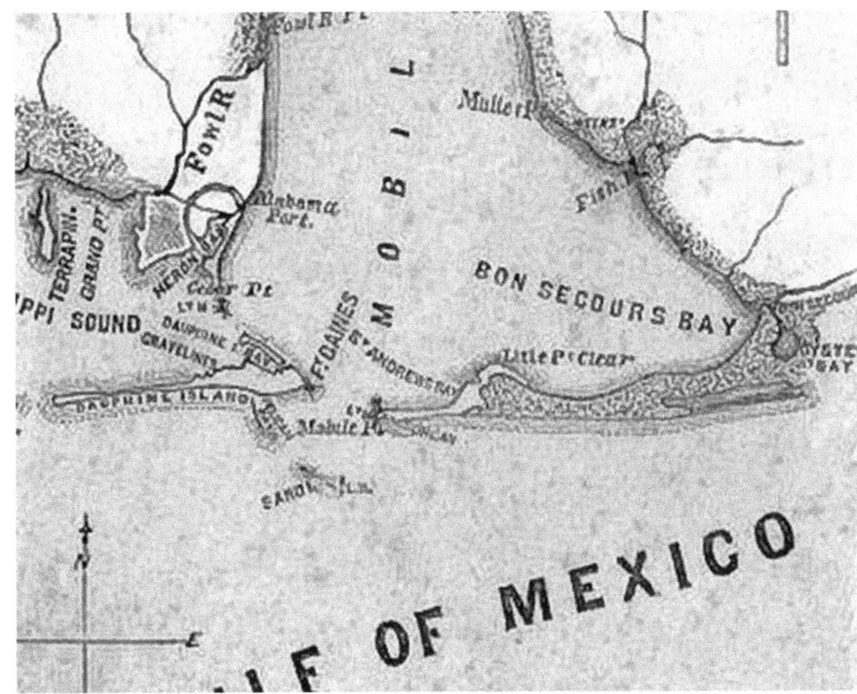


**The entrance to Mobile Bay. The forts' locations are marked with the red "X"'s.**

## August 3, 1864

In Atlanta, Carrie Berry writes in her diary: "Aug. 3. Wednesday, this was my birthday. I was ten years old, But I did not have a cake times were too hard so I celebrated with ironing. I hope by my next birthday we will have peace in our land so that I can have a nice dinner."

In Georgia, near Jug Tavern (later Winder), the two divisions of Union Cavalry that escaped the capture at Sunshine Church have moved around Athens, and the brigade, under Brig. Gen. Adams, heads on north, then west and will make it safely back to Sherman's lines, but the division under Brig. Gen. Capron turns west on the Hog Mountain Rd. to Jug Tavern, where, last night, they fed and watered their horses, then marched about 1/4 mile to King's Tanyard to rest for a couple of hours. Just before dawn, this morning, Brig. General Williams' Confederates, yelling loudly, charge over the Federal pickets and into a large group of escaped negroes, throwing them into a panic. The panic spreads to Capron's men and a stampede toward Mulberry River results. About 430 of the Yankees are captured, and the remainder escape temporarily into the woods. Capron himself, with only six men, will reach safety in Marietta four days from now,--on foot. This is the final chapter of the great "Stoneman Raid".

***

In the Gulf of Mexico, outside Mobile Bay, the combined army / navy effort is preparing for the actions of day after tomorrow. They are waiting on one more iron-clad Monitor to arrive to bring the total of those to four. It will arrive late today and be in position by tomorrow night. The army landing force, 1500 men, under Major General Gordon Granger, invades the western end of Dauphine Island and moves up to fortify in siege positions next to Fort Gaines today. Granger only has a small force, but he is one of the best field commanders the Union has; he always does well with what he has.

**Union Admiral David Farragut (left) and Major General Gordon Granger**

## August 4, 1864

In Atlanta, Carrie Berry writes in her diary: "Aug. 4. Thurs. The shells have ben flying all day and we have stayed in the cellar. Mama put me on some stockings this morning and I will try to finish them before school commences.".

***

In the Gulf of Mexico, Union Admiral Farragut has sent a wooden steamer to tow the slowly approaching monitor that will be the fourth one to arrive outside Mobile Bay. The wooden warships are pairing up and lashing themselves to their partners, so that, in the event that an engine should fail while under the guns of the forts, the other ship can power both. Early tomorrow morning the fleet will attempt to capture the bay by entering it and defeating the 3-vessel Confederate fleet, then it will just be a matter of time until the forts fall. The entry path will have to be chosen perfectly because the mouth of the bay is partially blocked by heavy, contact, torpedoes, forcing any ship to have to pass close to the guns of Fort Morgan.

***

Outside Atlanta, Union General Sherman has moved General Schofield's Army of the Ohio from the Decatur area, northward, then westward, all the way around to the extreme Federal right to establish new positions and try to creep the lines further south to cut the railroad supplying the Rebels in Atlanta. He assigned the Army of the Cumberland's 14th Corps, under the command of General John Palmer to reinforce Schofield.

Yesterday the Northern Force arrived at Utoy Creek, and this morning Schofield orders the crossing of the creek, but Palmer refuses to obey any commands, believing himself to be the senior officer. By the time Sherman can intercede, the Rebels have reinforced the defensive positions and repel any efforts for the Yankees to advance. Sherman will try this again tomorrow.

**Union General John Palmer**

## August 5, 1864

In Atlanta, Carrie Berry writes in her diary: "Aug. 5. Friday. I knit all the morning. In the evening we had to run to Auntie's and get in the cellar. We did not feel safe in our cellar, they fell so thick and fast."

Near Atlanta, on Utoy Creek, Union General Palmer has tendered his command resignation because Sherman has ruled that he is Junior in rank to General Schofield, but he has agreed to cooperate with today's fighting. The attacks by the 14th Corps really never develop past the stage of overrunning the Confederate pickets. The attacking Federals lie down and fortify themselves as soon as the Rebs start shooting back, giving their enemy another day to strengthen their works.

***

In the Gulf of Mexico at Mobile Bay, this morning at 6:47, the lead attack monitor "Tecumseh" fires on Fort Morgan and enters the bay, followed by three other monitors, 12 wooden ships, and 2 armored gunboats. The wooden boats are supposed to keep the iron-clads between them and the guns of the fort but stay to the right of the mine fields of torpedoes. Smoke is heavy on the scene and "Tecumseh" strays into the minefield where she is blown up and sunk by a torpedo. A lead ship, "Brooklyn" stops for, her captain to become unconfused as to his responsibilities, holding up the advancement, so Union Admiral Farragut commands his ship to lead the way through the minefield and around the obstruction with the cry "Damn the torpedoes, full speed ahead!".

None of the torpedoes explode, and the Union fleet is able to get inside the bay. After a vicious fight with "CSS Tennessee" the overwhelming numbers are able to capture the iron-clad and two of the three Confederate wooden ships. This afternoon Admiral Farragut is in control of Mobile Bay, but not of the City of Mobile or the three forts on the shores of the bay.

**Federal fleet passing Fort Morgan**

## August 6, 1864

In Atlanta, 10-year-old, Carrie Berry pens in her diary: "Aug. 6. Sat. We have ben in the cellar all day. Cousin Henry Beatty came this evening and brought some Yankee coffee for me to grind for him. some he had captured yesterday in a skirmish."

***

In Springfield , Massachusetts, the temperature will reach 102 degrees today, down from the 108 of earlier this week. The Northeast has been in a drought with high heat and almost no rain for over two months now, and water supplies are drying up.

***

In Mobile Bay, the Union ships are shelling the three Confederate forts and being shelled by them. Fort Howard, the weakest of the three, was designed to fight invasion from the Gulf and is not as strong on the Bay side. The fort commander, Lt. Col Williams, is declaring the defense of the fort is untenable and has his men spike the guns, blow the magazine, then everybody wades to shore and on to Mobile.

Union Army Commander, Granger, is shelling Fort Gaines from emplacements adjacent to the fort on Dauphine Island.

***

Near Atlanta, on Utoy Creek, having no success hurling the demoralized XIV Corps of General Palmer against the defenses of Confederate William Bate, Union General Schofield has decided to order his own division under Jacob Cox to move against the Rebels. Early this morning, Reilly's Brigade, of Cox's Division, charges and easily pushes the pickets in, but as they advance, suddenly, there is a wall of lead from the fortified positions. Yankees fall by the scores and have to retreat. Regrouping, Reilly has them try it again, and once more the formations are ripped apart. This action will convince Sherman that his tactics of extending his right to cut the railroads will not work. He will have to think of something else. The Federals lose 306 in Today's action, and Bates loses 15 or 20.

**Confederate Major General William B Bate (Future Governor of Tennessee)**

## August 7, 1864

In Atlanta, GA, 10-year-old Carrie Berry writes in her diary: "Aug. 7. Sun. We have had a quiet day it all most seems like Sunday of old. Papa and I went to Trinity Church. Mr. Haygood preached. It is the first time I have been to Church in a month.".

In Mobile Bay, while the Federal gunboats shell Fort Morgan, the large land force of General Granger blasts away at the weak side of Fort Gaines. Although the actual number of defenders of the fort is unknown, it is certain that they are vastly outnumbered, and there is no way to get reinforcements to them. The fort cannot hold out for long.

***

Near Moorefield West Virginia, Confederate Brig. Gen. John McCausland with 3,000 horsemen has pulled back across the Potomac after his destructive raid on Chambersburg. Three days ago, he was unsuccessful in a raid on the B&O Railroad at New Creek, foiled by Union artillery high on a mountainside, raining down on him. He is currently camped with each of his two divisions separated from each other by the South Branch Potomac River. Having been unopposed since he left Virginia, he is careless in his camp's security as well as his army's position, and Union Brig. Gen. William Averell makes him pay for it.

At three o'clock this morning Averell and 1400 men attack the camp across the river from McCausland, surprising everybody, and a rout and capture ensues. With the Confederates in confusion, Averell then attacks the other side of the river with the effect of destroying McCausland's force temporarily.

The Union victory causes 488 Rebel casualties, including 377 captured, while suffering 33 casualties, including 13 captured. An interesting note about General Averell is that after the war, he will become a gifted inventor, and will become quite wealthy with his invention of American Asphalt Paving.

**Confederate Gen. John McCausland.**

**Federal Gen. William Averell**

## August 8, 1864

In Atlanta, 10-year-old Carrie Berry writes about her day in her diary: "Aug. 8. Mon. I got up early this morning and cleaned up the house for Mama. I nursed Sister while Mama got dinner. We had Cousin Eddie Stow to take dinner with us to day. I did not knit much to day. I went up to Auntie's in the afternoon. We have not had many shells to day."

In Mobile Bay early this morning, Fort Gaines, on Dauphine Island, surrenders unconditionally to the Land forces of Union General Granger. This, coming after a two-day discussion between the Federals and the fort, and constant demands by telegraph from Confederate Brigadier General Page to Colonel Anderson to not surrender yet. Anderson knows his fort cannot defend his men against the available force against him. He probably also knows that Page will not be able to defend Fort Morgan, the strongest of the forts in the Bay, for much longer.

***

Outside Atlanta, Union General Sherman wants one more attempt on confederates under Bate in front of Union General Schofield at Utoy Creek, so he develops a plan of distraction that should help Schofield pull it off. He orders Cavalry General Garrard to move southward on the eastern side of the City to attract attention there. He also orders Cavalry General Kilpatrick to move southward on the western side of the city against the Rebel cavalry now supporting Bates. And he orders all artillery to fire at least fifty rounds on downtown Atlanta tomorrow. This is all designed to occupy the Confederates so that Schofield can make one final push to get to the railroad southwest of the city. Atlanta is going to have a bad day tomorrow.

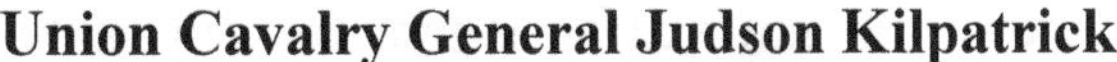

**Union Cavalry General Judson Kilpatrick**

## August 9, 1864:

In Atlanta, a tired Carrie Berry writes in her diary: "Aug. 9. Tues. We have had to stay in the cellar all day the shells have ben falling so thick around the house. Two have fallen in the garden, but none of us were hurt. Cousin Henry Beatty came in a and wanted us to move, he thought that we were in danger, but we will try it a little longer.".

Yesterday, Union General Sherman ordered all artillery units to fire on downtown Atlanta today, as part of his "diversion" plan, to allow General Schofield to advance at Utoy Creek. This morning a bombardment of over 3,000 shells and solid shot began and lasted all day, but Confederate General Bates' defensive works hold, and Schofield is able to gain nothing. There are no casualties inside the City in spite of a terrifying day of noise and destruction.

***

At Grant's headquarters at City Point, Virginia, a horrific explosion occurs late this morning when a timed ignition device is placed on an ammunition barge by Confederate Secret Service agent, John Maxwell. Maxwell has posed as a dock workman and has convince Federal guards that the box is supposed to be stored on board. No one has ever heard of such a device because Maxwell has just invented it.

One of Grant's officers writes, "Such a rain of shot, shell, bullets, pieces of wood, iron bars and bolts, chains and missiles of every kind was never witnessed." There are even saddles falling from the sky, originating on a barge adjacent to the ammo barge. 43 men are killed instantly and 126 are wounded. The wharf is entirely destroyed, and all glass and plaster in the buildings of the town are shaken from their structures. The entire affair is thought by Grant and the rest of the Union to have been an accident. Only after Confederate records are examined will the truth come out.

**By Alfred Waud for Harper's Weekly**

## August 10, 1864

In Atlanta, Carrie Berry has this to say in her diary, "Aug. 10. Wed. We have had but few shells to day. It has ben raining nearly all day and we had to stay in the house very close."

In Atlanta, it has been quiet most of the day, until General Sherman's new toys come into play. Late this afternoon, he has three (expecting a fourth) new guns, 4.5" ordinance weapons, rifled cannon set up just off Howell Mill Rd, on the bluff above the bridge over Peachtree Creek. He calls them "Parrott Guns". and most historians will call them "Rodman guns"; they are neither. "Parrott Guns" have a reinforcing band welded at the breech, but Sherman's guns do not. "Rodman" guns are cast differently than Sherman's guns, but they are still lethal with their 33-pound payload of devastation, at a range of miles, not yards. From the new perch of his guns, well placed for receiving ammunition on the well-traveled, Howell's Mill Road, he can deliver his hateful message of pompous superiority to the citizens of Atlanta with round after round of explosives, hour after hour.

From Atlanta, Confederate Lt. General Hood sends forth, against the supply lines of Union General Sherman, Cavalry General Wheeler with over 4,000 horsemen, in high hopes of forcing starving Yankees back to the North where they all belong.

**Confederate Cavalry Commander Joe Wheeler**

## August 11, 1864

In Atlanta, 10-year-old Carrie Berry writes in her diary: "Aug. 11. Thurs. Mama has ben very buisy to day and I have ben trying to help her all I could. We had to go in the cellar often out of the shells. How I wish the federals would quit shelling us so that we could get our and get some fresh air."

Near Atlanta, in his own words, Sherman has said to General Halleck, "*I am too impatient for a siege*". Today he has ordered General Schofield to send a division out to cut the West Point Railroad, and Schofield points out that it will be very dangerous. Sherman replies, *"to fight Hood the earliest possible moment he will come out of his trenches, and would risk a great deal to draw him out...I feel mortified that he holds us in check by the aid of his militia. It seems we are more besieged than he is.*".

***

In the Shenandoah Valley, confederate General Early and his 14,000 men have had their way all over the Valley, and the Union opposition has done little, except to brutalize the population with smaller independent commands. Now all the Union forces have been united under the new command of Phil Sheridan. Although Sheridan is still building his force, he already has enough men to be a threat to Early, and he moves to get southward of the Confederates who are in Winchester. Early realizes the movement and pulls his own force southward to much better defensive positions, just north of Strasburg, Virginia.

***

Since May the Cavalry Corps of the Army of Northern Virginia has been without a formal commander, following the death of Maj. Gen. JEB Stuart. However, Wade Hampton of South Carolina who assumed temporary command when Stuart was killed, and a month later defeated a numerically superior Union force under Sheridan at Trevilian Station, just southeast of Gordonsville, has performed very well. Today, he is given formal command.

**Confederate Cavalry Major General Wade Hampton**

## August 12, 1864

In Atlanta, Carrie Berry shares her 10-year-old world in her diary: "Aug. 12. Fri. Mary came home yesterday and we have not had so much wirk to do so I have ben knitting on my stocking. We had a present to day of a bag of nice pears fro our friend Mrs. Green. We enjoyed them very much. We do not get any nice fruit since the army has been here."

Near Atlanta, Union General Sherman is worried about his supplies and his own lack of progress. In all his warehouses and supply stations he has only enough food to last until the middle of September, and only enough animal feed to last until the 1st of September. After getting word from a lookout that three trainloads of Confederate troops entered the City today, Sherman sends word to his Army commanders to meet with him at 10 o'clock tomorrow morning to discuss a major movement to the Union right.

***

In the Shenandoah Valley of Virginia, Confederate General Early is in sound defensive position on Fisher's Hill, south of Strausburg with 14, 000 men and is confident he can defend himself against Union General Sheridan with 21,000 men, and growing in strength, but he is concerned that part of Sheridan's force might slip south up the parallel Lauray Valley to cut him off from Richmond. To guard against that, he sends John Imboden, with a brigade of Cavalry, to Lauray Valley. Confederate General Anderson, commanding Longstreet's Corps, is at Culpepper with 6,000 infantry, and Lee orders him to move into the direction of Early in case he is needed.

**Confederate Cavalry Brig. Gen. John Imboden**

## August 13, 1864

In Atlanta, 10-year-old Carrie Berry has this to say about today in her diary: "Aug. 13. Sat. We have had a very quiet day to day. We have all ben very buisy trying to work some while we could get out in safety. We fear that we will have shells to night. We can hear muskets so plane."

Actually, Carrie could not know, but the Federals have run out of ammunition for the siege guns that are Sherman's favorite toy right now. Fear not for him; his supply will be replenished in the morning

At ten o'clock, Sherman meets with his Army Commanders, Thomas, Howard, and Schofield to explain his plan and ask them to provide plans for implementing it. He has already informed General Halleck a couple of hours ago: *"Leave one corps strongly entrenched at the Chattahoochee bridge in charge of our surplus wagon trains and artillery; with 60,000 men, reduced to fighting trim, to make a circuit of devastation around the town, with a radius of fifteen or twenty miles. I go on the faith that the militia in Atlanta are only good for the defense of it parapets and will not come out."* Sherman begins to get news of Confederate General Wheeler's men doing damage to his railroad, so he assumes a substantial raid is under way.

In northern Virginia, antagonists Early and Sheridan's forces collide several times today with heavy skirmishes., each to determine the strength of the other

In New York City, the most popular periodical of the day, "Harper's Weekly" publishes a cartoon that probably only makes sense to Northerners

PENNSYLVANIA PREPARED FOR THE NEXT INVASION.

OLD Dutch FARMER. " O yes ! I's all ready. T'ose plame Rascals no cotch me again. I got ebery ting pack up all on de vagon ! Rebs come; Off I go! Rebs no cotch me!"

## . August 14, 1864

In Atlanta, GA, 10-year-old Carrie Berry has this to say in her diary today: "Aug. 14. Sun. Sure enough we had shells in abundance last night. We averaged one every moment during the night. We expected every one would come through and hurt some of us but to our joy nothing on the lot was hurt. They have ben throwing them at us all day to day but they have not ben dangerous. Papa has ben at work all day making the cellar safe. Now we feel like we could stay at home in safety. I dislike to stay in the cellar so close but our soldiers have to stay in ditches."

In Dalton, Ga, elements of Confederate Cavalry, under Joe Wheeler, demand surrender of a small contingency of Union troops in well-fortified position, who refuse, and are able to hold their position against attacks well into the evening. Wheeler's men pull away near midnight.

***

In the Shenandoah Valley of Virginia, Union General Sheridan finds out that Early's Confederates are being reinforced to almost equal his own strength. This news gravely concerns General Grant and almost panics Washington.

Near Petersburg, in an effort to keep Confederate General Lee from sending any more reinforcements to Early, Grant has decided to threaten Richmond again. Last night he sent Maj General Winfield Hancock with 28,000 men across the James River, at Deep Bottom, to attack the Confederate left which he believes to be drastically weakened by the removal of Anderson's Corps to the Shenandoah. At first, after finally getting his force across the river, Hancock makes good progress (There are only about 8,500 Rebs defending at first), but then runs into Anderson's Brigade (7th and 8th GA, among others) at Fussell's Mill, where most progress is stopped. It is a bitterly hot day, and the Yanks are suffering many heat strokes in their offensive maneuvers. Fighting will continue tomorrow.

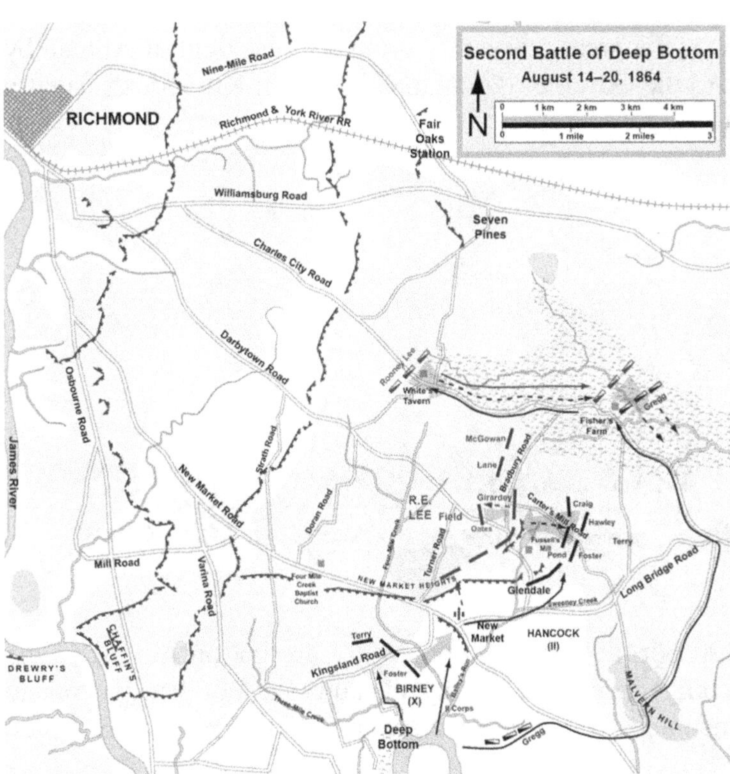

## August 15, 1864

In Atlanta, 10-year-old Carrie Berry writes in her diary about a scary day: "Aug. 15. Mon. We had no shells this morning when we got up and we thought that we would not have any to day (but, my, when will they stop) but soon after breakfast Zuie and I were standing on the platform between the house and the dining room. It made a very large hole in the garden and threw the dirt all over the yard. I never was so frightened in my life. Zuie was as pale as a corpse and I expect I was too. It did not take us long to fly to the cellar. We stayed out till night though we had them all day but they did not come so near us again"

In the Shenandoah Valley of Virginia, Major Union General Phil Sheridan skirmishes with Early's Confederates near Strausburg at Cedar Creek and determines the Rebel positions to be too solid to attack. He also knows that Early is about to be reinforced to parity with his own strength so this evening he begins a withdrawal, back toward Winchester

Near Richmond, the attacking force under Union General Hancock has made little progress since crossing the James River two days ago. Every time progress is made, the Confederates counter and take it away from them.

***

In Georgia, Sherman begins to prepare for the great movement around to the right of Atlanta by slyly having all supply wagons brought to the extreme right and all horses in Kilpatrick's cavalry command re-shod.

***

**"CSS Tallahassee"** originated on the River Thames in London as "Atalanta", an opium and blockade runner. Acquired by the Confederacy, equipped, and armed, she is commanded by President Zachary Taylor's Grandson, Commander John Taylor Wood. She left port at Wilmington, North Carolina on August 6, and has become the scourge of Yankee shipping since then. Today she adds six more cargo ships to her inventory of conquests. Northern insurance companies are screaming for the US Navy to do something about her.

## August 16, 1864

In Atlanta, Georgia, Carrie Berry writes about the twenty-four hours of pounding by the guns of Sherman: "Aug. 16. Tues., We had shells all night. There was a large piece came through Mama's room directly after we went to bed and fell on the little bed and I expect if we had been sleeping there some of us would have ben hurt. Cousin Henry and Cousin Eddy came to see us to day. They told us that they did not think the Federals would be here much longer to torment us and I hope that it may be so for we are getting very tired of living so."

Near Atlanta, since the Confederate cavalry has been greatly weakened by the absence of Joe Wheeler's raiding force, General Sherman decides to send Kilpatrick's cavalry on a scout to help determine routes and defenses pertaining to his big troop movement, the one planned for the western side of the City on the 18th. Kilpatrick has a fine time with his expedition, reaching Fairburn with no problem, then Lovejoy, and can see no reason why he could not go on into Jonesboro. He will report to Sherman in the morning.

***

In the Deep Bottom area of Virginia, the fighting is heavy again today, the heaviest day yet. General Hancock's Yankees attack the Confederates at Fussell's Mills, and have success driving the Rebels from their trenches, but the counter-attacks from the graycoats are successful in taking victory away. During the counter-attack, Confederate General John Chambliss is killed behind the Yankee lines and his West Point classmate, General David Gregg, recovers his body, burying it with ceremony. On the body, is discovered possession of a map of all the Confederate defensive positions around Richmond. Yankee engineers trace the map and lay it over a sheet of photographic paper which is then exposed to the sunlight. When developed, the paper is black except for where the tracing shaded it, and the Yanks can produce enough copies within 48 hours, that all their field commanders have a copy.

**Chambliss' map**

## August 17, 1864

In Atlanta, GA, it seems as if 10-year-old Carrie Berry is getting accustomed to the bombardment because today she writes in her diary: "Aug. 17. Wed. Nothing of interest has hapined to day. We have stayed very closed in the cellar. Mama ran up to Aunties to see how a shell had ruined her house yesterday".

***

In the Shenandoah Valley of Virginia, elements of Confederate General Early's Corps follow, to harass, the withdrawal of Union General Sheridan and involve in a sharp action at Winchester where Sheridan has left a well-fortified rearguard.

***

In Mobile Bay, Union General Gordon Granger still has Fort Morgan under siege. Yesterday, the Confederates abandoned two batteries of the outer defenses and today Granger is moving his siege mortars within 500 yards of the fort and his 30- pounder rifled guns to within 1,200 yards. There is no sign of surrender of the fort.

***

Near Atlanta, Union General Sherman, who is preparing major elements of his army for a grand movement around the Confederate left, is having second thoughts on what to do. This morning, Judson Kilpatrick reports to him that he can easily take a souped-up cavalry force around the Confederates and demolish the railroad at Jonesboro in one day's effort, so Sherman orders him to prepare his men and horses and leave in the morning, meanwhile he informs his bosses and army commanders the movement, already designed for tomorrow, is delayed, waiting to be cancelled upon Kilpatrick's success. Sherman is giving Kilpatrick two brigades of Garrard's Cavalry to assist in this project. Kilpatrick has been described by a staff office in the Army of the Potomac, where he was serving last year, as "*a frothy braggart without brains*".

**Union Cavalry General Judson Kilpatrick**

## August 18, 1864

In Atlanta, after a frightful night, Carrie Berry writes the following in her diary: "Aug. 18. Thurs. When I woke this morning I thought the hole town would be torn up. The cannons were so near and so loud but we soon found out that it was our guns so we have ben very well content all day. We have had less shells to day than we have had in a week.".

Near Atlanta, late this afternoon just after sundown, Union cavalry under Judson Kilpatrick, 4,700 strong, starts toward Sandtown. Arming the force are many Spencer repeating rifles and two batteries of horse artillery. Resistance is limited to Confederate Brig. Gen. Ross's Texas Brigade with 400 men, but by destroying bridges, sniping from the bushes and well-placed ambushes, Ross is able to effectively slow the advance of the thousands tonight.

***

In Virginia, just south of Petersburg, General Grant's Yankee army is trying to cut Lee's railroad supply at Globe Tavern on the Weldon Railroad, which connects Petersburg to Weldon, North Carolina. The attack force is led by V Corps Commander, Major General Gouverneur K. Warren, with about 20,000 men. At dawn, this morning Warren's men overrun pickets and a cavalry brigade at Globe Tavern. Part of the force goes to work tearing up track and others begin to fortify their position, anticipating a counter-attack.

Confederate General A.P. Hill sends two brigades of Henry Heth's division, along with one brigade of Robert Hoke's division, combined, about 2 o'clock, they launch a strong attack and push the Union troops back to within a mile of Globe Tavern.

Warren, then counter-attacks effectively, regaining his lost ground. Everybody fortifies for the night and will resume tomorrow.

**Globe Tavern**

## August 19, 1864

In Atlanta, 10-year-old Carrie Berry writes in her diary: "Aug. 19. Fri. Auntie went down to Grandpa's this morning and I missed her so much. That is the only place I had to run to. I have ben knitting on my stocking some today and sewing some to day."

Near Atlanta, Union General Kilpatrick has sent a diversionary unit of 309 horsemen off toward Griffin while he proceeds with his main force of 4,400 toward Jonesboro. The Confederate forces stationed in Jonesboro learn of the approach of the decoy force and leave out after it. This means that any defense will have to be done by the 400 Texans of Lawrence Ross, who have been fighting all night. The Rebs make a strong showing, ambushing from the town buildings, but the 10 to 1 odds are overwhelming, and at 5 in the afternoon when Kilpatrick's forces fully arrive, they have to leave in a hurry. Kilpatrick's men find a store of whisky, so they have the unit band strike up lively tunes to enjoy as they burn the buildings of the small town and tear up railroad track, but they are not able to heat and bend the rails because of heavy rainfall. At ten in the evening the Federals pull out of Jonesboro and head toward Lovejoy's Station.

***

Near Globe Tavern, Virginia, During the night last night both combatants were reinforced by elements of Maj. Gen. William Mahone's division of the Confederacy and Union Maj Gen. John Parke's IX Corps. For most of the day, heavy rain prevents much contact until late in the afternoon when Mahone finds a weak spot in the Yankee line, charges into it and sends the bluecoats into a panic with many surrendering. As daylight fades, the IX Corps counterattacks the Rebels, and widespread hand-to-hand combat ends the day as a rainy darkness makes fighting impossible.

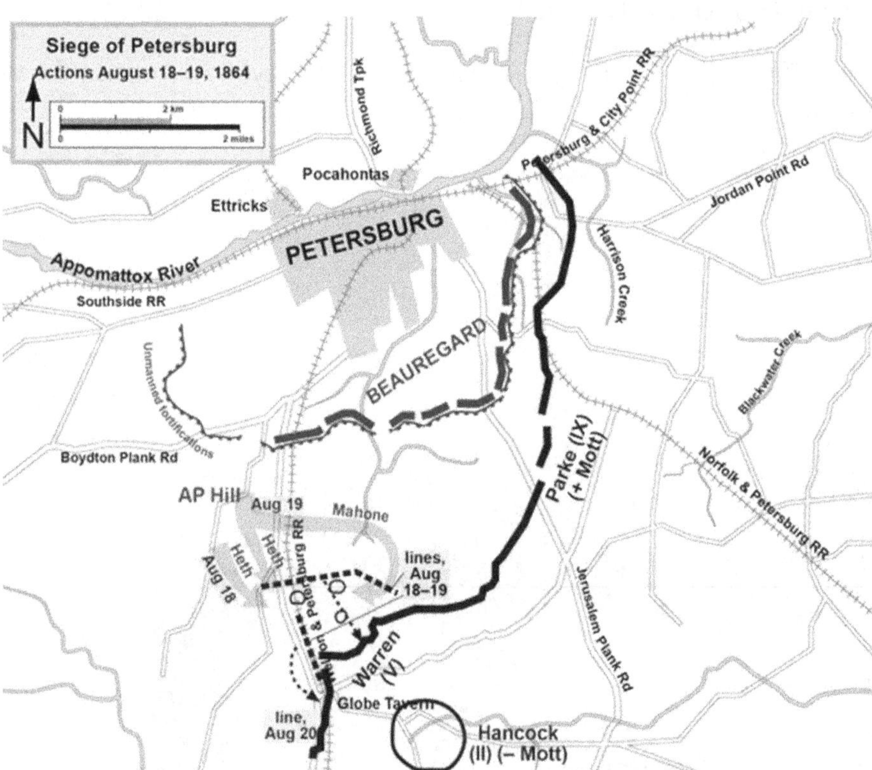

## August 20, 1864

In Atlanta Georgia, 10-year-old Carrie Berry writes in her diary: "Aug 20. Sat. We have had shells all day. They have not ben hitting very close to us but they have been giving them to Uncle Markham. He like to had his house burnt up by one passing through the house and set some cotton on fire which they had layed on the flore. I expect if they had ben at home some of them would have ben hurt."

***

In Virginia, on the Weldon Railroad south of Petersburg, the Federals stay on ready, in a constant downpour of rain, for an attack by the Confederates that does not come. Reb General Beauregard is using the day to bolster his forces for an attack tomorrow morning in hopes of breaking the Federals' new hold on the railroad. Union General Warren will pull back to better fortified positions, still on the railroad, tonight and also receive reinforcements.

***

Early this morning, in Georgia below Atlanta, Confederate Generals Ross and Frank Armstrong combine their small forces and attack Kilpatrick's 4,700 at Jonesboro, not knowing that Kilpatrick left town late last night and is probably camped on the way to Lovejoy's. Ross takes his Texans and moves down the McDonough Rd and then toward Lovejoy. Armstrong takes his Mississippians and moves straight up the railroad, hoping to beat Kilpatrick to Lovejoy, and he does. Just outside Lovejoy, Armstrong meets up with General Reynolds and his Arkansas Brigade, conspiring with them for an ambush to treat Kilpatrick's arrival. When Kilpatrick moves up, about 11 am, a deadly fire erupts from the woods and gullies from the small, combined force in front of him, then Ross, with his 400 moves on him from behind. For three hours they fight, then Kilpatrick decides to abandon the raid and get back to General Garrard and safety. With sabres drawn, he charges his 4,700 over the small group of Texans who scatter and run toward Nash's farm in the direction of McDonough. As Ross tries to stop his men and make a stand, the larger force runs over him again, fully dissipating his command. Kilpatrick will pass through McDonough about midnight tonight and move toward the Flat Shoals at Panola.

**Future Governor of Texas, Conf. Gen. Lawrence S Ross**

## August 21, 1864

In Atlanta, Carrie Berry writes: "Aug. 21. Sun. This was a dark rainy morning and we thought we would have a quiet Sunday but we were disappointed. Papa says that we will have to move down town some where. Our cellar is not safe."

Near Atlanta, on the western side, General Sherman anxiously awaits word from cavalry commander Kilpatrick who is in Henry County trying to make it back to safety in Decatur

***

In Virginia this morning, the reinforced infantry of Confederate General A.P. Hill resumes the attack of the 19th on the defenses of Union General Warren who has been reinforced also. Warren has also changed his entrenchments by using his new men to form a line along the railroad from the point of his extreme left on the 19th and perpendicular to the original line. Unaware of this change, Hill's attack swings around the Union left, but instead of being behind the lines, Hill's men are swept with an enfilading fire and refused by their new front which is now on their left. After an hour's fighting, the Confederates pull away to try the lines no more. The Federals have effectively blocked the Weldon Railroad, making the Rebels have to haul their supplies about thirty miles by wagon. This, first victory of the campaign for Grant, has cost him dearly. Of over 20,000 men involved, he has lost 4455. Beauregard, of about 14,000, has lost about 1,600.

***

Memphis is occupied by 6,000 Federal soldiers, and Confederate Nathan B. Forrest has only 2,000 cavalry, but Forrest assails the City today with three goals in mind: to capture three Union generals posted there; to release Southern prisoners from Irving Block Prison; and to cause the recall of Union forces from Northern Mississippi. None of the generals are captured, but Forrest's men capture Union General Washburn's uniform while he escapes in his nightshirt. The attack on the prison fails, but the raid does have the effect of Union soldiers being pulled out of northern Mississippi, and Forrest takes 500 prisoners, much supplies, and many horses.

**Forrest's attack on Irving Block Prison in Memphis**

## August 22, 1864

In Atlanta, conditions have improved somewhat for Carrie Berry as she writes in her diary: "Aug 22. Mon. I got up this morning and helped Mama pact up to move. We were glad to get out of our small cellar. We have a nice large cellar here where we can run as much as we please and enjoy it. Mama says that we make so much noise that she can't here the shells. *(Cellar of house on Alabama street between Pryor and Central Avenue)."*

***

In the Shenandoah Valley, Union General Phil Sheridan is feeling secure. Having found himself near the Confederate fortifications with almost as many men as he had (20,000), he denied himself the opportunity to be slaughtered, by withdrawing back to Harper's Ferry. Meanwhile, his promised reinforcements have been arriving daily, bringing his strength to about 40,000, well fortified and well fed. He explains his defensive tactics in a telegram to Washington today, " *"My position at best being a very bad one, and, as there is much depending on this army, I fell back and took a new position in front of Halltown, without loss or opposition."* Confederate General Early is not going to attack him, but every hour of every day, he is going to remind Sheridan that he is there.

***

In Decatur, Georgia, Union cavalry commander, Judson Kilpatrick, and his exhausted raiding force reach safety from their mission of railroad devastation south of Atlanta. He reports to General Sherman that the railroad is damaged to the point that it will take 10 days to get it operating again, but tomorrow night three trains will reach Atlanta from the south.

***

In Geneva, Switzerland, at the Geneva Convention, the first codified international treaty that covers the sick and injured soldiers in the battlefield, is adopted by 12 nations. The code provides for a permanent relief agency (Red Cross) for humanitarian aid in times of war, and a government treaty recognizing the neutrality of the agency, allowing it to provide humanitarian aid in times of war. American Clara Barton, who is heading up the Army hospitals along the James River in Virginia, is a huge proponent of this treaty and will be the motivating factor in the United States' adoption of it in 1881.

**Clara Barton**

## August 23, 1864

In Atlanta, 10-year-old Carrie Berry writes in her daily journal: "Aug. 23. Tues. We feel very comfortable since we have moved but Mama is fretted to death all the time for fear of fire. There is a fire in town nearly every day. I get so tired of being housed up all the time. The shells get worse and worse every day. O that something would stop them."

Near Atlanta, Union General Sherman, after consulting with his army commanders, orders his entire army to be ready to move around the City to the west, then south, day after tomorrow.

***

In Washington, President Lincoln sends all his cabinet members a note, asking them to help him finish his term effectively after the upcoming election: *"This morning, as for some days past, it seems exceedingly probable that this Administration will not be re-elected. Then it will be my duty to so co-operate with the President elect, as to save the Union between the election and the inauguration; as he will have secured his election on such ground that he cannot possibly save it afterwards.".*

***

In Mobile Bay, Fort Morgan has been under siege for two weeks since the fall of Fort Gaines. Finally, from the constant pounding of the guns of the land forces and of the warships, the fort is so damaged that it cannot be defended. After a threatening fire raged most of the night last night, early this morning, Confederate Brig. Gen. Page orders all guns to be spiked and orders the white flag to be raised, giving the Union full control of Mobile Bay, the last port to remain in Confederate control east of the Mississippi River on the Gulf of Mexico.

**Fort Morgan just after the surrender**

## August 24, 1864

In Atlanta, multiple fires have been ignited by the incendiary shells falling on the city, as reported by Carrie Berry in her diary: "Aug 24. Wed. We have ben frightened twice to day by fire. I have ben wanting to go home all day to get some grapes but it has ben too dangerous." The observing Federals have been puzzled by the smoke coming from the City. They think the Johnnies are planning some big movement. In reality, most of it is from 500 flaming bales of cotton in P. E. McDaniel's warehouse, set afire by Sherman's shells.

***

In Virginia, on the Weldon Railroad near Ream's Station, Union General Hancock's men are busy destroying the road bed, burning the ties, and heating to deformation the iron rails, when word reaches them that a substantial Rebel force is heading their way. General Lee has pulled 8-10 thousand of A.P. Hill's defenders from the line and sent them under the field direction of General Heth to stop the rail destruction, handing Grant a defeat for the Northern papers to talk about. Hancock has about 9,000 men so it should be a good fight tomorrow afternoon.

***

Near Atlanta, General Sherman is making final preparations to pull his entire force away from the trenches tomorrow night, northward, then westward, then southward around the left of the southern defenders. His words to his army commanders, *"During today and tomorrow morning our troops will send all the surplus men, horses, wagons, ammunition and baggage wagons, &c. and material not absolutely necessary for the success of the expedition, to Vining's Station, on the other side of the Chattahoochee River, each unit will send a small force to the same place to guard such. Let all preparations for this campaign be completed by tomorrow noon. Place a good and reliable division officer of the day, or commander of your division pickets, on duty tomorrow. A staff officer will be sent to you to point out the route of march for your division, and further instructions will be given in reference to the time and manner of withdrawing your pickets."*

**Sherman meeting with his generals about the coming army movement**

## August 25, 1864

The Federal guns around Atlanta are being readied for movement this morning as evidenced by the diary entry of Carrie Berry: "Aug. 25. Thurs. Mama woke me up irly this morning and told me there were no shells falling and told me I must run over and see what had become of Aunt Healy. We had not herd from her in so long. I stayed til after dinner. We had such a nice dinner and so many nice grapes but best of all we had no shells all day."

Early this evening, about 8 o'clock, the Federal armies begin to pull away from Atlanta, leaving a strong picket presence to keep up the appearance of occupancy until the movement can get well under way toward Jonesboro.

***

In Virginia, the Union force of about 9,000 under General Hancock is busy destroying the Weldon Railroad near Ream's Station, basing themselves in fortifications at the station. All workmen are recalled to base when news of the approach of Rebel cavalry reaches Hancock. The first attacks come about two PM and are repulsed with heavy fighting. Charge after charge is denied until about 5:30 when the Confederates are able to develop a gap, panicking two Union regiments, and throw the defenders into an absolute rout. Hancock is able to gather enough force to counter attack and stall the Rebel progress to allow for an orderly Union withdrawal to Petersburg after dark. Of the 9,000 Federals involved, 2,747 are casualties, compared to the similar strength of the Confederates having only 814 casualties.

**Engraving below from "Leslie's Illustrated"**

## August 26, 1864

In Atlanta, joy is expressed by Carrie Berry in her diary, typical for the City on this date: "Aug. 26. Fri. Cousin Henry came in this morning and told us we need not fear the shells any more. The Yankees left there brest works and he hoped they were on the way back to Tennessee. We have had such a delightful day. We all wanted to move to day but we will wait til to morrow and see if the Yankees have gone" The townspeople have discovered the Yankees are gone, and the prevailing opinion is that Wheeler has so interrupted their supply lines that starvation is causing the withdrawal. Confederate General Hood is not buying it. As much as he would like to believe it, he is reinforcing all the entrenchments on his left, very suspicious of all the Federal activity around East Point. As the Confederates occupy the abandoned Federal lines they find large quantities of blankets, clothing, hardtack, bacon, and even sutler's stores, no evidence of a starving army, but moods are high among the populace, just being without the shells falling is cause to celebrate.

***

In Virginia, Union Major General Hancock is lamenting the defeat he suffered yesterday at Ream's Station by a force unfortified and of similar strength as his own. In my opinion, Hancock is probably the best General Officer in the Union Army, but he is a totally defeated man today. Charles Morgan, Hancock's Chief of Staff is quoted as saying, "*It is not surprising that General Hancock was deeply stirred by the situation, for it was the first time he had felt the bitterness of defeat during the war. He had seen his troops fail in their attempts to carry the intrenched positions of the enemy; but he had never before had the mortification of seeing them driven, and his lines and guns taken, as on this occasion."*

**Union Major General Winfield Scott Hancock**

## August 27, 1864

In Atlanta, Carrie Berry gets to move back to her house: "Aug. 27. Sat. We moved home this morning and we have ben buisy trying to get things regulated. I feel so glad to get home and have no shells around us.".

The population of Atlanta is still in celebratory mood today, with most believing that the Federals have drawn back north to Chattanooga. Reb General Hardee knows better; he can see them, Schofield's Army of the Ohio, in force, just outside his defensive lines at East Point. General Sherman has set up headquarters at the Utoy Post Office (located where one day will be the intersection of I-285 and Cascade Rd.) The Army of the Tennessee, after marching all night in the rain, arrives this morning on Camp Creek, about 4 miles from Sherman, and elements of General Thomas' Army of the Cumberland are camped at Gilgal Church on the Fairburn Road. Confederate General Hood only has a vague idea of the Federal forces location, but he has deduced that their target is probably either Rough and Ready (Hapeville) or Jonesboro. There are good roads by which you could move an army to either of these places and access the railroad for damage and devastation. Hood can't do anything, until Sherman indicates his plans, but strengthen his own forces under Major General Hardee that are nearest the enemy,

**Confederate Lt. General William J. Hardee**

## August 28, 1864

In Atlanta, GA, still enjoying the quiet from the Yankee guns, Carrie Berry writes in her diary: "Aug. 28. Sun. Everything seemed so quiet this morning. I wish the people would come back so we could have Church and Sunday School. Mr. came in this morning and brought some shells which Cousin Henry sent us. He got them from the Yankees. Cousin Eddy came in this morning to tell us goodby. We feel sorry he was going to move so far. We all ways love to see him and Cousin Henry.".

***

In the Shenandoah Valley of Virginia, the dwindling force of Reb General Early has moved away from the growing, fortified Force of Union General Sheridan at Harper's Ferry and is now advancing, unopposed, on Charles Town, W. VA.

***

In Georgia, near Atlanta, Union General Thomas reaches Fairburn on the West Point Railroad this afternoon, and General Howard's Army of the Tennessee attains the same railroad at Red Oak. Union General Slocum is occupying the area around Gilgal Church, east of Fairburn. Confederate General Hood knows the approximate locations of the Federals, but he still can't tell what they are up to. Hood is moving troops from the eastern side of Atlanta to Rough and Ready and to Jonesboro in case Sherman wants to try another raid on the rail lines at those places. Losing the West Point railroad is not a powerful blow to Hood. That line has been very hard to protect from Federal raids and has not been used much lately. He must protect the Macon Road or move his army further south.

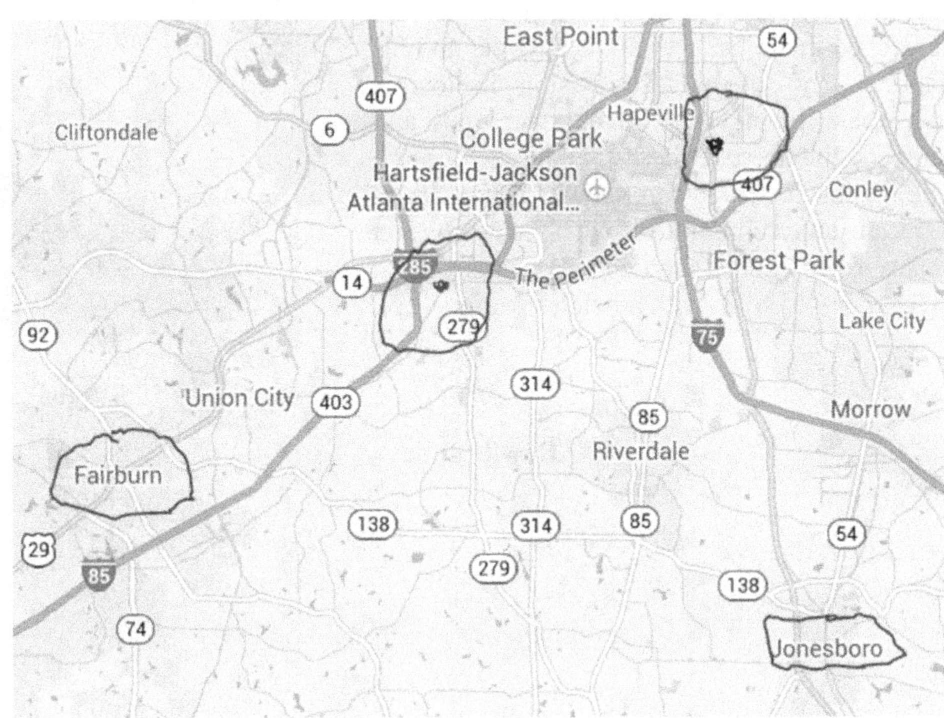


**Old places on a future map (The red dot marks Red Oak, the blue dot marks Rough and Ready)**

## August 29, 1864

In Atlanta, GA, 10-year-old Carrie Berry writes in her diary: "Aug. 29. Mon. Zuie and I went over to Aunt Hattie Smiths this morning to see if we could find our school teacher We stayed all day with her. We had a very pleasant time playing with Ellen."

Near Atlanta, the Federal Army spends the day destroying the West Point Railroad between Red Oak and Fairburn, about 12 miles. First the workers lift one side of the track, ties and all. Then they knock the ties loose with big hammers and stack them into a hot fire, laying the iron tracks on top. When the tracks are red hot they are twisted into unusable shapes and piled into the railroad cuts which are then filled in, with trees, dirt, and booby traps to entertain future excavation.

***

In Chicago, the Democratic National Convention opens today, to adopt a platform that will make peace with the South and stop the War. Their candidate will be General George B. McClellan, still in the army, until election day when he will resign his commission.

***

In Tennessee, south of Nashville, confederate courier Dewitt Jobe is captured, today, by 15 Federal soldiers who become irate when they discover that Jobe has eaten and swallowed the papers he was carrying. When he refuses to disclose the contents of the papers, or who dispatched them, his eyes are destroyed, and his tongue is cut out, he still refusing disclosure. They then tie his head to a horse's tail and stampede the horse, effectively hanging poor D. Jobe. When Jobe's cousin, Dewitt Smith, hears of the atrocities committed to his kin, he goes on a private war against the Federals and is able to kill as many as fifty, with a butcher knife.

**Dewitt Jobe**

## August 30, 1864

In Atlanta, Carrie Berry wants her life back to normal, as noted in her diary today: "Aug. 30. Tues. Miss Fannie Homes came around this morning to see about her school. I was so glad to see my old teacher once more. I hope she will commence her school. I am tired of staying at home."

South of Atlanta, after a day of railroad destruction on the West Point Rd., Union General Sherman has his armies in motion toward Jonesboro. General Howard is ordered to march toward Jonesboro, stopping four miles away at Renfroe Place, the intersection of Fairburn and Fayetteville Rds., but finding no water there, he is forced to move ahead to the Flint River, very near, indeed, to Jonesboro. General Thomas is moving his Army of the Cumberland corps to a point 3 miles north of Renfroe Place to wait for movement on Jonesboro in the morning. General Schofield follows Thomas and moves on to Morrow's Mill and entrenches, facing the Confederate forces, in order to protect the Federal left. The Federals will get a good night's rest, but some Confederates will get none. General Hood is placing all the force he can muster on the roads tonight to occupy Jonesboro in the morning, mainly Stephen Lee's Corps and Hardee's Corps, under the field direction of Pat Cleburne. Their orders are not to hold Jonesboro, but to attack the moving Yankees at first opportunity.

***

In Chicago, the Democratic National Convention establishes its platform, mostly the work of the Copperheads and peace democrats, very critical of the Lincoln government. The names placed today in nomination for Presidential candidate are Thomas H. Seymore, of Connecticut, and Maj. General George B. McClellan.

**George B. McClellan**

## August 31, 1864

In Atlanta, oblivious of the drama playing south of the City, 10-year-old Carrie Berry writes about her world in her diary: "Aug. 31. Wed. I have ben knitting all the morning and Zuie and I are going over to spend the night with Aunt Healy. I know we will enjoy ourselves."

In Atlanta, last night, Confederate General Hood met with Generals Hardee and S. D. Lee about 9 PM. His orders to them are to attack the Union Force under Oliver Howard, defeat him and drive him away from the railroad at Jonesboro. The combined Confederate force will be about 20,000 men with Lee's Corps and Hardee's Corps, under the field command of Pat Cleburne. Hardee will be in over-all command.

The Yankees are across the Flint River early in the morning but see activity in Jonesboro, so they prepare defenses and are reinforced to numbers that approximately equal the Rebel force coming at them, with Union General Thomas' army nearby if needed. It is almost noon by the time Cleburne can get all of his men into Jonesboro and several more hours until Lee's Corps arrive; all men in gray are exhausted from the march, but they form up for attack about 3 PM, in a line about a mile and half long. The attack is supposed to be en-echelon, but when Lee hears the sound of battle, he orders his men forward, leaving Cleburne's flank poorly protected.

It does not matter because the well-fortified entrenchments erupt a murderous fire on the Southern boys, and they have to fall back and start preparing to be attacked. The Yanks have cut the telegraph, so no communication is possible with Atlanta, but Hood sends a courier ordering Lee to bring his Corps back for the attack that Hood feels that he is about to befall there. Hardee will face tomorrow alone. He has lost 2,200 men today, only inflicting 172 on the men in blue.

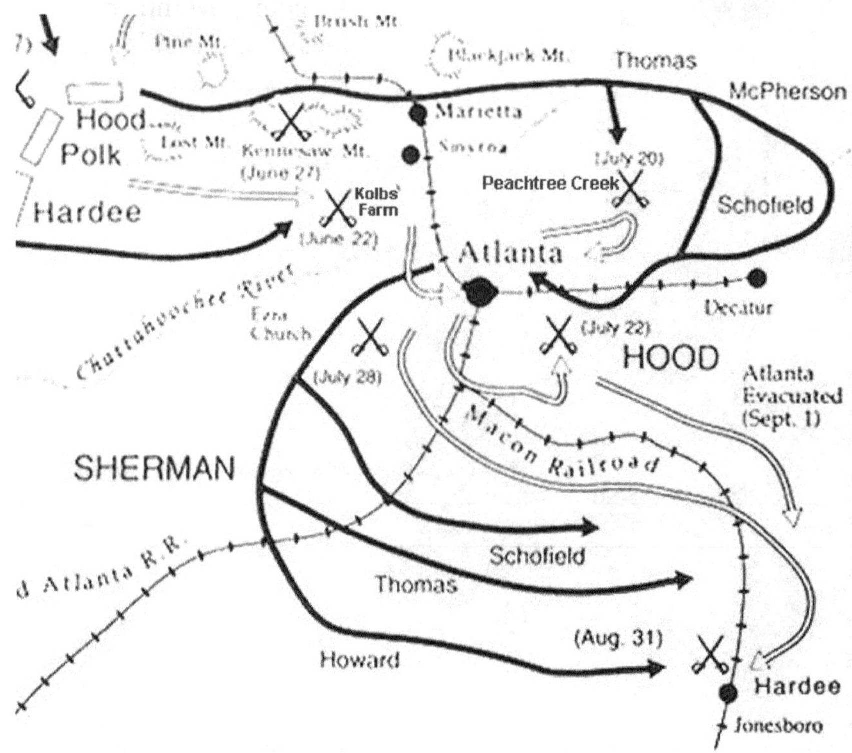

## September 1, 1864

In Atlanta, Georgia, 10-year-old Carrie Berry writes in her diary: "Sept. 1. Thurs. We did not get home untill twelve o'clock. We had a very pleasant time and every thing seemed quiet. Directly after dinner Cousin Emma came down and told us that Atlanta would be evacuated this evening and we might look for the federals in the morning. It was not long till the hole town found it out and such excitement there was. We have ben looking for them all the evening but they have not come yet. Mr. came in to tell us that dear Cousin Henry was wounded and he thought he would not get well. We are so sory to here it. We loved him so much. I finished my stockings to day."

In Jonesboro, GA, Confederate General Hardee, alone with one corps, defends very well against six Federal corps from, quickly developed but strong, defensive positions. He knows that General Hood is preparing to leave Atlanta, and he has been ordered to protect Macon and do whatever he can to keep Sherman's troops at Jonesboro so that Hood can pull out the McDonough Rd., the only avenue still open for major travel. In fighting this afternoon, the Federals are able to overrun a portion of Hardee's line, but others hold, with heavy casualties. There are so many Yankees that everyone knows that tomorrow they will be able to overwhelm the Rebs, but tonight Hood will be out of Atlanta, and Hardee will be able to withdraw his exhausted corps southward to Lovejoy's Station, then on to Macon.

As Hood is leaving the city, his men are destroying everything they cannot carry, that would be of use to the Federals. On the train tracks, just outside the City Graveyard (later Oakland), there is a supply train to be destroyed, consisting of 5 locomotives and 81 boxcars of supplies, including 28 boxcars of ammunition. The fiery destruction of the trains is a most spectacular event, with the sounds of the explosions reaching Sherman's ears all the way to Jonesboro.

**(aftermath of the ordinance train destruction (Note the boxcar wheels all rolled together and the adjacent ruins of the rolling mill)**

## September 2, 1864

In Atlanta, after a tumultuous night and bewildering day, 10-year-old Carrie Berry tells her diary about this day: "Sept. 2. Fri. We all woke up this morning without sleeping much last night. The Confederates had four engenes and a long train of box cars filled with amunition and set it on fire last night which caused a grate explosion which kept us all awake. It reminded us of the shells - of all the days of excitement we have had it to day. Every one has been trying to get all they could before the Federals come in the morning. They have ben running with saques of meal, salt and tobacco. They did act rediculous breaking open stores and robbing them. About twelve o'clock there were a few federals came in. They were all frightened. We were afraid they were going to treat us badly. It was not long till the Infantry came in. They were orderely and behaved very well. I think I shall like the Yankees very well." Bless your heart child, you have no idea.

This morning, in Atlanta, historian Wallace Putnam Reed, future Oakland resident, will tell the situation best: " *Then came the awful hours of waiting—waiting for the unknown! Delicate women, as well as stalwart men, looked after their weapons and put them in order. There was no thought of resisting insults and robbery, but some outrages they were resolved to defend themselves against to the death. Men with wives and daughters stayed at home, to be ready for any emergency. But the center of the town was filled with the riffraff, with stragglers and deserters, with negroes delirious over their strange sense of freedom, and with lean and haggard men and women of the lowest class, who were going through the stores, picking up such odds and ends as had been left behind by their owners. This was the state of affairs on the morning of the 2d of September, when Atlanta, worn out and shattered by the storm of war, lay panting between two flags, under the protection of neither, abandoned by one, and with no hope of mercy from the other."*

Mayor Calhoun with a small contingency of responsible citizens rides out the Marietta Rd and meets a reconnaissance patrol of Federal soldiers under Captain Scott who sends a message from the Mayor to Brig. General Ward, his commander: "S*ir: The fortune of war has placed Atlanta in your hands. As mayor of the city, I ask protection to non-combatants and private property."*

## September 3, 1864

In Atlanta, Ga where the rain is casting its gloom across a defeated City, Carrie Berry writes in her diary: "Sept. 3. Sat. 1864. The soldiers have ben coming in all day. I went up to Aunties this morning and she said that she had a yankee officer to spend the night with her. We have not seen much of them. Only two of them have ben here to beg some thing to eat. We have had a rainy day and we all feel gloomy."

South of Atlanta, near Jonesboro, telegraph service to Atlanta is restored and Union General Sherman is notified of the Confederate evacuation and his own army's occupation by courier from General Slocum. By telegram, he notifies all the army and declares the campaign finished and won. He states he will rest the soldiers for at least 30 days while planning for another, winter-time, campaign.

Confederate General Hood has reinforced Hardee's position just north of Lovejoy's Station with his remaining men, and the armies are stalemated there in strong defensive positions. If Sherman is going to further damage the Southern Army, he will have to do another, wide, flanking movement to require them to fall back southward where they still have supply lines.

***

**In the North there is jubilation in most parts, but Sherman's news is not good for the Democrats. A vast swing in the political mood will occur because of this Lincoln victory. In fact, today Lincoln calls for a National day of celebration on September 5 for the victories at Mobile Bay and Atlanta. It was just three days ago when this banner was the toast of Chicago at the Democratic National Convention.**

## September 4, 1864

It is Sunday in Atlanta, and Carrie Berry's diary has this to say about the day: "Sun. Sept 4. Another long and lonesome Sunday. How I wish we could have Church and Sunday School. We have ben looking at the soldiers all day. They have come in by the thousand. They were playing bands and they seemed to be rejoiced. It has not seemed like Sunday."

Carrie thinks there are a lot of Federal soldiers in Atlanta now, just she waits a few days. General Sherman orders today that General Thomas' Army of the Cumberland will move from Lovejoy's Station to occupy Atlanta. The Army of the Tennessee under General Howard will occupy East Point, and Schofield's Army of the Ohio will protect the left flank from Decatur. The cavalry will occupy Sandtown, Roswell, and other points on the flanks. Both armies rest today, still facing each other at Lovejoy's.

***

In Greenville, Tennessee, things have not been going well for John Hunt Morgan lately. After his escape from Federal prison in Ohio, he has raised another command, on his own, from, largely, deserters and other misfits of the Army of Tennessee. In his last raiding venture into Kentucky, because of the pillaging of his men, he no longer holds the sympathies of the community. The recent antics of his command include two bank robberies and multiple attacks on private citizens' property. This morning he has been betrayed by the hostess of the mansion where he has been planning his next raid into eastern Tennessee. He is still sleeping when the property is surrounded by Federal soldiers who know he is there and have come to kill him. He makes it out of the house, but cannot escape, shot before he can surrender.

**Morgan is still regarded a National hero by the Confederacy and is mourned as such. In 1911, the United Daughters of the Confederacy, with the State of Kentucky will erect this statue to him in Lexington.**

## September 5, 1864

In Atlanta, GA, Carrie Berry writes in her diary: "Mon. Sept. 5. I helped Papa tick a matress and it blistered my hands but it was for my bed and I think I shall sleep so nice that it will pay me. We have seen nothing to day."

Near Stephenson's Depot, north of Winchester, VA, portions of the Confederate and Union forces skirmish, probing each other's strength in different places. Confederate General Early is reluctant to attack the main Union force because he has only 20,000 men to fight 40,000 Yankees. Union General Sheridan is reluctant to attack the main Confederate force because he only has 40,000 men to fight 20,000 Rebels.

***

In Massachusetts, the Society of Jesus has founded Boston College, and it opens its doors on this day, with 3 teachers and 22 students.

***

In Atlanta, GA, today, acting on orders from General Sherman (Still at Lovejoy), the Union Provost Guard orders all families of Confederate soldiers to prepare to leave the city. Sherman has already told General Slocum, in temporary command of Atlanta, to "advise people to quit now. There can be no trade or commerce until the war is over."

The map below shows the final positions of the Federal Army and Confederate Army, facing each other in strong defensive positions just north of Lovejoy's Station. The confederate line runs straight across the future intersection of Hwy 41 (Tara Blvd) and the McDonough Rd.

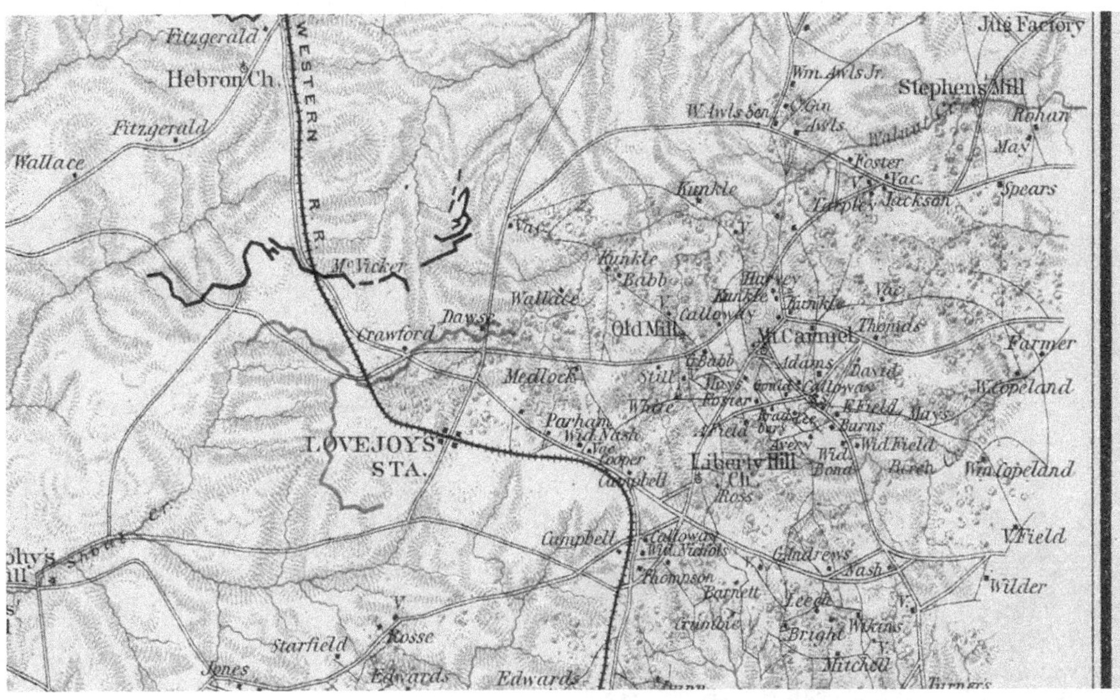

## September 6, 1864

In Atlanta, Carrie Berry has this to say in her diary: "Tues. Sept. 6. This has been a dark gloomy day and we feel gloomy too. I have ben wanting to see Grandma all day. I commenced knitting me a pair of gloves, but I don't know when I will get them done."

South of the city of Atlanta, just north of Lovejoy's Station, the Southerners view a dawn without Yankee gun-barrels looking at them. Sherman's armies have pulled out, retreating back and into, the limits of Atlanta, East Point, and Decatur. Sherman has wired Grant that he will take a couple of days to move back, having his army graze the corn crops and gardens of the locals as he moves, probably arriving in Atlanta tomorrow.

***

In Maryland, the state adopts its new constitution, outlawing slavery. Remember, the Emancipation Proclamation did not apply to Maryland, a slave state, because it was not "in rebellion" at the time of issuance.

***

Mostly, the major battle fronts of the War are quiet today, but a new bombardment of Fort Sumter and Charleston begins, lasting nine days.

Confederate Lt. General Richard Taylor is promoted today to command of the Confederate Department of Alabama, Mississippi, and East Louisiana. He is the brother-in-law of Jefferson Davis, the son of President Zachary Taylor, and very nearly the finest General in the Southern Armies. He learned much under Stonewall Jackson, where he was Jackson's "go to" guy, and the work he did with a small force against Union General Banks in the Red River Campaign was brilliant, all this while suffering terribly with crippling arthritis.

**Confederate Lt. General, Richard Taylor**

## September 7, 1864

In Atlanta, Carrie Berry writes in her diary: "Wed. Sept. 7. The times get a little worse every day. Mary went of this evening and I don't expect that she will come back any more but we can do very well without her. I will have to go to work to help Mama."

In Atlanta, without fanfare, Union General Sherman comes into town and takes his quarters in the headquarters set up in the John Neal (one day resident of Historic Oakland Cemetery) home at 68 Mitchell St, across from City Hall (City Hall will later be torn down and the Georgia State Capitol building constructed on its site). Without wasting any time, he composes a letter and sends it to General Hood proposing a two-day truce to remove all citizens from Atlanta. *"I have deemed it to the interest of the United States that the citizens now residing in Atlanta should remove, those who prefer it to go south and the rest north."* Sherman states that he will provide transportation to destination to all who want to go north, and he will provide transportation to all who want to go south to Rough and Ready Station, where they are to be met with cooperating Confederate transportation to distribute them in the South. This will be a blow to hundreds of people who have no place to go, maybe Sherman can be persuaded to change his mind

**The Neal Home, providing Sherman his headquarters building, is never to be occupied as a home again. It will be a girl's school among other things, including the home of Oglethorpe College for a while. In the late 1920"s it will be torn down and Atlanta City Hall will be constructed on the site.**

## September 8, 1864

In Atlanta, 10-year-old Carrie Berry reports to herself in her diary: "Thurs. Sept. 8. We all went to wirk in glad spirits this morning. Me and Tilo went to ironing. Mama was buisy regulating things when Papa came and told us that Gen. Sherman had ordered us to move. It broke all into our rangements."

This morning in Atlanta, Mayor Calhoun issues this to the population: "*Major-General Sherman instructs me to say to you that you must all leave Atlanta; that as many of you as want to go North can do so, and that as many as want to go South can do so, and that all can take with them their movable property, servants included, if they want to go, but that no force is to be used. He will furnish transportation for persons and property as far as Rough and Ready, from whence it is expected General Hood will assist in carrying it on. Like transportation will be furnished for people and property going North, and it is required that all* contemplated by this notice will be *carried into execution as soon as possible.*"

Carrie Berry and her family ultimately will not have to go. Through the influence of family and business relations from the north, local unionists, he will find employment that will allow the family to stay, one of about fifty families that do. I had originally said I would include Carrie's diary in my posts through August, but from feedback I am getting, I am leaning toward going with the remaining posts that are available to me, through January 5, 1865. I believe that is when she will stop her writing. This is the only picture I have of her so here it is again.

**Carrie Berry**

## September 9, 1864

In Atlanta, a despondent Carrie Berry laments over the news of the townspeople's' imminent removal: "Fri. Sept. 9. We all comenced this morning to prepare for moving. We don't know how long we will get to stay here. We are all in so much trouble."

***

In the Confederate trenches of Petersburg, Virginia, there is great cheering and celebration over the news that General Hood has retaken the City of Atlanta. What a letdown prevails when the news is deemed to be false...oh well, it was fun for a few minutes.

In Atlanta, word reaches the population of the death of John Hunt Morgan last week near Greenville, Tennessee. You will recall the large reception given to General Morgan in the Trout House last February when he visited the City for a few days. Another much-loved Southern hero is gone away.

Confederate General Hood responds to the letter from General Sherman asking for his cooperation in removal of the Citizenry:...."*GENERAL: Your letter of yesterday's date, borne by James M. Ball and James R. Crew, citizens of Atlanta, is received. You say therein, "I deem it to be to the interest of the United States that the citizens now residing in Atlanta should remove," etc. I do not consider that I have any alternative in this matter. I therefore accept your proposition to declare a truce of two days, or such time as may be necessary to accomplish the purpose mentioned, and shall render all assistance in my power to expedite the transportation of citizens in this direction. I suggest that a staff officer be appointed by you to superintend the removal from the city to Rough and Ready, while I appoint a like officer to control their removal farther south; that a guard of one hundred men be sent by either party as you propose, to maintain order at that place, and that the removal begin on Monday next. And now, sir, permit me to say that the unprecedented measure you propose transcends, in studied and ingenious cruelty, all acts ever before brought to my attention in the dark history of war....In the name of God and humanity, I protest, believing that you will find that you are expelling from their homes and firesides the wives and children of a brave people."*

**Confederate General Hood**

## September 10, 1864

In Atlanta, Carrie Berry tells in her diary today: "Sat. Sept. 10. Every one I see seems sad. The citizens all think that it is the most cruel thing to drive us from our home but I think it would be so funny to move. Mama seems so troubled and she can't do any thing. Papa says he don't know where on earth to go."

Confederate lines near Lovejoy, GA, Reb Cavalry General Wheeler returns today, on his 28th birthday, from the raid on Sherman's supply lines, minus 1,000 of the 2,000 men he left with last month. Wheeler is the only Confederate General that will also serve as United States General after this war is over (In the Spanish American War).

In the Neal house on Mitchell Street in Atlanta, General Sherman pens his response to the scolding from Reb General Hood of yesterday: "*GENERAL: I have the honor to acknowledge the receipt of your letter of this date, at the hands of Messrs. Ball and Crew, consenting to the arrangements I had proposed to facilitate the removal south of the people of Atlanta, who prefer to go in that direction. I enclose you a copy of my orders, which will, I am satisfied, accomplish my purpose perfectly....You style the measures proposed "unprecedented," and appeal to the dark history of war for a parallel, as an act of "studied and ingenious cruelty." It is not unprecedented; for General Johnston himself very wisely and properly removed the families all the way from Dalton down, and I see no reason why Atlanta should be excepted. Nor is it necessary to appeal to the dark history of war, when recent and modern examples are so handy. You yourself burned dwelling-houses along your parapet, and I have seen to-day fifty houses that you have rendered uninhabitable because they stood in the way of your forts and men. You defended Atlanta on a line so close to town that every cannon-shot and many musket-shots from our line of investment, that overshot their mark, went into the habitations of women and children. General Hardee did the same at Jonesboro, and General Johnston did the same, last summer, at Jackson, Mississippi...In the name of common-sense, I ask you not to appeal to a just God in such a sacrilegious manner. You who, in the midst of peace and prosperity, have plunged a nation into war–dark and cruel war–who dared and badgered us to battle, insulted our flag, seized our arsenals and forts that were left in the honorable custody of peaceful ordnance-sergeants, seized and made "prisoners of war" the very garrisons sent to protect your people against negroes and Indians...Talk thus to the marines, but not to me, who have seen these things, and who will this day make as much sacrifice for the peace and honor of the South as the best-born Southerner among you! If we must be enemies, let us be men, and fight it out as we propose to do, and not deal in arch hypocritical appeals to God and humanity. God will judge us in due time, and he will pronounce whether it be more humane to fight with a town full of women and the families of a brave people at our back or to remove them in time to places of safety among their own friends and people.*"

**Union General William T. Sherman**

## September 11, 1864

In Atlanta, 10-year-old Carrie Berry writes in her diary: "Sun. Sept. 11. We all have been trying to rest to day and feel contented. Mama went over to see Aunt Healy this evening and she felt as sad as we."

***

In the Shenandoah Valley of Virginia, parity of strength between the warring parties is threatened. Confederate General Robert E Lee desperately needs Longstreet's Corps, now temporarily under the command of R.H. Anderson and serving under Early. It is unlikely that Early can do well without those men.

In Atlanta, Mayor Calhoun and two City Councilmen render a written appeal to General Sherman about the civilian evacuation: *"We, the undersigned, mayor and two of the council for the city of Atlanta, for the time being the only legal organ of the people of the said city to express their wants and wishes, ask leave most earnestly, but respectfully, to petition you to reconsider the order requiring them to leave Atlanta. At first view it struck us that the measure would involve extraordinary hardship and loss, but since we have seen the practical execution of it so far as it has progressed, and the individual condition of the people, and heard their statements as to the inconveniences, loss, and suffering attending it, we are satisfied that the amount of it will involve in the aggregate consequences appalling and heart-rending. Many poor women are in advanced state of pregnancy; others now having young children, and whose husbands, for the greater part, are either in the army, prisoners, or dead. Some say, "I have such an one sick at my house; who will wait on them when I am gone?" Others say, "what are we to do? We have no house to go to, and no means to buy, build, or rent any; no parents, relatives, or friends to go to.... and that on more reflection you, we hope, would not make this people an exception to all mankind, for we know of no such instance ever having occurred; surely none such in the United States..... In conclusion, we most earnestly and solemnly petition you to reconsider this order, or modify it, and suffer this unfortunate people to remain at home and enjoy what little means they have. Respectfully submitted. JAMES M. CALHOUN, Mayor."*

**James M. Calhoun, Mayor of Atlanta**

## September 12, 1864

In Atlanta, Carrie Berry writes in her diary: "Mon. Sept. 12. We commenced packing up to move. We did not do much. Papa herd up town there was a chance for us to stay if he could get into business." (Her father is a building contractor, and evidently is trying for some sort of government contract).

In Atlanta, the first of the railroad cars loaded with household goods leaves today for Rough and Ready to be moved on further south by the Confederates....General Sherman, in a rambling oration, tries to make his case to God that he should go to Heaven and stay clear of hell, in spite of the things he has done. His soap box is the response letter to Mayor Calhoun and two City Councilmen.

"Gentlemen:

*I have your letter of the 11th, in the nature of a petition to revoke my orders removing all the inhabitants from Atlanta. I have read it carefully, and give full credit to your statements of the distress that will be occasioned, and yet shall not revoke my orders, because they were not designed to meet the humanities of the case, but to prepare for the future struggles in which millions of good people outside of Atlanta have a deep interest. .... You cannot qualify war in harsher terms than I will. War is cruelty, and you cannot refine it; and those who brought war into our country deserve all the curses and maledictions a people can pour out. I know I had no hand in making this war, and I know I will make more sacrifices today than any of you to secure peace. But you cannot have peace and a division of our country. If the United States submits to a division now, it will not stop, but will go on until we reap the fate of Mexico, which is eternal war. .... You might as well appeal against the thunder-storm as against these terrible hardships of war. They are inevitable, and the only way the people of Atlanta can hope once more to live in peace and quiet at home, is to stop the war, which can only be done by admitting that it began in error and is perpetuated in pride. ....We don't want your negroes, or your horses, or your houses, or your lands, or any thing you have, but we do want and will have a just obedience to the laws of the United States. That we will have, and, if it involves the destruction of your improvements, we cannot help it."*

**Union General William T. Sherman**

## September 13, 1864

In Atlanta, a jubilant Carrie Berry writes to herself in her diary: Tues. Sept. 13. Papa got into business to day and the rest of us went to wirk in good earnest thinking that we will get to stay. I hope that we will get to stay. Mama dislikes to move so much."

In the Shenandoah Valley of Virginia, skirmish fighting is heating up as the opposing armies feel each other for strength in position, with action at Bunker Hill, near Berryville, and Opequion Creek.....In Atlanta, General Hood's response to Sherman's chastisement was written over several days, finished yesterday, and delivered this morning:

> "You order into exile the whole population of a city, drive men, women, and children from their homes at the point of the bayonet, under the plea that it is to the interest of your Government, and on the claim that it is an act of "kindness to these families of Atlanta.".... And because I characterized what you call a kindness as being real cruelty you presume to sit in judgment between me and my God and you decide that my earnest prayer to the Almighty Father to save our women and children from what you call kindness is a "sacrilegious, hypocritical appeal." You came into our country with your army avowedly for the purpose of subjugating free white men, women, and children, and not only intend to rule over them, but you make negroes your allies and desire to place over us an inferior race, which we have raised from barbarism to its present position, which is the highest ever attained by that race in any country in all time... . I feel no other emotion than pain in reading that portion of your letter which attempts to justify your shelling Atlanta without notice under pretense that I defended Atlanta upon a line so close to town that every cannon shot, and many musket balls from your line of investment, that over-shot their mark went into the habitations of women and children. I made no complaint of your firing into Atlanta in any way you thought proper. I make none now, but there are a hundred thousand witnesses that you fired into the habitations of women and children for weeks, firing far above and miles beyond my line of defense. I have too good an opinion, founded both upon observation and experience, of the skill of your artillerists to credit the insinuation that they for several weeks unintentionally fired too high for my modest field-works, and slaughtered women and children by accident and want of skill..... You say, "let us fight it out like men." To this my reply is, for myself, and, I believe, for all the true men, aye, and women and children, in my country, we will fight you to the death. Better die a thousand deaths than submit to live under you or your Government and your negro allies....."

*General John B. Hood*

## September 14, 1864

In Atlanta, here is what 10-year-old Carrie Berry thinks of this day, from her diary: "Wed. Sept. 14. I helpt to wash till dinner time and then I got dinner by myself. It made me very warm and tired but I supose I will have to learn to wirk. I have ben resting all the evening and I think I will sleep right sound to night if the musquitoes dont bite me too much."

In the Shenandoah Valley, Confederate General R. H. Anderson's Corps (Longstreet's Corps) leaves General Early's command, ordered back to the lines of Petersburg by General Lee. This reduces Early's force to about 14, 000 men, much less than Opposing Union General Phil Sheridan's 35,000+

In Atlanta, Union General Sherman is composing an epic to counter the latest scolding by Reb. General Hood, and Atlanta citizens continue to be moved out of the city by wagon and train.

***

50 years ago, today: Lawyer and part-time poet, Francis Scott Key is on a British ship in the Patapsco River, just outside of, but within sight of, Fort McHenry, Baltimore Maryland. He is on the ship to secure the release of his dear friend, Dr. Beanes, who was falsely charged with causing the capture of British officers. The British have agreed to release the doctor, but nobody can leave the ship because the fleet is attacking Baltimore and Fort McHenry. All night long Key has watched the spectacular bombardment of the fort and can see the American flag, tattered and torn, still flying above the fort. As the dawn occurs, the Americans run down the small "storm flag" and raise a larger American flag that inspires Key to write his famous poem, that will be set to music, composed by John Stafford Smith, and on March 3, 1931 will become the Official National Anthem of the United States, having already served that purpose at events for years. It will then be known as "The Star-Spangled Banner".

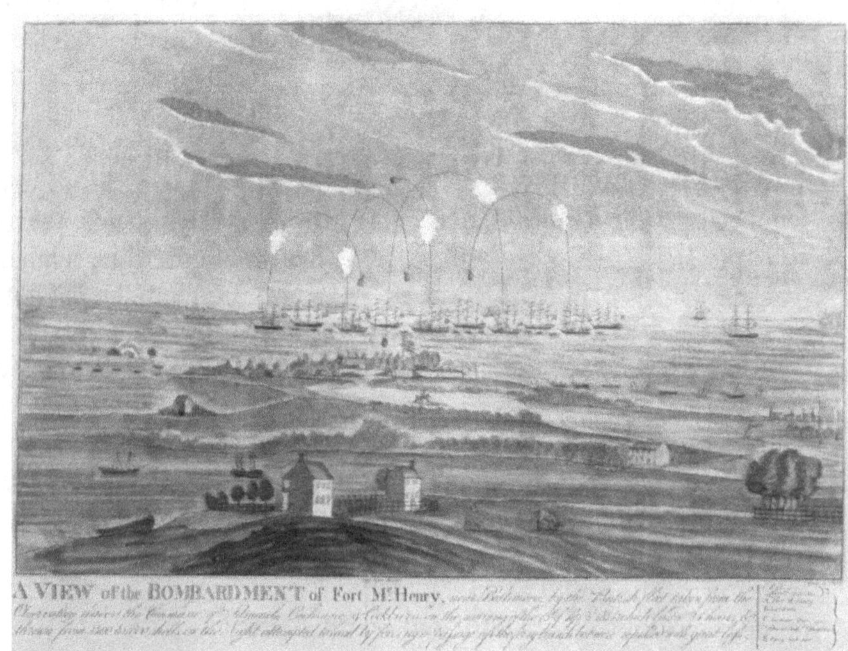


**Bombardment of Fort McHenry September 13 and 14, 1814**

## September 15, 1864

From Carrie Berry's diary: "Thurs. Sept 15. We had a general cleaning up this morning. Everything seems so clean and I hope that it would stay so."

From Atlanta, Union General Sherman reports to General Halleck in Washington that he has learned that Georgia Governor, Brown, has disbanded the State Militia so that the members can go home and gather the corn and sorghum crops. He also informs Halleck that he will participate with Confederate General Hood in the exchange of 2,000 prisoners with each side delivering the last 2,000 men captured. Also, Sherman delivers the last letter in the debate with Hood and finishes the correspondence by stating that his is the final word, and he will not play anymore.

HDQRS. MILITARY DIVISION OF THE MISSISSIPPI, In the Field, Atlanta, Ga., September 14, 1864

"General J. B. HOOD, C. S. Army, Commanding Army of Tennessee:
Yours of September 12 is received and has been carefully perused. I agree with you that this discussion by two soldiers is out of place and profitless, but you must admit that you began the controversy by characterizing an official act of mine in unfair and improper terms.

I reiterate my former answer, and to the only new matter contained in your rejoinder I add, we have no "negro allies" in this army; not a single negro soldier left Chattanooga with this army or is with it now. There are a few guarding Chattanooga, which General Steedman sent to drive Wheeler out of Dalton.

I was not bound by the laws of war to give notice of the shelling of Atlanta, a "fortified town" with magazines, arsenals, foundries, and public stores. You were bound to take notice. See the books. This is the conclusion of our correspondence, which I did not begin, and terminate with satisfaction.

I am, with respect, your obedient servant,
W. T. SHERMAN, Major-General, Commanding"

## September 16, 1864

In Atlanta, GA, with her diary, Carrie Berry reports to herself: " Fri. Sept. 16. I ironed till dinner and got through and I had a hollowday the rest of the evening. We have had a nice time playing and I think I will sleep sound to night."

At Fort Barrancas near Pensacola, Union Brig. General Alexander Asboth has received intelligence that the Confederates are fortifying the city of Marianna, the largest community in Northwest Florida. He also has reason to believe that 300 Union prisoners are being held there. He makes the decision today to cross Pensacola Bay and lead a raid on Marianna, so we will follow him and observe his success. Or lack of it.

***

From the Confederate defenses outside Richmond and Petersburg, Virginia, General Lee is watching his men hunger because of his dwindling supply sources. His problem will be increased when General Anderson returns his corps to the lines and all have to be fed. Confederate General Wade Hampton left the lines the day before yesterday chasing intelligence that a large number of cattle are being held on Edmund Ruffin's Federally-occupied plantation on Coggan's Point, near Harrison's Landing. This morning, with 3,000 Rebel soldiers, Hampton overwhelms the small defensive force guarding the cattle and captures 2, 468 head of walking beefsteak. Now he has to fight his way back to his lines while conducting a cattle drive....

**The Great Beefsteak Raid by Wade Hampton**

THE GREAT CATTLE RAID AT HARRISON'S LANDING,

## September 17, 1864

In Atlanta, GA, 10-year-old Carrie Berry writes in her diary: "Sat. Sept. 17. Mama went up to Aunties this morning and I had to keep house for her. I hemmed Sisters dress this evening."

In Atlanta, one of the many letters Union General Sherman writes today is addressed to President Lincoln, and in the letter, he tells Lincoln that A Mr. Wright, former member of Congress, from Rome, Ga., and a Mr. King, of Marietta, are now going between Governor Brown and himself, discussing making a separate deal from the Confederate Government. He says, "*Georgia can now save herself from the devastation of war preparing for her only by withdrawing her quota out of the Confederate army and aiding me to repel Hood from the borders of the State. In which event, instead of desolating the land as we progress, I will keep our men to the high roads and commons and pay for the corn and meat we need and take*".

***

In Charleston West Virginia, Union Generals Grant and Sheridan conclude their planning about defeating Confederate General Early in the Shenandoah Valley. Sending Anderson's Corps back to Petersburg has left Early with about 12,000 men. Sheridan has been reinforced up to about 40,000 and is feeling confident that he can whip Early now. Grant approves all the plans that Sheridan has laid out for him, to move against Early's supply lines south of Winchester.

After traveling and fighting all day and all night, Confederate Cavalry General Wade Hampton returns to Confederate lines near Richmond with all of his men, except 61. He also has over 2,400 head of cattle and over 300 Federal prisoners. There will be steak on every plate tonight and many nights into the future. The problem is that there is no cattle feed for the animals, and they will all have to be slaughtered soon. There is little resource for preserving meat, so starvation will return in a couple of weeks, but right now....boy o' boy!!

## September 18, 1864

In Atlanta, Georgia, on a gloomy Sunday, Carrie Berry writes: "Sun. Sept 18. This has ben a dark rainy day. We had stewed chickens for dinner."

Outside Atlanta, the parade of trains and wagons to Rough and Ready and toward Chattanooga continues as families leave their homes for adventures unknown to them at present. There are three more days remaining in the eviction truce and many families remaining in Atlanta, although the exit has been steady and continuous.

General Hood's Army of Tennessee, begins to move from its fortified position at Lovejoy, GA, toward the West Point Railroad, and on to Palmetto, where he intends to locate headquarters and can be supplied

***

In the Shenandoah Valley, Confederate General Early moves a division of his force under John B Gordon from Bunker Hill to Martinsburg where they encounter heavy Union presence under Cavalry General Averell. After driving the cavalry away, Gordon retraces his march back to the previous fortification where he is soon joined by Generals Rodes and Breckinridge. Ramseur's division is about a mile west of Winchester and closest to the enemy in force. There will be heavy fighting here tomorrow, and General Rodes will be killed. I will use a map tomorrow and wanted to get his picture before you.

**Confederate Major General Robert Rodes**

## September 19, 1864

In Atlanta, Carrie Berry writes in her diary: "Mon. Sept. 19. I went over to Aunt Healy this morning. She is packing up to move and I feel sorry that she is going away. We will miss her so much."

In Northeastern Indian Territory, Confederate Generals Stand Waite and Richard Gano combine forces to capture a large Federal wagon train, 202 wagons, enough to sustain them in the war for a while longer

In the Shenandoah Valley, Confederate General Early had split his 12,000 men between Winchester, VA, and Martinsburg, WV. When Union General Sheridan learned of the positions, he sent his entire force of 40,000 toward Winchester along the Berryville Pike. Learning of this movement, General Early orders all his forces to unite at Winchester, and they arrive about ten o'clock to support General Ramseur who has been engaged with lead elements of Sheridan since dawn. With hard fighting, the Confederates are able to defeat the forces brought to bear, but the Federals keep on, keeping on, arriving on the field, giving the impression of surrounding the Rebels, sending them into a panicked withdrawal, quickly becoming a rout. The withdrawing Confederates are pushed back to some old field fortifications near Winchester, on the opposite side, where they are able to stop the advance of the bluecoats. The result is a Union victory, with heavy losses on both sides. The Yankees lose 5,020 casualties, and the South loses 3,610 casualties, about one-fourth of their total force in the Valley. The North loses General David Russell, killed and three generals wounded. The Confederates lose General Rodes killed, and three Generals wounded. The South also loses Colonel George S. Patton, killed, whose grandson, Lt General George S Patton, will lead my father, and many other Americans, in battle eighty years from now in World War II.

**Reb Col. George S. Patton**

**Lt. General George S. Patton**

## September 20, 1864

In Atlanta, GA, Carrie Berry writes in her diary, "Tues. Sept. 20. It has ben raining nearly all day. I went up to Aunties this evening to see Willie. He is mighty cute and took three or four steps while I was there. Cousin Emma is packing up to leave."

In the Shenandoah Valley, Union General Sheridan's army is following closely on the heels of retreating Rebels under Jubal Early, with skirmishing occurring at Middletown, Strasburg, and Cedarville. By nightfall, the Yanks are fortifying themselves on high ground north of Strasburg, the Rebs, moving into strong positions on Fisher's Hill, just south of Strasburg. Caught as he was, with his forces spread all over the place, and an army three time his size attacking him in the open, the fact that Early is even able to field a force today speaks volumes about the poor generalship of Sheridan. Even Early, although he was able to survive the battle and keep a substantial force, showed poor judgment in spreading his generals so far apart with poor roads to connect them, in the shadow of the massive Federal presence. He will have a hard time defending this wonderful position because he does not have enough men to properly fortress the terrain. He needs Anderson's corps back, and he needs the men he wasted away yesterday back in position.

***

In Georgia, Federal Major General Sherman's supply lines are suffering from skirmishes with Rebel cavalry near Cartersville. Also, Major General Nathan Bedford Forrest has organized a raiding force of about 4,500 men and is moving from northern Alabama into Tennessee for supply disruption.

***

Confederate President Jefferson Davis leaves Richmond today, heading for Georgia to see for himself the condition of his army there, and what can be done to make it productive toward the Confederate cause.

**Confederate President Jefferson Davis**

## September 21, 1864

In Atlanta, 10-year-old Carrie Berry writes to herself in her diary, "Wed. Sept. 21. It is still raining. I have ben making Mama an apron. We are feeling so sad. We have received a letter from Aunt Maggie Shaw that dear Cousin Maggie was dead. She died the 8th of the month. I am so sorry. I loved her so much."

***

In the Neal home in Atlanta, General Sherman writes the following to Secretary of War, E.M. Stanton in Washington: "*In my dispatch today I reported that Hood was falling back. Reports just in seem indicate he has shifted from the Macon road at Lovejoy's over to the WEST Point road about Palmetto Station, where his men are intrenching. I will watch him, as I do not see what he designs by this movement.*"

***

In Virginia, Reb General Early has to make changes in his army. Major General Breckinridge has been called to the lines around Petersburg, leaving his command without a leader. Major General John B. Gordon is promoted to corps commander to take Breckinridge's place. He will also command his own division within his corps until next month when General Clement A. Evans will take command of that division upon returning from wound recovery

The Union Generals are in heavy discussion most of the afternoon about how best to attack Early on Fisher's Hill. General Wright is insisting that his corps should attack the right flank, and General Crook is insisting that any movement on the right would be seen by Confederate lookouts, but that an attack from the left could be hidden and implemented with success. Finally, Sheridan is convinced by arguments from future President General Rutherford B Hayes, and shortly after dark, Crook starts his silent, roundabout, trek to get into position for early tomorrow morning.

**Confederate Major General John B. Gordon (Future Oakland Cemetery Resident, note the heavy scar on his leftside face from the fifth bullet wound received on the Bloody Lane at Antietham Creek)**

## September 22, 1864

In Atlanta, little Carrie Berry writes in her diary today, "Thurs. Sept. 22. Mama and Buddy and I went over to see Aunt Healy for the last time. We felt so sorry to see her feel so grieved too. As we were coming home we were caught in the hardest rain and we got soaking wet and we fear that it will make us every one sick."

***

In the Shenandoah Valley, Union General Crook of Sheridan's army (30,000) has been stealthily moving his division away from and around the entrenched Confederate forces (9,000) on Fisher's Hill all night and most of the day, as the remainder of the Union army waits for attack. About four o'clock the hordes in blue pour onto the left of the Confederate line and behind it. The overwhelming numbers cause panic in the lightly defended ranks, and retreat becomes the order of the day. When the action begins the entire force of Federals in front attacks straight onto the hill, but the Rebels are quick-timing out of the area, losing about 1,300 men in the process (1,000 captured), and the Federals suffer about 500, total on the day. The battle plan is brilliantly conceived and masterfully executed, effectively utilizing the numerical superiority, and Sheridan is given, and accepts, all credit for it, excluding any praise for Crook. After the battle Union General Rutherford B Hayes, future President of the United States writes this, " *At Fisher's Hill the turning of the Rebel left was planned and executed by General Crook against the opinions of other generals....General Sheridan is a whole-souled brave man and believes in Crook, his old class and roommate at West Point. Intellectually he is not General Crook's equal, so that, as I said, General Crook is the brains of this army."*

**Union Major General George R. Crook (In 1877 Crazy Horse will surrender to him, as Geronimo will do the same in 1882)**

## September 23, 1864

In Atlanta, on a dismal day, Carrie Berry writes, "Fri. Sept. 23. Mama got up this morning and went to washing in the rain and we could not get them out. It was so cloudy she would not let me help her. My throat was so sore that I could not help her."

***

In the Shenandoah Valley, Confederate General Early moves his damaged army back through New Market, with his cavalry fighting at Front Royal, Woodstock and at Mount Jackson.

***

In Macon, Georgia, Confederate President Jefferson Davis, speaking to the citizens, is shouted down by wounded Confederates, chanting, "*Give us back old Joe!*". Davis replies, with defiance, that removing Johnston was the thing to do, and he urges all who have left the fighting forces unwounded should return, even half of them would return the army to winning strength. He also says, " *Sherman cannot keep up his long line of communication, and retreat sooner or later, he must. And when that day comes, the fate that befel the army of the French Empire and its retreat from Moscow will be reacted. Our cavalry and our people will harass and destroy his army as did the Cossacks that of Napoleon, and the Yankee General, like him will escape with only a body guard*".

***

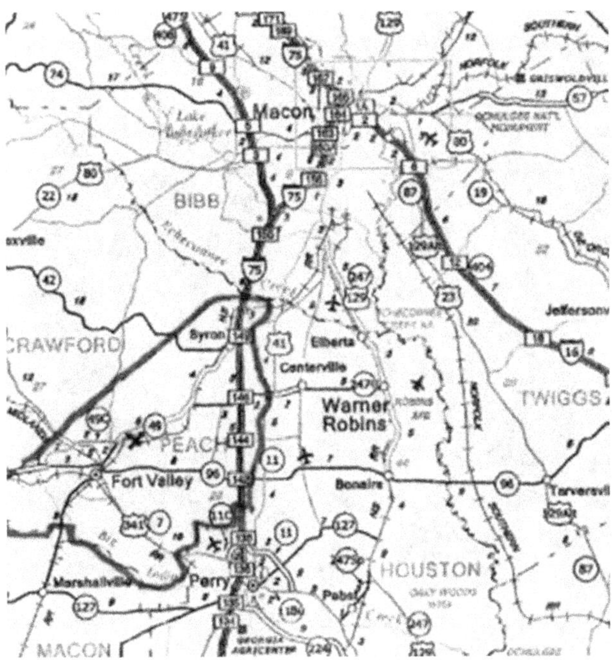


In northern Alabama, at Athens, General Forrest has the fortified town surrounded and has demanded surrender. The town is protected with about 450 Negro infantry and some white cavalry, heavily armed with repeating rifles and heavily fortified.

***

Near Fort Valley, Georgia, a northbound train has derailed, and the crash is quite deadly. Twenty Confederate soldiers, new recruits, heading to find Hood's Army, are killed and 37 others, military and civilian, are injured.

**Map from the "Macon Telegraph" (Crash location is yellow-shaded "X")**

## September 24, 1864

In much nicer weather in Atlanta, Carrie Berry writes, "Sat. Sept 24. This has ben a bright day and we all have ben ironing and cleaning up. We have had so much rain that a sun shiny day seems quite pleasant."

Also from Atlanta, General Sherman orders Army Commander Howard to order General Corse to take his division to Rome to help protect his flank from any mischief that the Rebels under Hood might have in mind: "*You may order General Corse to proceed to Rome by cars, and then unite his DIVISION to act against any force that my attempt to threaten Bridgeport from the direction of Gadsden. Let them march up to-morrow and take cars in the evening. The whole DIVISION will rejoin us before we take the field.*"

***

At Athens Alabama, the fortified city surrenders this afternoon after a show of overwhelming force is displayed by Reb General Forrest, surrounding the small Union (mostly black) garrison. A small reinforcement contingency is also captured just before it reaches the city. Sherman receives news of these events late this afternoon just before he attends a production by the Brass Band of the 33rd Massachusetts Volunteers at the Athenaeum, the theater on Decatur Street in Atlanta, built by future Oakland resident James Williams and will be demolished by Sherman on November 15.

***

The South has a new newspaper today. The "Marietta Times" begins its long career with its first publication as a weekly periodical.

In Florida, Union General Alexander Asboth, with his 700 soldiers, en route to Marianna to free Union prisoners, is camped today at Ponce De Leon Springs where he will suffer his first man killed on this expedition. It is an accidental gunshot wound that does the poor man in.

**Ponce De Leon Springs**

## September 25, 1864

In Atlanta, a quiet Sunday passes, according to Carrie Berry's diary, "*Sun. Sept. 25. Another long and lonely Sunday with out Church. So cloudy we all lay about and read until we are all tired.*"

In nearby Palmetto, GA, the President of the Confederate States, Jefferson Davis, is visiting the troops and meeting with his generals. He is here because General Hood wants him to remove General Hardee from his command. Hardee is whom Hood blames for his recent failures. Also, General Hardee wants to be removed as far as he can get from Hood's command; he does not like serving under, what he considers to be, a fool

***

In the Shenandoah Valley, Union General Sheridan's huge army is moving slowly toward Staunton and Waynesboro, Virginia, destroying railroads, looting, and burning farms as they move. The small force of Reb General Early's has no hope of preventing the complete destruction of the Valley.

***

In Florida, Union General Asboth and his 700 soldiers awaken to a continuous rain for the tenth straight day in the town of Cerrogordo on the Choctawhatchee River. They will spend an exhausting day moving their army and wagons across the wide expanse of water with a small ferry. What a great place for the Confederates to attack them, but it will not happen.

***

In Henry County Georgia, on the McDonough (later Kellytown) Road, Fulton County's first doctor (since 1829), William Gilbert is refugeeing with his family, but feeling miserable. They have been evicted from Atlanta, like almost everybody else, and are heading for McDonough. Dr. Gilbert tells the family to move on, that he will rest for a bit, then join them when he feels better, but he never shows up. When he is searched for, he is found dead, lying on the side of the road with his head on his saddlebag and his horse standing by his side. The Chafin family, nearby residents, help to bury him in their family graveyard where he will remain for at least 150 years.

**Dr. William Gilbert, 1st doctor in, what is now, Fulton, County, Georgia**

## September 26, 1864

In Atlanta, 10-year-old Carrie Berry writes in her diary, "Mon. Sept. 26. I have not done much to day. I have be up to Aunties several times to day to see Cousin Emma and Willie for the last time. They are going off to night for the north. Wee all feel so sorry to see her leave for we will feel so lonesome."

***

In the Florida panhandle at Campbellton, near Marianna, Union General Asboth runs into Rebel resistance from Captain A R Godwin's Campbellton Cavalry. The weak force can only generate "hit-and-run" tactics to delay the Federals as long as possible so that Colonel Montgomery in Marianna can be notified and gather as many defenders as he can. General Asboth helps some, by having his men take most of the day to rest and prepare for battle tomorrow.

***

In Palmetto, Georgia, President Davis meets with individual general officers and sees a somewhat different picture of past events than the one General Hood has painted. One thing is evident, Generals Hood and Hardee have to be separated. One of two things will probably occur. Either Hardee will be transferred out, or Hood will be relieved with Beauregard.

***

From Atlanta, Sherman is hearing the news of events of the last couple of days in Northern Alabama, and he is wiring both Halleck and Grant, begging for more troops in Central Tennessee to help defend against Forrest.

The day before yesterday, at Athens, Alabama, Forrest forced the surrender of the fort and the City. Yesterday, at Sulpher Creek Trestle, he defeated (1,000) the heavily defended fort and disrupted the railroad. In all, with a troop strength (4,500) twice his enemy's, he is able to wound, kill, or capture, all 2,350 of them. Most of the Yankees are black soldiers which Forrest neglects to massacre.

**Lt. General Nathan Bedford Forrest**

## September 27, 1864

In Atlanta, Carrie Berry has this to say in her diary: "Tues. Sept. 27. This has been wash day. I went up to Aunties this evening and she gave me some quilt peaces and some doll clothes." In southern Tennessee, Reb General Forrest continues Federal-held railroad destruction at Pulaski. With his large force (4,500) and his reputation, Forrest has had a fairly easy time of it until the Federals withdraw into their fort at Pulaski, and Forrest cannot trick them out. He decides to stick to his mission, by-pass the fort, and head eastward into Tennessee.

***

At Marianna, Florida, Union Colonel Asboth with his 700, attacks the local home guard and militia (300-400) this morning. The locals, with their scanty fortifications and primitive weapons, are at first successful in hurting the Federal force, but the higher numbers and physical condition of the participants finally prevail. In victory, the Federals lose more casualties than anticipated, including the severe wounding of Asboth himself, leading to the decision to withdraw back to Fort Barrancas near Pensacola.

***

A year ago, in Kansas, Union General Thomas Ewing (Sherman's wife's brother) had a group of relatives of Confederate partisans arrested and held hostage. The building they were held in, for some reason, collapsed, killing four of the women. William T. Anderson's sister was one of the women killed and his other sister was badly crippled. Anderson, probably already a psychopath, swore death to all Yankee soldiers and unionist civilians. Living up to his nickname, "Bloody Bill", today, with 80 men, he invades the town of Centralia, Missouri, and begins to loot it when the train arrives. Among the passengers on the train are 23 Union soldiers on leave from Sherman's army. 22 of them are executed, and one held, with hopes of a prisoner exchange in the future. About 3 p.m. 155 Union cavalrymen ride into town to confront Anderson's men. In the ensuing action, 123 of the Union soldiers are killed, 32 escape, no wounded, and no prisoners are taken. In the action, the Union leader, Major A.V.E. Johnson is killed by Jessie James, according to his brother Frank James.

**William T. Anderson (Bloody Bill)**

## September 28, 1864

In Atlanta, 10-year-old diarist, Carrie Berry writes to herself, "Wed. Sept. 28. His has been another rainy day. I have ben sewing some to day. I went up to Aunties and we brushed her hair for her."

In West Point, Georgia, after an overnight train ride from Newnan, President Davis makes a decision on the leadership of the Army of Tennessee. He will leave Hood in command, removing Hardee. This morning he sends a wire informing Hood of his decision. Hardee will be placed in command of the Department of South Carolina, Georgia, and Florida. Davis will bring General Beauregard into play somehow, but not under Hood, probably indirectly over Hood, perhaps in charge of an over-all Western Department. Hood takes it that the decision to keep him also blesses his operations plan, already presented to Davis, to take his army into North Georgia and Tennessee to disrupt Sherman's supply lines and force him to pull out of Georgia. Wasting no time, he issues orders immediately to move the army away from Palmetto and across the Chattahoochee at Pumpkin Town and Phillip's Ferry. He will headquarter tonight at Pray's Church on the west side of the river.

In Atlanta, the exodus of the citizenry is pretty much complete. Some wagons leave today, but the southbound wagon trains to Rough and Ready have been halted. Just before Sherman crossed the Chattahoochee in July, there were about 20,000 permanent residents in the City. Now only about 50 civilian families remain, probably about 250 people. From Russell Bond's book, "War like a Thunderbolt", I quote the "Cincinnati Commercial" newspaper: "*Grant walked into Vicksburg, McClellan walked around Richmond, but Sherman is walking upon Atlanta.*"

## September 29, 1864

In Atlanta, Carrie Berry writes about an uneventful day, "Thurs. Sept. 29. We and ironed to day and we got done by two o'clock and I went up to Aunties after I was done here and she gave me some rasenes."

***

In Virginia, between Richmond and Petersburg at five o'clock this morning, the Federals under Benjamin Butler mount a two-pronged attack on Confederate defenses near Richmond. The XVIII Corps under General Ord with 5,000 men easily overrun the 200 defenders of Fort Harrison.

The numbers are overwhelming, and the surprise is complete. The X Corps, under David Birney and 15,000 men cross the James River at Aiken's Landing and push down the New Market Road, toward the 1,800 defenders on New Market Heights. At first, the Federal casualties are so high, they have to withdraw from the battle line, but the second effort, reinforced by more battlefield arrivals, successfully pushes the Confederates back, after they have inflicted 850 casualties on the attackers, withdrawing into works the Union force cannot take.

Union general Grant's general plan with this action is to keep General Meade's forces poised at Petersburg, so that if it becomes known that Reb General Lee is moving substantial troops from Petersburg to reinforce the Richmond defenses, Mead will be able to attack the weak spots. The overall strategy of the entire operation is to keep pressure on Lee's forces so that he cannot reinforce Early in the Shenandoah Valley. Some of the strategy will work. Lee will bring 10,000 men tomorrow to try to retake Fort Harrison.

**Federal attack on Fort Harrison**

## September 30, 1864

In Atlanta, Carrie Berry writes in her diary, "Fri. Sept. 30. I have ben sewing some to day on my apron. There are so many soldiers pacing backward and forward."

***

In Virginia, between Petersburg and Richmond, two major actions are fought today. Yesterday, the Federal Army under Butler overran the slight defenses of the Confederates in Fort Harrison. Since that time, they have been strengthening the fort and have it defended by about 20,000 men by morning. Last night, Confederate General Lee sent 10,000 troops from Petersburg to take back the fort. Attacking early this morning, the Rebels are not organized well, and the poorly coordinated attacks fail quickly. The fort will remain in the hands of the Federals, the Confederates reestablishing their outer lines to accommodate.

Believing that Lee has weakened his lines at Petersburg to attack Fort Harrison, Union General Grant orders General Meade to find a weak spot and attack those lines. Meade has General Warren with two corps move toward Poplar Springs Church with initial success, but the Confederates under A. P. Hill counter-attack strongly and drive in between the two Yankee corps, forcing them to fall back. The Federals establish strong defensive lines on Squirrel Level Road, near Peebles' farm. At the end of the day, many men are dead and wounded, and the only real result is that the lines are repositioned.

**Battle of Poplar Springs Church from "Leslie's Illustrated"**

## October 1, 1864

In Atlanta, Carrie Berry reports on her day, "Sat. Oct. 1. It is very warm for the first day of October but we will look out for a frost before long. I have been making my doll a frock for Sunday.

Northwest of Atlanta, Confederate General Hood spent the last two days crossing his 40,000 men over the Chattahoochee River, moving north. By this evening, he will be about 8 miles from the river, near Marietta.

***

Through the rain of Virginia, Reb General Ewell throws two divisions, under Wilcox and Heth, from the Petersburg lines against the Federal lines, with little success. Union General Meade would like to return the attention, but he has trouble getting enough men to the party before late afternoon, so he will have to wait until tomorrow morning to counter-attack.

***

Near Wilmington, North Carolina, the blockade runner, "Condor", runs aground while evading the Union gunboat "USS Niphon." On board is Rose O'Neal Greenhow, the famous Confederate spy and diplomat, returning home after a two-year service for the Rebel Government in England. Two years ago, Rose was caught running a spy network in Washington DC. She spent four months in Old Capitol Prison and was banished forever into the Confederate States. In Richmond she was hailed as a hero, and President Davis enlisted her as a courier to Europe. Her duties included traveling through France and Britain, building support for the Confederacy with the aristocrats. While she was there, she wrote her memoirs, and she was rewarded handsomely with royalties, a portion of which she has with her, in the form of gold, sewn into her clothing, $2,000 worth. The gold turns out to not be an asset as her escape rowboat swamps, spilling her into the water, sending she and her gold to the bottom of the sea.

**Rose O'Neal Greenhow (The Confederate Rose)**

## October 2, 1864

In Atlanta, GA, 10-year-old Carrie Berry writes in her diary, "Sun. Oct. 2. This has ben a very pretty day. I went around to Mrs. Lesters. Ella and I took a walk to see how the soldiers had torn down the fine houses. It is a shame to see the fine houses torn down."

In Atlanta, news is reaching Sherman of the Progress of the Army of Tennessee around Marietta and of train disruptions further north, from the activities of Conf. Cavalry Generals Wheeler and Forrest. Sherman orders most of his army to prepare to move out to the north on short notice.

***

Near Petersburg, Virginia, the four-day Union offensive ends this morning with an attack by the Yankees that just fizzles away when they discover that the Confederates have conceded the area of the battlefield that they are assaulting. The Rebs have withdrawn into heavily prepared fortifications that should not be attempted. During the last four days, the Federals have extended their lines and kept any reinforcements from coming from the area to Early in the Shenandoah Valley, but the cost has been over 4,000 casualties. Grant's fifth offensive of the Petersburg Campaign has again ended in stalemate.

***

Confederate President Davis, in Augusta, GA., on his return journey to Richmond, tells General Beauregard to assume command of the two western departments now under Genls. Hood and Richard Taylor. He will have overall command but is not to interfere with field operations unless he is actually on the battlefield.

**Confederate General Pierre Gustave Toutant Beauregard**

## October 3, 1864

In Atlanta, Carrie Berry writes in her diary, "Mon. Oct 3. We herd that General Hood had go away around towards Chattanooga tearing up the railroad. The federals seemed very much trouble about it. I commenced Sister a little worsted dress. I love to sew for her because she loves me.".... (Little sister Mira will be 2-years old next month)

Indeed, General Hood has gone away toward Chattanooga, and today finds him and his force squarely on the railroad at Big Shanty, with Sherman's supply line stopped dead still. General Sherman, from Atlanta has begun to move 60,000 men across the Chattahoochee, towards Hood's forces, but Hood has plenty of time to destroy the functionality of the railroad and water tank. before moving on toward Acworth. Sherman has five of his corps with him, leaving General Slocum to hold Atlanta with one corps.....Anticipating Hood's direction of mischief, Sherman has already sent Major General Thomas to Nashville to assemble a force there for the combating of Reb General Forrest and protection of the railroads from Hood and Cavalry General, Wheeler. Thomas arrives in Nashville today.

***

In Augusta, Ga, as President Davis makes his way back to Richmond, he has met with Beauregard and Hardee to discuss their new jobs, and they join him in a political rally where they all get to speak. Davis tells the Augustans, "We must beat Sherman; we must march into Tennessee. There we will draw from 20,000 to 30,000 to our standard, and, so strengthened, we must push the enemy back to the banks of the Ohio and thus give the peace party of the North an accretion no puny editorial can give." Beauregard, who claims to have fired the first gun of the war, draws loud applause when he says he hope to fire the last. And, Hardee states that Hood has told him that "He intends to lay his claws upon the state road in rear of Sherman, and, having once fixed them there, it is not his intention to let them loose their hold."

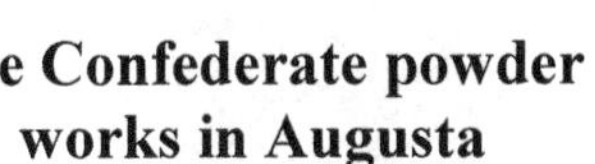

**The Confederate powder works in Augusta**

## October 4, 1864

Inside Atlanta, GA, Carrie Berry writes in her diary, "Tues. Oct. 4. I finished Sister's little dress to day and I have be up to Aunties once or twice. I feel so lonesome I cant stay at home. I wish it was so that I could go to school."

In New Orleans, the first black published newspaper in the United States hits the streets today. "*The New Orleans Tribune*", published in both French and English by Dr. Louis Charles Roundanez, is dedicated to social justice and civil rights.

***

In Georgia, north of Atlanta, Reb General Hood has split his men, with his main army located near Lost Mountain, west of Marietta, and divisions attacking the railroad stations north of Big Shanty (Kennesaw). Today there are skirmishes at Acworth and Moon's Station where the several hundred, badly outnumbered Federal defenders have to surrender. Hood knows about the great storage of supplies at Allatoona and the strong Yankee forts there, but he believes them to be lightly defended. This afternoon he sends General French with about 3,000 men to take the station and fill in the railroad gap in order to further render the line useless to the Federals. Sherman has already wired Union General Corse in Rome to order him to take his division to reinforce the Allatoona forts, on the high ground, each side of the railroad pass. Corse will arrive late tonight, increasing the defenders to about 2,000, many armed with repeating rifles and all, well fortified. So will French arrive during the night, moving carefully, positioning his men for early attack on the morrow.

**Allatoona Pass 1864**

## October 5, 1864

In Atlanta, Carrie Berry has this to say about this day in her diary, "Wed. Oct. 5. We and Tilo have ben washing. Mama cut her hand so that she could not wash. After I got done I went up to Aunties and she was selling out to go north. She is afraid that Gen. Hood will get back and commence shelling as the federals did. I don't blame her for I never would stay and be shelled again if I could get away, though we will be very sorry when she leaves.

In Georgia, north of Atlanta, the morning finds the Rebel Army under Hood camped in the Lost Mountain Community, near the battlefields of last May, where Johnston whipped Sherman sharply at New Hope Church and Pickett's Mill. Confederate General Hood, with almost 40,000, is trying to entice Sherman to come and fight again in the impossibly rugged terrain of the area. Sherman has 60,000 of his men camped around Kennesaw Mountain where he has a communications post on the heights with wig-wag flag operators in touch with various elements of his army.

This morning, at Allatoona Pass, Reb General French, with 3,200, waits until daylight and opens up his artillery on Yank General Corse, with 2,000, for a bombardment of over two hours, which is the time it takes French to get his men into position to attack the two fortified areas separated by the train track in a deep cut. At nine in the morning, French halts the bombardment to send a note to Corse that he is surrounded but can surrender the fort without loss of life. Corse has been notified by wig-wag "*General Sherman say hold fast. We are coming*" so he declines the opportunity, and the fight is on. The battle is furious with the South gaining ground and pushing the defenders into a concentration inside one of their forts. After about two and half hours of carnage, there is a lull. The Confederates are running low on ammo, and it will take some time to get it to the action. Also, French receives a false report that a Federal Division is approaching, so he decides to abandon the attempt and escape before darkness. Losses are high, with the Union losing just over 700 total.

**Battle of Allatoona Pass by Thure de Thulstrup, 1887.**

## October 6, 1864

In Atlanta, Carrie Berry writes in her diary, "Thurs. Oct. 6. I have ben up to Aunties' nearly all day getting quilt scraps and doll scraps. I am right sorry Auntie is going away. I don't know what I will do for some place to run to. It has ben raining nearly all day."

***

In Georgia, north of Atlanta, there is much cavalry activity today. Union General Sherman is puzzled about the intentions of General Hood's Confederates who have moved from their position about Lost Mountain, with lead elements reaching Dallas today, the right of the army occupying the old battlefield at New Hope Church. Sherman is headquartered at Kennesaw Mountain, spending much of his time on the mountain top with his signal station. He orders General Stanley's division to move northwestward to establish a signal station on Lost mountain, his cavalry patrolling a wide area, picking up Rebel deserters or stragglers for information about Hood's plans.

***

In Virginia, The "*Richmond Enquirer*" publishes an article suggesting the enlistment of Negro soldiers into the Confederate Army with the promise of freedom as incentive for the recruits. This idea is not popular, but is gaining support.

***

In the Shenandoah Valley, Union General Sheridan's army is having a grand time of destruction of homes and crops, rendering much of the Valley uninhabitable. He has assigned much of this task to General Custer who is attacked today at Brock's Gap by Confederate cavalry under Thomas Rosser. Custer repulses the attack, but it shows that the South still has teeth in the valley.

**Union Major General George Armstrong Custer**

## October 7, 1864

In Atlanta, GA., Carrie Berry writes in her diary, "Fri. Oct. 7. I have ben sick all day. I have not ben doing much of anything. It has cleared off but it is windy and we expect that it will turn cold and we may look out for frost.

Between Richmond and Petersburg, VA, Confederate General Lee sends two divisions against the Federal defenses on the Darbytown Road with initial successes. The bluecoats are routed from the field, and the Confederates follow, attacking further at New Market Road where they meet with stiff resistance and have to retreat. Texas Brigade Commander, Brig. Gen. John Gregg, is killed by a bullet through his neck. Losses are 458 Yankees and about 700 Johnny Rebs.

***

From the Shenandoah Valley, Union Major General Phil Sheridan writes to his boss, General Grant, describing how he is carrying out Grant's orders, "I have destroyed over 2,000 barns, filled with wheat, hay, and farming implements," begins the long list of destruction, "over 70 mills, filled with flour and wheat; have driven in front of the army over 4,000 head of stock, and have killed and issued to the troops not less than 3,000 sheep..."This destruction embraces the Luray Valley and Little Fort Valley, as well as the main valley. A large number of horses have been obtained, a proper estimate of which I cannot now make." .."tomorrow I will continue the destruction of wheat, forage, &c., down to Fisher's hill. When this is complete the Valley, from Winchester up to Staunton, ninety-two miles, will have but little in it for man or beast."

**Custer's Division doing Grant and Sheridan's work**

## October 8, 1864

In Atlanta, GA., 10-year-old, Carrie Berry has this to say in her diairy, " Sat. Oct. 8. I was sick this morning and did'nt get up until after breakfast but got better towards dinner and went up to Auntie's after dinner and she gave me so many nice scraps. It has ben right cold all day."

***

The dance in North Georgia continues with Confederate General Hood and the Army of Tennessee moving from Dallas to Van Wert, overnighting lead elements in Cedartown. Union General Sherman orders his three armies to proceed in the direction of Allatoona with the Army of the Ohio halting two or three miles south of Allatoona. The Army of the Cumberland halts on the south side of Acworth, and the Army of the Tennessee halts on the south side of Big Shanty (Kennesaw). The movement will be slow because of rain and the need to graze the animals.

***

In Liverpool, England, James Bulloch, of Roswell, Ga, has done it again. Bulloch is the Confederate agent who arranged for the construction or acquisition of the warships, "CSS Alabama", "CSS Florida", and "CSS Atlanta. He also acts as agent in the sale of smuggled southern cotton into Europe. Recently he has been able to acquire by purchase the "Sea King", which leaves England under his authority today, to be turned over to Captain James Iredell Waddell in international waters. Waddell will have the ship outfitted and crewed for war. It will be commissioned on the 18th of this month as "CSS Shenandoah".

**The picture shows James Dunwoody Bulloch on the left and his brother who served on the "CSS Alabama" with Admiral Semmes, on the right, Irvine Stephens Bulloch. Both of these men are uncles to future President Theodore Roosevelt, whose mother is Martha Bulloch, their sister.**

## October 9, 1864

In Atlanta, Ga., 10-year-old Carrie Berry writes in her diary: "Sun. Oct. 9. It has ben cold allmost like winter time. We herd that the federals had whipped Gen. Hood and driven him back."( Probably Carrie heard the Union soldiers talking about the Federals being able to hold the star-shaped fort at Allatoona last week)

In the Shenandoah Valley of Virginia, the Federal Cavalry under Alfred Torbert has been mercilessly harassed by the Confederates under Thomas Rosser as he takes his 3,500 against General Custer one day and Torbert another day with split forces. Today, in a well-planned move by Torbert, he attacks Rosser at Tom's Ford and has Custer attack a flank after he is engaged, giving him a combined force of 6,300 well placed horsemen that are able to defeat the Confederates, driving them from the field in a retreat that quickly becomes a rout. The Yankees lose 57 men in the action, while rendering 350 Rebel casualties.

***

In Northwest Georgia, General Hood is moving his army through Cedartown and into Cave spring. It is not clear if Hood is with the main army now, because I see dispatches, he sends today and tomorrow from Van Wert. Much of the Army will sleep in Cave Springs tonight before moving tomorrow to Veal's Ferry, on the Coosa River about 10 miles below Rome. Union General Sherman is moving his armies directly northward until he can determine the intent of Hood's Confederates. Today he is headquartered at Allatoona where he is overwhelmed with the task of protecting his long lines of communication and supply.

TO ULYSSES S. GRANT

Allatoona 7.30 p.m.
Oct. 9th 1864

Lt. Gen. Grant
City Point

It will be a physical impossibility to protect this road now that Hood, Forrest, Wheeler and the whole batch of Devils are turned loose without home or habitation. I think Hoods movements indicate a direction to the end of the Selma and Talladega road to Blue Mountain about sixty miles south west of Rome from which he will threaten Kingston, Bridgeport and Decatur and I propose we break up the road from Chattanooga and strike out with wagons for Milledgeville Millen and Savannah.

Until we can repopulate Georgia it is useless to occupy it, but the utter destruction of its roads, houses, and people will cripple their military resources. By attempting to hold the roads we will lose a thousand men monthly and will gain no result. I can make the march and make Georgia howl. We have over 8000 cattle and 3,000,000 pounds of bread but no corn, but we can forage in the interior of the state[.][1]

W. T. Sherman
M. Genl.

Telegram, DNA: RG 107, Records of the Office of the Secretary of War, Telegrams

**The picture is the telegram he sends to General Grant, explaining his future moves.**

## October 10, 1864

In Atlanta, 10-year-old Carrie Berry has this to say to herself, in her diary, "Mon. Oct. 10. Mama hired a black woman to work for her to day. I hemmed a towel and Ella came to see me. It is not so cold to day but we had a white frost last night."

In the Shenandoah Valley of Virginia, the Federal Forces under Sheridan are moving north across Cedar Creek to take strong defensive positions on both sides of the Valley Pike.

***

Arriving today, in St. Albans, Vermont, are the first of 21 Confederate soldiers, commanded by Lt. Bennett H. Young, who will drift into town in two's and three's until a whole force is assembled on the 19th, when they will attempt to take over the town. Hopefully, they will then rob the three banks, to use the proceeds to stoke the Confederate treasury. We will come back on that day.

In North Georgia, the game of chess continues between Generals Hood and Sherman. Sherman, not knowing what Hood will do, sends General Corse hell-bent to Rome, Ga to reinforce the defenses there. Sherman orders Corse to hold the town at all costs, promising to follow with the main army on the 12th (Where have we heard that before?...Allatoona?). Sherman, himself will spend the night in Cartersville, then move toward Rome in the morning of the 11th, but maybe not, instead going to Kingston. Meanwhile, the Rebels under Hood continue to move through, and out of Cave Spring toward Quinn's Ferry on the Coosa River about 12 miles below Rome, where they have erected a pontoon bridge for the crossing. Elements of Hood's Army are getting across today, and all will be across by late afternoon tomorrow.

**Cave Spring, Georgia**

## October 11, 1864

In Atlanta, GA., 10year-old Carrie Berry writes in her diary, "Tues. Oct. 11. We have ben ironing to day. We have got our clothes washed, ironed and put away. We will not have anything to do all the rest of the week."

In Kingston, GA., Union General Sherman is piling his troops on the train to Rome as fast as he can load them. He now believes that Confederate General Hood who has moved from Dallas to Van Wert, to Cedartown, to Cave Spring, is coming to try to take the City of Seven Hills and occupy it. In actuality, Hood is crossing the Coosa River today, from Cave Spring and will by-pass Rome, with lead elements up through Livingston and into Big Texas Valley, up through Everett Springs and into Sugar Valley, then to Resaca.

Hood has ordered cavalry Brigadier General Jackson to linger at Coosa until tomorrow when he is to proceed to Rome for a threatening show of force to encourage Sherman to continue to move his army there, rather than toward Resaca and Dalton. Jackson is to set up a communications line from Rome to wherever Hood happens to be. He has these instructions,"*..**Make a considerable demonstration from your side of the river; but be careful not to fire into the town. Communicate fully and frequently about all movements of the enemy."***

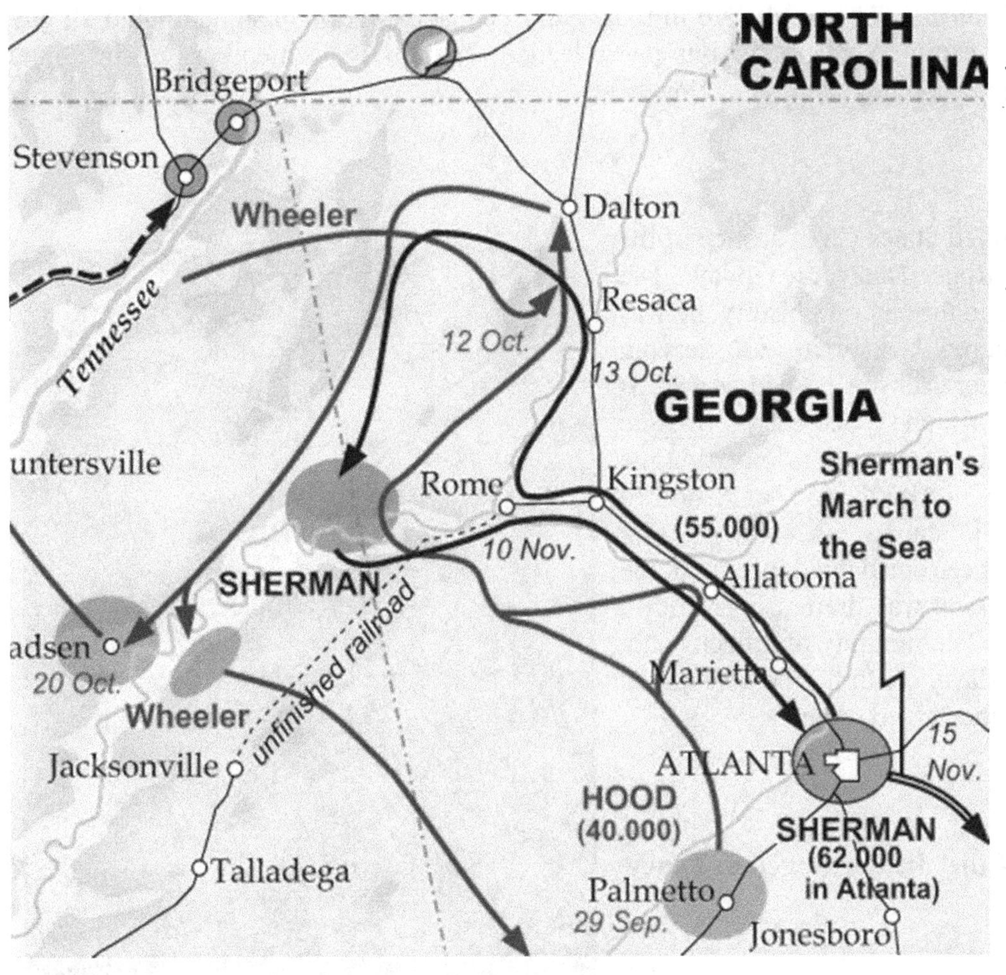

## October 12, 1864

In Atlanta, GA, Carrie Berry writes in her diary, "Wed. Oct 12. I mad me and apron today and my doll a dress, I did not get up to see Auntie to day. We are having nice and fine weather now."

In North Georgia, lead elements of Hood's Confederates under Stephen Lee reach Resaca, surround, the well-fortified bluecoats there, and demand surrender. The Federals refuse to surrender and Lee makes the decision that, while he could take the fort by storming it, the price in casualties would be too high for any gain, so his men begin tearing up the railroad track all the way to Tunnel Hill and move on up toward Dalton. Sherman remains in Rome and sends troops down both sides of the Coosa River to guard the pontoon bridge at Coosaville that the Confederates left in place after crossing.

***

In the North it was election day yesterday, for three states that hold their general elections one month before all others. The results are in today, and Pennsylvania, Indiana, and Ohio all gave the Republicans cause to celebrate, but party leaders caution their members against over-confidence in the upcoming contests in November.

***

In Maryland, United States Chief Justice of the Supreme Court, Roger Taney, dies today. The 5th Chief Justice in the Nation's history, he was appointed by Andrew Jackson in 1836, serving until today. Under Jackson he had served as Attorney General and Secretary of the Treasury. He is most famous for delivering the majority opinion in Dred Scott v. Sandford (1857) that ruled, among other things, that Africans, having been considered inferior at the time the Constitution was drafted, were not a part of the original community of citizens and, whether free or slave, could not be considered to be citizens of the United States.

**Chief Justice Roger B. Taney**

## October 13, 1864

In Atlanta, GA., Carrie Berry Writes in her diary, "Thurs. Oct. 13. We had quite a night here last night. Some body trying to steel our hogs. They did not get them though. They will be right smart if they do. I have hemmed a foot towel and that is all I have done to day."

In Virginia, in the Shenandoah Valley, Confederate General Lee has augmented Early's Army, and Early has pushed northward to Fisher's Hill. Learning of this, General Sheridan has recalled the VI Corps to his army's camp along Cedar Creek. Although the situation is worrisome, Sheridan still elects to attend a conference in Washington, leaving General Wright in command of his army.

In Virginia, between Richmond and Petersburg, there is a sharp action today on the Darbytown Road. The Southern forces attack to feel out the location and strength of the Federal lines but are repulsed. The Federals then reciprocate and they too, are repulsed. The Union loses just over 400 casualties for the day, and the South loses just over 500.

***

In Rome, Georgia, Union General Sherman receives from General Grant the permission he has been seeking to relieve North Georgia of his presence and take his Army down through the state to the Port of Savannah. But first, he must make sure that General Hood is not about to deal him a heavy blow of some sort. Sherman does get good news from the Coosaville area. Hood has taken his pontoon bridge from the Coosa River after all, indicating that he will not be going back toward Atlanta. If he goes on northward, he will become Thomas' problem and Sherman will go to the coast.

At Dalton, GA., Confederate General Bates demands surrender of the Federals posted there, but they refuse and fighting begins. Hood arrives on the scene with tens of thousands more Confederates, stops the action and gives the Federals another chance to surrender which they accept. Close to 1,000 prisoners are taken, most of whom are colored troops that will be returned to their masters. The white Yanks are paroled.

**Confederate General Bate**

## October 14, 1864

In Atlanta, GA, 10-year-old Carrie Berry writes in her diary, "Friday. Oct. 14. I went around to see Ella this evening. When I cam back Papa had killed a pig and while I was at Mrs. Lesters a little crazy girl came in and she cut up all sorts of shines."

In North Georgia, The Army of Tennessee under General Hood pulls out of Dalton with about 1,000 prisoners, heading in the direction of Gadsden and will camp tonight near Villanow. General Sherman is moving his 65,000 men by various routes to, and into, Snake Creek Gap, near Dalton, hoping to catch Hood for major battle. Hood has his eye out for the right place to stop and oblige.

***

In Jefferson County, West Virginia, Partisan Confederate Raiders, under John Mosby, de-rail and rob a passenger train bringing cash to Sheridan's army for payroll. Mosby relieves the train of $173,000, then has all the occupants disembark before firing the cars. Several Union soldiers on the train are taken prisoner, and passengers are robbed but not harmed.

***

In Danville, Missouri, "Bloody Bill" Anderson piles shame on the gray uniforms again today. You will remember that on September 27, Anderson's men, including Jessie and Frank James and Archie Clement, stopped a train at Centralia that contained 24 Union soldiers, unarmed, on furlough. Anderson had the soldiers executed mercilessly. Tonight, the raiders swoop down on Danville, murdering and robbing civilians, including at least one 12 year-old boy. They begin to torch the town and set fire to every building except the Female Academy which they spared because of begging from some of the students. Anderson has a fine time tonight, but he is not going to live much longer.

## October 15, 1864

In Atlanta, GA, Carrie Berry writes in her diary, "Sat. Oct. 15. This has ben a dark gloomy day. I have not done much wirk to say but make my doll a dress."

In Missouri, finally, Confederate General Sterling Price has some success in his campaign to overthrow the Federals controlling the State. His Brigadier Generals Jo Shelby and John Clark attack the Federal garrison at Glasgow. Outnumbered two-to-one, the Yanks fight bravely, but are soon worn down by the numerous opponents so they surrender, rewarding the victors with many new greatcoats and muskets. The prisoners are paroled and released, being allowed to keep their side arms and personal property.

***

In North Georgia, Confederate General Hood has his army together in a beautiful valley at a crossroad, about 9 miles south of Lafayette, near the future town of Trion. He will spend the day today and tomorrow at this place trying to figure out what he wants to do. He is having second thoughts about attacking Sherman, mainly because of the low morale of his men. Right now Hood's forces, about 35,000, are pretty much together, except for scouting parties, while Sherman has his forces, about 65,000, moving through hollows and gaps in separate, but strong, units with no real plan for coming together until they find Hood and determine his situation.

***

**In Harper's Weekly today, a sketch of the Western and Atlantic Railroad yard in Atlanta is published.**

VIEW OF THE STATE RAILROAD DEPOT AT ATLANTA, GEORGIA.—[SKETCHED BY A. W. GAREY.]

## October 16, 1864

In Atlanta, GA, food is on Carrie Berry's mind as she writes in her diary, "Sun. Oct. 16. We had some nice brains for breakfast and some stewed dumplings for dinner. I have ben at home all day."

In North Georgia, General Hood takes his second day of rest and contemplation in the beautiful valley between Taylor's Ridge and the Lookout Mountain Chain, about half way between Summerville and Lafayette, while Sherman moves on through the passes of Rocky Face Ridge and into the area of Villanow. Hood has a new plan, fairly complicated "*.....to make provision for twenty days supply of rations in the haversacks and wagons; to order a heavy reserve of artillery to accompany the army, in order to overcome any serious opposition by the Federal gunboats; to cross the Tennessee at or near Guntersville, and again destroy Sherman's communications at Stevenson and Bridgeport; to move upon Thomas and Schofield, and to attempt to rout and capture their army before it can reach Nashville. I intend to march upon that city where I would supply the army and reinforce it, if possible, by accessions from Tennessee.*". Implementation will begin tomorrow.

***

In the Shenandoah Valley, Union General Sheridan is seemingly perfectly entrenched on the north bank of Cedar Creek, too strong in numbers and position to be attacked. Confederate General Gordon, with the support of Confederate cartographer, Jed Hotchkiss, presents a plan to General Early whereby he, Gordon, will slip from the lines in the dark, move around to the enemy left and strike hard just at first light, then everybody else strike along the Federal lines. Early buys into the plan, and the morning of the 19th is set to go. A scar-faced David will attack Goliath.

**Major General John B. Gordon**

## October 17, 1864

In Atlanta, 10-year-old Carrie Berry writes in her diary, " Mon. Oct 17. I got up this morning and washed the dishes and cleaned up the house and nursed Sister while mama was washing. Sister was sick."

In the Shenandoah Valley of Virginia, Maj. General John B Gordon, and topographical engineer Jedediah Hotchkiss spend the day on Signal Knob on Massanutten Mountain, surveying the Union Camps below and developing a plan of battle to be implemented tomorrow night.

***

In North Georgia, Confederate General Hood moves his Army of Tennessee toward Gadsden, Alabama, leaving his beautiful two-day resting place peaceful and unblooded. Meanwhile, Union General Sherman prepares his armies for battle by sending all encumbrances in wagon trains to Chattanooga, keeping enough supplies for five days, and he heads his entire force toward Summerville, GA.

In Richmond, Virginia, Reb Lt. General Longstreet is back, and General Lee is happy about that. On May 6, of this year, Longstreet was shot by his own men in the heat of the Battle of the Wilderness. The bullet passed through his shoulder, severing nerves, and tearing a gash in his throat, a profoundly serious wound. He missed the remainder of the spring and summer campaign, and Lee missed his skill in handling the army. He was treated in Lynchburg, Virginia, and recuperated in Augusta, Georgia with his niece. He is back now, but his right arm is paralyzed and in a sling. He has taught himself to write left-handed.

**Confederate Lt. General James Longstreet**

## October 18, 1864

In Atlanta, Carrie Berry writes in her diary, "Tues. Oct. 18. I went up to auntie's this morning and Ella came to see me this evening and we had a good time. she is the only associate that I have now."

In the Northern trenches at Petersburg, the X Corps has sadness today. Their General, David Birney, who gave Grant good service in the Wilderness, Spotsylvania Court House (slightly wounded there), and Cold Harbor, became ill with malaria during the current Siege of Petersburg three months ago. He died of his sickness today, at home in Philadelphia, and will be buried in Woodlands Cemetery.

***

In North Georgia, Reb General Hood continues to move toward the Alabama line, and General Sherman's forces move through Subligna, Dirt Town, and Armuchee, in casual pursuit.

***

In the Shenandoah Valley, the morning is spent with meetings of Generals and other command officers in the 10,000-man Confederate forces of Jubal Early, planning the details of the attack tomorrow morning on Union General Sheridan's 30,000+ strong force. By plan, early this evening, after dark, General Gordon leads the Second Corps along a route that requires the men to proceed in Indian file. To keep the progress quiet, they have left behind their canteens and cooking utensils. "The long gray line, " Gordon will someday write, "like a giant serpent glides noiselessly along the dim pathway above the precipice." Moving all night, they will be in place, at Bowman's Ford, waiting and watching in the bright moonlight, just before the dawn.

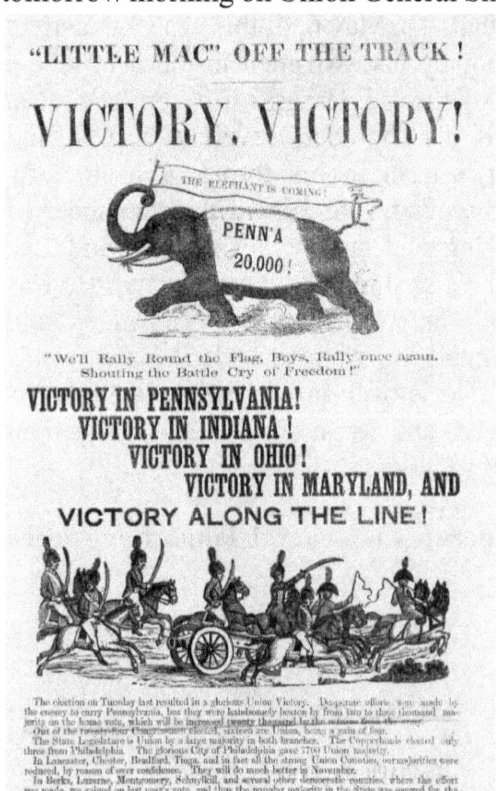


***

**The featured political illustration from today's issue of "Father Abraham", a Republican publication, is the first symbolizing of an elephant to represent the Republican Party.** "Seeing the elephant" is a slang expression among Civil War soldiers for engaging in combat, the symbol is a natural choice for honoring successful campaigns, military and political. The cartoon is accompanied by a listing of recent successes in early elections in the North.

## October 19, 1864

In Atlanta, GA., Carrie Berry writes in her diary, "Wed. Oct 19. We ironed today. We wirked in a hurry and got through by three o'clock and I went up to Auntie's and got her to cut out me an and I made it and I thought it was so pretty."

In St Albans, Vermont, the northernmost action of the War happens today. Twenty-one Confederate soldiers, who have escaped from Northern prisons and fled to Canada, have organized themselves and traveled here in pairs, discretely, over the last nine days. The leader of the group is Kentuckian Bennett H. Young, who was captured with John Hunt Morgan in Ohio last year. About 3 PM the soldiers announce to the town who they are and assemble the population on the village green while eight or nine Confederates hold them at gunpoint. The other soldiers simultaneously rob the three banks in town to capitalize the Confederate government. They take a total of $208,000 back into Canada with them.

***

In Virginia, near Belle Grove Plantation on Cedar Creek, Corps Commander John B. Gordon hurls his three divisions on the Federal left just after dawn. On the left of Gordon's effort is Clement A. Evans, commanding Gordon's old division. Ramseur's Division is on the right, and Peagram's supporting the other two. When Gordon's action begins, all others of Early's Confederates attack, routing the sleepy-eyed Yankee boys. In all quarters the Federals are running, in a panic their officers cannot quell. Reb General Early believes the victory to be complete and orders Gordon to stop the offensive, overruling Gordon's objections. By late in the afternoon, the Union Army Commander, Phil Sheridan, has returned to his army, utilized the reprieve by Early to reestablish order in his ranks and counter-charges. The Confederates, now scattered, surveying their booty from the Union camps, are forced into unorganized retreat, quickly turning into a rout, finally getting to defendable positions and safety. On this day, the Yankees lose 5,764 casualties and the Johnny Rebs lose 3060, ill-affordable for the South.

**Fighting at Belle Grove Plantation (Sheridan's Headquarters)**

## October 20, 1864

In Atlanta, Carrie Berry writes in her diary, "Thurs. Oct. 20. I went around to Mrs. Lesters this evening after I got through with my lessons. I have not done much wirk this week. Mama has been so buisy making Papa a coat to cut me any wirk out."

In Gadsden, Alabama, Reb General Hood notifies General Taylor that he will be headquartered in Guntersville tomorrow. It is at Gadsden that General Beauregard is able to catch up to Hood and they meet to discuss the plans for the Army of Tennessee. Sherman is at nearby Gaylesville and has his 60,000 men camped from Cedar Bluff to Centre. Sherman does not want to follow Hood any further, but to turn some of his men over to Thomas' growing force and make Hood Thomas' problem, while he can destroy and pillage Middle and South Georgia.

***

In Washington, President Lincoln, again this year, issues a proclamation that the last Thursday in November will be a national day of Thanksgiving. This will be the second, in a long tradition of this holiday...wonder if he will pardon a turkey?

***

In New York Harbor at Fort Hamilton, the newest and largest piece of ordinance in the world is tested and demonstrated with its inventor, Major Thomas Jefferson Rodman in attendance. The gun weighs 116,000 pounds, mounted on a carriage that weighs 36,000 pounds. It can fire a 1,000-pound shell, twenty inches in diameter for a distance of over five miles. The bore is so large that if the fuse tube becomes fouled, a man can crawl into the bore to the charge chamber and clear it. The new gun is not mounted inside the fort but in the tier of 15-inch guns extending along the embankment for a quarter of a mile below the fort, commanding the lower bay, and forming part of the defenses of New York harbor.

**Rodman 20-Inch Gun**

## October 21, 1864

In Atlanta, 10-year-old Carrie Berry writes to herself in her diary, "Fri. Oct. 21. Mama finished Papa's coat to day and it is very nice and I hope she will not be so buisy so that I can get some wirk. I went up to Auntie's and she said that she thought she would get off soon."

In Gadsden, Alabama, General Hood's Confederates have been delayed by news that Major General Beauregard, Confederate Regional Commander, is arriving this morning for an all-day conference with General Hood so that he can approve his actions and understand what he has to do to keep Hood's movements supplied. When the meeting concludes, he is in agreement with Hood that the Army of Tennessee is too demoralized and damaged to go head-on with Sherman's Yankees in Georgia, and that the proposed invasion of Tennessee should begin immediately.

***

The day before yesterday, a group of escaped prisoners of war, based in Canada, raided the town of St. Albans, Vermont, taking $208,000 from the three banks in the name of the Confederate Government. The US Government has complained to the Canadian Government, demanding the arrest of the men and return of the money. The Canadians have arrested the 21, but Canadian Courts will decide that they cannot be extradited and must be released. The court also rules that the money should be returned to the banks. There was only $88,000 recovered when the raiders were arrested.

***

Also, on the day before yesterday, at the battle of Cedar Creek, among the Southern casualties was one of the finest officers of either army. Major General Ramseur, a division commander under Gordon, had two horses shot from beneath him before taking a ball from his side that blew through both lungs. He fell in disputed ground and was captured by Union Soldiers of the 1st Vermont Cavalry, in whose company he passed away with this last request, ""Bear this message to my precious wife—I die a Christian and hope to meet her in heaven." The day before the battle, he received word of the birth of his first child, a baby daughter.

**Confederate Major General Stephen Dodson Ramseur**

## October 22, 1864

In Atlanta, Autumn has begun, as evidenced by Carrie Berry's diary, "Sat. Oct 22. This has ben a cold and rainy day. I have not be doing anything but sitting by the fire."

After receiving approval for his Tennessee invasion, last night, from General Beauregard, Confederate General Hood moves his Army of Tennessee out this morning toward Guntersville, Alabama. He will send all of Wheeler's Cavalry back into Georgia to continue to harass Sherman's supply lines and will join forces with Nathan B Forrest for cavalry support. Now he plans to stay on the south side of the Tennessee River until he can affect a union with Forrest, probably at Florence, Alabama.

Meanwhile General Sherman is headquartered at Gaylesville, Alabama and making plans to follow Hood for a while, but his heart is not in it. He writes the same song to Grant today that he has been singing for two weeks: *"I am now perfecting arrangements to put into Tennessee a force able to hold the line of the Tennessee whilst I break up the railroad in front of Dalton, including the city of Atlanta, and push into Georgia, and break up all its railroads and depots, capture its horses and negroes, make desolation everywhere, destroy the factories at Macon, Milledgeville, and Augusta, and bring up with 60,000 men on the seashore about Savannah or Charleston. I think this far better than defending a long line of railroad."*

He also writes to General Corse in Rome, Georgia , "October 22, 1864. I wrote you yesterday that I wanted you to send down the Coosa to Cedar Bluff, just above the Chattanooga, the spare pontoon bridge, and as accident may have interfered, I repeat the order. Also, that you cover the movement by a strong foraging expedition down the Vann's Valley, Cave Spring, and Center road. As soon as I get the pontoons, I will throw a force into Centre."

***

In Missouri, Confederate General Price has won his second battle in two days against the numerically superior Federal forces. Today at Independence, yesterday at Lexington, both victories are minor with few losses, but facing odds of more than two to one. However, this day leaves Price surrounded by his enemies. Now he needs a way out...what tomorrow?

**Confederate Major General Sterling Price**

## October 23, 1864

In Atlanta, Ga., Carrie Berry writes about damage already done to her City, "Sun. Oct 23. This has ben a beautiful day since the sun has come out. Mama and Papa took a walk this evening and they say that they never saw a place torn up like Atlanta is. Half of the houses are torn down."

In Missouri, near Kansas City at Westport, Confederate General Sterling Price has had two fights with a force commanded by Union General Samuel Curtis, over the past two days. Curtis has double the 8,000 men that Price has, but Price has been able to squeak out victories each day, and today seems to be developing no differently, in the morning. In the afternoon, another 6,000 troops sent by Union General Rosecrans brings the Federal force to 22,000, too much for Price's boys in gray when their ammunition begins to expend, and they begin to retreat. In some places the retreat becomes a rout, and the Rebels fall back about 24 miles, leaving 1,500 on the field as casualties. The Yankees lose about the same number, and they will vigorously pursue their enemy.

***

In Northwest Georgia and NE Alabama, the confederates under Hood, with Beauregard as observer, are making their way from Gadsden toward Guntersville. Their supply depot is in Jacksonville, capable of shooting supplies to them if the army can reach a rail head where they can be shipped to. Union General Sherman is still headquartered in Gaylesville but is intending to head back to Rome to meet his Chief Quartermaster, who is heading to Rome under orders from Sherman.

Today, Sherman has a new spin on his army's stealing from the citizenry. In three separate dispatches he says, "*If Georgia can afford to break our railroads, she can afford to feed us. Please preach this doctrine to men who go forth, likely to spread it.*" It is as if he is trying to justify his atrocities in his own mind.

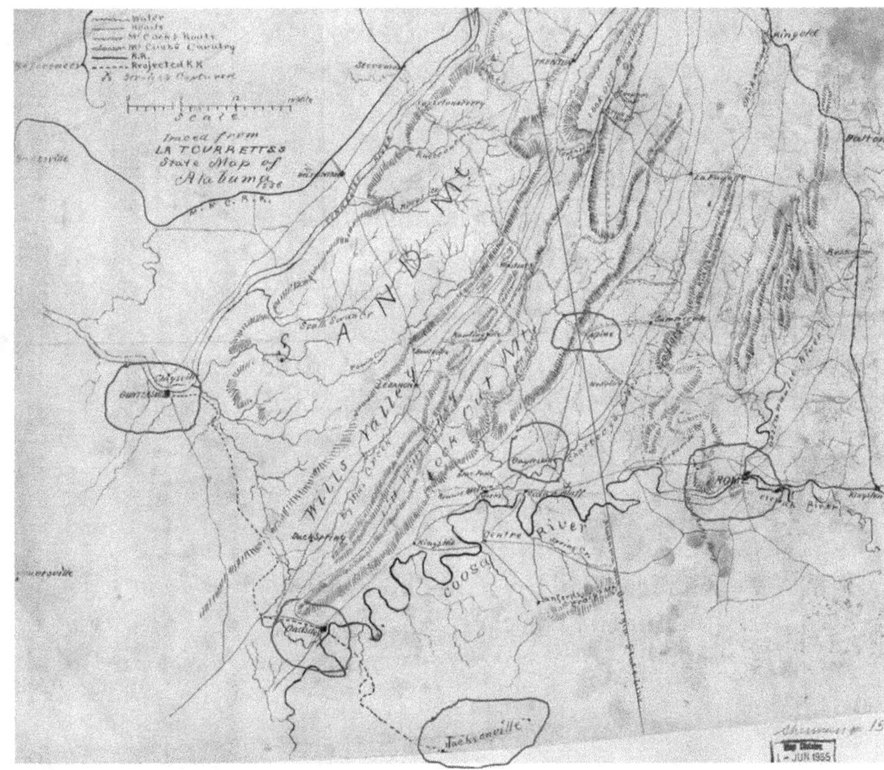

## October 24, 1864

In Atlanta, Ga, 10-year-old Carrie Berry writes in her diary, "Mon. Oct. 24. I went to see Ellen Flemming this evening, one of my old school mates. I had a nice time. She is a very nice little girl."

In Alabama near Cedar Bluff, the pontoons from Rome came down the river under the cover of darkness as planned, arriving about three in the morning. General Sherman came also, from Gaylesville, to personally supervise the construction of the bridge across the Coosa River. From here he sends word to Army Chief of staff, Halleck, that his forces have gathered 2,000 wagon loads of corn and forage, and that his troops are "living high on the hog". The town of Cedar Bluff has already been burned, but Sherman orders General Schofield to send a division to further dismantle the stone structure of the iron works here. Hood keeps moving westward.

***

In Missouri, Confederate General Price continues to move his crippled force, with its long wagon train of supplies and plunder, along the Kansas border in a running fight all day with pursuing Federals. It begins to rain late in the day, and the roads begin to quagmire. He goes into camp just south of Westport, Mo, and in the evening, the Yankees catch up, getting into positions, planning attack first thing in the morning.

***

In Richmond, Brigadier General Archer is dead. He bravely fought in all the major battles of the Eastern theater until he was captured at Gettysburg. During his active service he has been sick much of the time, sometimes conducting his men in battle from a wagon bed, but his year in prison caused his health to deteriorate even more. Upon release in late August, he joined General Lee in the trenches of Petersburg, fought in the battle of Peebles Farm, then became so ill he retired to Richmond where he died today. General Archer never married and has no family.

**Confederate Brigadier General James Jay Archer**

## October 25, 1864

In Atlanta, Ga., Carrie Berry writes this in her diary, "Tues. Oct. 25. Zuie and I went around to spend the evening and we had a very nice time playing with our dolls. That is all I have to interest me. Ella has had my doll a week or two and Ella made her so many nice clothes that she was dressed up so fine."

In Gaylesville, Alabama, General Sherman is still undecided what to do. He cannot figure out Hood's intent. For right now Sherman will just sit in Gaylesville and have his cavalry follow hood, keeping a goodly distance, trying to determine if he will come back this way and threaten Rome or Atlanta. If he keeps going, he will become General Thomas' problem, and Sherman will go to Savannah.

***

In Missouri, Confederate General Price has pushed toward Kansas City with a much smaller force than the Federal defenders. He has won hard victories in Lexington, Little Blue River, and the Big Blue River, but the day before yesterday the reinforced Federal army dealt him a stunning defeat, and their pursuit has been relentless. Today, the pursuers have caught up as the Confederates attempt to cross Mine Creek. The day is a constant downpour and the roads are a muddy quagmire. The four-to-five-foot creek bank is slippery and crumbling into the deep rushing water. The confederates have single-shot muzzle loader rifles and reloading in the weather conditions is difficult. Many of them have fired one time and are charging close enough to the enemy to use their rifles as clubs, while the Yanks all have breech-loading rifles that weather does not affect, and many of them have repeating carbines. Today marks the end of Confederate effectiveness on the western side of the Mississippi River. Now the remainder of the Johnnies have to try to escape the pursuit as best they can.

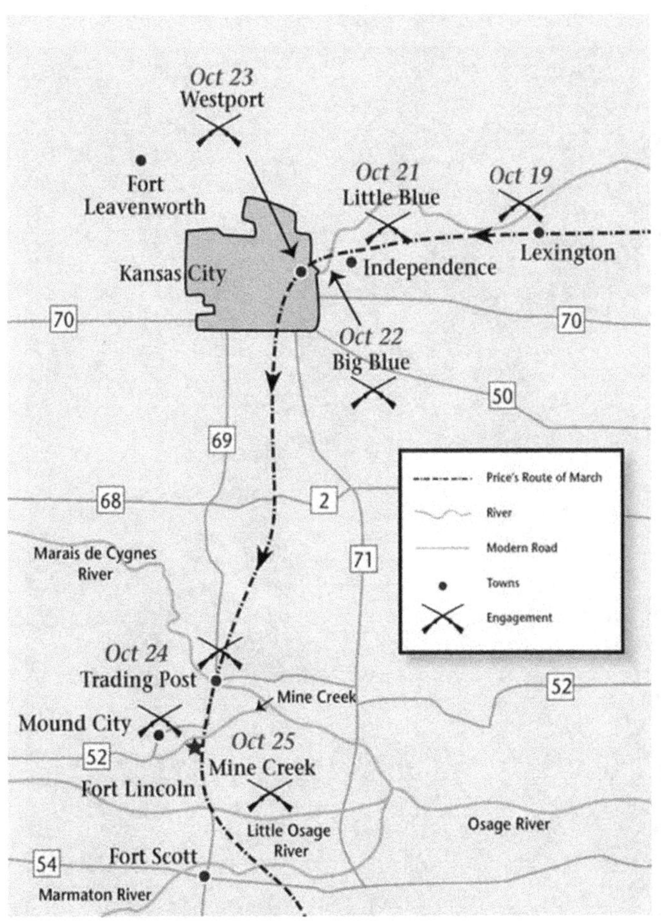


**Mine Creek Battle location**

## October 26, 1864

In Atlanta, GA, Carrie Berry writes in her diary, " Wednesday. Oct. 26. I have ben ironing nearly all day to day. I ran up to Aunties a little while this evening and she told me that she was going away, and I want to go too. I have ben begging Papa all of the evening."

In Northern Alabama, Confederate General Hood has learned, after he left Gadsden, that the Tennessee River Crossings at Guntersville are too heavily defended to affect a crossing without substantial loss of life, so he headed on toward Decatur. Today he receives word that Decatur is even heavier defended, so he moves on toward Florence.

***

In Virginia, the Petersburg and Richmond lines have been quiet for several weeks now, but there is increase of activity on the north side of the James. It looks as if the Federals are going to attack tomorrow.

***

In Missouri, after the slimiest man to wear the Confederate uniform, William T. Anderson, and his men pulled off the Centralia massacre last week, Union military leaders assigned Lt. Col. Samuel P Cox to kill Anderson, giving him 125 very experienced soldiers to help him do it. Soon after Anderson leaves Glasgow this morning, he is spotted, and Cox is told where he is. When attacked by Cox's force, Anderson charges them, continuing the charge after all the others, except one man, have retreated. His death is instantaneous when a bullet strikes his head just behind his ear. The murdering horse thief is photographed and displayed at the local courthouse for public viewing, then buried by the Union soldiers in a field near Richmond.

**William T. Anderson "Bloody Bill" having a bad day**

## October 27, 1864

In Atlanta, Carrie Berry writes in her diary, "Thurs. Oct. 27. I have ben running back and forth to Aunties all day carrying things what she gave me. She gave me so many things Mama says that I have got the house packing full of boxes, but I have got all I will get for Auntie is the last one that is left."

***

*Hancock attacking*

In Virginia, near the Petersburg lines, in an another attempt to cut General Lee's supply line of the Boydton Plank road, this morning Union General Hancock, with just over 30,000 troops, attacks Confederate General Heth with about 12,000 defenders all along the Confederate line. They run into Wade Hampton's Rebel cavalry, which is beaten back initially, but Heth and Hampton manage to put together a counter-attack that surrounds Hancock's forces, but are too thin in numbers and cannot take advantage.
Hancock then orders attacks on both Confederate flanks at Armstrong's Mill that are successful, being able to push into position to threaten encirclement of the Confederates, who have to withdraw away.

The Yankees are safe for the moment, outnumbering the Confederates in the area by a wide margin, but he is outside his own lines and in a very unstable position. He will withdraw his men back to the Federal lines under the cover of darkness, not knowing what Lee might send against him in the morning. Hancock is in poor health, never recovered from the wound that he received over a year ago at Gettysburg. Next month he will resign his field commission and go home. He will finish the war in non-combat positions, recovering from his wounds to run for President in 1880, narrowly losing to Republican Garfield.

## October 28, 1864

In Atlanta, GA, 10-year-old Carrie Berry is writing in her diary, "Fri. Oct. 28. Auntie left us this morning at eight o'clock. We all feel so sad to think that we are left alone. I don't know what I will do for some place to run to when I get lonesome."

In Virginia near Richmond and Petersburg, all the attacking Federals involved in yesterday's fighting that survived it are now withdrawn back into their works and probably will not come out again until spring.

***

In North Carolina on the Roanoke River, just outside Plymouth, as the Confederate ram "Albemarle" lay in mooring, Union Naval Lt. William Cushing moved into attack position late last night. He is commanding a launch with a 12-pound Dahlgren howitzer and a 14-foot spar, loaded with explosive and projecting into the water from the ship's bow. As he and his 22 -men crew approach, the sentries begin firing and ignite a huge signal bonfire to illuminate the action. Floating logs, chained together, protect the target from ramming, but Cushing orders full speed ahead and strikes the moss-covered barricade hard enough to slide his steam launch on top of the logs enough that the spar can slip beneath the ram, and the explosive is ignited with the pull of a rope attached to Cushing's hand. Almost simultaneously, "Albemarle's" gun blasts it's attacker point blank, destroying the launch and tossing it's crew into the water. The "Albemarle' quickly sinks, and Cushing strips off his uniform and swims to shore, where he hides until this afternoon, when he is able to steal a skiff from a Confederate patrol and venture downriver to Union forces and safety. Of his crew, one more escape, two drowned, and the remainder are captured. The much-feared Confederate ram "Albemarle" is done forever, and Lt Cushing is the North's newest hero.

## October 29, 1864

In Atlanta, Ga, 10-year-old Carrie Berry Writes in her diary, " Sat. Oct. 29. We all have felt very lonely to day. I went down to see Ella this evening and came by to see Aunt Marthy. She looks very lonely since Auntie has gone."

In Tennessee, near Paris Landing on the Tennessee River, Confederate General Nathan Bedford Forrest, who has not yet received the word that he is to join Hood in Alabama, has set up a gauntlet of hidden artillery that commands a mile stretch of the river. Today, his efforts pay off in the capture of the transport, "Mazeppa", towing a barge heavily laden with supplies, including 9,000 pairs of shoes. This is a pretty good gig, maybe he can milk it for a few more days, until word gets out he is here.

***

In St Louis Missouri, six Confederate prisoners held at the Gratiot Street prison have drawn black balls in the lottery among the prisoners. The ones who drew white balls are to be paroled, and the black-ball unfortunates are executed by firing squad today. This is a retaliation for the perceived murder of six Union soldiers and for the entertainment of the three thousand citizens that witness the event. Confederate Asa Ladd writes to his father about this day: *"Oct 29, 1864, My Dear Father, I am condemned to be shot today between the hours of two and four o'clock p.m.in retaliation for some men shot by Reeves (Major Wilson and six men). I am an innocent man and it is hard to die for another's sins. You can imagine my feelings when I think of you, my wife, and children. I want my family to come back to my old place. If you live till peace is made, I want you to settle up and pay off all my debts. You need have no uneasiness as to my future state for my faith is well founded and I fear no evil. God is my refuge and hiding place. Meet me in Heaven Good bye"*

***

**In New York, the weekly "Harper's Weekly" publishes today a drawing by their artist, Waud, portraying the absentee voting in the Presidential election by their soldiers.**

## October 30, 1864

In Atlanta, GA, Carrie Berry writes in her diary, " Sun. Oct. 30. I have ben over to Julia Lowry this evening. They are all ready to move and it looks like every body is going to leave here from the way the soldiers are moving about. Our sargent left us this morning. We all were sorry to part with him. He has ben a very good friend to us."

In Alabama, Reb Generals Hood and Beauregard continue to move across the State, now toward Tuscumbia.

General Sherman has moved his headquarters back to Rome where he is orchestrating movements all over the place. Major Gen Schofield is moving toward Resaca, taking responsibility for the railroad and will begin to be under the orders of General Thomas. Maj. Gen. Jeff C. Davis is moving to Kingston to await further orders. Major General Howard is moving to Coosa, there to cross the river, moving into Cave Spring, Cedartown, Van Wert, Dallas, and set up headquarters at Smyrna Campground. Brig. Gen. John Corse will hold his Division at Rome until further orders.

***

This morning, near Paris Tennessee, the steamer "Anna" is the first to run the gauntlet of Rebel guns on the Tennessee River under the command of Nathan B Forrest. "Anna" pretends to surrender, but as the guns silence, she makes a run and escapes, very severely damaged. Next the Federal gunboat, "Undine" convoying the transport "Venus" with two barges. This time the gunners are able to disable and capture both vessels, as well as another transport, the "Cheeseman". "Cheeseman' is irreparably damaged, so its cargo is salvaged, and the vessel is burned. The Confederates set about repairing the two damaged prizes to do service for the South

**Gunship "Undine"**

## October 31, 1864

In Atlanta, GA, Carrie Berry writes this in her diary, "Mon. Oct. 31. All of the soldiers have left from behind the garden and all ,but every thing seems so quiet. Ella came up this evening and spent the evening with me."

In Georgia, the Western and Atlantic Railroad is now operational, albeit patched together, rather than repaired, and it has much work to do. General Sherman has ordered all the surplus supplies and wounded men be sent from Atlanta to Chattanooga. General Thomas is screaming over the telegraph that Sherman has given him an adequate force to deal with Hood, but he doesn't have them yet, and Hood is crossing the Tennessee River at Florence. He needs the troops under Schofield that Sherman has sent to Resaca so Sherman orders the trains to pick up those troops as they arrive in Resaca and transport them to Columbia, Tennessee where they will be in good shape to help defend against Hood. This will help Thomas, but the troops ordered from Missouri and Mississippi have not arrived. Neither have the new recruits been seen either.

***

Near Paris Landing on the Tennessee River, Confederate Major General Nathan B. Forrest has decided to repair both the "Undine" and the "Venus" and equip them both to be Confederate gunboats. Already the "Undine" has twenty twelve-pounder guns, and Forrest adds two twenty-pound guns, making her more formidable than anything else on the river. He puts another pair of twenty-pounders on the "Venusm," creating a good "side kick" for the "Undine." Forrest is staffing the vessels with cavalrymen who are experienced seamen, calling them "Horse Marines." Their goal, when ready, is to proceed to Johnsonville and destroy the vast depot of supplies the Federals have accumulated and are relying on.

**There is great celebration in Carson City and Washington DC today because of the admission of Nevada to the United States. Although normally, a territory has to have 60,000 people to become a state, most of the 40,000 folks in Nevada will vote Republican in the election next week. Also, the 40,000 are more attractive than average because of their home being infested with silver, just beneath the soil.**

**Early Carson City**

## November 1, 1864

In Atlanta, GA, Carrie Berry writes in her diary, "Tues. Nov. 1. I have ben sewing on Sisters apron while Mama made me a pare of shoes and I have ben up to Aunt Marthy once or twice."

In northern Alabama, things are not going well with the plans of Confederate General Hood. The supplies he had thought would be waiting for him in Tuscumbia are not there, nor will they be for some time. The railroad has still not completed repairs, there being a ten-mile gap that has to be completed. Forrest has not even started to him yet, and the weather has turned really foul, impeding any progress of any sort.

In Rome, Georgia, in Union General Sherman's telegraph communication with General Grant, his boss, he can tell that Grant is having second thoughts about permitting his trip to the seacoast, wanting him to settle with Hood once and for all before he goes. Sherman, again, states his case, "*General Thomas has near Athens and Pulaski Stanley's corps, about 15,000 strong, and Schofield's corps, 10,000, en route by rail, and has at least 20,000 to 25,000 men, with new regiments and conscripts arriving all the time; also Rosecrans promises the two divisions of Smith and Mower, belonging to me, but I doubt if they can reach Tennessee in less than ten days.*" I don't know why Sherman didn't mention the 20,000 that Thomas has in Nashville, but he, Thomas, has plenty of men to deal with the Confederates under Hood, if he can just get them all together.

***

There is celebration among the 87,000 enslaved Negros of the State of Maryland today. The new State Constitution that abolishes slavery is adopted, and all slaves are freed. You will remember that the Emancipation Proclamation only freed those slaves *"in states now under rebellion against the United States."* Maryland never seceded because Lincoln had their legislature arrested so they could not vote for secession. But now, with the Republican legislature installed, emancipation is in the hands of Maryland, not of the Federal Govt.

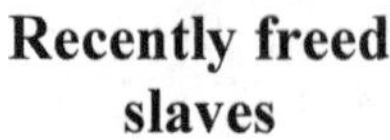

**Recently freed slaves**

## November 2, 1864

In Atlanta, GA, Carrie Berry writes in her diary, "Wed. Nov. 2. It has ben a cold and rainy day. I have ben sewing to day and studying some too. Papa has made my shoes and they are very nice."

In North Georgia, Union General Sherman is having a great day in spite of the weather. This morning he receives a telegram from General Grant finally granting full permission to take his army across the state of Georgia to the coast: *" I do not see that you can withdraw from where you are to follow Hood, without giving up all we have gained in territory. I say, then, go on as you propose. U. S. GRANT, Lieutenant-General".*

Sherman moves his headquarters from Rome to Kingston to be more centrally located to all his current interests, literally turning his back on Hood's army, waiting beside the Tennessee River at Tuscumbia.

Also, on the Tennessee River traveling upward from Paris Landing toward Johnsonville, Nathan B. Forrest's little navy of two gunboats is moving slowly, watching his artillery move on nearby roads, trying to keep up with the boats. In an encounter today, the smaller of the two gunboats, "Venus", is grounded by an attack of two Union gunboats, striking and moving on before the shore batteries can be brought to bear. "Undine" is slightly damaged but can continue, so the unusual force moves onward toward the fat Union supply depot ahead.

Today, English blockade runner "Lucy" is captured in the Gulfstream off the shores of North Carolina by a US Navy warship. A Confederate signal corpsman, serving as pilot, is on board and taken as a prisoner-of war. Sidney Clopton Lanier refuses the advice of the British officers to don one of their uniforms and pretend to be one of them. As a result of capture Lanier is taken for incarceration in a military prison at Point Lookout in Maryland where he will contract tuberculosis from which he will suffer the remainder of his shortened life before it finally kills him at the age of 39 years old, but not before he becomes one of the South's most beloved poets.

**Sidney Lanier**

## November 3, 1864

In Atlanta, GA., Carrie Berry makes her daily record in her diary, "Thurs. Nov. 3. I ironed some this morning and sewed some this evening. Me and Zuie went up to see Aunt Marthy."

In the East, the Petersburg-Richmond area, all is quiet. Grant has been ordered by the Secretary of War to not initiate any fights until after the upcoming election. Any loss or perceived loss would affect the President's chances for re-election.

***

In the West it is a time of waiting for the Rebels and troop movements for the Federals. For General Forrest, he is waiting until his men can get into position with their batteries tonight so that he can blast away at the Johnsonville depot defenses in the morning. Here is General Sherman's accurate description of the situation in the west today: *"Major-General HALLECK: The situation of affairs now is as follows: Beauregard, with Hood's army, is now at Florence, with a pontoon bridge, protected from our gun-boats below by the Colbert Shoals; from above by the Muscle Shoals. He has with him Wheeler's and Roddey's cavalry. Forrest's cavalry is down about Fort Heiman. The country round about Florence has been again and again devastated during the past three years, and Beauregard must be dependent on the Mobile and Ohio Railroad, which also has been broken and patched up in its whole extent. He purposes and promises his men to invade Middle Tennessee, for the purpose of making me let go Georgia. The moment I detected that he had passed Gadsden, I detached the Fourth Corps (General Stanley's) 15,000 strong, which is now at Pulaski, and subsequently the Twenty-third Corps (Schofield's), 10,000, which is now on the cars, moving to Nashville. This gives Thomas two full corps, and about 5,000 cavalry, besides, 10,000 dismounted cavalry and all the new troops recently sent to Tennessee, and the railroad guards, with which to encounter Beauregard, should he advance farther. In addition, Thomas will have the active co-operation of the gun-boats above and below the shoals, and the two Divisions of Smith and Mower, en route from Missouri. I therefore feel no uneasiness as to Tennessee, and have ordered Thomas to assume the offensive, in the direction of Selma, Ala."*

**Maj. Gen. Henry Halleck**

## November 4, 1864

In Atlanta, Carrie Berry writes, "Fri. Nov. 4. Nothing of interest has happened to day. It is the reporte that the federals are going to have to leave Atlanta and we are afraid that we will have to leave too."

From Kingston, GA, Union General Sherman issues orders to begin to destroy the Western and Atlantic Railroad from the Oostanaula bridge to Atlanta. He divides the road into three sections and assigns one corps per section for destruction. To General Corse in Rome, he orders, *"The commanding general directs that on receiving notice to evacuate Rome, by telegraph, of which he will give you as much notice in advance as circumstances will permit, that you destroy in the most effective manner, by fire or otherwise, all bridges, foundries, shops of all kinds and description, barracks, warehouses, and buildings especially adapted to armed use, lumber or timber, as also all cars off the track, or material that cannot be removed, and then remove your command, via Kingston and Allatoona, to Marietta, and report to General Howard, commanding Army of the Tennessee."*

On the Tennessee River at Johnsonville, TN, Confederate General Nathan B Forrest has moved his artillery into position to both restrict travel on the river and in three additional positions for destruction of the Federal depot and wharves. This morning the Federals send nine gunboats to engage the "Undine", recently captured and used by Forrest. The "Undine" is quickly overwhelmed, and the Rebels abandon ship, destroying her with fire. The shore batteries of Forrest's gunners open up a devastating fire on the enemy fleet, destroying three gunboats and removing the will to fight from the others who move away. The Confederate guns then destroy the supply vessels and warehouses that are filled with enemy ordinance. Union losses are 4 gunboats, 14 transports, 20 barges, 26 pieces of artillery, $6,700,000 worth of property, and 150 prisoners.

**Union Supply Depot at Johnsonville 1864**

## November 5, 1864

In Atlanta, Carrie Berry writes in her diary, "Sat. Nov. 5. I have hemmed Sister an apron and skirt. Mama has ben buisy drying up some tallow and I had to stay in the house."

On the Tennessee River, the Federal forces at Johnsonville are hunkered down to await the onslaught of Reb General Forrest. General Thomas, from Nashville, is trying frantically to get some help for them on the way. Forrest is already, silently moving away toward Corinth, leaving one battery for last, to send a few rounds into the fortifications, enough that the Yanks will keep their heads down for most of the day. Forrest receives his orders from General Taylor to join Hood at Florence, and he moves in that direction, with 9,000 pairs of Yankee shoes heading for Rebel feet.

In North Georgia, from Kingston, Union General Sherman issues orders that start General Howard's Corps to move from Smyrna to Atlanta to start filling their wagons with supplies for the trip. To make room for them he sends the following orders to General Slocum, occupying the City at present: " November 5, 1864. Major-General SLOCUM, Atlanta, Ga.: Load your trains and prepare your command at once for the march; move it out on the McDonough road some two miles and await your orders for the final move. You will leave your provost guard and such details as General Easton and Colonel Beckwith may wish."

SHERMAN, Major-General"

**Atlanta Depot Just before destruction**

## November 6, 1864

In Atlanta, GA, 10-year-old Carrie Berry writes in her diary, "Sun Nov. 6. Cold and cloudy day. Mama sent me around to Mrs. Lesters this morning to see if she was going away and she said she was going to stick tite to her house."

Mrs. Lester might change her mind if she could see the town of Cassville, GA this morning. Yesterday, General Sherman, headquartered a couple of miles away ordered the Fifth Ohio to destroy the town : *"that not a house be left within the limits of the incorporation, except the churches."* The 1300 residents were given time to get most of their things outside and the torch was applied to all except the three churches, one house being used as a hospital, and one house belonging to a Mason. This morning finds the citizens in make-shift tents huddled against the cold rain falling over the area. The thriving town will not be rebuilt; nearby Cartersville will gain in population.

From Tuscumbia, Alabama, General Hood communicates with President Davis, "*General Wheeler reports from Blue Mountain that Sherman is moving one corps to Chattanooga and one corps to Tennessee and three to Marietta. I hope to march for Middle Tennessee by the 8th or 9th instant. Should he move two or three corps south from Atlanta. I think it will be the best thing that could happen for our general good. General Beauregard agrees with me as to my plan of operations. Would like to be informed if any forces are sent from Grant or Sheridan to Nashville."*

***

In Chicago, Illinois, paroled Confederates and prominent Copperheads are arrested today in response to strong rumors that the detestable prisoner of war camp, Camp Douglas, is to be attacked and the prisoners freed to help disrupt the National election the day after tomorrow. Most of those arrested will be cleared and released. Several that have accumulated stashes of weapons will remain incarcerated.

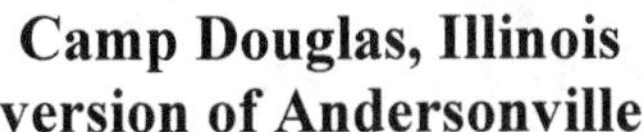

**Camp Douglas, Illinois version of Andersonville**

## November 7, 1864

In Atlanta, GA, Carrie Berry is distraught as she writes in her diary, "Mon Nov. 7. Every boddie seems to be in confusion. The black wimmen are running around trying to get up north for fear that the Rebels will come in and take them."

The word is out that the Federal Army is leaving. It will soon become even more apparent because of this order by General Sherman to his Chief Engineer: *"Captain O. M. POE, Atlanta, Ga.: I want you to take special charge of the destruction in Atlanta of all depots, car-houses, shops, factories, foundries, &c., being careful to knock down all furnace chimneys, and break down their arches; fire will do most of the work.".* From Kingston, Sherman issues a strange order to General Corse in Rome, "B*rigadier-General CORSE, Rome, Ga. :The 10th is as early as I expect to commence the movement. The Army of the Tennessee is being paid off. Send with your foraging party to Texas Valley tomorrow at least a brigade, and let them feel out to the gap. Stay there tomorrow night and come in next morning. I want it to produce a certain effect.*"

***

In Richmond, the second meeting of the Confederate Congress elected in 1862 begins work once more with a speech from President Davis who downplays the seriousness of the loss of Atlanta, "There are no vital points on the preservation of which the continued existence of the Confederacy depends." Then he suggests that the Army be allowed to purchase slaves for work in the War effort.

***

In the Shenandoah Valley, Union Generals Sheridan and Custer have started executing persons they suspect of being part of Mosby's Rangers. So far, they have executed seven men, and Mosby is now to retaliate. Yesterday he held a raffle with 27 Federal prisoners which decided which 7 of them would be killed this morning near the lines of General Sheridan. For various reasons, only three of the seven are hanged, but Mosby leaves Sheridan a note that will stop the executions for the duration of the war. The note said that Mosby would not execute any more unless the Yankees do.......

## November 8, 1864

In Atlanta, Carrie Berry writes about her day in her diary, "Tues. Nov. 8. This is Zuie's birthday and she has be very smart. We lost our last hog this morning early. Soldiers took him out of the pen. Me and Buddie went around to hunt for him and every where that we inquired, they would say that they saw two soldiers driving off to kill him. We will have to live on bread."

In Kingston, GA, at Sherman's headquarters he has his Aide de Camp issue the following field order announcing the reorganization of his command: "*The general commanding deems it proper at this time to inform the officers and men of the Fourteenth, Fifteenth, Seventeenth, and Twentieth Corps, that he has organized them into an army for a special purpose, well known to the War Department from our present base, and a long and difficult march to a new one. All the chances of war have been considered and provided for, as far as human sagacity can. All he asks of you is to maintain that discipline, patience, and courage, which have characterized you in the past; and he hopes, through you, to strike a blow at our enemy that will have a material effect in producing what we all so much desire, his complete overthrow. Of all things, the most important is, that the men, during marches and in camp, keep their places and do not scatter about as stragglers or foragers, to be picked up by a hostile people in detail. It is also of the utmost importance that our wagons should not be loaded with any thing but provisions and ammunition. All surplus servants, non-combatants, and refugees should now go to the rear, and none should be encouraged to encumber us on the march. At some future time, we will be able to provide for the poor whites and blacks who seek to escape the bondage under which they are now suffering. With these few simple cautions, he hopes to lead you to achievements equal in importance to those of the past.*"

***

**In the North, the long-anticipated election is held today with Abraham Lincoln securing 55 percent of the popular vote, 2,330,552 votes to McPherson's tally of 1,835,595.**

## November 9, 1864

In cold, rainy, Atlanta, GA, Carrie Berry writes in her diary, "Wed. Nov. 9. Aunt Marthy got fritened last night and began to pack to leave and we have ben bringing thing home that she gave us."

In southeast Missouri, a huge tornado touches down and crosses the Mississippi River into Chester, Ill., killing four people there and moving further into Illinois near Richview where it kills another, making it the most deadly weather event in Illinois history and for at least 150 years in the future.

***

In Georgia, William T. Sherman issues marching orders to his forces today. He starts with establishing a left wing (14th and 20th Corps, commander Gen. Henry Slocum) and a right wing (17th and 15th Corps, under Gen. O. O. Howard). These wing structures will be the main maneuvering and attack units of the campaign, and they will travel as nearly parallel as possible, by four roads, converging from time to time as ordered. Wagons will not accompany each regiment, only an ammunition wagon and an ambulance. The only supply wagons will be for ammunition and for ten days food and three days forage; these to follow each corps. General food supplies will be provided by foraging parties which will not be allowed to enter houses (Dream on), but only seize available food in the fields or in the barns. Livestock may be taken at will. Negros may be taken as long as they are fit to work and can be helpful to the movement, but are not to be. "just more mouths to feed". On the march, the roads are to be given to the artillery and wagons, and the troops are to march to the side, through the fields, coming to the assistance of the wagons at steep hills and bad crossings of streams.

***

In Dornum, Germany, Miene Schonberg is born. At the age of 16, she will immigrate to the US with her parents where she will eventually meet and marry Simon Marrix. They will Americanized their names and call themselves Sam and Minnie Marx. She will eventually give birth to six sons, five of whom will become show business familiars to the American public. In order of their birth they will be, Manfred (dead at two), Leonard (Chico), Adolph (Harpo), Julius Henry (Groucho), Milton (Gummo), and Herbert (Zeppo).

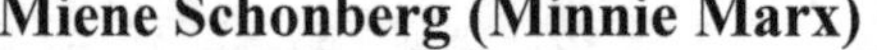

**Miene Schonberg (Minnie Marx)**

## November 10, 1864

In Atlanta, GA, Carrie Berry writes in her diary, "Thurs. Nov. 10. Me and silvie ironed to day and we were done by twelve o'clock and I hemmed Sister and apron in the afternoon. Aunt Marthy did not get off to day and we hope that she will stay."

In the Shenandoah Valley of Virginia, Confederate General Early is moving from New Market toward the forces of Union General Sheridan to try to make the Yanks think he is coming after them. In truth, he hasn't enough men to even get their attention.

In Washington, Abraham Lincoln is spending his days writing speeches to deliver to the groups who are coming every night to serenade him.

In Rome, Georgia, Union General Corse is accomplishing the work of the devil, per the orders of the devil himself, Sherman. During the day and night, tonight, the following are destroyed, as reported by Charles Norton of Rome: *"Cunningham's old store was burnt, full of cotton; both railroad depots; all of Noble's Foundry and rolling mill; Sloane and Cooper's warehouse with 200 or 300 bags of cotton; the Etowah House; the bank and buildings adjoining it, belonging to Meyerhardt. Sloan's house was not burnt. Ward's house, with three small buildings adjoining the back store, where I had cotton; the jail and the one-story dwelling of the Thomas R. Perry's, said to belong to C.H. Smith; Cohen's mill, Ford's house at the forks of the road, D. R. Mitchell's brick home near his steam mill, and the brick house out by the lime sink, owned by Mrs. Stevens."* The most spectacular fire of all is the burning of the temporary barracks, in the wee hours of tomorrow morning when all is ready to move toward Kingston. When the Federals leave, there being few healthy men in town, the marauding "scouts", deserters, renegades, and conscription evaders will begin to raid, stealing anything useful that is left.

**Rome, GA, during the Occupation of 1864**

## November 11, 1864

In Atlanta, GA, Carrie Berry writes in her diary, " Fri. Nov. 11. This is the last day that cars are going out to Chattanooga. We are erbliged to stay here now. Aunt Marthy went down to the carshed and I expect that she got off as she has not ben back."

In North Georgia, most of Union General Corse's Corps left Rome last night with their tents and surplus equipment in the camps. They slept until about 3 AM about six miles out the Kingston Rd, and this morning, they move on into Kingston where Sherman is headquartered. Lt. Cornelius C. Platter of the 81st Ohio Volunteer infantry writes in his diary, " The Railroad Depots Foundry and every thing of value to the enemy in Rome was destroyed. All the way from Rome to Kingston the road was lined with "contrabands" of all ages sizes and sexes - It was indeed a novel sight to see these people fleeing from Slavery. Every one was loaded - some with bundles of clothes and bedding larger than themselves.".

From Kingston, General Sherman has ordered all southbound shipping to cease and all rolling stock be sent northward to Chattanooga. All units of his armies that are going to the coast with him are ordered to move to Atlanta, or near there, to gain supplies and be organized into the two wings of his advancement. He issues the following ominous order to his commander of engineers in Atlanta: *"Captain O. M. POE, Atlanta, Ga.: You may commence the work of destruction at once, but don't use fire until toward the last moment. W. T. SHERMAN, Major-General"*

**Lt. Cornelius C. Platter of the 81st Ohio is a low-ranking officer and prolific writer whose work is made available to me by the Hargrett Rare Book and Manuscript Library of the University of Georgia. I can follow him through the end of the War. Carrie Berry's diary does not exist past the first week in January. The two of them will help me through the next few months.**

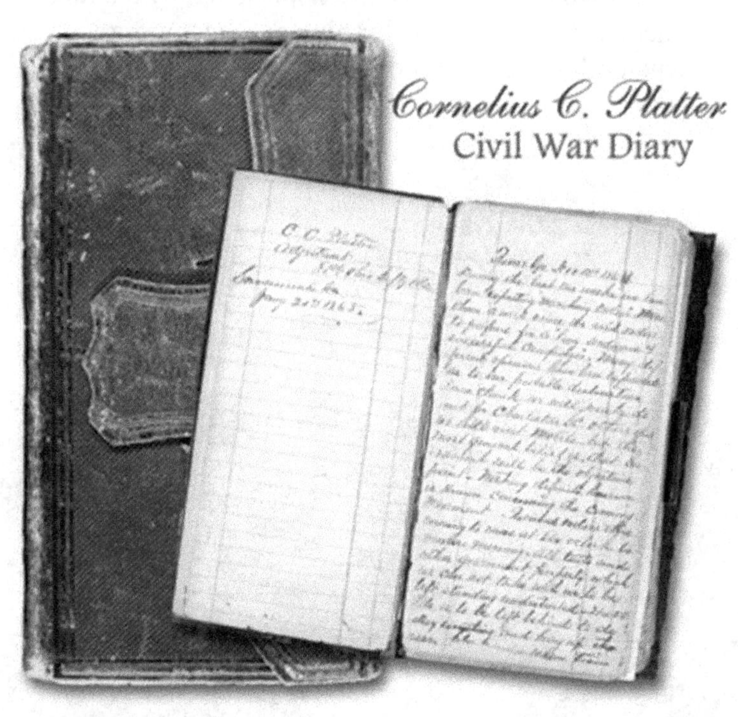

## November 12, 1864

In Atlanta, Ga, Carrie Berry is discovering who the "nice Yankee soldiers" really are, as evidenced in her diary entry for today, "Sat. Nov. 12. We were fritened almost to death last night. Some mean soldiers set several houses on fire in different parts of the town. I could not go to sleep for fear that they would set our house on fire. We all dred the next few days to come for they said that they would set the last house on fire if they had to leave this place."

Union General Sherman sends this to General Howard who is camped at Smyrna Campground: *"I start this morning. As soon as all the trains have passed north you may begin the work on the railroad. I want your army across the Chattahoochee on the third day. J. E. Smith and Corse are marching today. Davis will leave here in a few hours."*

General Corse asks permission to destroy Cedartown and Van Wert, but Sherman tells him to "wait", effectively saving the towns. That is probably why they did not burn the cave at Cave Spring also. Sherman too, leaves Kingston, heading for Atlanta, but will spend the night tonight at Allatoona.

Union Lt. Cornelius C Platter writes about his day in his diary, "Up at 2 A.M. had breakfast at 3 AM were under way at the appointed time our Brigade having the advance. Reached Cassville by daylight. The place was burned by our troops last Summer and presented nothing but a mass of ruins. Only two houses are standing and they are churches. Reached Cartersville at 10 AM where we halted several hours. Everything at Cartersville has been destroyed today." Platter must have been at Cartersville late in the day, because Sherman is there for lunch, at the local hotel, then the town is torched. Sherman sends his last message to General Thomas in Nashville from Cartersville before the line is cut. He will be out of communication until December 13. The railroad bridge across the Etowah at Emerson, just south of Cartersville is burned late this afternoon also. Although the bridge will be rebuilt, it will be abandoned in future years but the stone pillars, constructed by future Oakland Cemetery resident, Thomas Crusselle, will still be there at least 150 years from now.

## November 13, 1864

In Atlanta, GA., a very worried Carrie Berry writes in her diary, "Sun. Nov. 13. The federal soldiers have ben coming to day and burning houses and I have ben looking at them come in nearly all day."

***

On this Sunday morning in Bryantown, Maryland, John Wilkes Booth first meets Dr. Samuel Mudd, at St Mary's Church. It is to Dr. Mudd's house that Wilkes will flee to have his broken leg attended after the Lincoln assassination.

***

In Alabama, Confederate Generals Hood and Beauregard have about had enough of each other and today, Hood moves his headquarters from Tuscumbia across the Tennessee River to Florence where he can have some distance from Beauregard.

***

In Georgia, Union General Sherman travels from Allatoona to Marietta where he will spend the night. He finds that his cavalry under Kilpatrick has already been there, and the town is destroyed by fire, businesses, houses, everything. Sherman's infantry destroys Acworth as all forces move toward Atlanta where they will combine for the invasion of South Georgia. Destruction has already begun within the City and will take several days, but the combined force will be just over 65,000 men, including 5,000 cavalry. Union Lt. Cornelius Platter writes in his diary from the base of Kennesaw Mountain where he is camped tonight, "Up at 4 AM. and breakfast at 5 Rec'd a mail this morning just before starting. Suppose it will be our last mail for some time. Rec'd one letter from home - from "Sib" - We moved at 8 A.M. our Brigade having the rear. We passed over historic ground today Ackworth. Big Shanty. & Kennesaw Mt [Mountain] - they looked very familiar - the two former were entirely destroyed by fire which was done by the "Yankee vandals" The 14 were destroying the RR at Ackworth. - At Big Shanty we found the RR. completely destroyed - ties burnt and rails bent. We are now certain that we are entirely cut off from communication with the north and are an isolated command."......

**Federal Occupying camp near the railroad complex in Atlanta (Trout House Hotel and Masonic Lodge in the background)**

## November 14, 1864

In Atlanta, GA, Carrie Berry is having another frightful day as evidenced by her diary entry, "Mon. Nov. 14. They came burning Atlanta to day. We all dread it because they say that they will burn the last house before they stop. We will dread it."

In Alabama on the Tennessee River at Florence, the long-awaited, tired Confederate horsemen of Nathan Bedford Forrest reach General Hood's forces to support his campaign into Tennessee. Much of Hood's army is still across the rain-swollen river and cannot get across. It does not matter; the supply train isn't running yet anyway. There will be more delay.

In Atlanta, General Sherman's armies continue to come in to be better outfitted for the journey ahead. Some of them are departing; General Slocum is taking a division of the 20th Corps to Decatur and Stone Mountain for destruction today, and General Kilpatrick's cavalry is heading for Jonesboro and McDonough. General Sherman has arrived in town and resumed his headquarters in the Neal house (also known as Judge Lyon's). Sherman has this to say about conditions as he finds them: *"Colonel Poe, United States Engineers, of my staff, has been busy in his special task of destruction. He has a large force at work, has leveled the great depot, round house, and the machine-shops of the Georgia Railroad, and applied fire to the wreck. One of these machine-shops had been used by the rebels as an arsenal, and in it were stored piles of shot and shell, some of which proved to be loaded. Tonight, was made hideous by the bursting of shells, whose fragments came uncomfortably, near Judge Lyon's house, in which I am quartered. The fire also reached the block of stores near the depot, and the heart of the city was in flames all night, but the fire did not reach the parts of Atlanta where the court-house is, or the great mass of dwelling houses."*

Most of the fire destruction has not begun yet. There is much hand work to do on machinery and masonry that will not burn. The work force accomplishing this has grown to tens of thousands, breaking gears, pulling down metal and masonry buildings, **prying up rails**, etc. Much fire tomorrow.

## November 15, 1864

In Atlanta, a very distressed Carrie Berry writes in her diary, "Tues. Nov. 15. This has ben a dreadful day. Things have ben burning all around us. We dread to night because we do not know what moment that they will set our house on fire. We have had a gard a little while after dinner and we feel a little more protected.

In north Georgia, the cities of Cassville, Kingston, Rome, Cartersville, Acworth, and Marietta lie smoldering and devastated. The railroad, all the way from Atlanta to the Oostanaula River, is barren, devoid of rails, ties, and bridges. Even the telegraph poles have been cut down, leaving bark-less tree stumps as the only reminders they ever existed.

Most of Union General Sherman's army is now in, or about, Atlanta, engaged in destruction of the military, industrial buildings and machinery with sledge hammers, pry bars, improvising battering rams, as necessary. Fire has been used sparingly, mostly on the wood and tar of the commercial building roofs after the buildings are down. General Howard and his Corps moved out this morning toward Jonesboro intending to meet Sherman in Milledgeville in seven days. Likewise, General Slocum moved his Corps off the east by Decatur and Stone Mountain toward Madison, also to converge on Milledgeville in seven days. General Sherman is staying one more night in Atlanta with the 14th Corps to supervise the continuing destruction of the City.

Late this afternoon the fires start in earnest, some of them ordered and some not. The spirit of wantonness carries into the downtown and residential areas as well as the industrial. By darkness come, a fiery tempest storms across the Gate City of the South, blasting all before it, with few buildings escaping its wrath.......God help these people tonight.

## November 16, 1864

In Atlanta, GA, 10-year-old Carrie Berry writes in her diary, "Wed. Nov. 16. Oh, what a night we had. They came burning the store house and about night it looked like the whole town was on fire. We all set up all night. If we had not set up our house would have ben burnt up for the fire was very near and the soldiers were going around setting houses on fire where they were not watched. They behaved very badly. They all left the town about one o'clock this evening and we were glad when they left for no body know what we have suffered since they came in."

All night and through the morning columns of bluecoats are leaving Atlanta. Others are completing the devastation of the City with torches. Future Oakland Resident Dr. Noel D'Alvigny, who is in charge of the Atlanta Medical College hospital, goes there to see how much damage is done, and to his surprise, it has not been burned yet. Other staff are arriving for the same reason, so D'Alvigny bandages them and fills the empty beds with "fake" wounded. When the Yankees do come for the torching, not even they are pigs enough to torch a building full of wounded men, so they move on, warning that they would be back, but they moved out with the rest, leaving the building for good service in the future. Union General Sherman will have this to say about this morning when he writes his memoirs: "*...About 7 a.m. we rode out of Atlanta by the Decatur road, filled by the marching troops and wagons of the Fourteenth Corps; and reaching the hill, just outside of the old rebel works, we naturally paused to look back upon the scenes of our past battles. We stood upon the very ground whereon was fought the bloody battle of July 22d, and could see the copse of wood where McPherson fell. Behind us lies Atlanta, smoldering and in ruins, the black smoke rising high in air, and hanging like a pall over the ruined city.... We turned our horses' heads to the east; Atlanta was soon lost behind the screen of trees and became a thing of the past....*"

## November 17, 1864

In Atlanta, Carrie Berry writes in her diary, " Thurs. Nov. 17 Everything was so quiet we were afraid that the yankees will come back and finish burning the houses but they did not. They have left. Some Confederates came in here to day and the town is full of country people seeing what they can find. We have ben picking up some things."

In Northern Alabama, General Beauregard is ordering General Hood to send one division, Jackson's division, of Forrest's cavalry to Major General Wheeler who is trying to oppose the march toward the sea of the Union Army under Sherman. Forrest says he cannot spare the men so Hood will ignore the order. Every effort is being pushed on the construction of the last railroad bridge that will allow supplies to flow by train into the Rebel camps. It will be soon that the expedition can be on its way.

***

In Georgia, it is the second day of marching, and the left wing of the Union army with Sherman, reaches and passes through, Covington. Swarms of Negros are flocking around Sherman, hailing him as the Messiah. He allows them to worship for a bit, then sends them on their way, all but the young strong men, whom he allows to go with the army and perform laborer-type tasks. The right wing of the Army goes through McDonough and moves toward Jackson. Union Lt Platter describes it thusly: " We recd orders to move before daylight for we had the advance of the Division We took the McDonough road and passed through a country never plouted by the foot of a "Yankee". The country is more open today than it was yesterday and the marching much easier. than heretofore. We passed through McDonaugh. the county seat of Henry Co which is a village of not much importance....Had some splendid persimmons today - the best I ever ate - A fine day for marching."

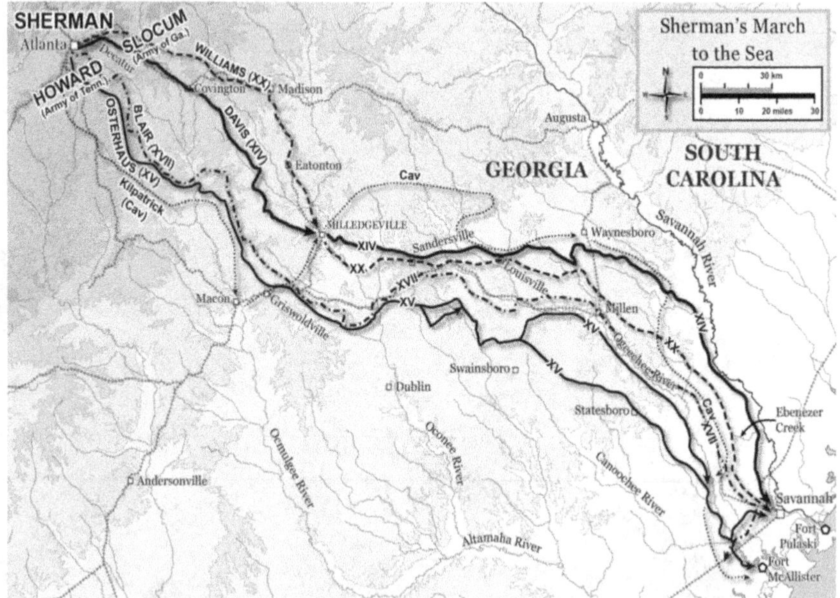


**The map showing the movements through Georgia by the Federals. Remember Sherman is with the left wing and Lt. Platter is with the right wing.**

## November 18, 1864

In Atlanta, GA, Carrie Berry writes in her diary, "Fri. Nov. 18. We children have ben plundering about to day seeing what we could find. Mama has been trying to straiten up for the house was torn up so bad."

In Northern Alabama, the working parties on the railroad have succeeded in making enough repairs that Confederate General Hood is now supplied well enough to start preparing to leave on his invasion of Tennessee.

Reb cavalry General, Joseph Wheeler arrives to defend Macon. Along with Howell Cobb, William Hardee and G. P. T. Beauregard, the city has about 10,000 men to defend it, about 3,000 soldiers and the remainder old men and boys, poorly armed.

In Georgia, the east wing of the Union Army's condition is reported by General Sherman, *"this corps turned south by Eatonton, for Milledgeville, the common objective. We find abundance of corn, molasses, meal, bacon, and sweet-potatoes. We take a good many cows and oxen, and a large number of mules. The country is quite rich, never before having been visited by a hostile army. The recent crop is excellent, just gathered and laid by for the winter... The skill and success of the men in collecting forage is exemplary. Each brigade commander has authority to detail a company of foragers, usually about fifty men, with one or two commissioned officers selected for their boldness and enterprise. This party is dispatched before daylight with a knowledge of the intended day's march and camp. They proceed on foot five or six miles from the route traveled by their brigade, and then visit every plantation and farm within range. They usually procure a wagon or family carriage, load it with bacon, corn-meal, turkeys, chickens, ducks, and every thing that could be used as food or forage, and then regain the main road, usually in advance of their train. When the trains come up, they deliver to the brigade commissary the supplies thus gathered by the way."* And the west wing is reported by Lt. Cornelius Platter, serving under General Corse, " We lived on the fat of the land today. The Reg't had more Fresh Pork Sweet Potatoes & etc than they could possibly use. Made a regular detail forage for the Regiment - We moved at 5 P.M and it was after dark when we passed through Jackson, which is an insignificant town. The C.H. was on fire when we passed through... we went about 6 mile and camped at 10 .PM. half way between Jackson & the ockmulgee River".

**Union Foragers**

## November 19, 1864

In Atlanta, GA, Carrie Berry writes in her diary, "Sat. Nov. 19. Mama and me have ben ironing all day. We have begun to feel at home but it does not look like Atlanta. The Citizens all met at the City Hall and . There are eighty men in town."

In Northern Alabama, Confederate General Hood starts his cavalry under Forrest, scouting ahead, toward Columbia. All others are preparing for the march, almost ready. The weather is terrible, cold, rainy, and sleet.

The second day of Yankee marching in Georgia finds Union Lt. Cornelius Platter in camp near the Okmulgee River writing in his diary: "Orders to march at 5 AM but it was seven oclock before we were under way. Has been a damp rainy day - We marched 4 mile to the ockmulgee River. at a point called the "7 Islands" - got there about 10 oclock and have been waiting for the 1st 2d and 3d Div. of our Corps to cross. - All the troops and wagons are over this evening except the 2d & 3d Brigades of our Div. Visited the "Ocmulgee Mills" and Factory this afternoon - both are very large and fine, especially the mill which is the finest I ever saw. Near the mill is a building containing 360 bales of cotton - suppose the Factory mill & cotton will be destroyed by our troops. There is quite a village here. Mostly women who were employed in the Factory. The "Ockmulgee" is nearly as large as the Chattahooche . is very rocky and Shallow. We have two pontoons to cross on. All surplus horses and mules are being taken to mount the 7th No news nor no fighting today -- Plenty to eat and every one enjoying the Campaign finely - We expect to cross the river tomorrow morning and then Ho! for Macon or Milledgeville - Distance 4 mile."

***

On the Eastern Coast the Federal blockade has been effective in keeping the South starved for goods, but the coast is so complicated around Wilmington, NC that some of the blockade runners are successful. Today the "CSS Chickamauga" returns from a cruise where she took several US Ships and is able to evade and outrun the opposition, bringing heavy cargo into the State.

**"CSS Chickamauga"**

## November 20, 1864

In Atlanta, as in Tennessee and middle Georgia, it is a cold, miserable day according to Carrie Berry," Sun. Nov 20. This has ben a cold and rainy day but the country people have ben in town plundering."

In Georgia, the two main directions of the Federal troops have been having a fine time of it, raiding, and pillaging the countryside. They are still getting wealthy on food and "stuff", but the November weather is turning against them. Sherman is with the most eastern column, the left wing and Lt. Platter is with the western column, the right wing: "We crossed the "Ocmulgee" this morning and advanced on the Monticello road passing through a country abounding in Hogs Cattle Chickens &c. On account of the recent rains the roads were very heavy. When we were about 4 mile from the river. we heard brisk firing in our rear - we supposed to be skirmishing, but it proved to be the Killing of worthless horses & mules at the "Crossing". The Citizens living near supposed a fight was on hands, and they were badly frightened -- The Factory & cotton were destroyed -- In our route we find many "Contrabands" but very few Citizens -- We marched 10 mile and went into camp at 8 P.M. in a beautiful pine grove. about half mile west of Monticello the County seat of Jasper Co. This has been a damp disagreeable day for marching -- Lost a very valuable ring today We are still in the dark as to our destination Rain in morning. Retired early."

Left Wing arrived in Rutledge yesterday. General John Geary is detached from the main column and ordered to make a feint on Augusta. He encounters resistance at Buckhead and burns bridges over the Oconee River and destroys a rail depot in the town. As the left wing approaches Madison, Georgia today, Joshua Hill, a Southern friend of Sherman's brother, John, rides out to meet the Federal forces hoping to meet with Sherman, whom he has met several times, to beg for the town to be spared. General Slocum, corps commander, grants the request, ordering the town to be spared destruction. In spite of the order, much looting occurs there, but the fine old houses are not destroyed.

**Madison, Georgia 1864**

## November 21, 1864

In Atlanta, Carrie Berry writes in her diary, "Mon. Nov. 21. This has ben such a bad day raining and snowing and we have stayed close by the fire."

In Northern Alabama, the remainder of the Confederate troops cross over the Tennessee River on a pontoon bridge to move into Florence where all of Hood's forces are moving out and into Tennessee, following the cavalry and Lee's Corps that left yesterday. The weather could be worse, but it is bad for travel, especially for the wagons and field pieces. General Beauregard has left this army to head for Augusta to see what can be done to impede the progress of Sherman's Army making havoc all through the State of Georgia.

In Georgia, Union Lt. Platter's diary says, "Up at 4 o'clock and found it raining very hard. it rained nearly all last night. Had orders to move at 4 am but did not move until 6.A.M. Brigade Hd. Qrs were "behind time" this morning and had to start without breakfast -- Passed through Monticello a very pretty village. Saw some beautiful gardens -- full of roses and flowers in full bloom. -- "Red white & blue" -- it was indeed strange to see such colors in "Dixie land" - "Pontoon train" in our front which delayed us very much - roads very heavy - rained most of the day - This has been about the most disagreeable day we have seen lately. Passed through Hillsboro. which was an insignificant town. but it is in ashes now - Went in camp half a mile south of Hillsboro in an open field - No wood nor rails near and a cold piercing wind blowing - We had rails hauled and made ourselves comfortable for the night - We came 11 mile. Our Div [Division] seems to be marching on a road by itself. Have not seen anything of the other Corps or Divisions since we left the Ocmulgee. We are still uncertain whether we will go to Macon or Milledgeville."

Confederate General Hardee has figured out that the Yankees are not going for Macon and orders the State guards (mostly old men and boys) to move to protect Augusta. Union General Walcutt's cavalry corps today moves into and destroys the foundry town of Griswoldville. Mostly a family-owned town and businesses, very proud of the pistols manufactured here for the Confederacy. In a few hours it is a perfect scene of devastation.

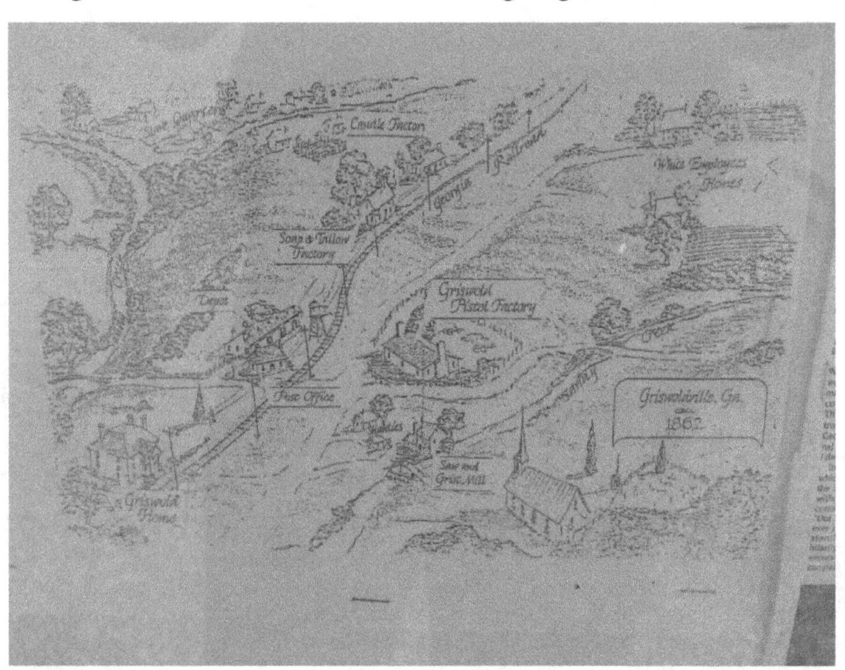

**Griswoldville, Georgia**

## November 22, 1864

In Atlanta, Carrie Berry writes in her diary, "Tues. Nov. 22. It is just a week to day since the federals were burning. Papa and Mama say that they feel very poor. We have not got anything but our little house. It is still very cold."

In Pulaski, Tennessee, Union General Schofield with 23,000 men learns of Hood's advancement across the Tennessee River and starts his own force toward Columbia, trying to arrive before Hood can. In effect, it is a race, because Hood is trying to get between Thomas in Nashville and Schofield.

In Middle Georgia, Union Lt. Platter describes the day, "A very very cold morning and continues cold and windy throughout the day - We enjoyed a snow storm in Central Georgia this morning. Roads still very heavy - Pontoon train delayed us very much."

Ten miles northeast of Macon, near Griswoldville, after burning much of the little town and destroying machinery, the Union forces have fortified themselves on the hill of a nearby farm and are waiting for the approaching Confederate force that the cavalry has informed them of. It is the division of about 3,000 irregulars (mainly old men and boys) that General Hardee ordered to Augusta yesterday. Apparently by accident, this Georgia Militia stumbled on this portion of Sherman's west wing and the sight of the damage to private property has clouded the wisdom of their inexperienced leaders. Militia General, Henry Kent McCay, a future state Supreme Court Justice and resident of Historic Oakland Cemetery is one of them. They attack in the bitter cold, across two creeks and marshy bottom land up the hill, against repeating rifles, and in spite of three valiant attempts they have to wilt away in the face of the veteran Union onslaught. Finally, those remaining retreat back to Macon. One of the Union officers will describe the scene later, ""*Old, gray-haired men and weakly looking men and little boys not over 15 years old lay dead or writhing in pain. I did pity those boys.*"

**Picture of map is by author**

## November 23, 1864

In Atlanta, GA, Carrie Berry writes, "Wed. Nov. 23. It has ben more pleasant to day. I went over with Ella to the city hall to get some hickery nuts but we did not get many. As we came home I went down with Ella to bery her guinea pig."

In Tennessee, the race to be the first to fortify Columbia is on between Hoods army and Schofield's Union army. Calvary of both sides are moving fast, but Schofield was nearer the mark when the race began and is the favorite right now.

In Middle Georgia, the right wing of Sherman's army is finding rough going, especially hauling the pontoons for temporary bridging, as told by Lt. Platter, "Wednesday, Nov 23rd 64, Up early, still very cold. Did not get started untill 10 am in consequence of the trains being so "mixed up" - Passed through Clinton County seat of Jones Co - A muddy dirty, delapidated Southern town --... Roads are still very heavy though they are better than they were yesterday. - We heard of the capture of Milledgeville which fell into our hands the 20th without a fight. When we left Clinton did not take the Macon road but proceeded towards Gordon - so I suppose we will not see Macon -.... Near Wallace at 10. P.M Distance marched 11 mile Soil sandy & productive. Country broken."

Yesterday, Union General Sherman, with the east wing of the Army, looted Reb General Howell Cobb's Plantation, and spent the night there. Today they ride into Milledgeville, taken by the cavalry two days ago. He uses Governor Brown's home as headquarters and in the State Capitol Union officers hold a mock legislature in which Georgia's ordinance of secession is repealed. Neither the Governor's Mansion nor the Capitol building is damaged, but many buildings are. More restraint is used here than in other places, but the railroad depot and factories and warehouses are burned, with flames spreading into residential areas in places. The State penitentiary is completely (see illustration) destroyed by fire (prisoners have been freed by Governor Brown and organized into fighting units, anticipating this destruction).

BURNING OF THE PENITENTIARY AT MILLEDGEVILLE, GA., NOVEMBER 23D, 1864.

## November 24, 1864

In Atlanta, Ga, 10-year-old Carrie Berry writes in her diary, "Thurs. Nov. 24. Papa went down to Grandpa's this morning and Mama has ben washing and I have ben nursing Sister for she was not very well. We all feel very lonesome."

In Tennessee, elements of Union General Schofield's army, under Jacob Cox reaches Columbia where the small garrison is under attack by portions of Reb General Forrest's cavalry. The blue infantry pushes the Confederates away, continuing to enter the little town, and fortify themselves on the south side. They are positioned so that they can interfere with any crossings General Hood might have planned when his numerically stronger force arrives.

This is the second year that US President Lincoln has proclaimed the last Thursday in November as Thanksgiving Day, and Northern troops in the South are celebrating as well as the citizens of the North. This, from Union Lt. Cornelius Platter "Thanksgiving Day" in Georgia. A most lovely day. Ordered to march at half past five and left at that time Our Brigade having the advance...Passed through Gordon at 9.A.M and went in camp 2 mile south of this town about 10.A.M. occupying works which our forces threw up some days ago - distance marched 10 mile - Country level and soil very sandy. roads splendid. Gordon is the Junction of the Milledgeville RR and the Macon & Augusta RR - We found the RR & depot buildings entirely destroyed - Do not know how much of the RR is destroyed. Most of our Corps was here but left for Irwinton this morning - Yesterday Walcotts Brigade had a sharp fight with the enemy near Johnsonville - our loss was 80 killed and wounded. and the enemy left 300 Dead in the field - their loss was 1000. All the Rebel forces seem to be in Macon Awaiting our arrival but they will be sadly disappointed for we seem to be taking a direct route to Savannah. - All are anxious to hear from the "outer world". We had our "Thanksgiving dinner" at supper. Bill of fare. - Fresh Pork Sweet Potatoes Corn Cakes Honey & Coffee -- We are living like "Kings" - We all enjoyed our rest finally this afternoon. - We changed 'our linen' and feel clean once more -- Was in Corinth Miss [Mississippi] one year ago today.". Do not forget, they are "living like Kings" on food, taken at gunpoint from Georgia farmers, leaving them nothing.

**The original drawing about Thanksgiving by Thomas Nast**

## November 25, 1864

In Atlanta, GA, 10-year-old Carrie Berry writes in her diary, " Fri. Nov. 25. We have ben very lonesome to day, Papa being gone. The Country people are picking up everything. Miss Hatttie Lester stayed all night with us."

In New York City, a group of eight Confederate officers, who have escaped from Federal prisons to Canada, attempt to burn the City by setting fires in, at least, 10 hotels. The local fire departments are able to contain the fires without much damage. All the Rebels escape for the time being.

***

In Georgia, Governor Joe E. Brown orders State Militia General and future Oakland Cemetery Resident, W. Pinkney Howard to inspect the State property in Atlanta and the city itself, and to protect the same. We will have his report on December 7.

From Sherman's right-wing Lt. Platter reports, " Left camp at half past five and took the Irwinton road which place we passed through about 10.a.m. It is the county seat of Wilkinson Co. - a small village - all the principal buildings have been burned. - Went into camp at Sundown 7 mile east of Irwinton at "Poplar Spring Church" - Nothing of interest happened today - distance marched 18 mile - Country broken and soil sandy..."

In Middle Georgia, left of Sherman's left wing, Union Cavalry General Judson Kilpatrick today reaches the Ogeechee River at the Shoals where his horsemen maraud the surrounding territory, burning the mills and damaging as they can. They do not destroy the stately home they use as headquarters, the Cheely-Coleman-Moore House. Not only do they leave the home intact, but they also leave their autographs, Kilpatrick, and his staff officers. These words are written on a bedroom wall with their signatures underneath *"May all the names engraved here, in the golden book appear,"*

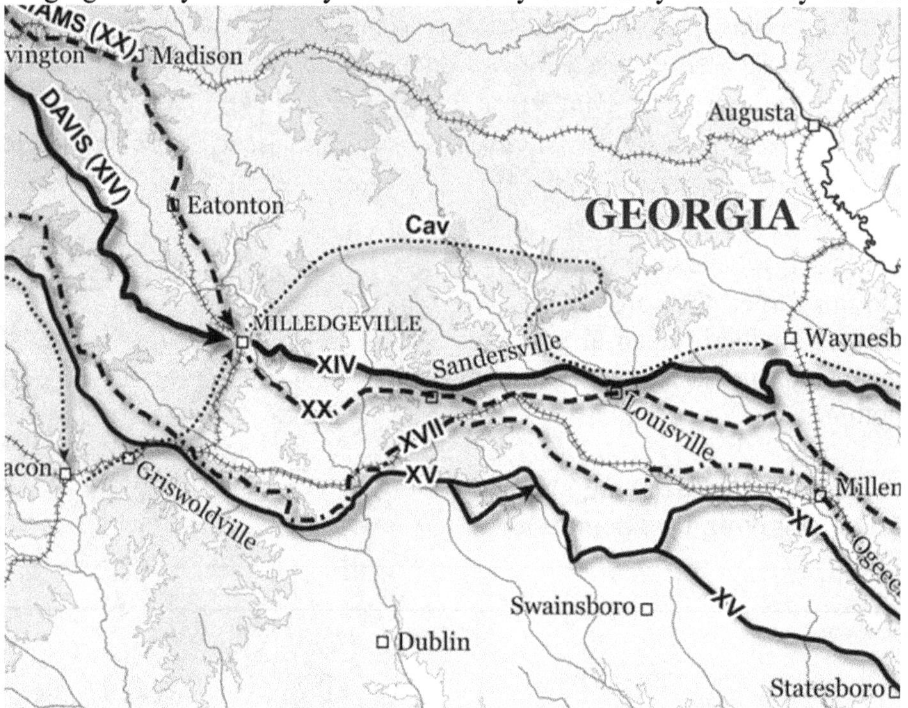


**The map is highlighted in yellow where Kilpatrick is today.**

## November 26, 1864

In Atlanta, GA., there is sadness in the Berry home as Carrie writes in her diary, "Sat. Nov. 26. I ironed this morning and in the afternoon I picked up nails and when I came home Papa and Grandpa were here. The Yankees payed Grandpa a visit and took every thing he had and they browt bad news that Uncle Osker was dead." (Oscar Berry, May 4, 1841 - Sept. 28, 1864) is buried at Noah's Ark Church Cemetery, near Jonesboro, and probably died of wounds received in the fighting thereabouts.)

In Tennessee, Confederate cavalry is swarming around Columbia, finding the fortifications of Union General Schofield to be substantial. The remainder of Hood's army is about a day away, and Hood will have big decisions to make upon arrival.

In South Georgia, Union General Sherman arrives at Sandersville. Wondering if he is close to the right wing, he interviews a Negro man from Tennille and asks if there are any Yankees at that place. The man responds, "First, there come along some cavalry-men, and they burned the depot; then come along some infantry-men, and they tore up the track, and burned it;" and just before he left they had "sot fire to the well."

In Sherman's right wing, Lt Cornelius Platter reports in his diary, "Ordered to march at 5 1/2 AM and we were on the road at that time. And reached the Oconee River about 12. M. [A. M.] at a point called "Morning Ferry" where the Uches Creek empties into the River -- Before reaching the river we had to pass through a fine swamp 3 of 4 miles wide. ... - Went into camp 10 mile from "Morning Ferry" and near a place called Irvine & Roads - distance marched 19 mile - Country this side of the river much better than what we have seen heretofore. We are now in Washington Co [County] about 4 mile from the R.R. - Saw plenty of "palm leaf" fans growing today. Also some beautiful "spanish moss".

***

Outside Petersburg, Virginia, in the Union camps, there is much grumbling by the fortified soldiers who are complaining that they have signed up for cavalry duty, but are assigned to manning breastworks. To appease the disgruntled, the Union officers have constructed a wooden horse that the complainers are required to spend four hours on, wielding a heavy wooden sabre. After this, horsemanship is much less attractive.---**Picture from this date's "Harper's Weekly"**

## November 27, 1864

In Atlanta, GA, 10-year-old Carrie Berry writes in her daily journal, "Sun. Nov. 27. This has ben a beautiful day and everything seems so quiet. There have ben a grate many cittizens coming back."

In South Georgia, Union General Sherman, with the left wing of his army, leaves Sandersville and moves to Tennille, where he has the following observations that he records, "*I rode down to the Tennille Station, and found General Corse's division of the Fifteenth Corps engaged in destroying the railroad, and saw the well which my negro informant had seen "burnt." It was a square pit about twenty-five feet deep, boarded up, with wooden steps leading to the bottom, wherein was a fine copper pump, to lift the water to a tank above. The soldiers had broken up the pump, heaved in the steps and lining, and set fire to the mass of lumber in the bottom of the well, which corroborated the negro's description.*"

***

In Tennessee, General Hood reaches Columbia and finds stiff fortifications keeping him from the bridges of the City. Not all of his force can reach here today so he waits for them before any attempts at dislodging Schofield's Federals, who cross to the north side of the river tonight, destroying all bridges and fortifying at river fords.

***

In Virginia, on the James River, the steamship "Greyhound" has been converted from a captured blockade runner into a luxurious headquarters ship for Union General Butler. Today Butler is transporting Union Rear Admiral David Porter from Dutch Gap to Hampton Roads, a very pleasant trip with these accommodations, when, suddenly, a great explosion rips through the engine room and catches the ship afire. All crewmen and passengers are evacuated with boats and survive to watch the fires smothered with water as the "Greyhound" slips beneath, and to the bottom. The cause of the explosion is a lump of coal that was shoveled into the engine furnace that was an iron casting loaded with explosives. It looks exactly like coal and is the brainchild of Gabriel James Rains, whose munitions experiments are known throughout the South.

USS Greyhound

## November 28, 1864

In Atlanta, GA., Carrie Berry's day is going like this, "Mon. Nov. 28. We have all ben picking up nails to day and we are all about tired down."

In Central Georgia, Union General Sherman talks about today in his journal, *"Baird's Division has crossed to Ogeechee River at Fenn's Bridge and camped on the other side. I shifted to the Right Wing, and accompanied the Blair's Seventeenth Corps from Tennille Station. General Howard, in person, is with the Fifteenth Corps, keeping farther to the right, and about one day's march ahead, ready to turn against the flank of any enemy who should oppose our progress. At Barton I learned that Kilpatrick's cavalry had reached the Augusta railroad about Waynesborough, where he ascertained that our prisoners had been removed from Millen, and therefore the purpose of rescuing them, upon which we had set our hearts, was an impossibility. The left wing is marching toward Louisville, Georgia."* In fact, Kilpatrick has convinced Reb Cavalry General Wheeler that Sherman is targeting Augusta and is concentrating his forces to give battle. There is heavy skirmishing around Waynesboro today.

In Tennessee Confederate General Hood and Union General Schofield are engaged in a deadly game of chess today. It begins with Hood sending Cavalry General Nathan B Forrest across hastily constructed pontoon bridges over the Duck River to drive the Federals away from the river crossings so that he can cross a major force of infantry tomorrow. Hood wants a major flanking movement against the now-entrenched Yankees on the North side of the Duck, with a substantial force pressuring the front, on the river, facing each other. There will be heavy fighting here tomorrow.

**Union General Schofield** **Confederate General Hood**

## November 29, 1864

In Atlanta, 10-year-old Carrie Berry is doing what she can to help her family survive in this terrible time, "Tues. Nov. 29. We have ben picking up nails again to day and it has made me sore."

In Middle Georgia, the left wing of Sherman's army under Slocum has proceeded near enough to Millen to be able to verify the rumors discovered by Kilpatrick yesterday that the prisoners in Camp Lawton have been moved way down south of Savannah. Sherman orders all infantry to not cross the Ogeechee River yet. He knows that Reb cavalry under Wheeler are looking for a strike opportunity and his army wings are scattered in travel.

***

In Eastern Colorado Territory, Black Kettle, Chief of a band of about 700 Southern Cheyenne is camped on Sand Creek. Most of his men are hunting buffalo, leaving about 75 men and the women and children in the camp. Having agreed to the peace treaty in September, Black Kettle is complying with the terms by flying an American flag over his lodge with a force of Colorado Cavalry, under US Army Colonel John Chivington attack the camp. Black Kettle raises a white flag with the American flag, but the attack continues in a brutal manner. Two Companies of cavalry refuse the attack order, but others, still drunk from the night before, commence a slaughter of women and children, scalping and removing genitalia from both. This is the lowest hour of an increasing attitude of brutality in the American Army. One famous Indian fighter, Kit Carson, has this to say about the day:

*"Jis to think of that dog Chivington and his dirty hounds, up thar at Sand Creek. His men shot down squaws, and blew the brains out of little innocent children. You call sich soldiers Christians, do ye? And Indians savages? What der yer 'spose our Heavenly Father, who made both them and us, thinks of these things? I tell you what, I don't like a hostile red skin any more than you do. And when they are hostile, I've fought 'em, hard as any man. But I never yet drew a bead on a squaw or papoose, and I despise the man who would."*

**Sand Creek massacre Robert Lindneaux**

## November 30, 1864

In Atlanta, Ga., Carrie Berry writes in her diary, "Wed. Nov. 30. We have ben resting to day. The cittizens are still coming in and it wont be very long untill they get the railroad fixed up from here to Macon and then I hope I can see Grandma.

"In South Central Georgia, with his left wing on the eastern side of the Ogeechee River and the right wing on the western side, Union General Sherman's plague approaches the Millen area.

***

In Tennessee, yesterday Confederate General Hood with his 40,000 men feints straight-on attack for this morning at General Schofield and his 27,000 men, but has a flanking movement all set to defeat Schofield at daylight this morning, only to discover that Schofield has sneaked away in the night and moved to Franklin. Hood hurries his army after Schofield who reaches Franklin well before Hood and occupies strong fortified positions, protected by the guns of Fort Granger. When about 20,000 of Hood's men arrive in the area, he hastily sends attacks forward over two miles of open ground into a cauldron of lead on the fly. Many of the Federals are armed with Spencer Repeating rifles and Fort Granger blasts the open attacks to pieces, especially the Rebel right. As attempts are driven back or destroyed, the efforts are reorganized and tried again, until darkness sets upon the field. Hood, although his army is badly injured, plans to attack again at dawn. Today he has lost six generals killed including, probably the best officer of either uniform, Pat Cleburne. He has lost six more generals wounded, and one, George W. Gordon was captured. Altogether, there are 6,252 Johnny Reb casualties and 2,326 Yankees....,and Hood wants to try this again?.....On the map below, I have circled the Confederate generals casualties of the day. Killed are circled in black, wounded in red, and captured in blue.

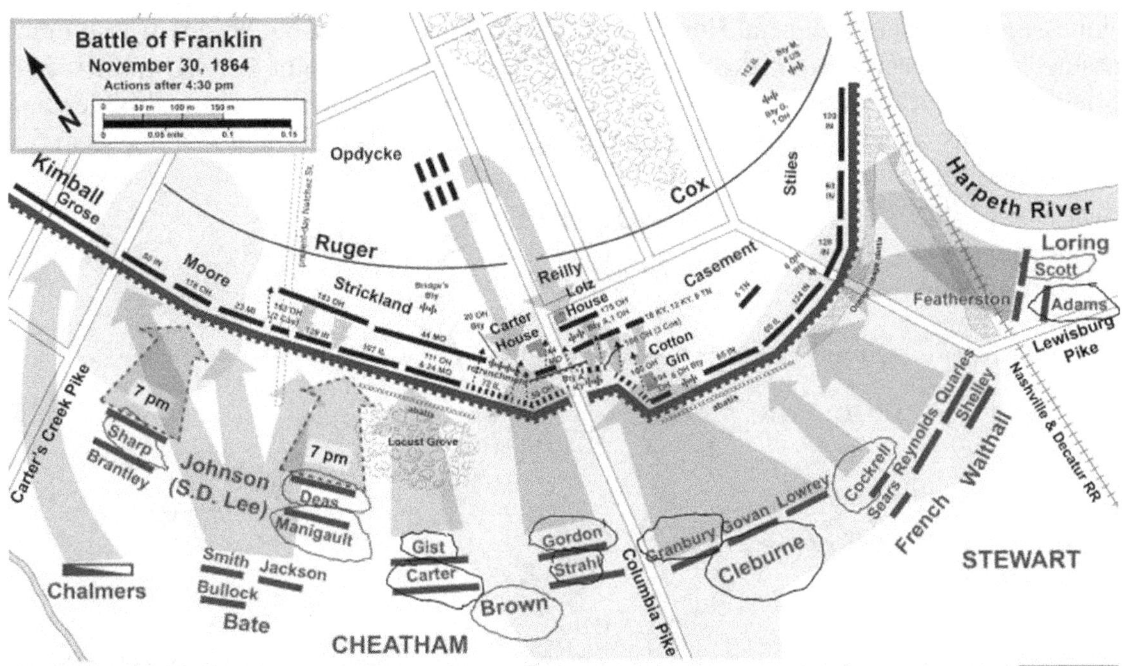

## December 1, 1864

In Atlanta, Carrie Berry writes in her diary, "Thurs. Dec. 1. This has ben such a pleasant day. I have ben ironing to day. It did not take me long."

In South Central Georgia, everyone in Sherman's Army is moving today, but the left wing is using a more circuitous route than the others, giving it further to travel so Sherman sends out orders for most units to take a day off tomorrow to get the movement closer in align. Union Lt. Platter, in the right wing, writes in his diary, "First day of Winter. and we can congratulate ourselves that we are in a more congenial clime than our friends at home. It was foggy again this morning but the sun soon came out and we had a warm pleasant day. Marched about 12 mile Country more fertile and thickly settled. We did not cross the River at Herndon as expected. When we were within two mile of the crossing, we took the Savannah road and travelled 8 mile down the Ogeechee and are still on the South bank of the River in Emmanuel Co. about two mile from the river and six from Milan Div. not known when we will cross the River perhaps not until we get within 18 mile of Savannah - Are in camp near 1st Div Engaged a "contraband" today to take care of my horse. Heard some splendid news. That Genl Granger has captured Mobile. Hood is badly whipped at Pulaski "and then we heard something that was not so agreeable "that the enemy had us (Shermans army) surrounded and it was only a question of time about his whole army being captured - but we cant see the 'surrounding force'.". The Army is completely cut off from communication with the world, no media of any kind, therefore rumors abound.

***

In Tennessee, Confederate General Hood was not whipped at Pulaski, but he sure was at Franklin. He has no "attack" decision to make this morning. Just before midnight last night, the victorious Schofield pulled out from his strong lines and moved toward Nashville. He will be leading his men into that City about noon today, combining with General Thomas and making them 55,000 strong, inside the fortifications that have been made ready with months of effort.

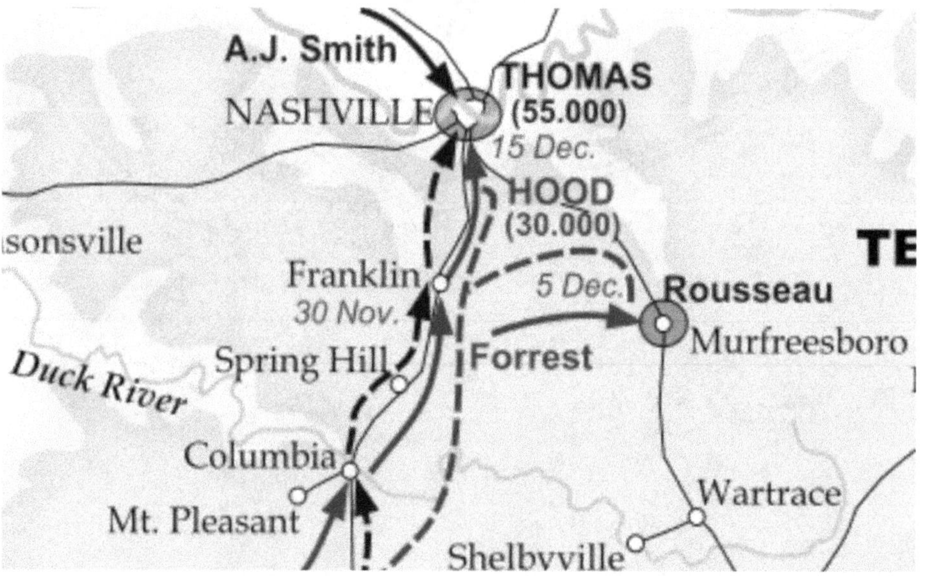

## December 2, 1864

In Atlanta, Ga, Carrie Berry has a brief diary entry for the day, "Fri. Dec. 2. Ella came up here this evening and me and her went off and made calls."

In Virginia, Confederate General Archibald Gracie III turned 32 yrs old yesterday, the same day his second daughter was born, and tomorrow he is to take a leave to go see her for the first time, but today as he peered about the trenches of Petersburg with a spyglass, an artillery round explodes just in front of him, breaking his neck and killing him instantly. Gracie was born and will be raised in New York, in the same house, Gracie Mansion, that the governor of New York will live in 150 years from now.

In Maury County, Tennessee, Ireland-born, Confederate General Pat Cleburne is buried at Ashwood, the private graveyard of the Polk family. His coffin is strewn with flowers by the ladies and the following lines were written by one of them, and read over the coffin:

""Fare thee well, departed chieftain!

Erin's land sends forth a wail.

And oh! my country sad laments thee,

Passed too soon through death's dark vale.

"Blow ye breezes soft on him,

Fan his brow with gentle breath,

Disturb ye not his peaceful slumber,

Cleburne sleeps the sleep of death!

"Rest thee, Cleburne, tears of sadness

Flow from hearts thou'st nobly won,

Memory ne'er will cease to cherish

Deeds of glory thou hast done."

**Confederate Major General Patrick Cleburne**

## December 3, 1864

In Atlanta, Georgia, Carrie Berry writes in her diary, "Sat. Dec. 3. I have ben buisy mending my pettacoats. Mama has be making Buddie a pair of pants."

In Tennessee near Nashville, as Reb General Hood fortifies his army, he sends elements of Forrest's Cavalry to blockade the Cumberland River just below Nashville. Today, about 300 horsemen and two cannon set up about 12 miles downriver, and are successful in capturing two transports laden with mules and horses and other supplies today.

***

In Southern Georgia, Sherman's army's right wing is partly on the south side of the Ogeechee River and Lt. Platter is reporting with his journal on the march there, "Up early and moved at 6.30 Our Brigade crossed the Ogeechee and occupied works made by the 1st Brigade - We lay in support of the Brigade who were tearing up the R.R. Remained there all day and then returned to the camp occupied last night Pontoons were taken up this evening Quite a number of negro came in today with Horses & mules. Saw plenty of "Live oak" Palm leaf" fans & Spanish moss today. Distance marched 4 mile"

Sherman, with the 15th Army Corps enters Millen with a bad attitude because of the town's involvement with Camp Millen, an abandoned prisoner camp nearby. When some of the soldiers visit the camp, they find much evidence of filth and starvation, including several unburied bodies of Federal soldiers in emaciated condition. Sherman issues the following orders: *"The general-in-chief does not expect you to move more than five miles [on the 3rd], to the vicinity of Paramore's Hill; but wishes you to make the most complete and perfect possible break of the railroad about Millen. Let it be more devilish than can be dreamed of."*

**Destruction of the Railroad station in Millen, GA**

## December 4, 1864

In Atlanta, Georgia, 10-year-old Carrie Berry writes in her diary, "Sun. Dec. 4. It is as cold a Sunday as usual. Ella came up this evening and we took a walk and we got some sweet gum"

In Southern Georgia, Union General Sherman leaves Millen where he received dispatches that informed him of Confederate General Bragg's presence in Augusta, but the dispatches couldn't have informed him of the death of his youngest son who dies today. As Sherman's men are busy destroying Southern people's property and livelihood, his own wife has to deal with the loss of an infant child alone, not knowing when he will actually learn of it. Meanwhile, across the Ogeechee River from Sherman, the extreme right wing of the invasion force marches on with Lt. Platter reporting on the day. "Marched at 6:30. Our route was down the south bank of the Ogeechee Went into camp at Sundown just opposite Cameron a station on the R.R. - distance marched 15 mile. Nothing of interest happened today. Country much better than any we have seen for 10 days - Forage for man and beast plenty." (Cameron Station is a couple of miles due north of a dusty crossroads called Statesborough).

Near Waynesboro, Georgia, well east of both Sherman and Lt. Platter, the cavalry of Union General Judson Kilpatrick (about 6,000) and cavalry of Confederate General Joseph Wheeler (about 4,000) have been moving in bands and snipping at each other for days. On November 28, Wheeler suddenly attacked Kilpatrick's camp south of Waynesboro and drove him southwest beyond Buckhead Creek toward Louisville. Today, Kilpatrick returns the favor. He assembles about 5,000 of his horsemen and attacks Wheeler's main camp, that is only at half strength, with the others out foraging for feed, and drives the Rebels through Waynesboro and across Briar Creek. The Yankees lose about 190 total casualties and the Rebels lose about 250. The Northern Press will make a big deal of this skirmish, and next month "Harper's Weekly" will print this picture of Kilpatrick in his "moment of glory".

## December 5, 1864

In Atlanta, Carrie Berry's life is getting a little more like normal with a school opening up, "Mon. Dec. 5. I was up by times this morning getting ready for school and about half past eight went to Miss Mat Lester. I like her very much and I think she is a very nice teacher."

In Tennessee, Confederate General John B. Hood has sent Maj Gen. Nathan B Forrest with two division of cavalry, assisted by General Bates division of infantry (about 7,000 altogether), to disrupt the operation of the Nashville and Chattanooga Railroad and cut Federal contact with the Union Army supply depot in Fort Rosecrans at Murfreesboro. Yesterday, Bate attacked the Blockhouse No 7, but was driven off. This morning Forrest split his cavalry, one column to attack the fort on the hill and the other to take Blockhouse No 4 at La Vergne. Upon Forrest's demand for surrender, both Union garrisons do so. Forrest and Bates now merge and advance to Murfreesboro, driving the Yankees into their Fortress Rosecrans fortifications. The Confederates settle into encampment on the edge of the City for the night

***

In Southern Georgia, Union Lt. Platter is enjoying the change of scenery in the State as he passes through, "Saw some splendid "live oaks" today - Marched 20 mile crossing "Belchers Mill Creek and when near the River each man was ordered to "shoulder a rail" and we marched down to a large swamp and left the rails for the Pioneers to build roads with. One of the most beautiful sights I ever saw was the trees in the swamp which were all thickly covered with "Spanish Moss" went into camp near by. We are just opposite Guyton -."

The left wing of Sherman's army is not having such a good day, as General Slocum reports,... *"Soon after my dispatch of 10 a.m. yesterday the enemy cut a mill-dam on Little Horse Creek, flooding the road to such an extent as to entirely stop that portion of the column on the other side. Being in the advance I did not hear of this until I had nearly reached this point. All of Geary's and part of Ward's division is still back of Little Horse Creek (ten miles from here), unable to cross."*

**Sherman mentions with pride, every day, the amount of Southern railroad track he destroys.**

## December 6, 1864

In Atlanta, GA, Carrie Berry writes in her diary, "Tues. Dec. 6. Cousin Pink Butler came here to day to see us. She was just from Macon. She had such a sweet little babe. She is trying to get back here and Aunt Katie."

In Tennessee, Union General Thomas is preparing to attack the Confederates who are fortifying about two miles from Nashville. Union General Grant is screaming for the attack and threatening to fire Thomas if he does not promptly comply with attack orders. Meanwhile, at nearby Murfreesboro, Confederate cavalry and infantry under Forrest and Bate attack the Federal fortifications, but do not make much gain. Both sides cease firing and glare at each other for the remainder of the daylight. More infantry shows up to help Forrest when Brig Generals Sears and Palmer bring their brigades to the show.

In Southern Georgia, there is more cavalry action every day as Sherman gets closer to the coast. He is resting some of the units today in order for other units to gather closer in to the main bodies. Union Lt Platter talks about this in his daily journal, "Did not cross the river last night - We are still in the camp which we occupied last night. This has been the first days rest we have had since leaving Rome. We washed, read, slept, &c. [Had Company "Inspection" - found arms in good condition & men well supplied with ammunition. The other Divs [of our corps proceeded down the river. Lt Pittman and 45 men were detailed to cross the river and "tap" the R.R. but on going to the River found nothing to cross on so returned to camp - Our Pioneer Corps has been busy all day fixing roads - No news from the 14 & 20 Corps - Suppose they have been fighting some as we heard distant Canonnading yesterday - We are now 35 mile from Savannah and by this time next week we hope to be enjoying the "balmy breezes" of the sea coast. Do not know whether we will proceed directly to Savannah - it may be we are only making a "feint" and instead of going to S. will Cross the Savannah River and tread the Sacred Soil of South Carolina". Heard today that Gen Foster had destroyed the fleet off Charleston and Savannah R.R. It is now 26 days since we left Rome and we are all hungry for "Northern news". It is no fun being "cut off" from the civilized world. Quite a number of Contrabands came in today and they afforded us a good deal of amusement dancing wrestling & c.

In Washington, President Lincoln delivers his annual message to Congress. It is quite interesting, long and rambling. He also announces the appointment of Salmon P. Chase as Chief Justice of the Supreme Court to replace deceased Roger B. Taney.

**Salmon Chase**

## December 7, 1864

In Atlanta, Ga, Carrie Berry Writes in her diary, "Wed. Dec. 7. This has ben a election day for Mayor and council men but the election was broken up. I had a little sister this morning at eight o'clock and Mama gave her to me. I think its very pretty. I had to cook breakfast and dinner and supper." It is election day, but I don't know what Carrie means by "broken up". I can find no irregularities in the process. James M. Calhoun is elected for his fourth term as Mayor, and ten City councilmen are elected for the five wards. Mayor Calhoun announces to the Council that there is $1.64 in the City Treasury. Last November 25th, a week after Sherman's army pulled out of Atlanta in ruins, Governor Brown ordered Militia General W. Pinkney Howard to inspect the State property in Atlanta and the city itself. He reports in full to the Governor today. You can read the full report in Mr. Garrett's "Atlanta and Environs" volume 1 page 653.

In Nashville, Tennessee, Union General Thomas would like to wait for more reinforcements, especially cavalry, to arrive before attacking Reb General Hood, but Grant is hot to get it done, so Thomas has ordered the army ready for attack tomorrow.

Meanwhile, near Murfreesboro, the Federals under Rousseau attacks the combined force of Bate's infantry and Forrest's cavalry. Fighting continues for several hours, then suddenly, the infantry of Bate's begins to run, infuriating Forrest. Forrest manages to organize an orderly retreat but felt he should have won the day. Actually, the entire raid of Forrest accomplishes very little, and it keeps him away from the coming Battle of Nashville.

The confederate batteries set up at Bell's bend on the Cumberland River, below Nashville, have been effective in closing the river, and today Union Lt. Commander Leroy Fitch takes two heavy ships, the ironclad "Carondelet" and the monitor "Neosho" to engage the batteries. When the smoke clears, both gunships are too badly damaged to continue the fight and have to withdraw, leaving the Rebel batteries in command of the river.

**"U.S.S. Neosho" at Bell's Bend**

## December 8, 1864

In Atlanta, Ga Carrie Berry writes in her diary, " Thurs. Dec. 8. I have ben cooking and cleaning house and waiting on Mama and little sister Maggy. I have learnt to make nice egg bread and how to cook very nice."

In Tennessee, although Union General Thomas in Nashville is not satisfied with his personnel situation, he is committed to moving his army into the field and attacking the flanks of the entrenched Rebels a couple of miles outside the city. He has been hoping that Confederate General Hood would be dumb enough to attack him, behind his strong works, but Hood proves to be too smart for that, at least. The action can come tomorrow, but late in this day the weather turns "iffy."

***

In Southern Georgia, the Federal troops under Sherman are getting very close to the coast now, and resistance is becoming more bothersome. The roads are obstructed with felled trees, and Rebel cavalry is nipping at the edges of the movements. There is no force in the South to oppose them, and they suspect that. Sherman sends a messenger to the Federal fleet off the coast with news that they have arrived nearby, and he will make his plans known to them presently. Confederate General Beauregard in Charleston and General Hardee in Savannah are discussing what to do about Sherman, and Beauregard offers this sound advice, "Having no army of relief to look to, and your forces being essential to the defense of Georgia and South Carolina, whenever you shall have to select between their safety and that of Savannah, sacrifice the latter, and form a junction with General Jones, holding the left bank of the Savannah River and the railroad to this place as long as possible." If he can keep moving, Sherman will have the land forces surrounded in a couple of days and sea forces will prevent any exodus or aid from that quarter.

## December 9, 1864

In Atlanta, Ga, Carrie Berry writes in her diary, "Fri. Dec. 9. I made up some buiskets last night and Mama says that they were nice. Every moment I can get I am making things to do on the tree. Ella and I are going to have one together. This has ben a cold sleaty day."

In the Nashville, Tennessee area, the weather has really turned miserable. It has been sleeting and freezing rain all night and the ground is covered with ice. Limbs are breaking from the trees, and other trees are uprooting. It is 12 degrees with a hard wind blowing, and the icy crust is so hard a knife will not penetrate. It has not affected telegraph service though, and General Grant is burning up the wires demanding that Thomas get his attack under way. Thomas responds to him thusly, "*I had nearly completed my preparations to attack the enemy tomorrow, but a terrible storm of freezing rain has come on today, which will make it impossible for our men to fight to any advantage. I am therefore compelled to wait... Major General Halleck informs me that you are very dissatisfied with my delay in attacking. I can only say I have done all in my power to prepare, and if you deem it necessary to relieve me. I shall submit without a murmur.*" The ice storm saves Thomas' job for the moment because Grant has already decided to replace Thomas with Schofield. (Wonder why Grant isn't attacking Lee today?)

In Southern Georgia, As Union General Jefferson Davis has moved through the state, a group of Negro camp followers has accumulated, and they have become pests to the General, so he devises a plan to be rid of them. As his troops are crossing Ebenezer Creek near Savannah, he orders all the Negros, except the young strong ones, to stay clear of the bridge until the entire army crosses. It is a pontoon bridge over a wide and deep expanse of water, and when the last soldier crosses, Davis has the bridge disengaged so that the end floats away from the 600 Negros waiting. Immediately, they jump into the river trying to cross over, and most of them drown, so many that it creates a human dam to stop the small river. Most other officers of the Union Army are furious with Davis, and the Northern press is going to have a field day with him.

**There are multiple sources about this event and multiple dates attributed to it. I believe it happened on the 8'th or 9'th, so this is the day I tell it.**

## December 10, 1864

In Atlanta, GA, 10 yrs old Carrie Berry writes in her diary, "Sat. Dec. 10. It has ben so cold that I couldnt make anything for the tree. I ran down to Mrs. Lester to see what Ella was making for the tree."

In Tennessee, near Nashville, everything is iced in, and more icy rain and sleet is falling. The Federal Army is poised to go after the badly outnumbered Confederates who are unable to complete their defensive works in the bad weather. The scantily clad Rebel boys are piled in close to each other, hoping their collective blankets will keep them from freezing to death.

In Southern Georgia, Union General Sherman is both elated and worried. It is a critical time in his march through Georgia. He has arrived near the outer defenses of Confederate General Hardee, and they are formidable. However, Hardee has only about 10,000 men to man them. For the first time since beginning this trek, the Yankees are on half rations because of the poor, swampy, land they have been passing through the past week or so. There has not been enough food to take from the farmers who grew it to feed. this many people, and the supply ships that lie off the Georgia Coast cannot come up the Ogeechee River to meet Sherman because of the guns of Fort McAllister. They have tried plenty of times before and been blasted out of the water. Sherman spreads his left wing in defensive, siege, positions all the way to the Savannah River on the north side of the City, and the right wing, all the way to the Savannah River, in like positions, on the south side, with about 4,000 troops under Brig. General Hazen moving in position to take Fort McAllister. Union Lt. Platter writes, "Regiment ordered to remain as Guards to Division train. Capt Vanpelt with a platoon of "A" Co was sent to the RR. but didn't not develop any enemy. 12th & 66th Ills went to the R.R. bridge over the Little Ogeechee River - 1st and 3d Brigades moved forward on the main Savannah road. ...Went up to the front could plainly see Rebel tents & works - A large swamp intervenes between us & the enemy -- They have opened the "flood gates" of the canal and have "flooded" the country to prevent our crossing. Heavy cannonading all day. but without any result. The "Seige of Savannah" may be said to have commenced today - As the City is entirely inverted ".

## December 11, 1864

In Atlanta, Ga, Carrie Berry writes in her diary, "Sun. Dec. 11. It has ben so cold to day that I have not done much cooking to day. came this evening and I the kitchen to her. I am glad that she came for I am getting tired of cooking."

In Southern Georgia, a few miles outside Savannah, the Federal troops are refining their positions and making plans for establishing a supply base on the Ogeechee River. Much scouting and noting of Confederate positions is going on. Due to the swamps and flooded fields the only approaches to the City are five causeways, heavily defended with big guns that Sherman's light filed pieces are no match for. He is still trying to make contact with the supply ships offshore, so another patrol is sent to the coast in canoes today.

***

In Nashville, the ice continues to fall and bitter cold rules the day. The armies are huddled in as best they can with very little movement stirring.

In Washington Lt. General Grant is beside himself, again on the telegraph demanding that Thomas attack the Rebels. He cannot seem to understand that no one can stand up outside, much less attack a hillside position. Grant writes, "If you delay attack longer the mortifying spectacle will be witnessed of a rebel army moving for the Ohio River, and you will be forced to act, accepting such weather as you find. Let there be no further delay… I am in hopes of receiving a dispatch from you today that you have moved. Delay no longer for weather or reinforcements." Thomas won't reply today but will send a message tomorrow.

**The Federal outer line at Nashville**

## December 12, 1864

In Atlanta, Ga, 10 yrs old Carrie Berry is trying to get in the holiday mood per her diary entry, "Mon Dec. 12. I have ben making things for the tree. Mama has been helping me make things for the tree."

In Nashville, Tennessee, both armies in the area are suffering from the extreme cold and freezing rain that is showing signs of letting up. Today is no different from yesterday, with US Grant on the wires demanding action from the Yankee Army under Thomas. Thomas has done his homework, he knows all there is to know about his enemy's positions, and he has had extensive meetings with the other army leaders in his command. Everybody knows what to do, as soon as the ice is thawed, he will strike.

It is cold in Southern Georgia also, with a hard wind blowing. Confederate Major George Anderson has 230 defenders of Fort McAllister, guarding the Ogeechee River, allowing no enemy boat traffic. Seven times during this war have enemy gunboats tried his guns, and seven times their withdrawal or destruction has been their result. It is a well-armed defensive fort from the seaward/river side, but poorly defended on the land side, where Sherman's army is fast approaching. Sherman has Brig. General Hazen with his 4,000 troops ready to cross the Ogeechee on Kings bridge just as soon as the engineers can complete repairs to it. Sherman himself, is there to oversee the construction, and will spend the night in Mr. King's house tonight.

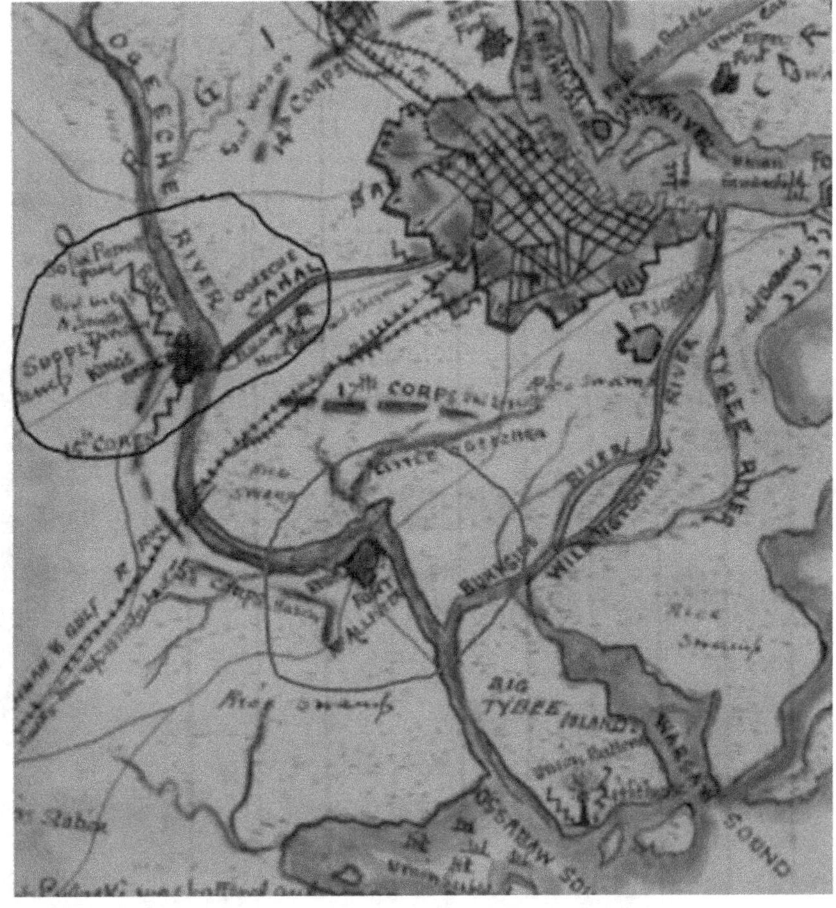


**On the map, Kings Bridge is circled with a blue line and Fort McAllister on the Ogeechee River is circled in red.**

## December 13, 1864

In Atlanta, Ga, Carrie Berry writes in her diary today, " Tues. Dec. 13. I have made Papa some buesket and pies to take with him to Macon. He is going to try to get in business."

In Tennessee, it is still sleeting, but the weather is a little warmer, indicating this storm may be about over. Still, nothing is moving in the Nashville area, but plans are made, everybody knowing what to do when Union General Thomas gives the word. Union General Grant has lost all patience. He has given General Logan a letter relieving Thomas of command and ordered him to Nashville to take over the army to attack Hood's Confederates.

***

In Southern Georgia, on the Ogeechee River, King's Bridge is repaired, and the 4,000 soldiers of Brig. General William Hazen have flooded into position at Fort McAllister. The fort, being a protection against the invasion of enemy ships, is poorly protected on its hindquarters, where Hazen has headed. About five o'clock the signal to begin is given, and the horde of Yankees tears through the abatis, down into the ditch, and up the walls of the bunkers into the fort. There are very few riflemen in the fort so after the big guns are passed, the combat is hand to hand, but the overwhelmed Confederates do not surrender. Every one of them has to be killed or subdued. Confederate battle losses are 71 of 230 participants. Of course, the remainder are captured. The Yanks suffer 134 killed and wounded. Sherman has the supply ships, that he can see in the distance, signaled to come on up the river, and he goes to meet them, to give them communications for Washington, the first news they have had of him in weeks. The City of Savannah is surrounded by land and sea. All rail, road, and telegraph communication are cut off. The Federals now have a supply line and supply base to keep them operating. Savannah is doomed.

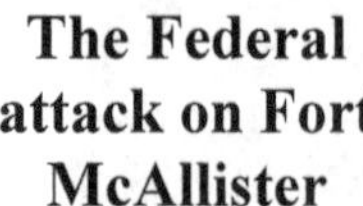
**The Federal attack on Fort McAllister**

## December 14, 1864

In Atlanta, GA, Carrie Berry writes in her diary, "Wed. Dec. 14. Papa started to Macon this morning. Mama and me have ben buisy making Fannie and Zuie a rag doll. We feel very lonesome with Papa so far away and the weather is so bad we cant get out."

In Southern Georgia, on the Ogeechee River, Sherman's Army refines its siege positions, and Sherman meets with various members of the United States Navy, including Admiral Dahlgren, who is on board the "Harvest Moon" in Ossabaw Sound. Dahlgren is very accommodating and agrees to help Sherman by furnishing him with big, rifled siege guns and to remove the torpedoes that still restrict traffic on the Ogeechee. Until that can be done, the supply ships will get as far up the river as they dare, and a wagon train will be set up to move supplies to those that need it. The army mainly needs bread, sugar, and coffee. They have plenty of meat on the hoof, needing a slaughterhouse operation set up.

In Tennessee, a warm rain yesterday and last night has melted the ice that has stymied military operations for a week. Union General Thomas spends most of the day meeting with his generals, discussing the written orders he is issuing, and keeping a critical eye on the weather. About Eight o'clock tonight, he wires General Halleck in Washington that the ice has melted, and that Hood will be attacked tomorrow morning. Union General Steedman will heavily feint toward the Confederate right, but the main attack will be a wheelhouse movement against the Confederate left. Union units will begin assembly at 6 AM.

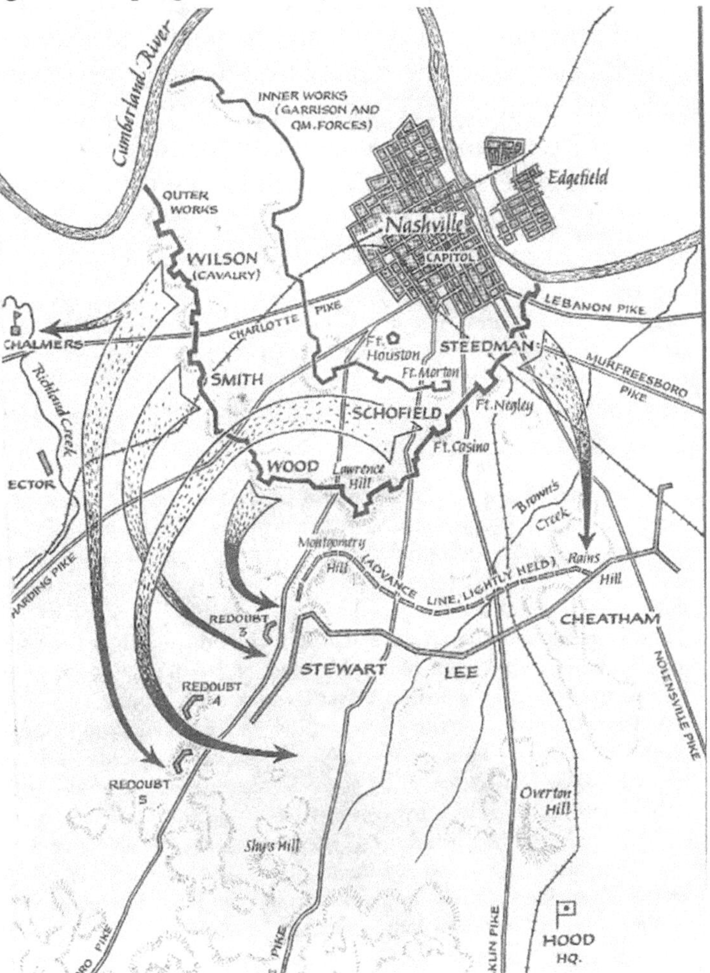

**Thomas' Attack Plan on Nashville**

## December 15, 1864

In Atlanta, GA, Carrie Berry writes in her diary, "Thurs. Dec. 15. We finished the dolls today and they look very nice. I went down to Mrs. Lesters and got Ella to come and we washed doll clothes."

In Southern Georgia, outside Savannah, the Federal Army is creeping elements around further toward Augusta in order to tighten the noose on the City of Savannah. Sherman still hasn't been able to supply his troops yet, and some of them are quite hungry as Lt. Platter states, "A very spirited Cannonading duel This morning - Our batteries seem to have the best of it. Spent the day in writing letters wrote three one to Father -- Lizzie and Lt H.R. S.R. 15 tons of mail said to be at the coast but cannot come up untill the obstructions in the "Ogeechee" are removed. But little firing on the Skirmish line. - The boys of Co "E" procured a small " guns" and took it out on the "skirmish line" It throws a formed ball and created quite a disturbance among the enemys It has been a nice day. cool and pleasant - No Rations & eating very slim."

Outside Nashville, the morning dawns with heavy fog obstructing the battlefield, and by the time the fog lifts and the complicated attack begins, it is almost noon. Thomas' battle plan works perfectly. He feints to the Confederate right and occupies them there as the bulk of his 55,000 men wheel around to their left and slam into the sparsely manned works of the Confederate left. Vastly outnumbered, the Rebel boys give a good accounting of themselves by first stalling the attacks, but as more surges pound them, they begin a fighting retreat, moving to a defendable line of hills at Brentwood, about a mile to the rear, where Hood establishes much shorter defensive lines, and darkness ends the fighting for the day. The general opinion is that Hood will pull out during the night, and the Federals prepare for a chase tomorrow. They will try to cut off his retreat and destroy the remainder of his army, but Hood will be right here tomorrow morning.

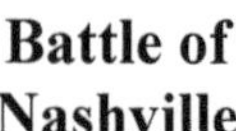

**Battle of Nashville**

## December 16, 1864

In Atlanta, Carrie Berry writes in her diary, "Fri. Dec. 16. I went down to Mrs. Lesters and ironed them and put them all away very nicely." (I think she is referring to the doll clothes she washed yesterday)

In Southern Georgia, the Ogeechee River has been cleared of torpedoes, but the large seagoing transports of the Federals can only make it to King's Bridge where the water becomes shallower. Transfer of freight to lighter boats is necessary for further transport. Huge shipments of mail reach the troops today. Lt Platter has this in his diary, "Was up early. Enemy threw shell in among us. Col Adams being afraid that some one would get hurt moved us back to where the rest of the Brigade was - 1/2 mile from our position occupied at morning. 12th Ills detailed as Guards to 13th AC. Rec'd large mail this morning -- got six letters 2 from Lizzie -- 2 from home, one from "Hugh R S." and one from Columbus - an official documents" -- also rec'd a huge lot Of Cincinnati Gazetts - Sat up very late reading the news was after 12 o'clock when I gave myself up to the arms of "Morpheus"

***

Outside Nashville, the left of Thomas' Yankee Army pushes against the Rebel right, while the main Federal force makes its way around to the left, with units moving far enough around to be able to attack in the rear. As the movement is occurring, Federal guns bombard the Confederates until all is ready, and the attacks begin. At first the boys in Gray hold their lines against overwhelming odds, but in mid-afternoon the left begins to yield to the pressure. They begin to withdraw, then retreat, then the line breaks, and the result would have been a rout, had the right side not fell in behind to cover the withdrawal down the roads toward Columbia. Of the almost 30,000 Confederates that began the fight yesterday, only about 24,000 walk away from it today. Of the 55,000 Federals that began the fight yesterday, about 52,000 walk away. The Yankees take 4,500 prisoners today...

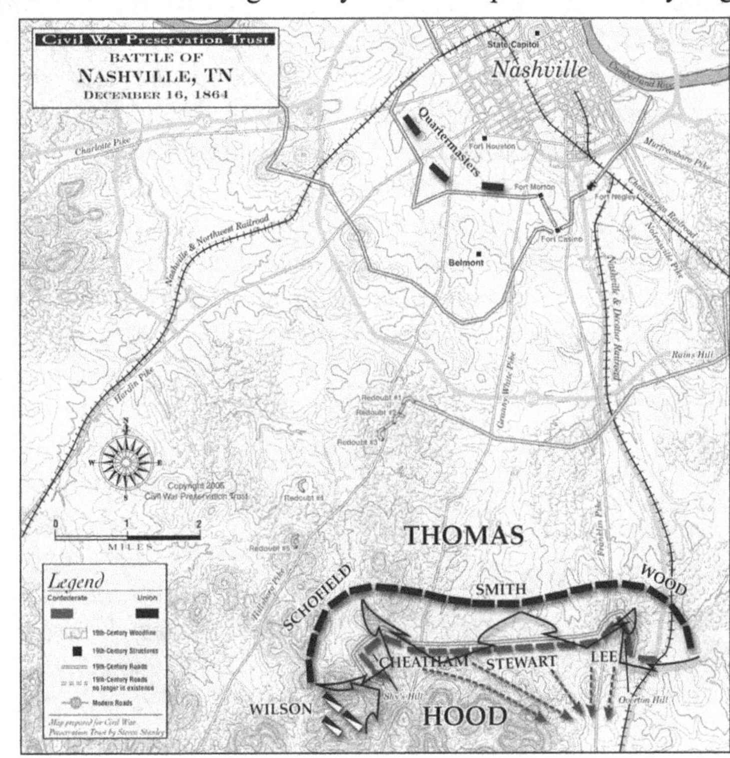

**Map is today's fighting**

## December 17, 1864

In Atlanta, Ga., Carrie berry writes in her diary," Sat. Dec. 17. Ella stayed all night with me. She is making her mother a present. We were looking for Papa home and he hasn't come."

In Tennessee, as the army of Hood withdraws toward Columbia, the Federal cavalry, under Wilson, keeps attacking the rear. There is sharp fighting at West Harpeth River.

***

Near Savannah, Union General Sherman sends a letter to Confederate General Hardee, making the following demand, *"I have already received guns that can cast heavy and destructive shot as far as the heart of your city; also, I have for some days held and controlled every avenue by which the people and garrison of Savannah can be supplied, and I am therefore justified in demanding the surrender of the city of Savannah, and its dependent forts, and shall wait a reasonable time for your answer, before opening with heavy ordnance. Should you entertain the proposition, I am prepared to grant liberal terms to the inhabitants and garrison; but should I be forced to resort to assault, or the slower and surer process of starvation, I shall then feel justified in resorting to the harshest measures, and shall make little effort to restrain my army—burning to avenge the national wrong which they attach to Savannah and other large cities which have been so prominent in dragging our country into civil war."...*

Lt. General Hardee replies, "*General: I have to acknowledge the receipt of a communication from you of this date, in which you demand "the surrender of Savannah and its dependent forts," on the ground that you "have received guns that can cast heavy and destructive shot into the heart of the city," and for the further reason that you "have, for some days, held and controlled every avenue by which the people and garrison can be supplied." You add that, should you be "forced to resort to assault, or to the slower and surer process of starvation, you will then feel justified in resorting to the harshest measures, and will make little effort to restrain your army," etc., etc. The position of your forces is, at the nearest point, at least four miles from the heart of the city. That and the interior line are both intact. Your statement that you have, for some days, held and controlled every avenue by which the people and garrison can be supplied, is incorrect. I am in free and constant communication with my department. Your demand for the surrender of Savannah and its dependent forts is refused. With respect to the threats you conveyed in the closing paragraphs of your letter (of what may be expected in case your demand is not complied with), I have to say that I have hitherto conducted the military operations entrusted to my direction in strict accordance with the rules of civilized warfare, and I should deeply regret the adoption of any course by you that may force me to deviate from them in future. I have the honor to be, very respectfully, your obedient servant."*

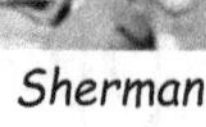

Sherman

Hardee

## December 18, 1864

In Atlanta, Ga., Carrie Berry writes in her diary as she worries over the absence of her Father, "Sun. Dec. 18. We are all very lonesome. Mama has ben lying down and I have ben trying to read. After dinner Ellen and me went to see Mrs. Spencer."

In Tennessee, the Federal cavalry pursuing General Hood's remaining army is not able to cross the flooded Rutherford Creek, and will be delayed in its efforts. Reb General Steven Lee was badly wounded yesterday, and his Corps is taken over by General Stevenson.

Near Savannah, Confederate General Beauregard has passed the word to General Hardee that President Davis will approve if he sacrifices Savannah to save his Army. Hardee knows that he has, only the newly constructed bridge across the Savannah River as a way out, and if it is destroyed, he will be trapped, but he still cannot make himself leave. Union General Sherman receives a letter from General Grant who tells him he has dispatched enough troop transports to bring Sherman and most of his army to Virginia to help him against General Lee. Sherman wants to continue his plundering stroll through the Carolinas, and he usually gets his way. We will see. In the meantime, distribution of supplies is very difficult, over the swamp roads.

Many of the Federal units are sending their soldiers to the new supply depot at King's Bridge to pick up supplies. Today Union Lt. Platter makes such a trek and describes it in his diary," Saturday Dec 18th 1864 for this date. Went to Kings bridge to day in company with Captain Lockwood, Lt Johnson and Hank Comstock -- Went to see the fleet and to get something for our men to eat -- only one boat at the bridge unloading Rations. A large no of soldiers at the landing. 12th Ills started for Hilton Head to day in charge of prisoners - After repeated efforts at the bridge we succeeded in getting some "Hard tack" & sugar for our men - Returned about dark. Had a rich dinner today - "Bill of Fare" "Dried Apples" - Men are living on "parched corn" to day" - Rations will be issued some time tonight. Men are very hungry -- A battery of 32 Rd Parrott guns arrived today from New York & was sent to the 20th AC on the left of our lines. - 17th AC are worse off than our corps for Rations - Capt Compton "[illegible] " was mustered out today & will start march soon.

## December 19, 1864

In Atlanta, Ga, there is some relief in the Maxwell Berry household tonight, per his daughter's diary, "Mon. Dec. 19. It has ben pleasant to day. Ella came to stay all night with me and just as we were going to supper Papa came in and such joy as we all had. We were so glad to hear from Aunt Dundie.

In Savannah, Confederate General Hardee has made the decision to pull out of the City. It is evident that Sherman is now trying to cut off the only route out, so it's time to leave before his enemy can do that. Preparations for movement are going on with departure time to be after darkness tomorrow night. As Hardee is making preparations to leave, Georgia Militia General (Future Oakland Resident) Henry Kent McKay, has two hundred militia, and two 32 pounder rifled cannons dug in at the Doctortown Railroad bridge, trying to defend the bridge from 1,000 of Kilpatrick's horsemen. After several attacks, the Federals withdraw, McKay faring much better than he did at Griswoldville. Casualty numbers are not available to me. McKay will, eventually, become a State Supreme Court Justice.

On the Ogeechee River, Union Lt. Platter writes in his diary, "Was up early and sent... Leut Pittman and 10 volunteers crossed the "Little Ogeechee" this evening at nine oclock and explored the ground on the opposite side -- he reported that a crossing could be made and Col Adams wanted to cross his Brigade immediately - but Gen Osterhaus would not let him I suppose we will cross the "Rubicon" tomorrow night - Gen Rice attempted to effect a crossing but failed - a few shells demoralized him Capt McCain & squad floated down the River in a boat right under the guns of a Rebel battery for which they deserve the thanks of the Div -- Still starving -- a full supply of Rations will by issued tonight."

In Tennessee, the Federal Army pursuit is still stalled at Rutherford Creek, north of Columbia. Hood is moving into Columbia on the line of the Duck River. As his men are marching now, they have added a verse to the popular song they sing, "The Yellow Rose of Texas". This has caused "the Yellow Rose of Texas" to no longer be General Hood's favorite jingle.

Now I'm headed southward
And my heart is full of woe.
I'm going back to Georgia
To see my Uncle Joe.
You may boast about your Beauregard
And sing of Bobby Lee
But the gallent Hood of Texas
Played hell in Tennessee!
*Chorus:*

## December 20, 1864

In Atlanta, Ga, Carrie Berry writes in her diary, "Tues. Dec. 20. I have ben buisy making presents all day. I went down to Mrs. Lesters to make Mamas. Miss Matt helped me. I think it is so pretty. I fear we will not get through with our presents Christmas is getting so near."

***

In Southwestern Virginia, a 7,000-man cavalry force of Union General George Stoneman pulls off a destructive raid, against the 1,000 defenders, destroying the important salt factory and iron mill there.

***

In Savannah, GA., the Confederates are preparing a way out of the City. With the bridges either destroyed or protected by the Federals, a new bridge, across makeshift pontoons is being constructed. Thirty 80ft long rice barges are being lashed together and boarded across, forming the road that is ready by early this morning, and will be utilized just after darkness falls this evening.....General Sherman has gone up the coast to confer with Union troops in Hilton Head, not under his command, about blocking any attempt the Confederates might make to move toward Charleston from Savannah, and will not return to his headquarters until the 22nd.

This evening, the Confederate guns have been firing into the Yankees all day, ceasing at dusk. The guns and ammunition are the first to cross the river to the South Carolina side. There are large fires built near the ends of the bridge and all the troops follow the guns across the water and over three islands to the state that is celebrating its fourth anniversary of secession today. The evacuation goes without a hitch.

## December 21, 1864

In Atlanta, Ga., 10 yrs old Carrie Berry writes in her diary, "Wed. Dec. 21. Papa has to go back to Macon next week and we fear he will be put in servis. He has ben buisy all day making me a pair of shoes. I do hope he will get off. the people are treating the citizens so mean that stayed here with the yankees.".(It seems Carrie is catching on that is not "business" that is taking him to Macon. He is answering questions about his collusion with the Federal army during Atlanta's occupation. He will be cleared)

In Savannah, the day dawns on empty troop positions. The guns are spiked, not manned, and the Union Army approaches the City cautiously. As Union General Geary's Division makes its way over the causeway, he is met by a contingency of citizens, composed of the Aldermen, Mayor Arnold, and some of the Ladies of the town. Their purpose is to offer a peaceful surrender in exchange for the promise of protection of lives and property. After consulting with Sherman by telegraph, Geary accepts their proposal and is given the key to the City by Mayor Arnold. The Union occupation begins immediately. Union Lt Platter has this to say about the events of the day, "This morning after breakfast we were informed that the "Rebs" had taken up their departure last night not believing it I went down to the front and seen for myself that the enemy had indeed left. We were immediately ordered to cross.... As soon as our horses arrived Maj [Major] H and I rode into the city -- with the exception of Huntsville it is the prettiest city I have seen in the 'Southern Confederacy" - The "Wharfs and docks" are magnificent but on account of the obstructions in the River below Jackson our fleet cannot come up. The town was quite full of Soldiers - quite a number of stores were plundered by soldiers assisted by negros and "poor white folks" who seemed delighted at having a chance to pillage - As a general thing the Citizens kept 'in doors". Saw the Rebel [illegible] Savannah and a gun boat laying on the opposite side of the river -- The enemy finished crossing this morning about daylight and are supposed to be making for Charleston. I think Sherman has rather been "out generaled" by Hardee. or since he couldn't have gotten away so easily - Who is to blame for allowing him to escape?

**"Picture is from "Harpers Weekly" of Geary's Division inside Savannah this afternoon.**

## December 22, 1864

In Atlanta, Ga, 10-year-old Carrie Berry writes in her yrs. ago today, diary, "Thurs. Dec. 22. We went to get our Christmas tree this evening. It was very cold but we did not feel it we were so excited about it.

Near Savannah, Union General Sherman is riding into the city after traveling all night from Port Royal by boat to the supply depot at King's Bridge. He is chastising himself for not anticipating the brilliant move by Reb General Hardee that liberated the 10,000-man capture that Sherman thought he would have upon the surrender of the City. But the City is his, with all its abandoned military stores and forts that protect it from the coast, and large stores of cotton, hidden and stored in small quantities all over the City. Most of the Union troops are not brought into Savannah but are remaining in their various camps in yesterday's positions. However Lt. Platter is allowed to go in and has this to say, in his diary, "- A cold windy morning - We obtained a house for Hd Qts and spent the day very pleasantly - Lt Johnson and I rode down town in the afternoon - The city of Savannah is much larger than I imagined it to be yesterday -- We visited the RR buildings. The enemy left a large amount of rolling stock - cars locomotives &c. &c. - We passed through many fine streets & seen many fine buildings - The city has some splendid Parks. saw the Pulaski & Greene Monuments. -- The enemy "blew up" the Rebel gunboat Savannah last night. it made a fearful and tremendous explosion, - 66 Ills detailed as Provost Guards and ordered to report to Col Woods Had a very disagreeable day. Have made our beds down on the floor and will try sleeping in a house tonight. Retired early."

Charles Green an English businessman welcomes Sherman into the City and invites him to use his fine house as his headquarters. Green only asks two rooms for his personal use and Sherman can have the remainder. After consideration, Sherman accepts the offer and moves his personal truck inside. One of his first acts, at the desk that will become familiar to him, is to pen a note to Abraham Lincoln.

*"His Excellency President LINCOLN: I beg to present you, as a Christmas gift, the city of Savannah, with 150 heavy guns and plenty of ammunition, and also about 25,000 bales of cotton."*

*W. T. SHERMAN, Major-General"*

**The Green House, Sherman's Savannah headquarters.**

## December 23, 1864

In Atlanta, Ga, Carrie Berry writes in her diary, "Fri. Dec. 23. I went down to Mrs. Lesters and Ella and me planted the tree and finished making the last presents. I came home and strained some pumpkins to make some pies for Christmas."

In Savannah, Union General Sherman is bringing more of his army into the City and organizing for long-time occupation. Nearby, Lt. Platter writes in his diary tonight, "Up early. Wind still blowing and quite cold. Had to move our quarters this morning - as the 3d Div of our Corps were to camp where we were -- We moved to a much better place 300 yds in rear of Brigade Hd Qrs. inside of the "Rebel Works" Our Hd Qrs are near a "dutchman's" house - will make him evacuate a room for us. Lt Johnson applied for "leave of absence" today, but it will not be granted. Rec'd a large mail this evening but "Nary letter" for me. Orders came to be ready for review tomorrow - our whole corps will be reviewed by Genl Sherman. No news. Retired early."

***

Wilmington, North Carolina remains the only Confederate sea port open to receiving blockade runners, and Union General Benjamin (Spoons) Butler is going to take it by destroying Fort Fisher, the guardian of Wilmington. This afternoon, the "USS Louisiana", laden with 200 tons of gunpowder, is grounded adjacent to the fort, and the huge planned explosion occurs, but does not damage the fort. There are 60 warships in Admiral Porter's fleet, plus the troop transports for land assault if needed. Upon failure of the explosion, Butler orders a fierce bombardment to begin.

***

In Washington, Dr. Samuel Mudd introduces actor, John Wilkes Booth, to a young Confederate spy, John Surratt, Jr. Surratt has been the small town postmaster of Surrattsville, Maryland, but has been working for the Confederate government for over a year, carrying messages to Confederate boats on the Potomac, keeping them informed on troop movements that he can find out about. His mother is Mary Surratt, who will be hanged for the murder of Abraham Lincoln.

**John Surratt Jr.**

## December 24, 1864

In Atlanta, GA, Carrie Berry writes in her diary, "Sat. Dec. 24. I have been buisy to day making cakes to trim the tree and Ella and I have it all ready trimed and we are all going to night to see it. I think it looks very pretty. We will be sorry when it is all over."

On the North Carolina coast, at the mouth of the Cape Fear River, the Federal fleet has maneuvered into bombardment positions. The "Ironsides" opens first with a devastating salvo that hushes the guns of the fort. It is then joined by a frigate, "USS Minnesota", then others, numbering up to 37 vessels. The Confederate defenders hunker down inside their bomb-proofs and listen to the show, as the multitude of guns plow up the surface of the earthen fort, doing little real damage. The Federals have plenty of ammunition so the action will continue into the night and on the morrow

***

In Savannah, Union Lt. Platter writes in his diary, "Was up early - As ordered, the Regt prepared for Review. 81st was attached to Gen Rice's Brigade. Our was formed on Broad St. Passed in review before Gen Sherman Howard Osterhaus &c presenting a fine appearance. Col Adams did not go on review as he had no command. -- Glorious news from Thomas. Hood has been badly defeated before Nashville. has lost 60 pieces of Artillery and 10.000 prisoners and he is retreating Southward rapidly. No mail today"

**In Washington, US President Abraham Lincoln receives Sherman's "Christmas Present" telegram and announces it at a dinner party.**

## December 25, 1864

In Atlanta, Ga, Carrie Berry writes in her diary, "Sun. Dec. 25, 1864. We all went down last night to see the tree and how pretty it looked. The room was full of ladies and children and Cap. gave us music on the pianno and tried to do all he could to make us enjoy our selves and we did have a merry time. All came home perfectly satisfied. This has ben a cold dark day, but we all went down to see how the tree looked in the day time but it was not as pretty as at night."

The war goes on, even on Christmas. About ten this morning the bombardment of Fort Fisher begins again, and Union General Butler unloads his invasion force. At first, he is successful in taking a Confederate battery, but then the resistance stiffens, and he suspects the Rebs are reinforced, so he withdraws back to the ships and sails away. The Confederates have won a victory and are not sure how, because their reinforcements have not arrived yet.

***

In Savannah, GA, Union Lt Platter writes about his Christmas, "-- Was up early - Lt Johnson and I attended preaching this morning at the Presbyterian Church and heard a splendid sermon by the Rev Dr Axson. a noted DD. Quite a number of citizens were out. - In Afternoon went to 17th AC and saw Dave Plattes, Capt Simpson &c Sent a wagon after Oysters this morning - but they did not have very good success. House sacking was carried on quite extensively all day on the road between camp and town. The city was full of drunken soldiers and officers -- Had a splendid oyster supper this evening. No news today. Retired early" (Dr Axson, the minister, is the Grandfather of Ellen Axson, of Rome, Ga, who will marry Woodrow Wilson and become first Lady of the United States on March 4, 1913)

In Atlanta, the small, returned population is treated to a Christmas service in the 1st Baptist Church, the first such since the devastation. Dr. Hornady, the pastor has cleaned up and decorated as best he can. I am not privy to the particulars except that he brings forth the message of hope, and of prophecy. The music probably included songs that will be sung 150 years from now, such as "Deck the Halls", "Oh Come all Ye Faithful", "Hark the Herald Angels Sing", "It Came Upon A Midnight Clear", and "We Three Kings of Orient Are". Other seasonal singing, not in church, would include "Jingle Bells" and "Up on the Housetop".

**Thomas Nast's Christmas drawing is a conciliatory one, showing Lee and Grant shaking hands while Lincoln invites the cold hungry Confederates into the banquet hall.**

## December 26, 1864

In Atlanta, Ga, a worried Carrie Berry writes in her diary, "Mon. Dec. 26. Papa left us this morning. He has gone to Macon to be tried for staying here with the yankees. We are afraid they will put him in the army. We all feel very sad."

In Savannah, Union Lt. Platter writes in his diary, "It has been a nice clear and pleasant day. - Considerable talks about our Div garrisoning Savannah, but there is no foundation for the Rumor - We were informed to - day that we could fix up our quarters - for we would remain here 2 or 3 weeks. -- We moved our camp forward, so as to give room for the 12th Ills who came back a few days since. Several boats came up to - day but no mail. Co "C" was transferred to "E" & "F" and "B" to "D" ".

From Washington, President Lincoln writes to General Sherman, "*Many, many thanks for your Christmas gift, the capture of Savannah. When you were about leaving Atlanta for the Atlantic coast, I was anxious, if not fearful; but feeling that you were the better judge, and remembering that "nothing risked, nothing gained," I did not interfere. Now, the undertaking being a success, the honor is all yours; for I believe none of us went further than to acquiesce.*"

***

In southern Tennessee, as Reb General Hood retreats toward the Tennessee River, the Union Cavalry under General Wilson is in hot pursuit and has had many engagements with the Confederate rearguard under General Forrest with General Walthall supporting. This morning, as the Federals approach Sugar Creek, the Confederates are doing something different. They are fortified in a strong position, and the Federals cannot see them through the fog until they are within 100 yds. A murderous fire blasts forth, with the Yankees quickly retreating to form for a charge. Before they can act, Forrest charges them, running over them and chasing them for over a mile before returning to his strong position. The Federals are not coming back for more, but will keep position for two days as Forrest waits for the Gray Army to escape to safety into Alabama, and on into Mississippi.

**Reb Lt. General Forrest...Yank Major General Wilson**

## December 27, 1864

In Atlanta, Georgia, 10-year-old Carrie Berry gets confused about the date as she posts in her diary, "Tues. Dec. 28. Some little girls came up here last night and we had a concert and enjoyed our selves very much. At one o'clock we let the tree fall and then came home and had a party. Now our Christmas ended with a hail storm."

In northern Alabama, the last of Hood's Confederate Army crosses the Tennessee River, ending the Nashville Campaign. The group could hardly be called an army at this point. If not for Forrest, it would be easy pickings for the Federal cavalry who will move back into Tennessee now, not trying to force a river crossing against the Confederate Cavalry.

In Savannah, Union Lt. Cornelius Platter writes in his diary, "Was up early and went to work at nothing and continued at it all day -- Men busy fixing up quarters - Had a nice clear day The new Consolidation of Co's promises to work well. "Dave Murphy" was up to see us to day He has a furlough of 30 days in Ohio. Capt Lockwood sent in his resignation on Surgeons Certificate of disabilities --Rumor says Jeff Davis is dead, said to be official -- 17th AC was reviewed by Genl Sherman to - day - Had Dress Parade this evening - have orders to have Parade every evening and make a report of the same to Div Hd Qrs."

From Savannah, Sherman issues orders for the Tybee Island lighthouse be repaired and restored to working order, and the Savannah River again is to be made navigable. He also sends for Brigadier General J. D. Webster and his staff to come to Savannah from Nashville, thus moving the Military Division of the Mississippi business headquarters to Savannah.

Today, from off the shore of North Carolina, the U. S. Navy fleet Commander, Admiral David Porter writes a scathing letter of criticism of the recent actions of the Army to Navy Secretary Gideon Welles. He states that although General Butler unloaded 7,000 men off-ship, onto land, he made no real effort to surround Fort Fisher, and that if he had made that effort the undermanned garrison would have gladly surrendered to him. However, Butler heard a rumor of Rebel reinforcements and the weather turned sour, so he quit. There will be more about this in the days to come.

**Union Admiral David Dixon Porter**

## December 28, 1864

In Atlanta, GA, Carrie Berry is still confused about the date as she writes in her diary, "Wed. Dec. 29. I have had no Christmas to day. I have ben studying the multiplication to day. I have ben running about so much that it has made me sick."

In Northern Alabama, Lt. General Forrest is crossing his Confederate Cavalry across the Tennessee River today, and tomorrow General Walthall will cross, all Hood's Army of Tennessee will be across. The only threat to them then will be raiding parties.

***

In Savannah, General Sherman is approached by a group of Southerners who are loyal to the Union and want to organize for mutual benefit. They ask Sherman for Federal protection from the Rebels, which he quickly and eloquently avows.

In Savannah, Union Lt. Platter states in his diary, " It has rained nearly all day but has cleared off this evening Orders to have schools for Div Brigade Regiments & Companies and establishing drills, Camp Guards. Guard mounting &c. It looks as if we are going to stay awhile. The citizens had a meeting today and adopted a strong set of resolutions -- Sent a copy to Dr Miller."

***

From Washington, President Lincoln sends a wire to General Grant about the failure of the capture of Fort Fisher: "*If there is no objection, please tell me what you now understand of the Wilmington expedition, present & prospective.*"...Grant to Lincoln: "*The Wilmington expedition has proven a gross and culpable failure. Many of the troops are now back here. Delays and free talk of the object of the expedition enabled the enemy to move troops to Wilmington to defeat it. After the expedition sailed from Fort Monroe three days of fine weather was squandered, during which the enemy was without a force to protect himself. Who is to blame I hope will be known?*"......

**Union Major General Benjamin F. Butler**

## December 29, 1864

In Atlanta, Ga, Carrie Berry is once again straight with her diary dates, "Thurs. Dec. 29. I have ben studding the six line of the multiplication table and I think I will no it very well. We made some candy and wound up the Christmas. I went to take Miss Mary Come some and they thought it was very nice.

In southern Tennessee and northern Alabama, it is raining, the roads have becoming quagmires in the last few days, and Thomas' Union Army has become too spread away from Nashville to be properly supplied, so Thomas calls off all pursuit of Hood's Confederates, ordering his men into winter camps at Eastport, Huntsville, and Dalton, *"where they can be easily supplied, and from which points they can be readily assembled to make a spring campaign."*

In Savannah, Union Lt. Platter writes in his diary, " Capt Vanpelt and I rode into Savannah this morning and saw the 17th AC reviewed by Genl Sherman -- it presented a fine appearance. Capt Vanpelt officiated at Dress parade this evening and did fine. Several boys got quite happy -- Joe especially -- Dr Jacobs & Howell came over and had a game of "whist" -- The "dutch" family moved down town today and we have the whole house for Hd Qrs."

Since Sherman's chief engineer, Orlando Poe, constructed the defensive works of Nashville that Reb General Longstreet tried so hard to take last year, he has been invaluable to Sherman, causing him to write the following in his field journal, *"I sent recommendations for promotions among my engineering corp including Captain Poe, my chief engineer. I prefer that he should be brevet Brigadier-General in the Regular Army, in order that I may retain him near my person as long as I have the honor to exercise an active command in the Army of the United States. I find him so thoroughly qualified that I would be lost without him."*

**U.S. Brigadier General Orlando Metcalf Poe**

## December 30, 1864

In Atlanta, GA, Carrie Berry writes in her diary, "Fri. Dec. 30. I have ben studding the seventh line and I find it harder than the six. After I got the seven line I went down to Mrs. Lesters and me and Ella had a little dinner and we had turkee and rice and potato for dinner and we had a merry time of cooking."

In Washington, President Lincoln orders Grant to organize another operation against Fort Fisher, leaving the fleet under Porter in place, bombarding the fort every day. Lincoln tells his cabinet that he will fire Butler.

From Washington, powerful Maryland politician, Francis Blair Sr., a friend of both Lincoln and Jefferson Davis writes to Davis to request that he, Blair, come to Richmond for a meeting with Davis about the possibilities for peace.

In Savannah, Union General Sherman is preparing to move his army again, evidenced by the following order to his Quartermaster: "*I am instructed by Major-General Sherman to say that he wishes to accumulate at this place as soon as possible sixty days' forage for 35,000 animals. We have today but one day's grain on hand and none in the sound or river.*"

In Savannah, Union Lt. Platter writes in his diary, "A bright clear night . The 20th AC was reviewed today -- About the time the "review" commenced they fired a salute and we imagined Gen Grant had Arrived but it was just some of the 20th Corps style. They presented quite an indifferent appearance - Many who went to see them were very much, as they expected to see something "extra". Men are entirely out of something to eat -- Sent a wagon after Oysters for New Years. A Blockade runner ran up to day - not knowing Savannah was in our possession 15 AC to be reviewed next week "

***

In Bombay, India, a son is born to a British couple, John L Kipling, and Alice Macdonald Kipling. Rudyard Kipling will grow up to be one of the most popular authors in the world in the late 1800's and early 1900's. Legions of Children will be fascinated by the characterizations of the exotic animals of "The Jungle Book" and think that Mowgli is the luckiest boy on earth.

**Joseph Rudyard Kipling**

## December 31, 1864

In Atlanta, on this last day of the year, Carrie Berry writes in her diary, " Sat. Dec. 31. I learned the eight line and I learned it very well. It has ben a cold and we had to stay in the house very close."

In Savannah, Union General Sherman is resting his army and today turns out volumes of letters to his wife, brother, and Generals Grant and Halleck, all stating how well behaved his army is and how much he is loved by the citizens of the South. The army is resting to be able to put forth the effort of destruction in a couple of weeks in South Carolina.

***

In Atlanta, the citizens are returning, slowly. They are greeted with stark devastation, piles of rubble and burned shells of structures. Some residential areas are spared, because Sherman only gave his destruction crews a couple of days to ply their handiwork, the flames being mostly reserved until the end. The railroad is already being repaired to the southwest, and some citizens are attempting to rebuild. Future Oakland Cemetery residents, John Collier, and his sons, are cleaning bricks and accumulating nails and lumber to rebuild his law office and repair his cannonball damaged home.

The worst year in the State's history will soon be over, devastation from Dalton to Rome, to Atlanta, to Milledgeville, to Millen, and through the countryside of all those places. All citizens who have not quit, are looking to the new year with a sense of revitalization, facing the immediate future without the sense of dread that held forth this time a year ago. 1865 will mean the end of war, the beginning of true reconstruction along with the heavy hand of vindictive victors, not an easy year, but better than the one finishing now. For memory's sake, the picture for the day was taken by Barnard, Sherman's photographer, just days before the destruction. Two-thirds of the scene is now gone to dust and ashes. It is taken from the cupola of the Female Seminary at Courtland and Ellis, with City Hall in the center distance and the brick Atlanta Medical College (with the cupola) on the extreme left....

# INDEX

## A



## B

## C



## D

## E



## F



## G

## H



## I



## J

## K



## L



## M

## N



## O



## P

## Q



## R



## S

## T



## U



## V

## W



## Y

# Bibliography


Avery, A History of the State of Georgia, From 1850 to 1881, New York, 1881

Battey, A History of Rome and Floyd County, Cherokee Publishing Co. Atlanta, 1922

Bonds, War Like The Thunderbolt, Yardley, Pennsylvania, 2009

Catton, Never Call Retreat, New York, 1965

Clark, Atlanta Illustrated, third edition, Atlanta, 1881

Clarke, The Story of Decatur, 1823-1899, Atlanta, GA, 1973

Cooper, Official History of Fulton County, Atlanta, 1934

Cox, Atlanta, Morningside, 1987

Cunyus, History of Bartow County, Formerly Cass, Easley S.C., 1933

Eckert, John Brown Gordon, Soldier-Southerner-American, Baton Rouge, La., 1989

Evans, Georgia, Confederate Military History, Vol. VI., Secaucus NJ

Evans, Sherman's Horsemen, Union Cavalry Operations in the Atlanta Campaign, Indianapolis, 1996

Foote, The Civil War, A Narrative, Vol. III, Red River to Appomattox, New York, 1963

Freeman, R. E. Lee, Vol III, New York, 1934

Fretwell, This So Remote Frontier, The Chattahoochee Country of Alabama and Georgia, Tallahassee, 1980

Garrett, Atlanta and Environs, A Chronicle of Its People and Events, Athens, Ga., 1954

Garrison, Atlanta And The War, Nashville, 1995

Hoehling, A. A., Last Train From Atlanta, New York, 1958

Hood, Advance and Retreat, Personal Experiences in the United States & Confederate States Armies, New Orleans, 1880

Horn, The Army of Tennessee, A Military History, New York, 1941

Hubner-Walker, Charles W. Hubner, Poet Laureate of the South, Atlanta, 1976

Miles, Fields of Glory, A History and Tour Guide of the Atlanta Campaign, Nashville, 1989

Nichols, The Story of the Great March, From the Diary of a Staff Officer, by Major George Ward Nichols, New York, 1865

Patrick, Jefferson Davis and His Cabinet, Baton Rouge, 1944

Price, The History of Dekalb County, Georgia 1822-1900, Fernandina Beach, Fl., 1997

Reed, History of Atlanta, Georgia, With Illustrations and Biographical Sketches of Some of its Prominent Men and Pioneers, Syracuse, NY, 1889

Russell, Atlanta 1847-1890, City Building in the Old South and the New, Baton Rouge, 1988

Tankersley, John B. Gordon, A Study in Gallantry, Atlanta, 1955

Temple, The First Hundred Years, A Short History of Cobb County, in Georgia, Athens, GA, 1935

Walker, Secrets of a Civil War Submarine, Solving the Mysteries of the H. L. Hunley, Minneapolis, 2005

CPSIA information can be obtained
at www.ICGtesting.com
Printed in the USA
BVHW071141081120
592579BV00004B/5

9 781733 404471